Judicial Reform in Taiwan

This book examines Taiwan's judicial reform process, which began three years after the 1996 transition to democracy, in 1999, when Taiwanese legal and political leaders began discussing how to reform Taiwan's judicial system to meet the needs of the new social and political conditions. Covering different areas of the law in a comprehensive way, the book considers, for each legal area, problems related to rights and democracy in that field, the debates over reform, how foreign systems inspired reform proposals, the political process of change, and the substantive legal changes that ultimately emerged. The book also sets Taiwan's legal reforms in their historical and comparative context, and discusses how the reform process continues to evolve.

Neil Chisholm is a Visiting Scholar at the Academy of East Asian Studies at Sungkyunkwan University, South Korea.

Routledge Law in Asia
Series editors:
Randall Peerenboom and Pip Nicholson

10 **Freedom of Information Reform in China**
Information Flow Analysis
Weibing Xiao

11 **Law and Development in Asia**
Edited by Gerald Paul McAlinn and Caslav Pejovic

12 **The Judicialization of Politics in Asia**
Edited by Bjorn Dressel

13 **Juries in the Japanese Legal System**
The Continuing Struggle for Citizen Participation and Democracy
Dimitri Vanoverbeke

14 **Confucian Constitutionalism in East Asia**
Bui Ngoc Son

15 **Religion, Law and Intolerance in Indonesia**
Tim Lindsey and Helen Pausacker

16 **Constitutional Interpretation in Singapore**
Theory and Practice
Jaclyn L. Neo

17 **Politics and Constitutions in Southeast Asia**
Marco Bünte and Björn Dressel

18 **Law and Society in Malaysia**
Pluralism, Religion and Ethnicity
Edited by Andrew Harding and Dian Shah

19 **Judicial Reform in Taiwan**
Democratization and the Diffusion of Law
Edited by Neil Chisholm

Judicial Reform in Taiwan

Democratization and the Diffusion of Law

Edited by Neil Chisholm

Routledge
Taylor & Francis Group
LONDON AND NEW YORK

First published 2020
by Routledge
2 Park Square, Milton Park, Abingdon, Oxon OX14 4RN

and by Routledge
52 Vanderbilt Avenue, New York, NY 10017

Routledge is an imprint of the Taylor & Francis Group, an informa business

British Library Cataloguing-in-Publication Data
A catalogue record for this book is available from the British Library

Library of Congress Cataloging-in-Publication Data
A catalog record has been requested for this book

ISBN: 978-0-415-85529-7 (hbk)
ISBN: 978-0-203-73718-7 (ebk)

Typeset in Times New Roman
by Wearset Ltd, Boldon, Tyne and Wear

For the people of Taiwan,
that the story of your laws would be more widely known

Contents

Illustrations

Table

Figures

Contributors

Ching-Hui Chen is Assistant Professor of Law in the Department of Law at National Taipei University. She holds a doctorate in law from the University of Bonn and passed the Taiwanese Judicial Exam for Judge and Prosecutor Qualification and the Taiwan Bar Exam in 1999. She also worked from 2003 to 2005 as a Law Clerk for a Justice of the Constitutional Court and Judicial Yuan. Her areas of research are constitutional law, EU law, international law, and administrative law.

Hwei-Syin Chen is Professor of Law at National Chengchi University (NCCU). Her Dr. jur. is from the University of Regensburg. She has been head of the College of Law and served as advisor to the government in various capacities. She specializes, teaches, and writes on Chinese legal history, German legal history, family law, succession law, gender and law, and law and literature.

Mong-Hwa Chin is an Associate Professor at National Chiao Tung University School of Law. He received his S.J.D. degree from Duke University Law School. He teaches criminal law and procedure. He is interested in the fields of wrongful conviction, legal psychology, and lay participation.

Neil Chisholm is a Visiting Scholar at the Academy of East Asian Studies at Sungkyunkwan University. He holds a BA in Law from the University of Cambridge and a D.Phil. in Socio-Legal Studies from the University of Oxford. His research focuses on comparative law in East Asia.

Heng-da Hsu is Associate Professor of Criminal Law at National Chengchi University, Taiwan. He received his Dr. iur. degree from Goethe-Universität Frankfurt am Main, Germany in 2008. His scholarship focuses on doctrinal studies of criminal law, penal policy, and the intellectual history of punishment.

Chia-Wen Lee is a Professor in the Department of Law at National Cheng Kung University in Taiwan. She received her S.J.D. (Doctor of Juridical Science) degree at the Maurer School of Law, Indiana University-Bloomington. Her publications include two books, *Punishment in the Neo-Liberal Order* and *Justice on a Tightrope: Essays on Criminal Justice*, and various essays on criminal procedure, the death penalty, and policies against sex crimes.

Chien-Liang Lee is Director and Research Professor at the Institutum Iurisprudentiae, Academia Sinica and Professor of Law at National Taiwan University (NTU). He obtained his Dr. jur. degree from Göttingen University. His main fields of research include constitutional law, administrative law, and environmental protection law, and he emphasizes the local application of legal theory.

Rong-Geng Li is Professor of Law at National Taipei University. He received his S.J.D. degree at Indiana University Maurer School of Law in Bloomington. His research focuses on criminal procedure.

Jing-Huey Shao is Associate Professor of Law at National Cheng Kung University in Taiwan. She obtained her LL.B. and MBA at National Taiwan University, LL.M. at Columbia University, and J.S.D. at Washington University in St. Louis, US. She was an attorney at law admitted to the Taiwan, New York, and PRC bars, and practiced in Taiwan. Her research interests include empirical studies, civil procedure, and comparative law.

Puma Shen is an Assistant Professor of Criminology at National Taipei University. He holds a Ph.D. in Criminology and Law and Society from the University of California, Irvine and received his law degrees from the University of Pennsylvania and National Taiwan University.

Yen-tu Su is Associate Research Professor at the Institutum Iurisprudentiae, Academia Sinica. He received his S.J.D. degree from Harvard University in 2010. His research interests include the law of democracy, democratic theory, constitutional law, and judicial politics.

Yueh-Sheng Weng is Adjunct Professor of Law at National Taiwan University and Honorary Professor of Law at National Chengchi University. He holds a Dr. jur. degree from Heidelberg University. His main fields of research include constitutional law and administrative law. He served as Justice of the Constitutional Court in Taiwan from 1972 to 1999 and from 2003 to 2007. He was the President of Judicial Yuan from 1999 to 2007.

Tzung-Mou Wu is Associate Research Professor at the Institutum Iurisprudentiae, Academia Sinica. He received a doctorate from the School for Advanced Studies in the Social Sciences (EHESS) in France and Roma Tre University in Italy. His research specializes in nineteenth- and early-twentieth-century French and German law and jurisprudence, their migration to East Asia, and their relevance to contemporary issues, such as institutional reforms for indigenous empowerment.

Foreword

In contemporary constitutional democracies, judicial power greatly impacts citizens' lives. Courts must protect human rights and judges need to reach just outcomes in individual cases. In liberal democratic states, the judiciary should not be used as a tool by governments, and courts should not be places of ingrained bureaucratic habits. The legal system must keep pace with the times and satisfy peoples' needs, providing people with dignified and efficient services. These have been the goals of judicial reforms in countries over the world, and Taiwan is no exception.

As a former Justice of the Constitutional Court (formerly known as the Council of Grand Justices) and having worked at the Judicial Yuan for 35 years,[1] I have not only seen the development of constitutional interpretation, but I have also dedicated myself to judicial reform in Taiwan. I served as the Chairman of the National Judicial Reform Conference (July 6–8, 1999), and took part in a series of judicial reforms undertaken afterwards. The judicial reforms were very complicated and could not be achieved through one person or a single authority, and so the process relied on cooperation between authorities, scholars, and the legal community. The reforms after the 1999 Conference were meant to bring the legal system into step with developments of democratization and modernization over the past half century. Although I have retired from my judicial position, I am still concerned about the development of the judiciary in Taiwan and hope that the pace of judicial reform could be accelerated.

It is with great pleasure that I have heard that Dr. Neil Chisholm, a Postdoctoral Research Fellow at the Institutum Iurisprudentiae at Academia Sinica, has been dedicated to studying and discussing problems of judicial reform and judicial independence, and, after years of academic research and discussion with Taiwan's scholars and legal professionals, has managed to get a book published on this subject. The content of this book covers the history of Taiwan's judicial

1 Until a Constitutional revision in 2004, the President of the Judicial Yuan was not a Justice. Therefore, while I worked at the Judicial Yuan since 1972, I did not serve as Justice from 1999 to 2004.

system, legal education reform, the creation of a jury system, reform of the appeals system, reform of the prosecution, developments in the right to counsel, reform of the status of the Judicial Yuan, criminal procedure reform, civil procedure reform, administrative law reform, and several other important issues regarding judicial reform in Taiwan. The book will enable countries all over the world to understand the work of the judicial reform process in Taiwan, and can surely improve the course of events here in Taiwan.

Judicial reforms take time and communication. I hope that in the future the judicial reforms can be carried out through good interactions and rational discussions and that a reliable legal system can be built to make the court a sacred place where justice is realized and the rights of the people are protected.

Yueh-Sheng Weng

Grand Justice (appointed 1972) and President of the Judicial Yuan (1999–2007)

Preface

This book is a product of my postdoctoral work at the law institute of Academia Sinica during 2012–15. My research at the Institutum Iurisprudentiae focused on Taiwan's judicial reforms. Since my doctoral thesis was on the influence of American law on South Korea, I had learned a great deal about judicial reform there in the 2000s. In Taiwan, I discovered a fascinatingly parallel judicial reform movement and discourse. Both jurisdictions' reforms appeared to be driven by the aftermath of democratization and shaped by the diffusion of law. A clash of newer American and older German legal influences was underway. This compelling comparative law story deserves much more attention than it has received.

Although I had wanted to write comprehensively on Taiwan's judicial reforms, it quickly became clear that I lacked the technical expertise and local insights to do so. I decided to edit a volume on this topic because it would be the only practical way to recount the saga of judicial reform. But I desired to avoid the common pitfall of edited volumes containing a jumble of loosely connected chapters. It was necessary to carefully commission chapters such that major areas of judicial reform would be covered, with minimal overlap or omission. For this, I sincerely thank Tzung-Mou Wu, who assisted me with determining the conceptual "lay of the land" and locating suitable authors. As a comparativist par excellence, his insights and help were invaluable throughout my time in Taiwan.

The people to thank for the creation of this book are too many to name. I think especially of the Instititum Iurisprudentiae at Academia Sinica (IIAS) professors charged with overseeing my work, Fort Fu-Te Liao, K.C. Huang, and Tzu-Yi Lin. It was a surreal experience to learn from K.C. while he became a political celebrity, formed the New Power Party, and resigned to enter the legislature. Afterwards, like K.C., former Director Lin helped my research enormously. There are also the authors of this book's chapters. Most were peer reviewed by Hwei-Syin Chen, except the one we co-authored, which was reviewed by Chia-Wen Lee. My Introduction was reviewed by Yen-tu Su and the Afterword by Heng-da Hsu. I benefitted from meeting with dozens of interviewees, many unnamed in my chapters, who explained their work and perspectives. Particularly helpful people, in addition to the aforementioned, include

Judicial Yuan Vice President Su Yeong-chin, Kao Jung-chih at the Judicial Reform Foundation, Judge Huang, Shwu-Fann Liou, Tay-Sheng Wang, and John Chen of Formosa Transnational. Finally, the IIAS made this book possible through its generous support of my postdoctoral research, which was ultimately funded by the people of Taiwan. Thank you.

Taiwan is a very special place. Beyond its natural beauty and friendly people, it is one of the world's rare success stories of modern economic development and democratization. Formosa is blessed with remarkably talented people, including world-class comparative legal scholars on all sides of judicial reform debates. I hope that Taiwan will continue to advance and become as much a successful model in law as in economics and politics.

Part I

Taiwan's judicial reforms in comparative and historical context

1 Taiwan's judicial reform process

East Asian context, democratization, and diffusion

Neil Chisholm

Introduction

In 1999, a gathering of Taiwan's legal elites and civil society agreed to enact sweeping changes to the island's legal institutions. Wide-ranging judicial reforms were proposed to the ways citizens engage in civil litigation, challenge executive decisions in administrative court, how authorities prosecute crime, the nature and functions of the Judicial Yuan, judicial independence, and quality control of judges. On the surface, the main motivations for the reforms were, foremost, the restoration of collapsing public trust in the judiciary as well as enhancing its efficiency. Behind the key issue of public confidence, however, were Taiwan's democratization and its aftermath. Many reform proposals aimed at rebalancing the power of the people vis-à-vis the government in favor of the citizenry. Empowered citizens and ex-dissident elites sought to infuse a democratic ethos into tarnished judicial institutions inherited from the authoritarian past.

Taiwan's legal system derives not only from the Republic of China's modernization efforts on the mainland in the early twentieth century, but the Japanese and German laws that inspired them and have continued to inform legal development in Taiwan. Judicial reform discussions have often implicitly questioned the legitimacy of Taiwan's Continental legal tradition. In many fields of reform, debates between reformists and traditionalists have involved a contest of comparative law – whether to maintain continuity with the civil law tradition, or depart from it by adopting Anglo-American legal ideas. Roughly speaking, traditionalists have usually advocated solving local problems by keeping with the civilian spirit of Taiwanese law, while reformists have often proposed the radical medicine of common law solutions.[1] Comparative law analyses have thus shaped judicial reform discourse and motivated participants' proposals.

1 To be sure, coalitions for reform varied over time and by issue. For example, there were German-trained jurists on both sides, the Judicial Yuan and Ministry of Justice were often "pro-tradition" yet had many disagreements, and reform advocates in civil society, the judiciary, and prosecution often distrusted each other.

Meanwhile, as Taiwan debated reforming its judiciary, Japan and South Korea initiated judicial reform processes of their own. These judicial reforms were noteworthy not only for their parallels to Taiwan's process, but also because these jurisdictions of shared legal heritage each undertook systemic reform at roughly the same times. Japan and the two systems it has significantly influenced seemed to simultaneously declare their dissatisfaction with their legal traditions and adjusted them, often by adopting American ideas. Moreover, as the three jurisdictions' judicial reforms progressed, developments in Korea and Japan began to exercise an influence on Taiwan's more slow-moving process, especially in the discussions over adopting a type of jury system. Analyzing Taiwan's judicial reforms in East Asian comparative context can uncover such regional borrowing, highlight similarities that suggest common root causes and factors in reform, and also reveal divergences that indicate local particularities as well as offer benchmarks for assessing progress or success.

Taiwan's judicial reform process has attracted too little attention, given its importance as a case study of the legal dimension of democratization as well as of the transnational diffusion of law. This book's aim is to publicize Taiwan's remarkable story of judicial reform. While subsequent chapters examine specific fields of reform, this chapter introduces the overall judicial reform process. First, it outlines the main features of judicial reform in Japan, Korea, and Taiwan. Second, based on interviews, it offers a detailed analysis of how Taiwan's 1999 National Judicial Reform Conference was initiated, summarizes its results, and explains how the process then stretched out for years afterwards. Third, the chapter analyzes Taiwan's judicial reforms from the thematic perspectives of East Asian context, democratization, and legal diffusion. Fourth, the book's chapters on specific areas of reform are summarized.

Judicial reform in Japan, Korea, and Taiwan: a (legal) family affair

Judicial reform in Taiwan has occurred at a time of similar systemic reforms in its most closely related jurisdictions. Taiwan is twice the legal offspring of Japan: first, the Japanese Empire's law was administered during the 1895–1945 colonization period, and second, after World War II Taiwan received the Republic of China's (ROC) Japanese-influenced legal system. The similarity of the two legal regimes allowed for a smooth transition, in the legal sphere, to ROC rule in 1945.[2] Modern Japan's legal system, formed after the 1868 Meiji Restoration, followed the Continental European style, with a particularly strong influence from the German Empire. The unification of Germany in 1871 led to a period of intense, contemplative legislative activity aimed at unification of state-level legal systems.

2 Tay-Sheng Wang, *Legal Reform in Taiwan under Japanese Colonial Rule, 1895–1945: The Reception of Western Law* (Seattle: University of Washington Press, 2000).

The laws and institutions that emerged were seen in Japan, and much of the world, as modern, enlightened, and attractive. For example, Germany's 1877 Courts Constitution Act (*Gerichtsverfassungsgesetz*) was essentially adopted by Japan in 1890 (*Saibansho kōsei hō*, 裁判所構成法).[3] The same was true for the codes of criminal and civil procedure. Japan's translation of these codes linguistically, and culturally into Asian context, made them accessible and desirable to ROC legal reformers. Korea also experienced the transplantation of Japanese-style civil law during its 1910–45 colonization. And after liberation, South Korea effectively maintained Japanese-style procedural laws and judicial institutions.[4]

Thus, by the end of World War II, an unspoken legal familial relationship existed among Japan, Korea, and Taiwan. The three jurisdictions had court systems substantially influenced by German law. In the decades following the War, some in these places continued to look to Germany for legal inspiration. For example, aspiring legal scholars in these jurisdictions have often traveled to Germany to obtain law doctorates, a practice facilitated by the low cost of higher education there. Moreover, in South Korea and Taiwan, jurists would often pay close attention to Japanese laws, court decisions, regulations, and legal scholarship, as they sought to emulate its successful economic development.

However, the end of World War II brought an American military occupation to Japan that engaged in systemic legal reform, imparting US influences to Japanese institutions and procedural codes. Korea and Taiwan did not experience such an enforced Americanizing reform of their prewar legal system.[5] Therefore, while the postwar procedural laws of Japan moved closer to the American style, those of South Korea and Taiwan maintained relative continuity with their illiberal prewar legal inheritance, which suited the authoritarian governments in the two places. This general point is crucial for understanding the later East Asian judicial reforms.

By the 1990s, there were drives for judicial reform in all three jurisdictions. Why was this? In Japan, the precise motivations for the emergence of judicial reform are still mysterious, but they seemed to be designed to "reinvigorate" the country, as one senior Japanese law professor told the author in 2014. What is clear is that a longstanding "administrative reform" political discourse, on streamlining bureaucracy, merged with a push by the Japan Business Federation (*Keidanren*, 日本経済団体連合会), an influential business lobbying association, to overhaul the judicial system. It is unknown why *Keidanren* agitated for

3 Neil Chisholm, "The Faces of Judicial Independence: Democratic versus Bureaucratic Accountability in Judicial Selection, Training, and Promotion in South Korea and Taiwan," *American Journal of Comparative Law* 62 (2014): 904–5.

4 Joon-Young Moon, "The Making of the Constitution and the Civil Code in Postliberation Korea," in Marie Seong-Hak Kim, ed., *The Spirit of Korean Law: Korean Legal History in Context* (Leiden: Brill Nijhoff, 2016), 177–8.

5 South Korea experienced an American occupation, but its legal reforms were not intensive or enduring. Gregory Henderson, "Human Rights in South Korea, 1945–1953," in William Shaw, ed., *Human Rights in Korea: Historical and Policy Perspectives* (Cambridge: Harvard University, 1991), 125.

judicial reform, but Setsuo Miyazawa has theorized that, because of the prolonged economic slump, big business sought to change the nation's economic paradigm. It wanted to reduce the traditionally powerful bureaucracy's role in the economy, as well as its costly maintenance, and instead switch to a more market-oriented economic model in which the legal system would play a greater role.[6] As he put it, "because deregulation will reduce government intervention in many aspects of life, the public should be given better access to the judicial system and legal profession to ensure their protection."[7]

The government heeded *Keidanren's* call for reform and created the Justice System Reform Council (JSRC, 司法制度改革審議会) to discuss and propose fundamental reforms to the country's postwar judicial configuration. Almost unexpectedly, reform-minded groups were invited to provide input into a process they were not mainly responsible for initiating. The Committee was designed to deliberate over transformative ideas outside of the ordinary legislative process and in such a way that the judicial establishment (i.e., the Ministry of Justice and Supreme Court) could not easily block reform. The Committee was composed of 13 members, six from legal fields (three law professors and one representative each for the courts, Ministry of Justice, and bar), and the rest came from other areas of civil society. The Committee's structure gave an opportunity for reformists (i.e., typically from legal academia and the Japanese Federation of Bar Associations) to negotiate with traditionalists in a forum in which the latter were not in full control, as they normally were.

The JSRC started deliberations in July 27, 1999 and presented its final recommendations to the Prime Minister on June 12, 2001.[8] While the report made proposals across a variety of issues, the top three reforms were the expansion of the number of lawyers, the establishment of an American-style law school system, and the creation of a lay participation system. The first two proposals related to the perceived problem of limited access to justice on account of there being too few lawyers in society. The law school reform was designed to train a greater number of lawyers and improve their quality by providing superior education, compared to the old system. Prewar Japan had followed the German *Staatsexamen* and *Referendariat* systems, under which aspiring jurists would be qualified by examination and undertake rotating internships within the judiciary, with passers classified into judges, prosecutors, and lawyers based on their examination scores. After World War II, Japan retained the "judicial examination" system, but transformed the *Referendar* internship into the Legal Training and Research Institute (LTRI), a Supreme Court-operated school for exam passers. By the 1990s, reformists had come to believe that the jurists produced by the LTRI and examination-centric

6 Setsuo Miyazawa, "The Politics of Judicial Reform in Japan: The Rule of Law at Last," *Asian-Pacific Law & Policy Journal* 1 (2001): 102.

7 Ibid., 99.

8 Justice System Reform Council, *Recommendations of the Justice System Reform Council – For a Justice System to Support Japan in the 21st Century*, June 12, 2001, https://japan.kantei.go.jp/policy/sihou/singikai/990612_e.html.

education system were too narrow-minded and too few in number. Their solution was the importation of American-style, graduate-level legal education and a modified examination with a higher pass rate.

The third key reform involved adoption of a German-style lay participation system in which ordinary citizens deliberate and vote with judges in certain criminal trials. A unique feature is that the lay judges' finding of guilt can be ignored if all professional judges are united in disagreement with the finding made by the lay judges. This reform did not address any widely perceived problem, but rather aimed to resolve a vague sense of public detachment from the legal system by introducing civic involvement in the courts.[9] One of the JSRC's objectives was to shift the postwar national paradigm from reliance on administrative guidance to the rule of law.[10] This entailed, in the JSRC's words, encouraging individuals to "grow out of the sense of being a governed object and … participate in making a free and fair society in mutual cooperation as an autonomous governing subject with social responsibility in hand."[11]

After the JSRC proposed these three reforms, and a number of other important reforms that cannot be considered in this space, the task of drafting laws to implement the JSRC's proposals was left to a special "Promotion Office" under the Prime Minister, rather than the ordinary political process, to protect reform from dilution.

In Korea, pressure for judicial reform had been building since the 1988 democratization. In 1995, the Globalization Promotion Committee (세계화추진위원회/世界化推進委員會), created by President Kim Young-Sam, suggested adopting an American-style law school system to replace the Japanese-derived judicial examination and Judicial Research and Training Institute (JRTI) system for qualifying jurists. As in Japan, it was believed that the system produced too few lawyers. Traditionalists in the judicial establishment (Supreme Court, Ministry of Justice, and the Korean Bar Association) were able to defeat this proposal, although pass rates for the examination were gradually raised so as to qualify 1,000 lawyers per year as a compromise. Furthermore, an influential legal activist NGO, People's Solidarity for Participatory Democracy (PSPD, 참여연대/參與連帶), was founded in 1994 to fight perceived vestiges of the authoritarian era, and judicial reform has been one of its core focuses. Meanwhile, a growing problem with no parallel in Japan began to emerge – collapse of public faith in the judiciary. Opinion polls showed this declining trust and protests around courts became a common occurrence. At times, a hidden battalion of riot police was stationed behind the Supreme Court building.[12]

9 Ibid., Chapter IV.

10 Tom Ginsburg has suggested that this was a key motivation of Japan's judicial reforms, and this is clearly supported by the JSRC's public statements. Tom Ginsburg, "Korea and the Reform of the Northeast Asian Legal Complex," in Marie Seong-Hak Kim, ed., *The Spirit of Korean Law: Korean Legal History in Context* (Leiden: Brill Nijhoff, 2016), 233.

11 Justice System Reform Council, *The Points at Issue in the Justice Reform*, December 21, 1999, https://japan.kantei.go.jp/policy/sihou/singikai/991221_e.html.

12 The author recalls this from a 2008 tour of the Supreme Court.

Judicial reform became a political issue, and President Roh Moo-Hyun was elected after campaigning to undertake it. He assumed office in February 2003, and later that year established the Judicial Reform Committee (사법개혁위원회/司法改革委員會). It was composed of 21 members from legal academia, legal professions, and civil society. It started deliberations on October 28, 2003 and delivered its final recommendations on December 31, 2004.[13] Thereafter, an implementation committee was established, the Judicial Reform Promotion Committee (사법개혁추진위원회/司法改革推進委員會), under the Prime Minister's Office. This Committee translated the first Committee's proposals into legislation because it was believed that reform would be watered down or prevented if it were left to the legislature. A range of reforms to procedure and judicial organization were proposed, but the centerpieces were expanding the number of lawyers, adopting an American-style law school system, and establishing an experimental jury system that inclined more towards the US model than the German or Japanese.

Numerous Korean law professors and judges explained to the author that the Japanese judicial reform process was consciously benchmarked and improved upon where weaknesses were perceived. For example, in Japan, undergraduate law departments were not closed upon the establishment of law schools, resulting in too many law students and a still relatively low examination pass rate. Japanese judicial traditionalists also forced a compromise on civil participation, leading to the adoption of a variation on the German lay judge system instead of the more radical American alternative. Korean reformists met with Japanese scholars and jurists to learn from their judicial reform experience. Subsequently, Korea's Judicial Reform Committee (JRC) recommended limiting the number of law schools and creating a jury system whose verdicts would be virtually binding on judges.

Just as Japan's JSRC report spoke of transformative change, Korea's JRC explained its importance and purpose in its final report:

> Our judicial system has reached a moment at which it must boldly transform by taking on a new paradigm that can respond to a rapidly changing environment, in order to regain the people's trust, actualize justice and universal values, and effectively support the national development of the future.... The JRC deliberated … according to the basic concepts of realizing:
>
> 1. A judicial system that can establish and root the rule of law;
> 2. A judicial system that can enhance the people's trust in the judiciary and its suitability for democracy;
> 3. A speedy and fair judicial system that the people can use easily;
> 4. A judicial system that strengthens human rights protections, and;

13 Supreme Court of Korea, "Reform," https://eng.scourt.go.kr/eng/judiciary/history/reform.jsp.

5. A judicial system that can train excellent legal personnel with specialist legal knowledge, international competitiveness, and professional ethics.[14]

While the Japanese reform seems to have been motivated more by a desire to shake up the national model to end an intractable period of economic stagnation, Korea's reforms were more driven by democratization-related concerns. Korea's judicial institutions had become deeply unpopular and needed to be altered to meet the expectations of an angry public. The judicial establishment understood this. For example, a 2008 internal judicial report admitted that,

> It is said that inside the judiciary the principles of democracy and the rule of law are not sufficiently guaranteed, and we have come to be afflicted with the endless criticism of outsiders who point this out. And we are disregarded by the people for the reason that, they say, in such a judiciary the output, as expected, lacks suitability for democracy. In the end, this can lead to the result that, because of the people's loss of trust, the judiciary can come to be unable to carry out its mission.[15]

The diffusion of law also played a role in the reform process. Political, legal, and civil society leaders harnessed the public outcry and crafted solutions based on their interpretations of foreign legal ideas. Leading reformists, such as Professors Cho Kuk and Han In-Sŏp, studied in the US and argued in the JRC process for the adoption of many American ideas. For example, Cho Kuk is most well-known for the establishment of sentencing guidelines and Han In-Sŏp for jury trials. Additionally, Japan's earlier launch of judicial reform strengthened the hand of reformists in Korea because Japan's legal example is prestigious in legal circles there. In the face of reformists' invocations of both American ideas and Japanese legal developments, and amidst the collapse of public trust in the judiciary, Korean legal traditionalists faced strong pressure to compromise.

Another factor was also important: strong political support from President Roh, a former dissident lawyer who grasped the importance of reforming the machinery of justice. Moreover, his political party won a majority in the legislature in April 2004 (after the failed impeachment effort against Roh), clearing the way for passage of legislation drawn up by the Judicial Reform Promotion Committee. Korea's judicial reforms thus occurred at an ideal political moment for reformists.

What about Taiwan? Its judicial reform process predated both the Japanese and Korean processes. Like Korea, in Taiwan there existed popular discontent with the judiciary, a legal reformist movement descended from the democratization movement, agitation for the adoption of some American legal ideas, and,

14 사법개혁위원회 [Judicial Reform Committee], 사법개혁을 위한 건의문 [Recommendations for Judicial Reform], December 31, 2004: 1–2.

15 대법원 [The Supreme Court], 사법부의 어제와 오늘, 그리고 내일 [The Judiciary's Yesterday, Today, and Tomorrow], September 29, 2008: 214.

at one stage, a dissident lawyer-turned-President, Chen Shui-Bian. However, unlike Japan and Korea, the key reform issues were not increasing numbers of lawyers, legal education reform, and adopting the jury – although jury reform became a major issue later. Rather, the main issues were the reorganization of the institutional roles of the Supreme Court and Judicial Yuan, reform of the judicial personnel system, and criminal procedure reform. And crucially, unlike Japan and Korea, Taiwan did not utilize the Japanese and Korean model of a deliberative committee (meeting for one–two years) followed by an implementation committee. Rather, Taiwan held a three-day conference and left implementation in the hands of the ordinary political process and judiciary. Consequently, implementation of judicial reform stalled for years and went in new directions when the presidency changed hands. It continues even to this day, while the Japanese and Korean reforms are considered essentially concluded.[16]

The comparative sketch above has passed over the three jurisdictions' reforms to criminal, civil, and administrative litigation procedure. These were important, but they cannot be fully discussed here. To summarize, as mentioned above, it is generally true that Japan's postwar occupation reformed its procedural laws to make them more American and soften Continental features. The most visible examples may be criminal procedure's shift toward adversarialism, the reduction in headcount of Japanese Supreme Court judges from over 100 to 15, and the abolition of the administrative jurisdiction for government-versus-citizen litigation. As stated above, South Korea and the Republic of China did not have such reforms imposed on them in the postwar era, although they both followed certain Japanese developments independently – for example, mimicking its institutions for judicial selection, training, and promotion. But they maintained an old, prewar style of procedural law, which in Korea's case was an illiberal colonial law, and in the Republic of China's case coincided with a period of authoritarianism. The retention of these laws in the postwar era empowered the government and judiciary at the expense of the citizenry. For example, in criminal procedure, neither Korean nor Taiwanese prosecutors needed judicial permission for searches, detention, or other coercive measures.[17] In civil procedure, trial by dossier was the norm and oral

16 In Korea, judicial reform discourse has recently returned because of scandals flowing from the 2017 impeachment of President Park Geun-Hye. Current issues relate to reform of prosecutorial organization and judicial administration, both of which are suspected of independence-related failures.

17 In Taiwan, judicial approval for detention warrants became a requirement in 1997, and the same occurred for search warrants in 2001. See, Chapter 3 in this volume, Heng-da Hsu, "The Development and Reform of Taiwan's Prosecutorial System: 1945–2014." In Korea, prosecutors could conduct searches and seizures within 48 hours of a warrantless detention, but thereafter they needed to seek judicial permission to continue the detention, search, or seizure. Warrant requirements were symbolically established by Article 12 of the new Constitution in 1987. Jibong Lim, "Korean Constitutional Court and the Due Process Clause," in Kuk Cho, ed., *Litigation in Korea* (Cheltenham: Edward Elgar, 2010), 160–74. These constitutional protections were more fully realized in revisions to the Criminal Procedure Code in the 1990s and 2000s.

proceedings were limited. In administrative litigation, the government regularly defeated citizens. Taiwan's postwar Administrative Court was nicknamed "the court of rejection" (駁回法院) by the public.[18] Thus, in Korea and Taiwan, revising the procedural law of the authoritarian era was a high priority for reformists.

In light of the many East Asian parallels, it is natural to ask why Taiwan's judicial reform process was similar to those of Japan and Korea in many ways but different in others, especially process, agenda, and outcome. To begin to answer this question, the course of Taiwan's judicial reforms must be closely examined.

Taiwan's judicial reforms: a difficult start and changes of direction

The 1999 National Judicial Reform Conference and its results

The judicial reform process in Taiwan took the form of a deliberative, three-day conference in 1999, the "National Judicial Reform Conference" (全國司法改革會議). Before this, there had been some precursor movements for judicial reform, including the "National Judicial Conference" (全國司法會議), which was held in 1980 and 1988. These occurred under the shadow of the authoritarian era and so are not highly regarded as successes by contemporary reformists.

Efforts to accomplish fundamental reforms to the judicial system began after Taiwan's political democratization. The political transformation proceeded in two stages: first, President Chiang Ching-Kuo ended 38 years of martial law in 1987, and, second, in 1991 President Lee Teng-Hui announced the termination of the Period of National Mobilization for the Suppression of the Communist Rebellion (動員戡亂時期). President Lee was a democracy supporter from a liberal wing of the *Kuomintang* (KMT, 中國國民黨), the Chinese Nationalist Party that presided over authoritarian rule. These and other measures of political reform culminated in Taiwan's first fair legislative elections in 1992 and competitive presidential elections in 1996. During this period of liberalization, activist lawyers were organizing and demanding reforms.[19] In 1990, the Taipei Bar Association experienced a revolt against its pro-government leadership and replaced its board of directors with pro-democracy lawyers. Then, in 1995, the Judicial Reform Foundation (JRF, 民間司法改革基金會) was founded as an offshoot of the Taipei Bar Association to mobilize for judicial reform full-time.

18 Tzung-Mou Wu's Chapter 2 in this volume relates this amusing fact. Tzung-Mou Wu, "The Long Century of Taiwan's Westernized Justice System: Historicizing the Dynamics of Her Judicial Reform of 1999."

19 For a timeline of landmark events in judicial reform activism from 1995 to 2005, see: 民間司法改革基金會 [Judicial Reform Foundation], 理與力: 十年發聲, 十年思辨 [Reason and Power: Ten Years of Voicing, Ten Years of Thinking] (Taipei: 五南 [Wu Nan], 2005), 319–24.

The activist lawyers and legal scholars associated with the JRF saw judicial reform as a necessary follow-up to democratization. They saw themselves as leading a social movement for transformative change in the legal system and drew strength from public dissatisfaction with the courts. Miscarriages of justice during the authoritarian years had diminished public trust in the machinery of justice. For example, in the 1982 case of Wang Ying-Xian (王迎先), the police tortured an innocent man into confessing to a bank robbery, and shortly thereafter he committed suicide in custody.[20] Although this scandal shocked society and led to expanded rights to counsel, defense lawyers were still ill-treated. Wellington Koo (顧立雄), an activist lawyer and former JRF leader, explained in an interview that defense lawyers had to remain silent during police interviews. Once, when he spoke up to say "my client didn't say this, please change the record," the police asked him to leave for interrupting the interrogation. When he refused, the officers grabbed him by his tie and physically threw him and a fellow lawyer out, breaking the latter's glasses on the doorframe.

But by the 1990s, activist lawyers were newly empowered to fight back against injustices. For example, the JRF publicly attacked the judiciary over the "Hsi-Chih Trio" case (蘇建和案), in which three men were dubiously convicted of a 1991 double murder in the Hsi-Chih area (汐止區, *xìzhǐqū*). The case ping-ponged between the courts, resulting in 13 retrials whose outcomes alternated between death-sentences and acquittals.[21] Taiwan's Supreme Court added to the problems of allegations of torture and procedural missteps by refusing to decide the case conclusively and simply remanding it several times, as it commonly does. The overall result was 21 years of trials and appeals, until the trio's ultimate exoneration in 2012. The case symbolized systemic flaws in the island's justice system.

In 1994, President Lee Teng-Hui appointed a new President of the Judicial Yuan, which is the body responsible for administering the court system under the Republic of China's five-part separation of powers regime. President Lee instructed the new President, Shih Chi-Yang (施啟揚), to pursue judicial reform. Under Shih's direction, the Judicial Yuan established the "Judicial Reform Committee" (司法改革委員會) in 1994 to study the issue. The Committee was composed of 24 Members, two of whom were lawyers. This was later increased to four after protests. According to John Chen (陳傳岳), a founder of the JRF, the Committee conducted research and discussed judicial reform, but ultimately "did nothing" except publish a three-volume set of books.[22] Chen, and other activists, agreed with the thrust of the research but were dismayed by the lack of tangible reform.

20 For further details, see Chapter 10 in this volume, Rong-Geng Li, "The Evolution of the Right to Counsel in Taiwan."

21 Rich Chang, "'Hsichih Trio' Are Finally Freed," *Taipei Times* (September 1, 2012), www.taipeitimes.com/News/front/archives/2012/09/01/2003541675/1.

22 司法院 [Judicial Yuan], 司法改革委員會會議實錄 [Judicial Reform Committee Meeting Records] (Taipei: Judicial Yuan, 1996).

In May 1997, a delegation of reformists – representing the Taipei Bar Association, Prosecutor Reform Association, pro-reform judges, and the Judicial Reform Foundation – visited President Lee Teng-Hui to request that he organize and chair a judicial reform conference.[23] President Lee agreed to order the conference, but he refused to preside over it on the grounds that it would violate the separation of powers for him to interfere in a judicial matter. Shih, who was present at the meeting, was persuaded to accept responsibility for organizing the conference within six months. Although Shih was "reluctant," according to interviewees who were at the meeting, the JRF was satisfied. Wellington Koo stated to the author that the purpose of proposing a conference was to generate media pressure to push the Judicial Yuan to undertake reforms it had been dragging its feet over.

But reform was delayed again. After several months, Huang Kun-Huei (黃昆輝), President Lee's Secretary-General (總統府秘書長, equivalent to Chief of Staff), had not heard any news of the conference's organization. He arranged a meeting, and Shih told Huang that he was still making preparations.[24] A few months later, Huang had still heard no news of the conference. At their second meeting, Shih announced that a judicial reform conference was unnecessary. Huang and President Lee again directed him to hold the conference. In the months afterwards, Shih did not provide Huang with direct answers about progress on the conference. Huang heard from sources at the Judicial Yuan that Shih feared the difficulty of organizing the conference and arguing with reformist JRF figures at such a forum. Eventually, Shih asked Huang to pass a message to President Lee that a judicial reform conference was not necessary. Huang replied that he would not dare to do so, and thus Shih met the President to tell him. Lee now realized that he had to request Shih's resignation and put a more reform-minded person into the presidency of the Judicial Yuan.[25] The ideal replacement seemed to be Weng Yueh-Sheng (翁岳生), who was already inside the Judicial Yuan as a Justice of the Constitutional Court and was recommended to Lee by leaders in the legal community. Weng accepted Lee's offer of the Presidency of the Judicial Yuan at a secret meeting at Lee's residence, and he expressed enthusiasm for planning the conference.[26] On February 1, 1999, Weng assumed office. A conference would open in five months.

23 They also demanded budgetary independence for the Judicial Yuan, which was soon granted.

24 Interview with Huang Kun-Hwei.

25 In fairness to Shih, one scholar suggested that he may have refused to hold the conference because he did not want to cede control over the reform agenda to JRF activists. And Shih did accomplish reform in some areas. He appointed outspoken reformist judges to the Judicial Yuan committee responsible for determining judicial promotions, notably Lu Tai-Lang (呂太郎) in 1998. This was a major milestone in Taiwan's judicial independence reforms. Chin-shou Wang, "The Movement Strategy in Taiwan's Judicial Independence Reform," *Journal of Current Chinese Affairs* 39 (2010): 135–7.

26 Interview with Huang Kun-Hwei.

Why was a conference format selected for Taiwan's judicial reform process? According to interviewees, national conferences called by political leaders had then recently been used for democratization-related reform. In 1990, in response to the Wild Lily Student Movement (野百合學運), President Lee met with student protest leaders and promised to hold the National Affairs Conference (國是會議).[27] It produced additional steps toward democratization, such as ending the Period of National Mobilization for the Suppression of the Communist Rebellion and its associated police state institutions (e.g., the Taiwan Garrison Command, 臺灣警備總司令部). In 1996, President Lee held the National Development Conference (國家發展會議), which discussed political and economic reforms as well as the island's relationship with mainland China. The judicial reform Conference may thus be understood as another in a series of major reform conferences in a period of political liberalization.

The National Judicial Reform Conference (NJRC) was held from July 6 to July 8, 1999. It was composed of 125 representatives drawn from lawyers, judges, prosecutors, scholars, and civil society, including some with no legal background. They were tasked with debating 57 specific reform ideas, submitted to the conference beforehand, relating to 12 thematic issues. Representatives and reform proposals were divided into three panels. Panel One discussed five themes: (1) the Judicial Yuan's "position" (定位, i.e., its role in the judiciary), (2) improving "the people's right to litigation" (人民訴訟權), mainly in the context of the criminal defense lawyer system, (3) further research on adopting civil participation in court proceedings, (4) civil procedure reform (including limiting appeals), and (5) how to harmonize conflicting judgments made by different panels within appellate courts. Panel Two examined two themes: (1) introducing adversarialism into criminal procedure and (2) reducing appeals in criminal cases, which, as with civil procedure, focused on enhancing the finality of first-instance judgments. Panel Three considered five themes: (1) judge personnel reforms (including to the appointment system and self-governance measures), (2) prosecutor personnel reforms, (3) how to better evaluate, supervise, and fire judges or prosecutors, (4) establishing judicial independence (including anti-corruption policies), and (5) improving training for judges and prosecutors.[28]

The first two days of the Conference were devoted to deliberation within the panels while the last day was set aside for the Conference as a whole to vote on each panel's decisions.[29] The NJRC voting rules were as follows. The panels were tasked with reaching a consensus on each assigned topic and then sending

27 The Chinese name of this Conference connotes "correcting the nation's wrongs."

28 Descriptions of the each panel's work and conclusions can be found at: 司法院 [Judicial Yuan], 全國司法改革會議結論具體措施時間表 [Timetable of Specific Measures from the Conclusions of the National Judicial Reform Conference], July 26, 1999, www.judicial.gov.tw/aboutus/aboutus05/aboutus05-05.asp.

29 司法院 [Judicial Yuan], 全國司法改革會議實錄 [National Judicial Conference Records] (Taipei: Judicial Yuan, 1999): 1581–3.

them as preliminary resolutions to the grand assembly, where a majority of all representatives was required for the Conference to endorse any proposal. Alternatively, if no consensus could be found for an issue, the panel could submit two or three temporary resolutions to the grand assembly. Then, the four vice presidents of the NJRC would need to reach a consensus on a temporary resolution and submit it to the grand assembly for a vote. If the four vice presidents could not unanimously approve a temporary resolution, it could not be given the grand assembly and no final resolution would be made. These consensus-based voting rules were designed to ensure that judicial reform had strong support from the legal community.[30] In total, the Conference decided on 49 resolutions for reform.

Out of the issues discussed by the NJRC, the three most important were the position of the Judicial Yuan, judicial personnel policy, and criminal procedure reform. The debate over the position of the Judicial Yuan involved the question of whether the Judicial Yuan should be mainly a judicial administrative body or mainly an adjudicative body. Although the Judicial Yuan has inclined towards administration, many reformists believed that both the Constitution and common sense required that the Judicial Yuan be "tribunalized" – converted into Taiwan's highest court for all jurisdictions. This had almost happened in the past, but failed when the Judicial Yuan lost a power struggle in 1947 with the Supreme Court, Administrative Court, and Ministry of Judicial Administration. Thereafter, the Judicial Yuan's adjudicative side developed into a German-style Constitutional Court (大法官會議, formerly known in English as the "Council of Grand Justices"), with a limited jurisdiction, existing alongside final courts for other jurisdictions (the Supreme Court, Administrative Court, and Commission on the Disciplinary Sanctions of Functionaries).

A key motivation for the "position" debate was the perceived failures of the Supreme Court, which, as aforementioned, has habitually refused to decide cases and instead remands them to lower courts for retrial, often on minor procedural pretexts. Additionally, the Supreme Court maintained its aloof place in the judiciary by refusing to accept appointees it had not requested, in defiance of the Judicial Yuan's administrative authority. To make matters worse for some reformists, the Supreme Court has been staffed by around 100 judges at times, a fact that seems inappropriate to American or Japanese-trained jurists. Yet this may appear natural for those educated in Germany, whose highest ordinary court is comparably large. The reformers' plan was to replace the Supreme Court, and other final courts, with a tribunalized Judicial Yuan heading all jurisdictions, with only 13–15 Justices.[31] Thus, the debate over the Judicial Yuan's position

30 The workings of the NJRC are also explained in Chapters 9 and 11 in this volume: Chia-Wen Lee, "Conscience and Convenience: Taiwan's Rocky Road to Adopting the Adversarial System in Criminal Procedure" and Jing-Huey Shao, "A Leap Forward Not Yet Achieved: Civil Procedure Reform in Taiwan."

31 See Yen-tu Su's Chapter 5 for details on the Judicial Yuan position debate: Yen-tu Su, "Regime *Un*changed: The Organization and Failed Reorganization of Taiwan's Judicial Yuan." See Puma Shen's Chapter 6 for the controversy over Taiwan's Supreme Court: Puma Shen, "Reform and

was, to an extent, a contest over the propriety of German versus American-style judicial organization. At the NJRC, the reformists' proposal was adopted.

Second, the controversy over judicial personnel policy was aimed at enhancing judicial independence and competence. Judicial independence had been harmed during the decades of dictatorship as the judiciary had suffered interference from political authorities. Moreover, there was a problem of judicial independence from the prosecution, as prosecutors in the Republic of China had historically been considered "judicial officers" (司法官), existing in the same category as judges. This view was reinforced by their joint post-examination training at the Judges and Prosecutors Training Institute (JPTI, 司法官訓練所). This had implications for criminal procedure, as prosecutors came to expect judicial deference to their arguments and could scarcely conceive of themselves as acting as a mere party to proceedings, equivalent to the presumptively-guilty defendant. Indeed, historically, the prosecutor sat next to the judges in court, facing the defendant, symbolizing his cooperation with judges at trial. Reformists' main remedy for these independence problems was the Judges Act (法官法).[32] The inspiration for this law came from West Germany's *Richtergesetz* ("Judges Law"), an act adopted after World War II to protect judicial independence. Judicial Yuan President Weng, who had studied in Germany, had long championed passing such a law. The Judges Act would recognize judges as a special class of civil servant, codify their decisional independence (審判獨立), and contain specific provisions forbidding their participation in political parties or activities.[33] It was also hoped that the Act would accomplish the "separation of the judiciary and prosecution" (審檢分隸) by excluding any mention of prosecutors and establishing a separate training system for judges alone. Prosecutorial resistance on these items had long delayed the law.

The judicial personnel policy discussion also aimed at elevating the competence of judges. In Taiwan, when there are media reports of cases decided in ways that run counter to common sense, there is a tendency for people to criticize judges as simply too young and socially inexperienced. As in other civil law jurisdictions, Taiwan selects judges by examination from former law students in their early-to-mid-twenties and trains them within the judiciary. Continental positivistic legal ideology demands that social values external to law must not influence adjudication, which should instead be rigorously logical and based on

Resistance: Restructuring Taiwan's Appeals Process and the Internal Culture of Taiwan's Supreme Court."

32 Pro-reform voices in the prosecution (e.g., the Prosecutor Reform Association, 檢察官改革協會) usually disagreed with other pro-reform groups on this issue and wanted to keep their "judicial officer" status.

33 范光群 [Fan Kuang-Chun], "台灣的司法改革 (2000–08): 本文以審判體系的改革為重心" [Taiwan's Judicial Reforms: Focusing on Reform of the Adjudication System], (unpublished paper): 4–5. Fan supplied this article to the author. Versions with similar titles and slightly different content have been published elsewhere.

written law. The brightest young minds are seen as ideal candidates for judicial careers in such a system of "logical legalism."[34] But this judicial style may not fully suit Taiwan, since young judges have come to be widely derided as "baby judges" (娃娃法官) or even "pacifier judges" (奶嘴法官). And those whose decisions defy common sense (but often narrowly follow the law) have been labelled out-of-touch "dinosaur judges" (恐龍法官). Reformists, who have often attacked judges using these terms, believed that much of the solution to this socially perceived problem involved firing judges who demonstrated a lack of competence.[35] The NJRC recommended passing a Judges Act with provisions on evaluating and "eliminating" (淘汰) judges.[36]

The third major reform discussion at the NJRC was on importing elements of Anglo-American criminal procedure. Pro-reform figures have believed that Taiwan's Continental-style criminal procedure did not function properly in Taiwan. One JRF leader, Fan Kuang-Chun (范光群), described it as "too inquisitorial" and "too authoritarian" in an interview. It required judges to investigate the facts of cases for themselves, which is normal for civil law systems. However, it was believed that Taiwan's judges were unusually overly reliant on prosecutors' pretrial investigations, whose findings were embodied in the dossier they provided judges at the start of the trial. Many in society perceived that judges and prosecutors were essentially working together to punish criminals rather than maintaining a healthy tension in a truth-uncovering trial process. Wellington Koo, a reformist former defense lawyer, explained that he wanted to

> establish a fair trial system … it seemed not to have a triangular structure – it was an interrogation by police, an interrogation by prosecutors, and an interrogation by judges. There was never a neutral judge to look at the case.

He added that

> there was no real oral proceeding. Judges didn't allow cross-examination of witnesses, only submission of a written statement. The judges already had the file and already decided their conclusion. Everything that happened in court was just … not a real trial, just a ceremony with no real substance. The court wouldn't listen to what you had to say.

34 Mirjan Damaška, *The Faces of Justice and State Authority* (New Haven: Yale University Press, 1986): 21–3.

35 The reformists also wanted to abolish the judicial exam and JPTI system for training judges. As John Chen explained in an interview:

> After graduating law school, they enter training, and become judges. But they have no experience and don't know society.… If they don't know the facts of society, how can they apply the law? … In the early days [of the ROC] the exam was good, because without the exam it would be easy to make political appointments.… But now, society has changed.

36 范光群 [Fan Kuang-Chun], "台灣的司法改革" [Taiwan's Judicial Reforms], 10–11.

To remedy this picture of the criminal trial as a mere "ceremony," the NJRC considered restricting judicial access to the prosecutor's dossier before the trial, limiting judges' power to expand the charges during the trial, and removing the judicial duty to investigate evidence. These proposed changes amounted an overturning of the Continental tradition in favor of Anglo-American adversarialism. How did reformists arrive at these proposals? Koo described how he and other JRF figures devised their planning that influenced the NJRC's agenda:

> We all studied in the US, we like to borrow its concepts, but when we write down [our ideas], we actually copy Japan. Japan is still civil law and we are civil law. We copy from Japan because it's easier than writing [our own Criminal] Code.

In other words, America's postwar imposition of adversarial criminal procedure in Japan had created a powerful example for Taiwan to follow – and one which was already translated into civilian conceptual terms, making it more easily adoptable.

However, at the NJRC these reform ideas were blocked. Panel Two could not come to a consensus on them, and the majority's conclusions were sent to the four vice presidents of the conference. One of them – the Minister of Justice, who heads the prosecutorial hierarchy – vetoed the proposals.[37] Prosecutors objected to the reforms because they reduced the relative power of prosecutors and increased their workload in the courtroom. It is important to understand that Taiwanese prosecutors were not (and are not) like American prosecutors in that their work involves making detailed arguments at trial. Rather, they are primarily investigators focused on pre-trial investigation and compiling the all-important dossier. If they appeared in court, and often they did not, they would typically refer to the dossier. Indeed, making courtroom appearances is a specialized type of prosecutorial job within Taiwan's prosecutorial organization, and it has been considered undesirable.[38] Accepting adversarialism would mean that the prosecution would have to expand its capacity for oral proceedings and engage in careful argumentation in court. Meanwhile, their high, quasi-judicial status would fall to the level of the socially stigmatized defendant and his lawyer.

Despite the failure of the criminal procedure reforms at the NJRC, the Conference was widely viewed as a success for the reformist side of Taiwan's legal community. But hopes for rapid implementation of judicial reform were soon dashed, and the problem was largely political. In 2000, within a year of the NJRC, Democratic Progressive Party candidate Chen Shui-Bian (陳水扁) was elected to the presidency. This was the first time the KMT was ousted from the

37 See Chia-Wen Lee's chapter on criminal procedure reform.

38 This was conveyed to the author in interviews with numerous Taiwanese prosecutors.

executive, although it retained control of the legislature, the Legislative Yuan. The result produced a legislative impasse during Chen's first term (2000–04) and second term (2004–08). Even though he strongly endorsed judicial reform as a candidate,[39] he was unable to accomplish many important reforms. Several interviewees from the legal community also believed that President Chen did not prioritize the issue sufficiently, but left it mostly to Weng Yueh-Sheng, who continued as President of the Judicial Yuan, to implement internally as far as he could. Huang Kuo-Chang (黃國昌), a reformist of a younger generation,[40] told the author that "I think that was [Chen's] biggest mistake … he must really regret that now. He trusted his teacher [Weng]" rather than resolutely pursue reform himself.[41] In any case, judicial reform became politicized amidst the KMT–DPP partisan warfare that characterized Chen's terms in office. And, as explained below, the KMT eventually came to adopt a view of judicial reform that in some ways reflected traditionalist dissent to the NJRC's outcome. Wellington Koo, a DPP supporter, stated in an interview that he believed that if the KMT had won the 2000 presidential election, the NJRC's vision for judicial reform would probably have been carried out more smoothly.

The faltering progress of judicial reform can be seen in how, in 2001, the Judicial Yuan attempted to force the Legislative Yuan into passing a law adopting the NJRC's proposed reform for the "position" issue. Its adjudicative section, the Constitutional Court, issued Interpretation No. 530, which required the legislature to act within two years. The Legislative Yuan refused.[42] Meanwhile, judicial personnel policy reform stalled, as the Ministry of Justice objected to passing the Judges Act because it did not include provisions on prosecutors. On the criminal procedure front, the NJRC's failed proposals unexpectedly re-emerged. The Judicial Yuan continued negotiations with the Ministry of Justice, and judges began to press prosecutors to more actively participate in trials. Under pressure, the Ministry of Justice relented and put forward a compromise position, the "improved adversarial system" (改良式當事人進行主義). According to this theory, although the prosecutor would become more active at trial, the judge still had a duty to investigate the facts of a criminal case. The Judicial Yuan accepted the new system, which represented middle ground between reform and tradition. It was codified in a series of laws passed in 2002–04.[43] Some suggest that this reform was the most important, since criminal procedure affects the role of the judge and mission of appeals courts.

39 陳水扁總統競選 [Chen Shui-Bian Presidential Campaign], "司法政策白皮書" [Judicial Policy White Paper], https://forums.chinatimes.com/report/newgov/paper/520-6.htm.

40 Huang Kuo-Chang is a JRF-linked professor-turned-politician who became active in the 2000s.

41 Reformists often respectfully refer to Weng as their "teacher" because he taught law part-time at National Taiwan University for many years, educating many pro-reform lawyers, including Chen Shui-Bian.

42 See Yen-tu Su's chapter for details.

43 See Chia-Wen Lee's chapter.

At the same time, there was progress on some of the still-important but secondary issues. Civil procedure reforms suggested by the NJRC were passed in 2000 and 2003. These efficiency-driven measures mainly sought to accelerate adjudication by adopting concentrated proceedings (i.e., holding trials on consecutive days) and limiting appeals. These policies fit with the larger reformist vision of "pyramidizing" (金字塔化) the judiciary – reducing citizens' need to appeal, in criminal or civil litigation, to the High and Supreme Court levels in order to obtain finalized justice, as is common in Continental legal systems. Their goal reflected an affinity with Anglo-American justice, in which presumptively final decisions are made at the first instance, and appeals are effectively restricted to cases with extraordinary errors of law or procedure. However, the civil procedure reforms are widely viewed as having not achieved a reduction in the time needed to decide a case.[44] Some reformists believed the reforms did not go far enough, citing the failure to adopt common law discovery.[45] Others blame the failures of the new civil procedure on the lack of progress in judicial personnel reform – specifically, moving senior judges to lower levels of the judiciary in order to conclude cases at the first instance. This has been resisted because it inverts the Continental ethos of hierarchical review by more capable judges and bureaucratic-style judicial promotion to higher courts over the course of a judge's career. Pro-reform figures also point to the failure to recast the Judicial Yuan as a new final court, which would likely reduce appeals dramatically.

Administrative litigation procedure reforms also proceeded as planned, although they were somewhat outside the scope of the NJRC because they were decided before it took place. The JRF's "Judicial Reform Blueprint," released in January 1999, called for the administrative court to be absorbed into the ordinary jurisdiction and to utilize adversarial-style procedure and oral proceedings.[46] Although administrative litigation reform was largely undiscussed at the NJRC, it was believed that the Judicial Yuan's repositioning as the new Supreme Court for every jurisdiction would resolve reformists' concerns. When that reform was indefinitely postponed, the Judicial Yuan carried out the pre-existing reform agenda, which generally expanded access to justice and created a Supreme Administrative Court in 2000.[47]

44 See Jing-Huey Shao's chapter.

45 For example, Huang Kuo-Chang's Cornell Law School doctoral dissertation on civil procedure advocated importing discovery. See Kuo-Chang Huang, *Introducing Discovery into Civil Law* (Durham: Carolina Academic Press, 2003).

46 民間司法改革基金會 [Judicial Reform Foundation], 司法改革藍皮書 [Judicial Reform Blueprint], (Taipei: Judicial Reform Foundation Press, 1999): 22–4.

47 翁岳生 [Weng Yueh-Sheng], 司法改革十週年的回顧與展望 (主題演說) [Looking Back and Ahead at the 10-Year Anniversary of Judicial Reform (Keynote Speech)], in 湯德宗 and 黃國昌 主編 [Dennis Te-Chung Tang and Huang Kuo-Chang, eds.], 司法改革十週年的回顧與展望 [Looking Back and Ahead at the 10-Year Anniversary of Judicial Reform] (Taipei: Academia Sinica, 2010), 40–4.

As a side note, the issue of legal education reform, barely examined at the NJRC, suddenly emerged in 2005. The decisions in Japan, in 2001, and Korea, in 2005, to adopt the American-style graduate-level law school system weighed heavily on the minds of certain leading reformist law professors who had experienced and admired the US system. Vice President Annette Lu (呂秀蓮), desiring a policy accomplishment to prepare for a possible presidential run in 2008, appointed Professor Lo Chang-Fa (羅昌發) to oversee an effort for law school reform. But the plan failed after it met with resistance from the majority of legal educators.[48]

Judicial reform under the KMT (2008–16): a new direction

The 2008 election of Ma Ying-Jeou to the presidency ushered in a new era for judicial reform. Politically, there was no longer divided government, as the KMT controlled both the legislature and executive. However, to many reformists it seemed that President Ma was not deeply interested in judicial reform and did not prioritize it. One major reform in his first term came with the April 2010 passage of the Fair and Speedy Criminal Trials Act (刑事妥速審判法), which aimed to reduce trial delays and limit criminal appeals.[49] Under the law, prosecutors are not permitted to appeal a case if the defendant has been acquitted three times, which resulted in the release of the high-profile "Hsi-Chih Trio" defendants in 2012.[50] Although the Act curbed some egregious abuses, reformers, many of whom were anti-KMT, were not invited to participate in its drafting and subsequently criticized it.[51] One JRF leader stated to the author that JRF activists felt unwilling to criticize judicial reform efforts during President Chen's years. But under President Ma, the JRF became the government's antagonist over his judicial reform policies.

In October 2010, President Ma selected new Judicial Yuan leadership to oversee judicial reform. Rai Hau-min (賴浩敏) was appointed as President of the Judicial Yuan, and Su Yeong-chin (蘇永欽) was made Vice President. It was widely believed in Taiwan's legal community that Su, a law professor, was essentially in charge of the judicial reform agenda under President Ma. It was also well-known that he was a personal friend of President Ma and a top advisor to the KMT on constitutional and judicial affairs. One professor described him as "the KMT's legal brain." Before the 1999 NJRC, Su wrote a book, *Re-Reforming Judicial Reform*, anticipating many of the Conference's conclusions and offering a

48 See Chapter 8 in this volume: Neil Chisholm and Hwei-Syin Chen, "Transformation from the Top-down or Bottom-up? Legal Education Reform as a Microcosm of Taiwan's Inconclusive Judicial Reform Process."

49 "Legislature Passes Speedy Trial Bill," *Taiwan Today* (April 26, 2010), https://taiwantoday.tw/news.php?unit=2&post=1125.

50 Rich Chang, " 'Hsichih Trio' Are Finally Freed."

51 Wang Jaw-perng (王兆鵬), "The Judiciary's Ignorant Approach," *Taipei Times* (April 20, 2010), www.taipeitimes.com/News/editorials/archives/2010/04/20/2003471016.

pre-emptive minority report.[52] Su's dissenting views included objecting to the transformation of the Judicial Yuan into an all-jurisdictional Supreme Court, and he had voted against this proposal as a delegate to the NJRC. Instead he preferred that it continue as a primarily judicial administrative agency with only a Constitutional Court. This reflected his generally pro-Continental and even pro-German law outlook. To the JRF, the elevation of the traditionalist Su to the Judicial Yuan's leadership was a nightmare come true.

Su did not accept the NJRC's conclusions as the last word on the direction for judicial reform. In an interview with the author, he carefully stated his respect for the NJRC's proposals but also generally dismissed them as decided in advance without genuine deliberation and therefore not entirely legitimate. To lay the groundwork for a new direction, Su effectively restarted judicial reform by initiating a new process. The Judicial Yuan established the National Judicial Reform Policy Committee (全民司法改革策進會), which deliberated for about a year during 2011. On the surface, it resembled the Japanese and Korean-style deliberative committees because it was composed of 13 members drawn from the judiciary, prosecution, bar, academia, civil society, and media.[53] However, mainstream reformists were shut out of the new Committee and its membership represented traditionalist and pro-KMT perspectives. The Committee had five subcommittees that each considered separate parts of judicial reform: the Judicial Yuan's position, criminal procedure, civil procedure, judicial personnel policy, and civil participation in trials.

To summarize its decisions, the Committee recommended preserving the Judicial Yuan's "position." Su defended this to the author by arguing that separate specialized courts of final appeal are better equipped to deal with the factual complexity of the issues they face. He also contended that it would be impossible for a single Supreme Court of 13–15 justices to adjudicate the thousands of appeals that it ought to hear annually. This reflected Su's traditionalist preference for German rather than American legal models. In criminal procedure it was decided that the reforms already passed were sufficient. The civil procedure subcommittee similarly found that the existing reforms were adequate, but it attempted to strengthen the "pyramidization" effort by encouraging senior judges to remain at the District Court level. A judge in the Judicial Yuan's Civil Affairs Department, tasked with implementing the reform, stated that this was largely unsuccessful because senior judges did not want to remain in hierarchically inferior positions. With regards to judicial personnel policy, the prevailing methods of selecting and training judges were to be kept, and it was hoped that better internal supervision of judges would lead to improvements in the public's negative image of judges. For civil participation, it was suggested that a "lay

52 蘇永欽 [Su Yeong-chin], 司法改革的再改革 [Re-Reforming Judicial Reform] (Taipei: 元照出版 [Angle Press], 1998).

53 司法院 [Judicial Yuan], 司改策進會 [Judicial Reform Policy Committee], www.judicial.gov.tw/revolution/index2.asp.

observer" system would be preferable for Taiwan rather than the Anglo-American-style jury. The common theme in the new vision for reform was maintaining continuity with Taiwan's judicial traditions as far as possible.

Political reality soon intruded upon the new era of judicial reform as scandals elicited public outrage and calls for deeper reform. Beginning in 2010, there were a series of judicial corruption incidents as well as several cases of lenient judicial treatment for accused child sexual assault offenders. Outraged mothers formed the White Rose Movement (白玫瑰運動) and held protest rallies against the judiciary, whose standing in opinion polls was collapsing.[54] As President Ma was preparing to run for re-election in 2012, he arranged for the passage of the long-delayed Judges Act. Its return from the political grave was made possible not only by the public pressure to reform judicial personnel policy, but by a concession to the Ministry of Justice – namely that prosecutors would be regulated in one of its chapters and therefore keep their foot in the door of "judicial officer" status. The JRF believed the Act did not go far enough in transforming the judiciary by abolishing judicial selection by exam, training within a school, and more intensively eliminating "dinosaur" judges. But reformist judges were happy with the Act's benefits for judicial independence.

As the JRF used the scandals to condemn the judiciary and press for judicial reform, a new flashpoint issue emerged: civil participation in trials. Activists began to suggest that the solution to problematic judicial decisions was to bring ordinary citizens into the trial process. Declining public confidence in the judiciary made that prospect realistic. Traditionalists like Su did not favor[55] such a radical watering-down of the Continental ethos of expert adjudication and argued that lay participation represented an unconstitutional infringement of the principle of trial by judges found in Article 80 of the Constitution.[56] However, Su admitted in an interview that because Japan and Korea adopted lay participation systems in their judicial reforms, traditionalists like himself felt a pull to move in a similar direction. Su's 1998 argument, that Japan rejected lay participation and so Taiwan ought to as well, had become outmoded.[57] Facing public and comparative pressures, Su's Judicial Yuan in January 2012 recommended that Taiwan follow Japan's example in adopting a weakened version of the German-style lay judge system (*Schöffengericht*).[58] It would have enabled five citizens to

54 Kai-Ping Su, "Criminal Court Reform in Taiwan: A Case of Fragmented Reform in a Not-Fragmented Court System," *Pacific Rim Law & Policy Journal* 27 (2017): 221–4.

55 蘇永欽 [Su Yeong-chin], 司法改革的再改革 [Re-Reforming Judicial Reform], 75–83.

56 "Judges shall be above partisanship and shall, in accordance with law, *hold trials* independently, free from any interference." [Emphasis added]. Constitution of the Republic of China, 1947.

57 蘇永欽 [Su Yeong-chin], 司法改革的再改革 [Re-Reforming Judicial Reform], 80.

58 In Germany, the votes of the lay judges can prevail in situations in which only one professional judge deliberates with two lay judges. Where there are three professional judges and two lay judges, the former can out-vote the lay judges. Thomas Rönnau, "Lay Judges in the German Criminal Justice System: A Critical Review," 早稲田大学法務研究論叢 [Waseda Law School Journal] 2 (2017): 187–8.

join three judges to hear a case and vote for a verdict, by simple majority, that could be disregarded by the professional judges.[59] The goal was to enhance transparency by opening up courts to citizens.

Reformists and the JRF seized the political opportunity to denounce the Judicial Yuan's "lay observer system" proposal (觀審制). They ridiculed it as a "tourist" judge system – a play on the terms' common use of the character "to observe" (觀) – implying citizen participants would be powerless onlookers in trials. According to the JRF's democratization-infused ideology, citizens would be fully capable of participating in adjudication and were needed to check the reasoning of error-prone "dinosaur judges." For example, one reformist lawyer has said that

> They do not want people to participate because they look down on the public. If what they said is true, we might as well shut down the legislature … since they [legal experts] are the ones who understand the laws best.[60]

Huang Kuo-Chang, a JRF-linked leader on this issue, advocated for the adoption of an Anglo-American-style jury system. He conducted empirical research showing that 80 percent of the public desired a lay participation system.[61] To address the counter-argument that, when facing limited evidence, Taiwanese citizens would be more likely to wrongfully convict than acquit a defendant, Huang carried out another empirical study to show that this danger would be significantly mitigated by a unanimity rule.[62] Huang's research supported his and the JRF's vocal pushback on the Judicial Yuan's plan. Ultimately, although the KMT controlled both the presidency and legislature, the reformists' public campaign against the Judicial Yuan's proposed lay observer bill, and the DPP's parliamentary obstruction tactics, stopped it from being ratified.

Finally, a new judicial reform issue unexpectedly arose during President Ma's second term: prosecutorial independence. On September 7, 2013, President Ma called a press conference to accuse the KMT President of the Legislative Yuan, Wang Jin-Pyng (王金平), of improper influence peddling. The Supreme Prosecutors Office Special Investigation Division (SID, 特別偵查組) wiretapped a DPP politician asking Wang to lobby the Minister of Justice to terminate the appeal of his first-instance acquittal. The SID prosecutors informed the Prosecutor General, Huang Shih-Ming (黃世銘), who told President Ma. This violated rules on

59 See Chapter 7 in this volume: Mong-Hwa Chin, "Adopting a Lay Participation System in Taiwan: The Trial Observer Reform Attempt."

60 Jason Pan, "Advocates, Experts Urge Jury System," *Taipei Times* (March 17, 2017), www.taipeitimes.com/News/taiwan/archives/2017/03/17/2003666935.

61 Kuo-Chang Huang and Chang-Ching Lin, "Rescuing Confidence in the Judicial System: Introducing Lay Participation in Taiwan," *Journal of Empirical Legal Studies* 10 (2013): 542.

62 Kuo-Chang Huang and Chang-Ching Lin, "Mock Jury Trials in Taiwan – Paving the Ground for Introducing Lay Participation," *Law and Human Behavior* 38 (2014): 367.

disclosure of information related to an investigation, and President Ma's public denunciation of Wang appeared to involve the politicization of prosecutorial power. A scandal ensued, known as the September Strife (九月政爭), in which President Ma unsuccessfully attempted to eject Wang from the KMT, while Wang received DPP support.[63] The September Strife had political consequences. It influenced the course of the Sunflower Student Movement (太陽花學運) six months later, as Wang refused to order the Legislative Yuan's police to evict students that had occupied the legislative chamber in order to stop a service trade agreement with China.[64] Wang used the opportunity to embarrass President Ma.

In terms of legal consequences, in the immediate aftermath of the September Strife, reformists denounced the prosecution as abusing its powers and called for reforms to strengthen prosecutorial independence. The issue of prosecutorial independence had existed earlier as a relatively minor issue, but it became far more prominent.[65] In the end, while no major systematic reforms took place, in 2015 the High Court convicted Prosecutor General Huang of improperly leaking investigation information, and in 2017 former President Ma was indicted on similar charges.[66] In late 2016, the DPP-controlled legislature, with President Tsai Ing-wen's (蔡英文) approval, agreed to abolish the SID over its perceived politicization. This was mostly a symbolic gesture because lower levels of the prosecution can still undertake politicized investigations. Reformers believe the prosecution requires systemic reforms.

Taiwan's judicial reform process has taken several twists and turns from the early 1990s until now. The 1999 NJRC process was initiated with great difficulty, and its implementation has been incomplete. Some reforms, like the Judicial Yuan's reorganization, were not implemented, while others, such as those to judicial personnel policy, are viewed by reformists as not having gone far enough. As the reforms dragged on, judicial traditionalists were able to gain control of the process in 2011 and steer it in new directions. Yet that effort largely stalled as well. Continued judicial controversies have fueled public outrage and energized reformists' attacks on the status quo, as traditionalists still object to their vision of reform. In August 2017, President Tsai initiated yet another judicial reform process, the National Conference on Judicial Reform (司法改革國是會議). As the Afterword explains, it promised several reforms, including changes to judicial personnel policy and a lay participation system.

63 See Heng-da Hsu's chapter.

64 See generally, Brian Christopher Jones and Yen-tu Su, "Confrontational Contestation and Democratic Compromise: The Sunflower Movement and Its Aftermath," *Hong Kong Law Journal* 45 (2015): 193.

65 王金壽 [Wang Chin-shou], 解釋台灣法院改革和檢察改革之差異: 一個政治機會結構的觀點 [Explaining the Difference between Taiwan's Court Reform and Prosecution Reform: A Political Opportunity Structure Perspective], 臺灣民主季刊 [*Taiwan Democracy Quarterly*] 9 (2012): 97.

66 Jason Pan, "Ma Indicted for September Strife," *Taipei Times* (March 15, 2017), www.taipeitimes.com/News/front/archives/2017/03/15/2003666788.

But as of this writing, one key theme of Taiwan's judicial reforms is threatening to reassert itself: inconclusive implementation.

Analytical perspectives on Taiwan's judicial reforms

Taiwan's legal systemic reforms can be understood more deeply when examined from relevant conceptual angles. The following sections highlight salient themes in Taiwan's judicial reforms.

East Asian context: Taiwan in a reforming legal family

This chapter began by introducing the judicial reforms in Japan and Korea as comparative context for Taiwan's reforms. Table 1.1 compares the three jurisdictions' processes.

How did Taiwan's judicial reform process resemble and differ from those of its legal family members? Consider process, agenda, and outcome. Taiwan pursued judicial reform through a three-day Conference, the 1999 NJRC, and implementation of the Conference's decisions was left to the judiciary and ordinary legislative process. This was because Taiwan's then-President, Lee Teng-Hui, believed that it would violate the separation of powers for him to lead judicial reform, despite the JRF's urging him to do so. The brief conference format reflected similar extraordinary conferences held in the 1990s. In Japan and Korea, reform was decided through deliberative committees that met for over one year, while implementation was entrusted to special law-drafting committees organized under the prime minister's office. The committee process reflected the Japanese governmental culture of rulemaking through consultative committees (*shingikai*, 審議会). Korea's governance culture is very similar, and its reformers self-consciously emulated the process in Japan, whose example is highly compelling in Korea.

In terms of reform agenda, the top three items in Japan and Korea were similar: increasing the number of lawyers (which the government had been purposely keeping low), creating law schools to improve lawyers' quality, and establishing lay participation in the judiciary. Where Japan's motivations were economic, Korean reformers' were more political – they believed in expanding access to justice. In Taiwan, however, the problem of the low number of lawyers had existed but was resolved earlier, in 1989, when the Examination Yuan raised the pass rate of the qualifying examination. Jury reform demands, in Taiwan and Korea, were driven by democratization-related concerns.

Perceptions of outcome differ in Japan, Korea, and Taiwan. In Japan and Korea, judicial reform, despite its compromises, is considered essentially concluded if not perfectly successful. The number of lawyers in both countries has grown to levels that alarm many, although reformers still want more, while law schools are viewed as problematic for various reasons. It is said that Japanese and Korean law students are still too focused on passing the qualifying exams rather than intellectual enrichment. Observers also believe that Japan's lay participation system is losing public

Table 1.1 Judicial reforms across East Asia compared

	Japan	*Korea*	*Taiwan*
Main perceived problem	Long economic slump; seemed national model exhausted	Loss of faith in judiciary; authoritarian ethos in machinery of justice	Loss of faith in judiciary; authoritarian ethos in machinery of justice
Judicial reform's main goals	Decisively transform legal system; reinvigorate society and economy	*Reformers*: "Democratize" legal system; *Traditionalists*: Restore faith with minimum change	*Reformers*: "Democratize" legal system, restructure judiciary; *Traditionalists*: Restore faith with minimum change
Who initiated the process?	Political and legal establishment	Reformists	Reformists
Main process	2-year committee	1-year committee	3-day conference
Year started	1999 (July)	2004	1999 (July)
Most important reforms	Increase number of lawyers Adopt US-style law schools Introduce jury system	Increase number of lawyers Adopt US-style law schools Introduce jury system	Judicial Yuan "position" (定位) Fix judicial personnel system Criminal procedure reform
Conflict lines (generally)	Supreme Court, Prosecutors v. Bar, Professors	Supreme Court, Prosecutors, Bar v. Professors, NGOs	Judicial Yuan, Prosecutors v. Professors, NGOs
Antagonism between the two sides?	Relatively low	High but decreased over time	High and increased over time
Executive support for reform?	Yes	Yes	Sometimes/Complicated
Drafting process	Promotion Committee	Promotion Committee	Ordinary legislative process
Did reformists mostly succeed?	Yes	Yes	No

support,[67] and Korea's jury system has been left unfinished in an experimental mode. Meanwhile, in Taiwan, judicial reform has been far more inconclusive. Although changes to criminal procedure were enacted, and are seen as a mixed success, the Judicial Yuan position reform failed and judicial personnel reform was partial. Later, the prolonged judicial reform process fell into the hands of traditionalists, who steered it in a new direction. Public distrust in Taiwan's judiciary has persisted, and a new reform process was initiated in 2017.

How can we explain the lower degree of reform success in Taiwan than in Japan and Korea? First, and probably most importantly, in the latter countries judicial reform was undertaken when the executive and legislature were controlled by the same party. This condition existed in Taiwan under the KMT in 1999, but disappeared when the DPP won the presidency the following year and judicial reform became politicized. Thereafter, the KMT and DPP visions of judicial reform diverged over eight years of divided government. Had Chen Shui-Bian not become President in 2000, judicial reform might have occurred more smoothly. Alternatively, had Judicial Yuan President Shih Chi-Yang not delayed the NJRC for years, significant reforms might have occurred under President Lee.

Second, executive branch heads in Japan and Korea prioritized judicial reform implementation, but their Taiwanese counterparts largely have not. The clearest manifestation of this is the special care taken in Japan and Korea to avoid leaving the drafting of judicial reform bills to the ordinary legislative process.

Third, in Korea's Judicial Reform Committee, the Supreme Court defected from the traditionalist side to join the reformers on many issues. The reasons were not only its new leadership appointed by President Roh Moo-hyun, but also the long-term impact of an "overseas training" (해외연수/海外研修) program that pays for judges to visit foreign law schools and undertake LLM degrees. The program sends about 100 judges abroad annually, and most choose the US as a destination. Judges who participate in the program are considered elite and are usually promoted to higher levels in the courts. The effect of the program has been to increase the influence of American law on senior judges, which has made them more sympathetic to reformers' views. A similar program exists in Taiwan's judiciary, but it is less well-funded, less in demand, and less prestigious.[68] Taiwan's judiciary thus remained firmly traditionalist and an obstacle to reformists. As a side note, pro-reform judges in Korea generally enjoyed a good working relationship with reformist NGOs and professors, strengthening the cause of reform, while such relations in Taiwan were much worse.

Fourth, it is possible that had Taiwan pursued reform in a longer, committee-based process, as in Japan and Korea, rather than a three-day conference, reformers and traditionalists may have been able to negotiate lasting compromises. Traditionalists believed that the NJRC's conclusions were rushed, although

67 Julian Ryall, "Japanese Opting out of Serving as Lay Judges," *DW.com* (June 14, 2016), https://p.dw.com/p/1J6BI.

68 Interviews with Korean and Taiwanese judges.

reformers thought that the three-day conference implicitly included years of pre-existing debates within the legal community. But it may be wishful thinking to think that the Japanese or Korean style of political decision-making could be applied in Taiwan. There, the culture of leadership and collective decision-making is simply very different.

Finally, what does Taiwan's experience contribute to the bigger picture of judicial reform in East Asia? A few scholars have compared the reforms in Japan, Korea, and Taiwan, noting similarities and searching for unifying themes or causes. Malcolm Feeley has suggested that judicial reforms in the region (including China) have achieved moderate success compared to court reforms in America decades earlier, which he evaluates as failures. Feeley attributes the accomplishments of East Asian reforms to two factors: that their court systems are relatively new creations, inspiring little allegiance from society, and they are managed centrally nationwide. This makes implementing change relatively easier, he argues. In contrast, US justice institutions are "well established" and decentralized, making them "entrenched" and "almost impervious to efforts at systemic change."[69]

Tom Ginsburg has interpreted the reforms in terms of political change. He argues that judicial (and other) reforms in Japan, Korea, and Taiwan represent a transformation of what he terms "the Northeast Asian legal complex" – the competent hierarchical judiciary, small legal profession, and government-favoring administrative law systems that existed in each of the jurisdictions. This complex was oriented toward generating high economic growth and "performance legitimacy" for the government, but it "ran out of steam" in the early 1990s because of economic decline in Japan and democratization in Korea and Taiwan.[70] Reforms that aimed to expand the bar, provide freedom of information, judicialize politics, and generally "open up" the legal system represented a push to increase transparency and participation. On the political economy level, these changes signify a shift away from the performance legitimacy of the developmental state era and toward a new epoch of "participation legitimacy," Ginsburg suggests.[71] "Northeast Asian political systems now derive their legitimacy from the *appearance* of involvement by the public. Participation legitimates the law."[72]

The significance of Taiwan's example for understanding judicial reform in East Asia is that it completes the picture of the Japanese legal family's repudiation of much of its procedural inheritance. Essentially, the three jurisdictions independently elected to overhaul their machinery of justice. All three, to some degree, drew greater inspiration for reform from American instead of German

69 Malcolm M. Feeley, "East Asian Court Reform on Trial: Comments on the Contributions," *Pacific Rim Law & Policy Journal* 27 (2017): 292–4.

70 Tom Ginsburg, "Korea and the Reform of the Northeast Asian Legal Complex," 233–4.

71 Ibid., 258–9.

72 Ibid., 234.

law, which is unexpected given their legal histories. And in Taiwan, as in Korea, the animating force of the reform efforts was the extension of democratization from the political realm into the law.

Democratization

Law reform in the context of democratization can be interpreted in two ways. First, it may be seen as part of "democratic consolidation," which is the set of post-democratization changes that serve to prevent a return to undemocratic government.[73] Second, legal reform may represent "democratic deepening"[74] or improving the "quality of democracy."[75] These theories only partly fit Taiwan's case: some reforms involved preventing the reoccurrence of authoritarian abuses, notably in criminal procedure, and all aimed at enhancing the quality of governance. But Taiwan's reformers went further – they wanted to impart a democratic ethos to the island's judicial institutions.

As described above, a major segment of Taiwan's judicial reform advocates, the JRF, were institutional descendants of democratization activists. The JRF and its associated figures were also legal elites who offered concrete solutions to an exasperated public that had lost faith in the judiciary. The JRF's early slogan was "the judiciary for the people" (司法為民), and this spirit guided their vision for reform. Its 1999 "Judicial Reform Blueprint" stated that

> … in the old days law took the people as its object, law as a tool for ruling the people; in the current age … it should take the people as its subject, law's purpose, and now safeguard people's value and dignity. With this, the state judiciary's task should be to listen to the people's voice, it should accept the people's supervision, and take protection of basic human rights, the realization of social justice, and promoting democracy and the rule of law as its supreme mission.[76]

Fan Kuang-Chun was an active JRF member and later Secretary General of the Judicial Yuan from 2003–07. Looking back, he summarized the main idea of judicial reform as follows:

> The courts of the past authoritarian era emphasized judges' and prosecutors' high and out of touch (高高在上) authority, whether the court or courtroom layout, both emphasize majesty with a stern atmosphere, making the people

73 Andreas Schedler, "What Is Democratic Consolidation?" *Journal of Democracy* 9 (1998): 91.

74 Joseph Wong, "Deepening Democracy in Taiwan," *Pacific Affairs* (2003): 235.

75 Larry Diamond and Leonardo Morlino, "The Quality of Democracy: An Overview," *Journal of Democracy* 15 (2004): 20.

76 民間司法改革基金會 [Judicial Reform Foundation], 司法改革藍皮書 [Judicial Reform Blueprint], 2.

> feel dread. Procedural laws also ignored the parties' status as the subjects of litigation, treating litigant parties as objects to be judged, especially criminal defendants, of course. However, after removing martial law in 1987, our country then rapidly took steps to become a highly democratized state, and the judiciary certainly needed democratization. That is to say, under the concept of the people's sovereignty, the judiciary exists for the people, it must serve the people, and it is not to suppress the people.... Therefore, in a democratized judiciary, courts should be the institution and place that highly values human rights and makes people feel they have dignity. Judicial reform is actually the leading of our courts toward this direction of improvement, causing people to feel they enter the court with dignity, leave the court with dignity, and have a feeling of being the owner of the country.[77]

Weng Yueh-Sheng wrote similar things in his retrospective article on the tenth anniversary of the NJRC.[78] Indeed, even former Vice President Su, a staunch traditionalist, agreed in interviews that democratization was a major motivation for judicial reform.

How did specific reforms relate to democratization? For reformers, the Judicial Yuan position reform was a linchpin reform in that it aimed at transforming the culture of appeals within the judiciary. It would set aside the dysfunctional Supreme Court, reduce the constant appeals that frustrated litigants, strengthen the first instance, and offer an administrative jurisprudence that was less biased against the people. Reforms to judicial personnel policy were meant to strengthen judicial independence through a Taiwanese *Richtergesetz* and also respond to public outrage over judges' perceived incompetence. Criminal procedure reforms were intended to strengthen the position of the accused in investigations and in court, while reducing the expansive powers of prosecutors and judges. The picture that emerges is one of reformers pushing to rebalance the relationship between the government and individual citizen in favor of the latter.

Motivations for Taiwan's reforms closely resembled Korea's. There also, descendants of the democratization movement took a leading role in pressing for reform. As for Japan, democratization was obviously not an issue, although a loose interpretation of the JSRC's rhetoric on establishing "the rule of law" may make some connection debatable.[79]

What does the Taiwan's experience suggest for theories of democratization? Taiwan's example offers a case study of how a judiciary can be gradually transformed from an instrument of authoritarian rule into a cornerstone of democratic governance. Democratization can generate strong public demand for reform of

77 范光群 [Fan Kuang-Chun], "台灣的司法改革" [Taiwan's Judicial Reforms], 3.

78 翁岳生 [Weng Yueh-Sheng], "司法改革十週年的回顧與展望" [Looking Back and Ahead at the 10-Year Anniversary of Judicial Reform], 60–3.

79 See generally, Justice System Reform Council, *Recommendations of the Justice System Reform Council.*

the judiciary, especially where the courts have been abused to help a non-democratic government remain in power. In such situations, the national community can feel alienated from judicial institutions and consequently distrust them. Legal elites can harness public mistrust of the judiciary and, using their technical knowledge of the law, articulate visions for reform. Legal elitist reform ideas may or may not correspond to the people's more generalized grievances, and it is also possible for rival judicial reform agendas to be adopted by political parties in electoral competition.

Taiwan's more recent 2017 judicial reform conference also suggests another possibility: the public can be invited to offer its ideas and complaints, and legal specialists can translate these into policy proposals to be debated and voted on by legal elites and ordinary citizens in a committee or conference format.[80] This creative model of judicial reform can help to bridge the gap between the public and legal elites, and it can also serve as a viable alternative to the electoral politicization of reform that may lead to its frustration. Such a model may help to transcend the partisan gridlock for societies that cannot, like Japan or Korea, keep judicial reform above politics and accomplish it rapidly.

Finally, Taiwan's case suggests that theories of post-democratization legal reform must move beyond the basics. Judicial independence and constitutional review of legislation and executive acts have been much discussed in this context, and they are important. But there are many other important and technical areas of judicial reform. In criminal, civil, and administrative litigation, procedural rules and institutional configurations shape the way justice is dispensed. One goal of judicial reform is to bring these into line with society's perceptions of fairness and demands for efficiency. Theories of post-democratization law reform should look more closely at how inherited procedural rules and institutional designs can fail to meet social expectations in new democracies. Reforming the judiciary may involve making litigation procedures friendlier to citizens, possibly by expanding the roles of parties in litigation, diminishing the powers of judges, or adopting civil participation in adjudication. These ideas represent the democratic spirit of empowering individuals rather than government agents. Such changes may not be demanded in every post-authoritarian society, but Taiwan offers a case study of how they can be. There are many policy choices when it comes to restructuring legal institutions and procedural rules to make them more amenable to democracy. Indeed, there are vast differences between the Continental and Anglo-American traditions of judicial organization that represent the main options for reformers.[81]

80 See, in this volume: Neil Chisholm, "Afterword: President Tsai's 2017 National Conference on Judicial Reform."

81 Neil Chisholm, "The Faces of Judicial Independence: Democratic versus Bureaucratic Accountability in Judicial Selection, Training, and Promotion in South Korea and Taiwan."

The diffusion of law

The transnational spread of law and legal ideas is a pervasive phenomenon. Discovering legal diffusion in Taiwan's judicial reform process may not be surprising, but the degree to which participants in reform debates relied on comparative legal analyses may be.

As in Japan and Korea, in Taiwan there was a split between the traditionalists' and reformists' visions for reform. Generally, traditionalists favored German and Continental legal solutions to Taiwan's problems, while reformists were more influenced by American ideas. Japan was an important reference for all sides, probably more so for reformers. With regards to the Judicial Yuan position reform, the pro-American inclination of reformists can be seen in how they desired to transform it into the final court for all jurisdictions, with only 13–15 justices, and relinquish much of its judicial administrative role. Many believed it was essentially inappropriate for a Supreme Court to have around 100 judges, despite this being normal, although not universal,[82] in the Continental tradition. For judicial personnel problems, reformists mainly rejected the selection of judges by examination and training within the judiciary. They wanted to select judges from experienced lawyers, as in the US, in order to increase the judicial stock of common sense and life wisdom, considerations which should be less relevant in a positivistic civil law system. Conversely, one traditionalist judge boasted to the author that Taiwan's judicial school was founded a few years before France's *École nationale de la magistrature*. In criminal procedure, provisions introducing adversarialism were borrowed from American law, via Japan, while prosecutors played the role of ardent traditionalists in trying to maintain trial by dossier.

Why did many reformers favor American law? Part of the explanation lies in legal educational patterns. Many pro-reform leaders obtained law master's degrees or doctorates in the US. Traditionalists have tended to receive training in Germany or domestically. People tend to advocate the law of the jurisdiction in which they have been trained. These tendencies were not exactly true, however, as pro-tradition Judicial Yuan leaders Shih Chi-Yang and Su Yeong-chin as well as pro-reform Weng Yueh-Sheng all obtained law doctorates in Germany. Another part of the explanation is that reformists perhaps implicitly felt that German law had failed Taiwan because it was associated with the legal system of the authoritarian years. Reformers seemed to believe that a radical departure from Taiwan's legal tradition was necessary. In the Anglo-American tradition

82 Some smaller civil law jurisdictions have Supreme Courts with fewer judges. Austria's currently has 60, and Switzerland's has 38. Der Oberste Gerichtshof [The Austrian Supreme Court], Richterinnen und Richter [Female Judges and Male Judges], www.ogh.gv.at/der-oberste-gerichtshof/richterinnen-und-richter. Schweizerisches Bundesgericht [Swiss Federal Court], Richter und Personal [Judge and Staff], www.bger.ch/index/federal/federal-inherit-template/federal-richter.htm.

they could find new methods of judicial appointment, another form of criminal procedure, strong juries, and a system that did not rely on repeated appeals.

The more intriguing question to the author is why German legal solutions were not obviously preferable to all sides. Many of Taiwan's judicial problems could be described as originating in a prewar, old-fashioned style of German or Japanese law that did not take account of Germany's postwar updates to procedure and institutions. Wouldn't modern German procedure contain straightforward solutions that would easily fit within Taiwan's existing civil law framework? No clear answer emerged from interviews. As aforementioned, perhaps local jurists felt the German tradition was tainted by its association with Taiwan's authoritarian period. Nevertheless, many German legal scholars visit the island annually for exchanges, but they seem to withhold practical advice. One German-educated Taiwanese professor complained that they take little interest in Taiwan and prefer to discuss law in abstract academic terms. Another explanation is that aspects of German law may not have fit Taiwan's society well in the first place.

A Continental transplant that possibly fits Taiwan poorly may be seen in the function of appeals. In the Anglo-American system, process fairness is primarily secured by strict procedural standards in the first-instance trial, which is presumptively final. Appeals to higher courts are extraordinary and normally limited in scope to questions of law. But in the Continental tradition, process fairness is obtained through routine hierarchical review by more capable judges. There, appeals are regular and intensive, typically covering issues of law and fact.[83] Indeed, the first instance judgment has "an aura of provisionality."[84] Civilian systems accept repeated appeals to obtain finalized justice as a necessary evil to be mitigated, a kind of counterpart to the common law's lengthy delays before the first-instance trial. But Taiwan's appeals system has been dysfunctional. The Supreme Court has refused to dispense justice and instead regularly remands cases to lower courts for retrial for minor reasons.

The poor fit of Continental-style appeals in Taiwan is either in the judiciary's failure to implement it or the growing public rejection of the need for repeated trials. The Taiwanese discourse on "pyramidizing" the judiciary thus represents a desire to escape rather than improve upon the civil law tradition of appeals as a fundamental source of process fairness. The corresponding effort to move senior judges to lower levels of the judiciary further undermines the hierarchical nature of the system.

The legal diffusion dimension of Taiwan's judicial reforms shows how a jurisdiction can become not just a laboratory of experimentation, but a comparative law battlefield. As Chia-Wen Lee puts it, "[reform] debates looked like a turf

83 Damaška, *The Faces of Justice and State Authority*, 47–70. It should be noted that Taiwan's appellate courts typically do not review all facts of a case, but do examine facts that were not assessed at a lower level. This is known as the "continued review system" (續審制).

84 Ibid., 49.

war between scholars who earned law degrees from Germany versus those who studied in the US or Japan."[85] This metaphor of a "turf war" is preferable to that of "palace war," which has been used to describe the diffusion of law in twentieth-century Latin America. There, US-educated lawyers and economists used their styles of technocratic knowledge to displace pre-existing European-educated elites.[86] In Taiwan's legal diffusion "turf war," traditionalists and reformists were motivated less by career advancement than by their senses of propriety regarding the correct image of a judicial system. Discussion of American versus Continental solutions to Taiwan's problems was often cast in terms of right versus wrong.

While there are many "mixed systems," few have attempted so thorough a reformation of their procedural and institutional machinery as Taiwan. For a civil law jurisdiction to adopt American commercial law concepts is relatively simple, but to alter the ways appeals work, how judges are appointed, how parties litigate, etc. is more fundamental. The Continental and Anglo-American judiciaries function according to logics that are philosophically alien to one another. Switching from one to another may prove extremely difficult. Practically, reformers' efforts have crashed into the civil law patriotism of traditionalists, especially existing judges and prosecutors. But greater conceptual difficulties await if reformists' advance further. How can positivistic logical legalism survive a jury system? Can the judicial workload be effectively shifted to the first instance? How can a judge promotion system accommodate that shift? How can competent and politically unbiased judges and prosecutors be selected if not by examination? Will the quality of judicial output suffer if judge training is abolished? The answers remain to be seen in Taiwan, and elsewhere in the Japanese legal family, as it moves in similar directions.

Chapter summaries

The chapters of this volume examine in detail the story sketched above. They are divided into three sections. In Part I, contributors place Taiwan's reforms into comparative and historical context. Chapter 2, by Tzung-Mou Wu, argues that Japan's colonization created a judiciary that was respected by Taiwanese society, but this respect was lost through the politicization of the courts and prosecution that followed the KMT takeover of the island. He further suggests that the executive branch still suffers from a lack of internal legal advice – "government lawyering" – and that this problem has been a blind spot of reforms. In Chapter 3, Heng-da Hsu reviews the history of the prosecution since 1945, laying particular stress on the post-democratization reforms of the 1990s. He also evaluates the

85 See Chia-Wen Lee's chapter.

86 Yves Dezalay and Bryant G. Garth, *The Internationalization of Palace Wars: Lawyers, Economists, and the Contest to Transform Latin American States* (Chicago: University of Chicago Press, 2002).

impact of the criminal procedure judicial reform and the 2013 September Strife scandal involving President Ma Ying-Jeou.

Part II of the book focuses on institutional transformations. Chapter 4, by former Judicial Yuan President Weng Yueh-Sheng and Chien-Liang Lee, examines the long struggle for judicial independence from the prosecution. Liberating judges from prosecutors, who have historically been jointly considered as "judicial officers," has improved judicial independence and thus been the cornerstone of judicial reform, Weng and Lee argue. Yen-tu Su explains the failed Judicial Yuan position reform in Chapter 5. According to Su, the reform was mainly a concern of the legal elite, and therefore reformists lacked public pressure, and the legislature had little political will to pass reform. When the legislature offered reformers a compromise to enact reforms but delay them, the Judicial Yuan refused, and the plan died. Chapter 6, by Puma Shen, analyzes reforms to the appeals system, with an emphasis on the changes that accompanied criminal procedure reform. The chapter covers the ways in which Taiwan's Supreme Court has resisted reform, the efforts of a judge-run association, the Supreme Court Reform Group, in advocating reform, and the growing influence of American ideas on reform discourse. In Chapter 7, Mong-Hwa Chin examines the recent history of lay participation reform discourse in Taiwan. Chin highlights problematic aspects of the "lay observer" reform proposal of the President Ma era and suggests that a more radical system is needed. Chapter 8, by Neil Chisholm and Hwei-Syin Chen, explains Taiwan's failed law school reform, placing it in the comparative context of the successfully passed systems in Japan and Korea. The reform failed in Taiwan because it lacked support from politicians and stakeholders. The chapter also highlights the tension between "top-down" and "bottom-up" reform approaches in legal education reform efforts.

Part III considers the procedural revolution dimension of judicial reform. Chapter 9, by Chia-Wen Lee, argues that criminal procedure reforms were driven by "conscience and convenience" – reformist idealism as well as the judiciary's desire to reduce its workload. She argues that the popular image of justice in Taiwan was shaped by the stories of "Judge Bao," centuries old tales of a clever activist judge who both investigated and adjudicated crimes. Recently, she contends, peoples' views have been influenced by American courtroom television dramas. These have boosted the reformers who favored US-style adversarialism at the expense of German-educated traditionalists. Yet Taiwan's "improved adversarial system" actually resembled an "improved inquisitorial system" until recently, Lee suggests, and it remains to be seen in which direction the law will move. Chapter 10 continues the discussion on criminal procedure by elaborating on the expansion of the right to counsel during investigation, arrest, and detention as well as the work of the Legal Aid Foundation. Rong-Geng Li argues that the right to counsel has been significantly enhanced by reforms.

In Chapter 11, Jing-Huey Shao analyzes civil procedure reforms aimed at reducing the time to resolve cases, a problem that has irritated society and judges alike. Reforms introduced the Anglo-American principle of concentration of proceedings, new case management powers, class action lawsuits, and strengthened

Alternative Dispute Resolution (ADR). The reforms have not been as effective as it was hoped: settlements have increased, the estimated time to resolve cases has decreased only slightly, and rates of appeal are unchanged. Reformers suggest that the voluntariness of many new rules has allowed judges to refuse to implement them. Chapter 12 provides an overview of the reform of administrative procedure, which was initiated before the 1999 NJRC process. Ching-Hui Chen describes how the new procedures, significantly influenced by American law, have evened the playing field between the government and citizens, making the law more suited to the democratic era. Finally, the Afterword, by Neil Chisholm, briefly explains recent developments surrounding the 2017 judicial reform process initiated by President Tsai.

Conclusion

Taiwan's still-ongoing judicial reform process has transformed governance on the island. The Republic of China's prewar German- and Japanese-influenced legal institutions and procedures have been updated in ways that accommodate them to the post-authoritarian age. Democratization permeated the judicial reform process both in motivating its participants to reshape the law and in guiding their efforts to empower individuals in relation to the government. At the same time, judicial reform has featured a real-life contest of comparative law, as traditionalists sought to preserve Taiwan's essentially Continental machinery of justice. Reformists, on the other hand, often proposed fundamental changes that involved the adoption of American legal concepts. German versus American legal educational patterns were often behind this struggle. From another perspective, Taiwan's judicial reforms had much in common with those undertaken in Japan and Korea at around the same time. Yet unlike those jurisdictions, reform in Taiwan moved at a slower pace, leading to frustration among reformers and the public. The goal of restoring public faith in the judiciary has not yet been achieved. As a new judicial reform process unfolds, the future of Taiwanese justice is uncertain.

2 The long century of Taiwan's Westernized justice system

Historicizing the dynamics of her judicial reform of 1999

Tzung-Mou Wu

> In civilized countries, by the side of a despot who governs, there is almost always a lawyer, who regularizes, and strives to render consistent with one another, the arbitrary and incoherent decrees of the monarch.... He who conceives the idea of the prince, without that of the lawyer, sees only one of the aspects of tyranny; to conceive it as a whole, it is necessary to contemplate them both at once.
>
> Alexis de Tocqueville[1]

Introduction

Like its national identity and political status, Taiwan's justice system is a work in progress.[2] Its history is short but complex, its integrity subject to skepticism, its functioning frequently attacked for various reasons.

The whole institution of Taiwan's justice system, as the country's constitutional and statutory documents show, appears similar to what exists in many Western countries. By "justice system," this chapter refers to the entirety of institutional mechanisms run by legal and paralegal professionals which resolve disputes in an authoritative way, enforce the decisions so rendered, or prevent disputes from occurring. In Taiwan's case, such professionals include judges,

1 Anonymous, 'Political and Social Condition of France: First Article,' *The London and Westminster Review* 25 (1836): 161. The translator was John Stuart Mill. For the French version in the Pléiade edition, see A. de Tocqueville, *Œuvres*, vol. 3 (Paris: Gallimard, 2004): 31. For this attribution of authorship and translation, see R. Swedberg, *Tocqueville's Political Economy* (Princeton, NJ: Princeton University Press, 2009): 239–40.

2 In this chapter, Taiwan, as one of the denominations of a political entity, refers to the archipelago that includes the island of Taiwan, the Penghu islands or Pescadores, and other smaller, accessory islands. Kinmen (Quemoy) and Matsu, which remained part of Chinese territory after Taiwan's annexation to Japan, are covered by this chapter only for the period between 1949 and the present. Note that both Kinmen and Matsu were deemed "frontlines" during the armed conflicts across the Taiwan Strait and thus have been subject to military government. The state of martial law on these islands survived that in Taiwan and Penghu by five years. They are the only territories of Fujian province which Taiwan's regime effectively possesses. Accordingly, Taiwan places them under the jurisdiction of the Fujian High Court.

public prosecutors, lawyers, civilian and military police officers, notaries public, and those who can be called court registrars, bailiffs, or *Rechtspflegers*, i.e., officials specialized in fact gathering and checking or the processing of non-litigious affairs. Yet despite the similarity to the West, Taiwan's justice system has been exposed to recurrent challenges. The system was scrutinized in the National Judicial Reform Conference (NJRC), a one-time, non-institutional, and somewhat elitist forum held in July 1999, where the Judicial Yuan, the highest authority of the country's judicial branch, made policy promises. Significant changes have since taken place, many of which are covered in detail by the other chapters of this book. In general, it is safe to assume that those who had earned their law degrees by 1999 would have to redo their constitutional, administrative, and procedural law courses to stay in the practice of law.

Some may be tempted to explain the reform process launched by the NJRC from perspectives like democratization, changes in the country's economic conditions, or its civil society. These approaches shed light on the background or context of the reform process, not the reform's target itself. Besides, such approaches may overlook the reciprocal and entangled relations between the justice system and the factors mentioned above.

If one looks to the justice system itself, the system's resilience, or even inertia, over time is striking. While the seven rounds of constitutional reform between 1990 and 2005 profoundly transformed both the executive and the legislature, most changes agreed in the NJRC occurred in the domain of procedural rules. To compare Taiwan's justice system to a historical castle, so far the reforms have renovated many parts of it, and made it a barrier-free, air-conditioned, more informative, and serviceable museum. Yet the edifice remains in place, and its personnel still behave as if some remained lords and knights acting above valets, maids, peasants, and the like.

This distinction between the institutional and procedural dimensions, however, is porous. Chronologically speaking, the institutional design preceded and thus conditioned the legislation on procedure. Yet the post-NJRC procedural reforms proceeded without an articulate, overarching institutional reform project, which would be as challenging to Taiwan as to any other country in a similar situation. As a result, the incrementally enacted twists in procedural law have amounted to demands for changes in the institutional design. Some of these demands, sometimes made by legal professionals, could be incompatible with or even contradictory to one another.

The lack of an articulate, overarching institutional reform project can be at least partly attributed to the conventional descriptions and criticisms of justice institutions which most scholars and officials share. These descriptions speak the language of legal reception or transplants, yet only underscore the genealogical aspect of Taiwan's existing institution by broadly labeling German, French, Austrian, Japanese, or US influences on the Republican Chinese regime between the end of the 1920s and 1949, or since 1949 to the present. Criticisms are thus often made based on perceived differences among countries' justice systems.

Dissatisfaction with the justice system became one of the top issues in Taiwan's 2016 elections. Promises of reform were made without any specific program. At the writing of this chapter, the October 2017 National Conference on Judicial Reform has made some recommendations. Yet debates are bound to go on in the formal lawmaking process.

The period studied here is the long century from 1895 to 1999, i.e., from Taiwan's annexation to Japan and the convening of the NJRC. This chapter draws heavily from Tay-Sheng Wang's works on Taiwan's legal history. Wang argues that "since 1919, an independent judiciary was to a large extent in existence," and that "[t]he colonial court basically possessed sufficient facilities and competent legal professionals to use Western-style positive law." Wang holds that it was not the judiciary, but Taiwan's colonial condition that was responsible for the partial reception of Western law under the Japanese regime. On the one hand, Wang points out, more and more individuals got to acquaint themselves with modern Western criminal and, above all, civil law. On the other, according to Wang, few grasped what Wang terms "the fundamental spirit of modern Western law," that is, the law's "primary function" being "to protect people from an arbitrary government and to realize justice."[3]

Wang's observation of a somewhat functional yet insufficiently liberal justice system unfortunately remains valid with respect to the mentality of Taiwanese society in the last decade. To take a recent example, the rising number of telephone impersonation scam victims shows that plenty of individuals still fail to distinguish between a judge and a public prosecutor, and tend to give in to an official's unlawful request instead of reacting to the perceived violation of their rights. The masterminds behind these organized fraud rings clearly understand Taiwanese people's limited legal consciousness. Police statistics show that since November 2005, more and more telephone scammers have impersonated officials from a court or a public prosecutor's office. A study finds that the police anti-scam hotline has registered more than 875,000 reports, or 55.2 percent of total reported scam calls between January 2007 and June 2009.[4] In 2016, the police still find it necessary to distribute flyers informing citizens that neither courts nor public prosecutors would summon anyone by telephone, seize any bank account without warrant, or send staff to receive cash in person. This particularly significant form of telephone scamming in Taiwan seems, at least in the period studied, as rare in Japan as in the United States.[5] As this chapter explains below, the Republican Chinese regime, especially under but not limited to the

3 T.-S. Wang, *Legal Reform in Taiwan under Japanese Colonial Rule, 1895–1945: The Reception of Western Law* (Seattle, WA: Washington University Press, 2015[2000]): 185–7.

4 蔡田木、周文勇、陳玉書 [Tsai Tyan-muh, Chou Wen-yung, Chen Yu-shu], 詐騙被害人屬性之研究 [*Study on the Characteristics of Fraud Victims*] (Taipei: 內政部警政署刑事警察局 [Taipei: Criminal Investigation Bureau, National Police Department, Ministry of the Interior], 2009): 68–9.

5 Ibid.

Chinese Nationalist Party (*Guomindang*, hereinafter KMT), has made it a practice to disregard the justice system's internal division of roles and functions for allegedly nobler causes.

Nonetheless, Wang may have misattributed to the "administrative civil mediation system and police summary judgment for criminal cases" the blame for Western law being unable to "penetrate Taiwanese society."[6] Similar mechanisms existed in nineteenth-century Europe, and some still stay in place. They may be deemed part of the justice system, though some may rule them out of the judiciary for lay participation or because police should be considered part of the executive. Wang's argument represents a widely shared, court-centered image of the justice system, which, this chapter argues, is a product of the United States' influence in the world after the Second World War. This image is better at undermining the KMT's ideological discourse than suggesting institutional design projects. Wang's argument seems also in line with a more recent understanding of the rule of law and human rights that would not apply to Western European jurisdictions between the 1860s and 1945. Indeed Wang's argument addresses the complex issue of evaluating colonial legacies. Yet, it is a bad idea to judge the colonial legacies with anachronistic criteria.

Every reform needs a baseline and a goal. Taiwan's judicial reforms lack both. To more adequately position Taiwan's justice system among the cases of Westernized jurisdictions, this chapter considers it necessary not only to historicize the system, but also to contextualize Taiwan's Continental and Japanese references, which were anything but static. This consideration of method matters because the justice system's temporality is, so to speak, "slower" than the legislature's and the executive's. Revolutionary events are much rarer in the history of any given European justice system than as regards legislative or executive power. The most significant one must be the fall of the *parlements* in the French Revolution. Unlike the Bourbons, Bonapartes, and Republicans, who all had their respective second chances, no one has ever since attempted to revive the practices and procedures of the *parlements*. The judiciary has henceforth been conditioned by the state-building process of different societies.

The paragraphs below provide, first of all, a timeline of Taiwan's justice system between 1895 and 1999. This period is divided in two, with one period from 1895 to 1945 and the other from 1945 to 1999. Then this chapter argues that Taiwan's judicial reforms may have overemphasized the judicial aspect and underestimated the executive's importance. Taiwan's executive branch drafts most statutes, enacts rules and regulations, and acts poorly in court. It controls and corrupts the public prosecutor's office, which, in the civil law tradition, is part of the judiciary though is to a certain extent subject to the executive's authority. This chapter concludes that Taiwan may have come to the verge of

6 Wang, *Legal Reform*, 185.

realizing that judicial reforms must be undertaken from a state-building perspective.

History

1895–1954

For fear that a strict chronological order may be confusing, the creation of a justice system on Taiwan and its subsequent modifications will be explained first. Subsequently, its forerunners in France, Germany, and its institutional parallel in metropolitan Japan of the late nineteenth century will be discussed.

The modernization of Taiwan's justice system and the rest of the government began in 1895, as Japan annexed the islands of Formosa, the Pescadores Group, and their inhabitants to Japan pursuant to Article 2, sections (b) and (c) of the Treaty of Shimonoseki she signed with the Great Qing Empire, which then ruled China. The Government-General of Taiwan (hereinafter GGT, *Taiwan Sōtokufu*) was established and vested with a wide array of powers over military, administrative, and even legislative matters of the new colony. This institution underpinned Taiwan's status as a special legal realm within the Japanese Empire throughout her reign over the island. The governor-general in Taiwan enjoyed extensive legislative authority to decide the contents of colonial law.[7] Unlike in the prefectures (*ken*), most laws and regulations were not automatically in effect in the colony, among which was the Court Organization Act (*saibansho kōseihō*, Law No. 6 of 1890), the bedrock of the Japanese justice system. Although Tokyo acknowledged reluctantly that the Meiji constitution also covered Taiwan,[8] its Article 60, which recognized military justice among other special jurisdictions, was the first provision of the whole chapter on the judiciary implemented on the island. By the military order (*nichirei*) of October 7, 1895, the GGT created a tribunal (*hōin*, instead of *saibansho* in metropolitan Japan) with 12 branches located in areas populated by Han Chinese and in which civil servants nominated by the governor-general tried defendants charged by a military or civilian police officer.[9]

Its military character notwithstanding,[10] this jurisdiction constituted a milestone of two novelties. First, it introduced into Taiwan a justice system operated by two offices, that is, the judge on the one hand and the prosecutor on the other,

7 Wang, *Legal Reform*, 44.

8 Wang, *Legal Reform*, 39.

9 Regulation regarding the Organization of the GGT Courts (*Taiwan sōtokufu hōin shokusei*), *Nichirei* no. 11, October 7, 1895. Penal Ordinance of Taiwan's Residents (*taiwan jūmin chizai rei*), *Nichirei* no. 21-1, November 17, 1895.

10 See 小金丸貴志 [Koganemaru Takashi], '匪徒刑罰令與其附屬法令之制定經緯' [Proclamation of the "Bandit Punishment Ordinance" and Its Subsidiary Legislation in Japanese Colonial Taiwan], 臺灣史研究 [*Taiwan Historical Research*] 19, no. 2 (June, 2012): 34–6.

though the officeholders were still bureaucrats. Second, it separated civil litigation from criminal. Besides, the sentence of imprisonment was introduced as a new form of punishment. These were clearly alien to both pre-Meiji Japanese and Qing Chinese institutions. The role played by the prosecutor's office to prevent the judge from being "inquisitorial," or initiating a criminal case that he would subsequently hear and judge, was also part of the legacy of the French Revolution. One should remember that the judgeship was further divided into the examining one (*yoshin hanji* in Japan, *juge d'instruction* in France, or *Untersuchungsrichter* in Germany until 1975) and the trial one. In certain cases, it was the examining judge that took charge of the pre-trial investigation in metropolitan Japan and, since 1899, also in Taiwan. In short, the ideal was that the powers of indictment, investigation, and trial should be separately assigned to three offices composed of equally qualified "magistrates" despite the difference in seniority.

However, Taiwan's colonial legislation transferred a large part of the examining judge's power to the prosecutor.[11] (Even so, no court or prosecutor's office was comparable to a Qing *yamen* or a traditional Japanese office of *yakusho* or *bugyōsho* anymore. The acting judges and prosecutors in this period were not yet legal professionals, but they nonetheless represented the end of the long tradition of multitasking mandarins, feudal lords, and samurai magistrates that T.-t. Ch'ü, Y. Ishii, and W. Röhl described.[12]) Of course, this military tribunal not only fell short of contemporary normative standards of a court of law, but it had limited effectiveness. Wang reports that only 41 of 345 criminal cases tried by this tribunal related to the armed resistance, and that most would-be convicts were killed untried in the name of "urgent disposition."[13] Some studies have estimated that about 32,000 people, or more than 1 percent of Taiwan's population (one out of every 25 young males) died because of resistance between 1895 and 1902.[14]

The justice system established in May 1896 by a GGT decree (*ritsurei*) was, according to Wang, the first Western-style one worthy of the name.[15] Modeled on the metropolitan Court Organization Act, the 1896 system created a hierarchy of tribunals, defined the offices of judge and prosecutor, and followed, with some exceptions, the Act's requirements for office holders. The Temporary Court created in July 1896, set up wherever the governor-general needed to try so-called bandits (mostly rebel fighters) without appeal, also appeared similar. This

11 Wang, *Legal Reform*, 129–30.

12 T.-T. Ch'ü, *Local Government in China under the Ch'ing* (Cambridge, MA: Harvard University Press, 1962): 15–18, 116–29. 石井良助 [Ishii Ryōsuke], 日本法制史概説 [An Outline of Japanese Legal History] (Tokyo: 創文社 [Sōbunsha], 1960): 470. W. Röhl, The Courts of Law, Appendix: Execution of Penalty, in *History of Law in Japan since 1868*, ed. by W. Röhl (Leiden: Brill, 2005): 711–12.

13 Wang, *Legal Reform*, 106.

14 Wang, *Legal Reform*, 111–12.

15 Wang, *Legal Reform*, 63.

military tribunal, while suspending the ordinary jurisdiction of the *locus delicti* and thus violating the right to be tried by one's "natural judge," was an institution run by civilian judges and prosecutors and was not particularly bloodthirsty.[16] T. Koganemaru underlines the fact that in the Temporary Court of Zhanghua, only 17 percent of the 421 arrested suspects were charged and 14 were convicted.[17] Without boasting of their virtue, Japanese professional jurists did in certain cases protect Taiwanese individuals against the arbitrary interference of the GGT.[18]

As mentioned above, the 1896 decree was based on the Court Organization Act of 1890, which was never applied in Taiwan. According to Article 4 of the decree, only judges (判事, *hanji*) in the sense of the metropolitan Act were allowed to be nominated to sit on the colonial bench, where the office bore the more authoritarian name of *hankan* (判官).[19] A similar provision regarding the office of prosecutor in the GGT Court was enacted in 1899. Except for the lowest level of the jurisdiction, all judges and prosecutors had to be qualified in two examinations and have 18 months of practical training.[20] The examination was open to all males of at least 20 years of age holding a diploma from an accredited educational institution.[21]

Taiwan's modernized justice system has stood fast ever since. Subsequent reforms in 1898, 1919, and 1927 were more about rearrangement and reassignment of posts and functions.[22] Despite challenges to its constitutionality raised

16 The "natural judge" is an anglicized French term. Originally it refers to the judge having jurisdiction over a citizen's case by predetermined criteria. U. Seif shows that many Continental countries, and, with some differences, England, share the idea against an *ad hoc*, *ex post* special court, and that neither the French term nor the German counterpart, "statutory judge" (*gesetzlicher Richter*), has become the vernacular. See French Constitution of 1791, ch. 5, tit. 3, art. 4. German Basic Law, art. 101, sec. 1, second sentence. U. Seif, *Recht und Justizhoheit: historische Grundlagen des gesetzlichen Richters in Deutschland, England und Frankreich* (Duncker und Humblot, 2003).

17 小金丸貴志 [Koganemaru Takashi], '匪徒刑罰令' [Proclamation of "Bandit Punishment Ordinance"], 35.

18 Ibid., 35–6.

19 The *kan* (*guan* in Mandarin) which substituted to *ji* (*shi* in Mandarin) in Japanese referred explicitly to the state authority in both the Japanese and Han Chinese contexts of the time, since it meant literally "official." The Republican Chinese legislation, however, made a different naming choice. While it kept the term of official for the prosecutor (檢察官, *jianchaguan*), it denied it to the judge, and followed a Qing legislation of 1907 to name it *tuishi* (推事). *Tuishi* was replaced by *faguan* (法官) in 1989, when the Court Organization Act was revised. Yet the term remains in use in, among other places, the Code of Criminal Procedure.

20 Article 57, Court Organization Act.

21 Article 5, 判事検事登用試験規則 [Hanji Kenji Tōyō Shiken Kisoku (Rule of Examination for the Recruitment of Judges and Prosecutors)] (Ordinance No. 3 of the Ministry of Justice, April 5, 1891). The gender barrier was partly broken by the reform of the Attorneys Act in 1933 (in force in 1936). Japan had her first three female attorneys in 1940 and first woman judge and woman prosecutor in 1949.

22 Wang, *Legal Reform*, 64–7.

by some metropolitan legal scholars of the time and all of its differences from the metropolitan *saibansho*, Taiwan's court system was officially one of the courts in the sense of Article 57 of the Meiji constitution.[23] From 1898 to 1919, there were two court levels forming a hierarchy of two instances. Between 1919 and 1943, there seemed to be two court levels from outside, and each of them consisted of two divisions. A single judge and a panel of three judges sat in the two divisions of the District Court. Another panel of three judges and still another of five judges handled appeals and re-appeals in the Higher Court. This re-appeal division was the forerunner of the Supreme Court.

In reality, Taiwan's justice system of this period was similar to the metropolitan one in that a litigant could have her case heard in three of the four divisions to get a final verdict, though no appeal to the Great Court of Cassation (*daishin'in*), the court of final instance in the metropolitan Japan, was admitted. In other words, Taiwan's jurisdiction was as insular as its geographical condition. The decision to keep the cases away from the metropolitan judiciary was made in 1898. It became a principle despite criticisms from Tokyo, and was later practiced in two other colonies, namely Karafuto (part of Sakhalin island south of the 50th parallel) (1907) and Korea (1910).[24] Indeed the arrangement freed the colonial government from judicial scrutiny, which neither the military nor the civilian political elite would welcome when the GGT was in their hands. The absence in Taiwan of the administrative jurisdiction (based on Article 61 of the Meiji constitution) occurred through the Constitution itself. The only possible remedy against an executive act was the administrative petition in effect since 1922.[25]

A legal subtlety stemming from Article 60 of Japan's Constitution of 1890 turned out to favor all but most indigenous individuals' freedom. It allowed the

23 小金丸貴志 [Koganemaru Takashi], '匪徒刑罰令' [Proclamation of "Bandit Punishment Ordinance"], 32–3. The key issue was the colonial court's constitutional basis. Japan's Constitution of 1890 provided no explicit rule for the governing of colonies. Hence, the institutional novelty of Taiwan's colonial government spurred some discussions in the Imperial Diet and among metropolitan legal scholars. Some members of the Diet challenged the constitutionality of Act No. 63 of 1896 (also known as "Law 63"), according to which colonial rule-making power was vested in the Governor-General. Koganemaru reports four theories regarding the constitutional status of the colonial court, the most popular one among scholars being that of vaguely interpreting the colonial court as part of the judiciary without specifying whether it pertained to the ordinary (art. 57) or the extraordinary (art. 60) jurisdiction.

24 山室信一 [Yamamuro Shinichi], '国民帝国日本における異法域の統合と格差' [Integration and Discrimination in the Japanese Nation-Empire], 人文学報 [*Journal of Humanities*] 101 (2011): 63–80. S. Yamamuro argues that the jurisdictionally separate legal realms embody Japan's rejection of a nation-state as well as her failure to build a nation-empire. Officials of these legal realms and interested groups (such as immigrants to metropolitan Japan) competed with each other for resources and honors. Unlike France, Japan did not have a "colonial school" to produce knowledge and teams of colonial administrators to manage the situation.

25 See 小野博司 [Ono Hiroshi], '植民地台湾における行政救済制度の成立：訴願法施行の経緯を中心に' [The Formation of the Administrative Remedy System in Taiwan under Japanese Colonial Rule], 神戸法學雜誌 [*Kobe Law Journal*] 63 (2013): 71–139.

Diet to create "special courts" alongside the judiciary defined by Article 57. As mentioned above, Article 60 was applied to Taiwan because the invading forces needed a court of law. Indeed the Constitution left some room for a more extensive use of court martial in Taiwan, as the last major armed conflict between the GGT and Han Chinese rebels occurred as late as 1915. Nonetheless, no military tribunal (*gunpōkaigi* or *conseils de guerre*), convened according to the Army and the Navy penal codes of 1883 and 1884, ever tried any individual of Han Chinese ethnicity in Japanese Formosa. Since the civil government took control on April 1, 1896, no military officer in service was ever allowed to judge any Han Chinese civilian. Nor did any military governor-general (10 between 1895 and 1918 and from 1937 to 1945) ever decide a lawsuit in person. In peacetime, the jurisdiction of the Japanese courts martial was confined to military personnel. Given that martial law was lifted on July 7, 1905, for most of the Qing's former territories, civilians of Japanese origin and other nationalities were thereafter under the ordinary jurisdiction until the end of the regime.

As for indigenous peoples, the GGT used dual criteria to decide whether an individual was subject to the court's jurisdiction, taking territoriality as principle and personality as exception. It is important to remember that the Qing only controlled the lower part of the island of Formosa when it was annexed. The rest of the island, mainly mountainous areas, was – and still is – occupied by over a dozen ethnic groups. There were borderlines between the two areas. For the former Qing territories, which were inhabited by Han Chinese settlers and some Sinicized ethnic groups, the territorial criterion would prevail, and the court could hear most cases involving an indigenous individual. The personal criterion was to be applied if such an individual was not or only slightly Sinicized, and these people usually originated from the other side of the border. Most of the less Sinicized indigenous peoples remained under direct police domination without access to court, be it civil or military, between 1895 and 1945.

Some exceptions existed. For instance, Wang cites an instruction of the GGT to show that it required its staff in 1900 to obtain the governor-general's approval before filing or dropping a criminal charge against an indigenous suspect.[26] This was also one of the very few places in criminal procedure where the governor-general gave a direct order or instruction to the public prosecutor. The scarcity of these kinds of cases and of archival evidence leaves the reality of this authority obscure. The requirement for such an approval was cancelled in 1920 whenever the indigenous suspect in question inhabited an ordinary administrative district, that is, far from his home tribe. Yet the police were still free to decide whatever appeared appropriate with respect to indigenous individuals.

26 王泰升 [Wang Tay-sheng], '日治時期高山族原住民族的現代法治初體驗：以關於惡行的制裁為中心' [Mountain Indigenous Peoples' Initial Encounter with Modern Law under Japanese Rule in Taiwan: On Criminal Sanctions], 臺大法學論叢 [*National Taiwan University Law Journal*] 40, no. 1 (March, 2011): 40–7, 50–2.

Back in the Han Chinese areas, Taiwan's judiciary was far from able to monopolize authority to resolve conflicts. The municipal administration and the police played some role as well, by means of aforementioned administrative mediation and police summary judgments. In addition to urging reconciliation with either personal charisma or the office's authority, the mediation section in every municipality was allowed to mediate, or dictate, in all kinds of civil disputes. Any resolution was to be documented and executed. This institution was copied to Korea in 1910. Its popularity in the first half of Japan's reign in Taiwan may be explained by its similarity to a Chinese method practiced by some of the Qing's mandarins and its low cost compared to a formal lawsuit. Yet the court seems to have won more and more confidence as time went on.[27] Unlike administrative mediation, which was only implemented in Taiwan and Korea, the police summary judgment system was enacted in metropolitan Japan in 1885 and remained valid until 1947. In Taiwan, this sanctioning tool began in 1896 and was extended in 1904, along with infamous legislation which restored flogging, as far as to the offenses punishable by detention or penal servitude for no more than three months. While petty offenses were thus screened from the ordinary criminal justice system, the police summary judgment enabled the GGT to procrastinate on investing in the judiciary.[28]

Although the Empire of Japan was comprised of separate legal realms, legal education, the recruitment of magistrates, and the rules for bar admission were uniform. Before Taihoku (the Japanese pronunciation of Taipei) Imperial University was founded in 1928, there had never been, unlike colonial Korea, a public nor private institution for legal education in Taiwan.[29] All law students from Taiwan were schooled in metropolitan Japan. In general, it is believed that, since the middle of the Meiji years, admission to higher education and the recruitment to bureaucracy, including judges and prosecutors, was meritocratic and achievement-oriented.[30] When Taiwan was annexed, Japanese graduates of

27 Wang, *Legal Reform*, 90–1.

28 Wang, *Legal Reform*, 99–101, 120–1.

29 An interesting but yet-to-be studied question concerns whether or not (and, if so, how many) Han Chinese students from Taiwan studied law in Korea, and vice versa. Korea's legal education started earlier and drew more support from local society than existed in Taiwan. Before the annexation, Korea founded a Judge Training School in 1895. Unlike Taiwan, several private institutions offered legal education in Korea before 1945. See Marie Seong-Hak Kim, *Law and Custom in Korea: Comparative Legal History* (Cambridge: Cambridge University Press, 2012): 129. For a more comprehensive account in Japanese, see 崔鍾庫 [Choi Chong-ko], 'ソウル大学校における京城帝大法学の遺産 – 法文学部法学科を中心に' [The Legacy of the Legal Scholarship of the Keijō Imperial University in the Seoul National University: Focusing on the Law Section of the Faculty of Law and Literature], trans. by 金炳辰 [Kim Byeong-jin], in 帝国と高等教育：東アジアの文脈から [*Empire and Higher Education in East Asia*], eds, 酒井哲哉 [Sakai Tetsuya] and 松田利彦 [Matsuda Toshihiko] (Kyoto: International Research Center for Japanese Studies, 2013): 213–28.

30 秦郁彦 [Hata Ikuhiko], ed., 日本官僚制総合事典: 1868–2000 [*Comprehensive Encyclopedia on the Japanese Government: 1868–2000*] (Tokyo: University of Tokyo Press, 2001): 383–8. Byung Chol Koh, *Japan's Administrative Elite* (Berkeley, CA: University of California Press, 1989): 11–12, 21, 30.

imperial universities and those who passed open and competitive examinations were on their way to replace, gradually, the ex-samurais and clients of powerful patrons who so far had dominated the administration.[31] Taiwan's judges were recruited from metropolitan Japan since its courts were founded. The same occurred with public prosecutors in 1899. This recruitment pattern remained, despite a few exceptions, until the end of Japanese rule.[32] Certain individuals even continued their judicial careers in metropolitan Japan after serving in Taiwan.[33] Unlike their senior colleagues in metropolitan Japan, who were hired when the state was meeting an urgent demand but had little choice, Taiwan's trainees were already preceded by a whole generation of law school teachers and practitioners. Thus they had to follow metropolitan legal doctrine and case law, except for issues relating to special rules whose validity was confined to the island.

The quality of judicial personnel largely explains the prestige that Taiwan's justice system enjoyed by at least 1945.[34] Magistrates were more respected than police officers, who had many more unwelcome duties. The courts' cost to the GGT's annual expenditure, though not necessarily significant, was, with few exceptions, somewhere between 0.9 and 1.2 percent of the budget for three decades, until 1937 when a military governor-general replaced his civilian predecessor. Since 1919, Taiwan's judges appeared to Wang as independent as their metropolitan brethren despite poorer tenure protections that were, unfortunately, still better than those in Korea.[35] Prosecutors in Taiwan never benefited from the tenure that existed in metropolitan Japan. Predominantly of Japanese origin,[36] some judges and prosecutors made blatantly discriminatory remarks in open

31 M. B. Jansen, *The Making of Modern Japan* (Cambridge, MA: Belknap Press, 2000): 453.

32 Wang, *Legal Reform*, 99–101, 120–1.

33 The existence of research literature being outside my knowledge, I found 和田一次 [Wada Kazutsugu] (1884–1949, judge – colonial official – Daishin'in), 北川信従 [Kitagawa Nobuyori or Nobutsugu] (1860–1924, prosecutor – Daishin'in), 川渕龍起 [Kawabuchi Ryūki] (1860–1941, prosecutor in leading positions), 岡長二郎 [Oka Chōjirō] (1900–1948, prosecutor in Tokyo, judge in Taiwan, then in post-war Japan). 林政佑 [Lin Cheng-Yu], Ph.D. candidate in Kyoto University, has helped me identify 古賀岩蔵 [Koga Iwazō (?)] (1896–?) in a 1970 pension case (Tokyo High Court, 1965-Gyo-Ko-39 and 1965-Gyo-Ko-51).

34 Alfred C. Oppler (1893–1982) provides a trustworthy observation. This former senior German judge, who communicated with eminent Japanese judges and law scholars in German or French, found that "the judges of Japan, although their social prestige did not measure up to the importance of their responsibilities, enjoyed a reputation of integrity and even of a degree of personal independence." A. C. Oppler, *Legal Reform in Occupied Japan: A Participant Looks Back* (Princeton, NJ: Princeton University Press, 1976): 87.

35 Wang, *Legal Reform*, 71.

36 Huang Yensheng (黃炎生), graduate of Kyoto Imperial University, became the first Taiwanese to be appointed judge in 1931. In 1943, about 10 percent of the 66 judges of the GGT courts were Taiwanese. No Taiwanese had been made prosecutor on the island, probably because of discrimination based on distrust and because the prosecutor was in charge of "thought control." Wang, *Legal Reform*, 80–3.

hearings, yet, by comparison to the police, which were occasionally alleged to take bribes, the honesty of judges and prosecutors was never questioned during the Japanese rule. While one prosecutor was convicted of corruption over 50 years, no judge was ever found guilty of such a crime.[37]

Ironically, the colonial era was the only period in the last three-and-a-half centuries of Taiwan's history when the public trusted the integrity of state officials in charge of dispute resolution.[38] The same can be said of practicing lawyers. While trial advocates (*soshōdainin*) without formal education were admitted to practice in the early years, more and more competent attorneys joined the bar after passing an exam or serving in the judiciary for a while, and they earned higher esteem.[39]

From the story told so far, it appears that all legal professionals working in Taiwan's justice system since 1895 were produced by the Japanese state. This feature has limited the public's understanding of the legal and paralegal professions. Conventionally, much less attention has been paid to, for instance, notaries public and judicial scriveners (*shihōshoshi*). Compared to the small number and official nature of notaries public, the judicial scriveners, whose work, according to Rabinowitz's translation of Article 1(1), Law No. 197 (1949), consisted in "the preparation of documents pertaining to the courts, the procuracy and the Ministry of Justice," became an important population, and the only legal profession in which Han Chinese outnumbered the Japanese.[40] Though the latter profession still exists in Japan and the Republic of Korea, it has been inadvertently transformed into a kind of specialist group dealing with land registration, known as *daishu* under the Republican Chinese regime.[41] As for the notary public, its function in Taiwan has been derisory compared to that in many Continental countries (or to the British solicitors) in spite of recent growth in importance since 2001. No requirement of legally documented evidence comparable to Article 1359 (formerly 1341) of the French civil code exists in Taiwanese law. While Continental notaries public or British solicitors provide important services in their respective markets of real property, buyers and sellers in Taiwan turn to the *daishu*. *Daishu* process formalities rather than produce documents with specific legal value.

37 Wang, *Legal Reform*, 86.

38 The magistrates in Qing China, along with their clerks and runners, remained under constant financial pressure because of the Empire's poor local finances. Phenomena that could be called "bribery" and "corruption" were not confined to the island of Taiwan. See Ch'ü, *Local Government*, 22–32, 49–53, 67–70. For the period of August 1945 to now, it should be enough to mention that four High Court judges, one prosecutor, and two prosecutors-turned-attorneys began to serve sentences in 2013 for corruption and related crimes.

39 Wang, *Legal Reform*, 46.

40 R. W. Rabinowitz, 'The Historical Development of the Japanese Bar,' *Harvard Law Review* 70 (1956): 79.

41 See 吳俊瑩 [Wu Chun-ying], 臺灣代書的歷史考察 [*Historical Study of Taiwan's Daishu*] (Taipei: Department of History, National Chengchi University, 2010).

1945–99

The justice system which the Republican Chinese regime transplanted to Taiwan after the Second World War requires much less explanation than that of the Japanese GGT. First, the Republican Chinese justice system borrowed directly from the Japanese model and indirectly from Germany and France. Second, few changes were made to Taiwan's existing justice system when Republican China took it over.

Taiwan's justice system under the Republican Chinese regime can be divided into two disproportional periods. The first part covers the first four years up to 1949 or early-1950, the second, the rest of the time. In the first era, Taiwan's justice system lost its insularity, and was de facto integrated into the Republican Chinese system and hence subject to a higher jurisdiction located in Nanjing, China. In the second, the "insularity" of Taiwan's justice system was restored and upgraded to the scale of a self-contained polity, because the whole Republican Chinese government, defeated by Communist forces, moved to Taiwan in exile.

The first part of the post-war period was characterized by China's disorganized yet triumphalist and assimilationist takeover of Japanese Formosa. China behaved during this period more as an impatient and self-righteous claimant of the island than an allied forces' trustee responsible for the colony's administration before its people would exercise their right to self-determination. Jiang Jieshi (conventionally transcribed as Chiang Kai-shek), the Allied Supreme Commander, China Theater, appointed Chen Yi (陳儀) as administrator-general and garrison commander of Taiwan. Under Chen's authority, three judges and one public prosecutor were dispatched to the island with a rough plan to set up a high court jurisdiction, a provincial-level court of appeal, and the first-instance, district courts below it. The process started officially on November 1, 1945. The fact, unknown to the Chinese officials, that the GGT's court, unlike the metropolitan Japanese one, was also two levels facilitated their task.

In addition, the functional similarity of the Formosan (not metropolitan Japanese) and Chinese judge and public prosecutor also smoothed the transition. The morphological and semantical similarity of the Japanese and Chinese legal and institutional vocabulary, too, helped the takeover.[42] The Chinese administrative jurisdiction was a novelty. Yet effective access to it was minimal. Its only tribunal was the Administrative Court in Nanjing. Those who would challenge an administrative act in Taiwan had to file petitions to request the administrative body reconsider its decision, which was almost identical to the procedure under the GGT.

42 It is well known that many Western political and legal terms translated into Japanese with *kanji* characters profoundly influenced Chinese terminology. In Taiwan's case, terms such as police (from *keisatsu* to *jingcha*), court (from *hōin* to *fayuan*), public prosecutor (from *kensatsukan* to *jianchaguan*), and notary public (from *kōshōnin* to *gongzhengren*) were borrowed.

In this period, the court and the public prosecutor's office was restaffed, had imposed on it a new working language, and was violently humiliated by the occupation forces.[43] The ethnically Japanese magistrates were successively relieved of their duties and then deported. H.-W. Liu finds that five Han Chinese magistrates and one veteran lawyer were made acting chief judges to look after two-thirds of the courts, and that in early 1946, nearly half of the magistrates in service were recruited locally.[44] The continuity regarding administrative personnel was much more significant. Yet the situation changed quickly as more mainlander magistrates arrived. The use of Chinese Mandarin was made mandatory at the beginning of the takeover. More importantly, the two sets of practices and values of legal professionals, however "Continental" they may have been, clashed with each other. Mainlanders, according to Liu, blamed islanders for writing and speaking the official language poorly, failing to comply with Chinese procedural rules and usages, having too much contact with lawyers and their clients (which would violate the "rule of avoidance" originating from imperial China when a lawyer was called to serve as judge in the jurisdiction where he had hitherto practiced), and being improperly lenient toward criminal suspects.[45] The stereotype that Taiwan's Han Chinese islanders were "poisoned" by the colonial regime and in need of re-education was prevalent among mainlanders in different branches of the Chinese government.[46] However, what the islander legal professionals were challenging was the illegality of Chinese procedural rules and usages.

Taiwan's justice system paid a heavy price in the Yuanlin incident of November 11, 1946. The mainland regime denied unabashedly the judicial and prosecutorial authority over the police and, more broadly, law's authority, which the islanders had learned under Japanese rule. Since the incident, the judiciary's reputation collapsed to the extent that the regime openly acknowledged it in March 1950. The incident arguably set the Taiwanese public's perception of the justice system for the next five or six decades. That is, that the judiciary was corrupt, inefficient, inconsistent, and that detention conditions were in urgent need of investment. The regime addressed its *mea culpa* to an audience that was greater

43 The public prosecutor in charge of the takeover, Jiang Weizu (蔣慰祖), was, according to some literature, arrested for corruption and taken back to the mainland on December 14, 1945. Yet *Shenbao*, a widely read newspaper based in Shanghai, offered a different account. A story published on January 1, 1946, mentioned rumors of the arrest, Jiang's conflict with the bench in Taipei, and the Ministry of Justice's denial. Jiang seems to have remained a judge and served in Xinjiang before returning to Taiwan as a practicing lawyer in April 1949.

44 劉恆妏 [Liu Heng-wen], '戰後初期臺灣司法接收（1945–1949）：人事、語言與文化的轉換' [Takeover of Judicial System in Early Post-war Years (1945–1949): Changes in Personnel, Language and Culture], 臺灣史研究 [*Taiwan Historical Research*] 17, no. 4 (December, 2010): 46–50.

45 Ibid., 71–4. Liu cites an instruction of 1946 requiring high-level officials to avoid being involved in affairs relating to their home province, and lower ones, those concerning their home county.

46 Ibid., 74.

than the islander community alone. Indeed, it was the Han Chinese islanders whom the incident traumatized more. Mainlander residents already understood the justice system's malfunctions from their experiences in China.

C.-y. Wu's recent study provides a well-documented account of the "Yuanlin incident."[47] In the evening of that day, a task force composed of the warden of a detention facility and 17 marshals and prison guards, was sent by the Taizhong District Court to arrest Xu Zongxi, a police officer involved in a battery case. After showing their bench warrant to Xu without resorting to coercion, Xu's colleagues entrapped three officers and then the warden himself in a conference room in the police headquarters of Taizhong county in Yuanlin (currently in Zhanghua county) before disarming them. In the meantime, the commander of the Taizhong county police, Commissioner Jiang Feng, learned about the arrival of the court's task force, and decided to dispatch more officers from neighboring police stations to resist the court's men. Lin Shimin, the head of police force of the nearby town of Beido, who arrived at Jiang's request, fired a warning shot first, then in the back of one of the task force's officer, and indiscriminately in the end. Two court officers were wounded but held without medical care until the early hours of the next day. The Chinese legislation of the time vested in the public prosecutor the power to command the county magistrate, police, and gendarmeries. Nevertheless, Taizhong's county magistrate Liu denounced the court, and wrote Chen Yi for support. The Taizhong police detained 11 officers of the court's task force until November 17, in spite of the Acting Chief Judge's request and the oral and written orders of a high court prosecutor, accompanied by police officers of the administrator-general's office.

The Taizhong police won not only physically but also judicially. Although all the police officers involved were indicted in Taipei district court, only Lin was found guilty on February 15, 1947. A newspaper published the entire decision on February 22 and 23, that is, five days before the even more explosive "228 incident." The high court found a second officer guilty. On July 21, 1948, the Supreme Court maintained the two guilty verdicts yet commuted the sentences. All the other officers were acquitted either officially "for lack of evidence" or because of the country-wide act of grace issued to celebrate the enactment of the Republic of China's constitution in 1947.

The different origins of the parties contributed to the public's outrage. The county magistrate and Taizhong's police officers were all mainlanders, mostly if not all Chinese nationals of Han Chinese ethnicity. On the other hand, lessons were taught to the islander judges, prosecutors, and warden who were carrying out their duties, and to the newspaper columnists and representatives of local bar associations who explicitly or implicitly criticized the police's outright disobedience

47 吳俊瑩 [Wu Chun-ying], '由「員林事件」看戰後初期臺灣法治的崩壞' [The Collapse of Rule by Law in Early Post-war Taiwan: A View from the Yuanlin Incident], 國史館館刊 [*Bulletin of Academia Historica*] 37 (2013): 89–92.

and contempt for the court's lawful order. These islanders were then Japanese nationals of Han Chinese ethnicity. In the aftermath of the incident of February 28, 1947, the former Acting Chief Judge in the court of Taizhong and the warden of his court's detention facility were detained. They were the luckier ones. Many others were either murdered or put under the intelligence service's surveillance for a long period.[48] It is worth noting that the justice system was gradually made accessible to indigenous individuals as time went on.

The Yuanlin incident exemplifies the dysfunction of the Republican Chinese justice system. The system bore the scars of China's decade-long upheaval. The judiciary, including the public prosecutor, was deemed one branch of the bureaucracy among others and was vested with jurisdiction only over civilians. Police officers still perceived themselves as military, as most of them had formerly served in the state's army or the militia of a certain warlord. They had little education and high personal dependence on the head of the local administration. They were unfamiliar with the practice of ruling by law,[49] let alone the rule of law, for the judiciary was a luxury in China by 1945. It was said that in two-thirds of municipalities with a district court, the police functioned as the public prosecutor and a section of the county government administered justice. The KMT government on the mainland could afford to equip only one-third of her municipalities with courts and judicial personnel.[50] The low investment in the judiciary, common to the Japanese and Chinese periods, had worse effects in the latter. The perception of corrupted judges seems to have been so alarming that the administration admitted the problem in general. In late March 1950, the Taiwan High Court made discipline or integrity (*fengji*) the top priority of the annual work program for all courts in its jurisdiction.[51] The timing is telling. The KMT regime was in desperate need of political legitimacy to secure its grip on Taiwan. Less than three weeks prior to the announcement of the High Court's program, Jiang Jieshi, who resigned from the presidency in January 1949, officially resumed, if not usurped, the office. The Korean War, which would stabilize the regime with US support, was yet to break out.

While the concept of judgeship was translatable into Chinese culture, challenges to the public prosecutor grew. This foreign institution was poorly understood. While it looked similar to its Japanese and French counterpart in the Qing legislation, its role and budget were reduced in the mid-1930s.[52] Compared to

48 Ibid., 114.

49 Ibid., 110–1.

50 王泰升 [Wang Tay-sheng], '清末及民國時代中國與西式法院的初次接觸－以法院制度及其設置為中心' [The Initial Encounter with Western-style Courts of Ch'ing and Republican China: A Discussion on the Institutions and Establishment of Courts], 中研院法學期刊 [*Academia Sinica Law Journal*] 1 (September 2007): 144.

51 Staff Writer, '高等法院施政方針及工作計畫' [Policies and Work Plans of the High Court], 中央日報 [*Central Daily News*] (March 20, 1950): 4.

52 王泰升 [Wang Tay-sheng], '清末及民國時代中國與西式法院的初次接觸' [The Initial Encounter with Western-style Courts of Ch'ing and Republican China], 140.

the police officers on the Chinese mainland, prosecutors in Taiwan impressed certain mainlander magistrates with not only their politeness but also their respect of legality.[53]

China's legal education, too, had been in chronic difficulty for decades. J. Escarra's first-hand observation made in 1935 is worth quoting. Among the array of deficiencies in China's legal education at that time – such as poor secondary education, low intellectual level of law teachers and the instability of their salary, the curricula and design of exam questions that awaited thorough reform, etc. – the education and promotion of young faculty members appeared a vicious circle that would impede the improvement of legal education. Escarra noticed that Chinese universities preferred holders of foreign doctoral degrees to the graduates of a Chinese institution. Alumni of foreign law schools, he said, took charge of the courses taught abroad by chair professors only with neither support nor requirements for serious publication or judicial experience, and that those who studied abroad would outperform their less fortunate colleagues only when they taught comparative law or a course of foreign law.[54] This French scholar described the situation of Chinese law students in France that, even today, would still fit some overseas Taiwanese students. "In a great number of cases," wrote Escarra, "a student arrives in France with his oftentimes mediocre level of general Chinese culture, superficial knowledge of Chinese law, and sometimes spoke very poor French." Such a Chinese student would fall behind in learning, yet would refuse any orientation for foreign students or special curricula because of the feeling of being disgraced or "losing face." Thus,

> This student, after some wasted years, may succeed in earning a bachelor degree that is given more or less out of indulgence and in a rush to move on. Or, after a dissertation that is below mediocrity, that no one would be able to check if it deals with Chinese law, he will go home with a doctor's degree which by no means corresponds to the value the diploma should have.[55]

The transfer of China's state institutions to Taiwan in 1949 laid the foundation of today's Taiwanese justice system, with its clear hierarchy of norms and the power of constitutional review. Indeed this institutional edifice, though updated by comparison to the Japanese one, was built on sandy political, social, and economic grounds. As Y.-H. Chu and J.-W. Lin argue, the KMT regime rested upon a four-fold basis that consisted of "an elaborate and centralized party apparatus, a system of extra-constitutional legal arrangements and emergency decrees, a controlled electoral pluralism implemented at the local level, and structural

53 吳俊瑩 [Wu Chun-ying], '由「員林事件」看戰後初期臺灣法治的崩壞' [The Collapse of Rule by Law in Early Post-war Taiwan], 112.

54 Jean Escarra, *Le Droit chinois. Conception et évolution, institutions législatives et judiciaires, science et enseignement* (Pékin: Vetch, 1936): 398–400.

55 Ibid., 421.

symbiosis between the party and the state."[56] All four elements impacted the justice system. In short, the justice system, though instrumental in legitimizing the continuity of the state's international legal personality for the KMT regime, was left with organizational inconsistencies. The function of the Judicial Yuan, a constitutional branch entrusted with the judicial power, has remained a patchwork and topped the agenda of the NJRC half a century after the institution's epochal migration.

The Republican Chinese constitution voted on in 1946 and in effect since 1947 assigns the judicial power to the Judicial Yuan (*sifa yuan*) in its chapter 7, "Administration of Justice (*sifa*)." This body literally appears to be a unitary court of final instance for civil, criminal, and administrative cases, as well as disciplinary proceedings of civil servants (Art. 77). More importantly, it is the ultimate interpreter of constitutional, statutory, and regulatory texts (Art. 78). A chief justice, a deputy chief justice, and a panel of "grand justices" (*dafaguan*) were to be politically appointed (Art. 79). Moreover, this constitution also enshrined the judge's independence and tenure with strict rules governing appointment, remuneration, dismissal, and transfer (Art. 80, 81).

Nonetheless, the application of the Constitution's judiciary went astray. Two organization acts of the Judicial Yuan were passed within less than nine months. In the version of March 1947, this body has five chambers: the Council of Grand Justices, with nine members as its chamber for constitutional cases, and four others for civil, criminal, administrative, and disciplinary suits. This version never entered into effect. In December 1947, the civil and criminal chambers were restored to the Supreme Court (*zuigao fayuan*), which the Judicial Yuan was set to replace, and the administrative chamber became a full-fledged court. In return, the Judicial Yuan got only eight more grand justices. Thus its power was essentially halved. This second version took effect on June 24, 1948, and remains with slight modifications. Apparently, professional judges won a battle over their entrenched interests against the politically-appointed president of the Judicial Yuan and the newborn constitutional court. This victory could have been short, had the outbreak of Korean war not secured the KMT regime in Taiwan. Reviving the design of March 1947 was on the official agenda from 1949 to 1951, as the civil war forced the regime to transfer, and, when it had nowhere to go, drastically downsize the central government.

Pursuant to Article 87 of the Act, it was the Ministry of Judicial Administration (*sifa xingzheng bu*) that supervised other courts after the takeover in 1945. It also should have overseen the prosecutor general, who stood at the peak of the prosecutorial hierarchy and represented the state before the Supreme Court in criminal cases. The Judicial Yuan's administrative authority covered only the

56 Y.-H. Chu and J.-W. Lin, 'Political Development in the 20th-Century Taiwan: State-Building, Regime Transformation and the Construction of National Identity,' *The China Quarterly* 165 (March, 2001): 113.

Supreme Court of ordinary jurisdiction, the Administrative Court, and the Commission on the Disciplinary Sanctions of Functionaries (*gongwuyuan chengjie weiyuanhui*). Although the Grand Justice Council of the Judicial Yuan declared such an executive supervisory arrangement unconstitutional in 1960 (Interpretation No. 86), the reorganization purportedly conforming to that decision occurred only in 1980. The public prosecutor remaining in the hands of the Ministry of Justice, all courts were finally under the auspices of the Judicial Yuan.

Whether before or after this belated reform, every judge's independence was at the mercy of a superior administrative power exercised by politically chosen leaders. The chief judges of courthouses appointed by these two agencies were effectively capable of vetoing their tenured colleagues' decisions until the end of 1995, even though this was blatantly illegal. Meanwhile, an incentive for judges to get promoted into this higher judicial bureaucracy emerged. Thus, behavioral differences between judges and prosecutors, which resulted from the career differences and which existed in the justice system before 1945, would decrease. Both groups became susceptible to influence and self-censorship, not for the sake of prestige accruing with performance, but hierarchically distributed power.

As under the GGT, most legal and paralegal functions, including the notaries public and bailiffs, were bureaucratized under the KMT regime. The public defender's office, however, was a Republican Chinese novelty. For public defenders, the same rules regarding the qualification, remuneration, and seniority of judges and prosecutors applied.

Despite this novelty, Taiwan's justice system since 1945 has been constantly struggling in vain for credibility because of the KMT regime's dualism of military and civil jurisdictions. The state of exception known as the "Period of Mobilization and Combating Rebellion" (*dongyuan kanluan shiqi*) between 1948 and 1991 and the illegal imposition of martial law in Taiwan in 1949 led to the wanton expansion of the military jurisdiction after 1950. Jiang Jieshi himself intervened in multiple cases in the capacity of commander-in-chief. Various intelligence services, secret police, and military police investigated political offenses. Meanwhile, the civilian police force, also headed by a high-ranking military officer until 1990, took care of the less sensitive charges that the ordinary justice system would process. The KMT regime's police enjoyed practically as much, if not more, power as under the GGT. Until 1990, it could, though it was twice declared unconstitutional, detain an individual, impose forced labor, shut down stores temporarily or for good with neither a court warrant nor a public prosecutor's order.[57] The intelligence services, military and civilian police were all known for torture, sloppy investigations, and corruption. Few, if any, agents were held accountable for wrongful official conduct.

57 Interpretations No. 166 of 1980 and No. 251 of 1990 underscored the unconstitutionality of the Law for the Punishment of Police Offenses (*weijingfafa*). This law was repealed in 1991.

The regime used military justice with such little care for the appearance of legality that the ordinarily criminal – that is, neither military nor "seditious" offenses – could be court-martialed at the government's discretion, both *ex ante* and *ex post*. The theoretical openness of court martial proceedings was also minimal. The media, controlled or censored, was allowed to cover some proceedings. The general public had little access to these trials as all were conducted in military facilities.[58] Since the 1970s, court-martialing certain kinds of criminal offenses had become a recurrent theme in Taiwan's political rhetoric. It survived the lifting of martial law and was translated into the broader theme of harshening punishment.

The KMT regime justified its military justice by not only the state of emergency and martial law, but also referring to the US counterpart, which was also present in Taiwan from 1954 to 1979. The Uniform Code of Military Justice (10 USC §§801–946) of 1950 inadvertently became a useful excuse for the regime to keep its armed forces segregated from civil society. Unlike the pre-war Japanese and war-time Continental – even the National Socialist German – practices, the KMT regime's military justice was administered, not by commissioned civilian judges, but by career judge advocates and, in some situations, non-lawyer officers. Many judge advocates became ordinary judges, public prosecutors, or, in particular, lawyers after years of service. This population enabled the regime to keep the admission rate of the bar exam at an extremely low level for decades, and it effectively had former officers control all the bar associations until 1989.[59]

The state of exception also resulted in low pay for all civil servants. Even judges and prosecutors, who received significantly more than civil servants of the same rank and seniority, could have problems making ends meet. The Judicial Yuan had little role to play in budget-setting until the constitutional amendment of 1994. Rumors of corrupted magistrates have never disappeared. Some judges or prosecutors who became lawyers were caught practicing what is called "justice brokerage" (司法黃牛, *sifa huangniu*): they improperly contacted judges in charge of their clients' cases with the intention of influencing the outcomes. The possibility of such brokerage has long remained in the public's perception. Some practitioners receive requests for this kind of improper contact with judges even though they have never served in the judiciary. In October 1957, Zhang Jinheng (張金衡), a public defender, sent his last words to newspapers, confessing to bribery and denouncing some of his colleagues' crimes, before he committed suicide.

Corruption was exacerbated by the justice system's involvement in the tug-of-war between the KMT and local political factions that the outnumbered

58 Military justice survived democratization, and remained in force even in times of peace until the reform in 2013, spurred by the wrongful death of sergeant Hong Zhongqiu (洪仲丘), whose compulsory military service was to be accomplished two days after his killing.

59 Between 1950 and 1988, 782 individuals passed the bar examination, while between 1989 and 2000, 8,404 were admitted to practice.

émigré régime had to "divide and rule." It was also involved in the tug-of-war among local headmen themselves. Politically sensitive lawsuits led to recurrent charges of conspiracy, bribery, and undue influence. There is a well-known saying in Taiwan that, "even the court belongs to the KMT" ("法院也是執政黨的," literally "the court also belongs to the ruling party"). A better known variant goes: "the court is run by KMT," "法院是國民黨開的"). This was said by Xu Shuide (許水德), then Party secretary-general, to his fellow party members in 1995 about criminal inquiries into alleged vote buying practices. This statement is so notorious that even a recent empirical study still takes pains to prove it obsolete.[60]

As for the Administrative Court, it was nicknamed the "court of rejection" (駁回法院, *buohui fayuan*) since the administrative law and its scholarship at the time would favor the state without the party's intervention. It was not until the 1990s that the reformed Constitutional Court ruled more and more frequently against the state and the pro-state Administrative Court.

Compared to pre-war Japan, the KMT regime made two positive contributions to the population of jurists: it expanded the capacity for legal education and allowed women access to legal education and legal professions. The migration of Chinese legal scholars boosted the teaching capacity and the number of departments of law in universities. While the bar was kept practically exclusive for mainlanders, the courts and the public prosecutors regularly recruited new magistrates and clerks. Women were admitted already in the early 1950s. On the other hand, indigenous individuals remained underrepresented in the legal professions despite the regime's officially more egalitarian and assimilationist approach in education and exams, compared to the Japanese segregation policy.

The judicial exam by 1995 and bar exam by 1999 were open not only to college graduates, but also those who could pass qualification tests. Difficult economic situations drove the less well-off to take the second track. Besides, many law degree holders preferred other career options, such as working in banking, to the legal professions. A notable population of degreeless practitioners consisted mainly of autodidactic elementary school teachers. They were fully sponsored and taken care of by the government. Students of a teacher's college were paid from their admission at the age of 15 and employed upon graduation at the age of 20, for women. Men waited until they finished their military service at 22 or 23. These teachers studied for qualification tests after their relatively manageable work at school. This population's presence in the justice system may have decreased the influence of university-based legal scholarship, especially when high-ranking officials gave questions for the judicial or bar exams.

60 C.-L. Wu, 'Charge Me If You Can: Assessing Political Biases in Vote-Buying Verdicts in Democratic Taiwan (2000–2010),' *The China Quarterly*, 211 (2012), 786–805.

Government lawyering: a marginalized issue in judicial reform

This chapter is too short to include an overall assessment of Taiwan's history of judicial reform attempts. Instead, the following paragraphs turn the focus on one institutional deficiency that has never interested any past reform and may trigger future efforts: the lack of an overarching mechanism for what may be called government lawyering. The term "lawyering" here refers to the provision of legal advice to governmental agencies by specialized individuals who are usually career civil servants rather than lawyers.

It is worrying that Taiwan, since the Nationalist Chinese takeover, has had no means of systematically coordinating the state's legal opinions in rule-drafting, rule-making, or litigating. Few, even in legal academia, seem aware of it. The sometimes low quality of legislation thus may leave the judiciary to serve as scapegoat when it does things by the book. Therefore it is suggested that the term usually translated as "judicial reform" (司法改革, *sifa gaige*) should be translated as "reform of the administration of justice." Put differently, the neglect in coordinating the state's legal opinions seems to have resulted in a particular type of "judicialized politics" that differs from Ferejohn's understanding.[61] Taiwan's justice system has been shouldering the blame for deficiencies in the administration of justice. But the executive branch is also liable for such deficiencies. Indifference to this problem remains widespread, while other issues occupy much reform discussion. There is little debate over how government lawyers should advise their "client" or draft rules on a given matter.

The discussions below are divided into three parts. First, some general features of government lawyering in Taiwan are explained, including a brief description of the roles that subdivisions of legal affairs play in Taiwan's governmental agencies, particularly in the central government. The second part bears on the Ministry of Justice and some of the Ministry's organizational characteristics related to weak government lawyering. The third part comments on the significance of Taiwan's case for the conventional wisdom on the introduction of Western law into East Asia.

Departmental and outsourceable government lawyering

The lawyering in Taiwan's executive branch is departmental and sometimes outsourceable to scholars or practitioners. Two features stem from a basic principle of governmental organization that each ministry-level agency may draft and propose bills concerning matters that pertain to its competence and that every statute names one or more competent authorities or agencies in charge (*zhuguan*

61 J. Ferejohn, 'Judicializing Politics, Politicizing Law,' *Law and Contemporary Problems* 65 (2002): 41–68.

jiguan).[62] Accordingly, standing in court proceedings is also departmental when a lawsuit against the government arises. Even when the constitutionality of a given statute is challenged, the agency (or agencies) responsible for interpreting or executing the law represents the state in the Constitutional Court. This is despite the fact that the enactment of statutes is an affair of state, a joint act of the executive and legislative branches theoretically authorized by the people.

Legal departments are an optional subdivision for the agencies. For those which choose to have a formal one, such a subdivision's organization varies from a small number of civil servants to a committee composed of higher-ranking officials and non-salaried, external members, who often are scholars or practicing lawyers. With respect to legislative bills and regulatory texts in particular, it is likely that those who draft them are civil servants without law degrees and that the legal department primarily edits texts. The processing of administrative appeals (*suyuan*) and tort claims is also agency-based and dependent on external participants, which may add credibility to but reduces the consistency of the agency's decisions. This role differs from the production of normative texts on two points. For administrative appeals, a uniform organizational regulation has governed all boards and committees of the kind under the Executive Yuan (EY) since 1972. External input and a quorum of members with legal qualifications were an innovation of the guideline's revision in 1993. As to tort claims against the government, over which civil justice has had jurisdiction since 1980, it is common practice to resort to outside counsel when an agency can afford it.

Some forms of centralized government lawyering exist. Leaving the Legislative Yuan's legal department aside, there are two principal bodies of legal advice in the executive branch. One is the Legal Affairs Committee (LAC, *fagui weiyuanhui*) of the Executive Yuan, and the other is the Ministry of Justice, which has some departments and committees in charge of legal advice for rule-drafting and rule-making. They both utilize external members. A formal process of consulting the two bodies in any law- or decision-making procedure is absent. So are definitions of the two bodies' competence and each's authority relative to the other. More importantly, the departmental feature of lawyering still dominates. None of the two bodies has authority over any other agencies, even if some agencies do ask for advice. The EY had been planning to concentrate the government's legal advice activities into a bureau of legislation in lieu of the LAC by 1967, yet aborted the plan in 1969. After the lifting of martial law, an organizational project for a bureau of legislation was drafted in 1996, but it seems to have been shelved since 1997. Unlike the central government, the legal service teams of six special municipalities (*zhixiashi*) and one county have become centralized, well-staffed agencies that have participated local cabinets since the late 2000s.

62 See, for example, art. 20 and arts. 23–5 of Central Regulation Standard Act (*Zhongyang Fagui Biaozhun Fa*). See also art. 153 of the Administrative Procedure Act.

The inconsistency of laws and regulations concerned the KMT regime when despair loomed over its last foothold. The problem already existed, and was aggravated by the new state organization set out in the Republican Chinese constitution of 1947 and the occupation of a territory hitherto governed by a different legal order. In response, the regime created, under the Ministry of Judicial Administration (renamed Ministry of Justice since 1980), the Committee for the Vetting of Legislation on the Administration of Justice (司法法規檢討整理委員會, *sifa fagui jiantao zhengli weiyuanhui*) on June 26, 1950. This CVLAJ, renamed the Legal Affairs Committee in 1980, was transformed into a substantial department of the Ministry in 2012. It included civil servants and around a dozen leading scholars during its first few decades. It produced a substantial output on civil law matters and Han Chinese customs preserved by the Japanese regime. The timing of its founding is also telling. The Committee's organizational rule was enacted one day before US President Harry Truman dispatched the Seventh Fleet to the Taiwan Strait because of the outbreak of the Korean War. The regime, distanced by the Truman administration, had been busy downsizing its bureaucracy and rationalizing its laws and regulations for survival.

The regime devoted similar efforts to administrative law. According to K. Hu, although the government failed once in the 1950s, it implemented two projects of systematizing administrative laws and regulations in the late 1960s and early 1970s.[63] Hu admitted that the two projects had reduced problems, but were still far from harmonizing conflicting or inconsistent administrative laws and regulations. He highlighted the problem that government agencies confused regulations with two kinds of texts: interpretations of regulations contained in their written responses to citizens' questions on the one hand and instructions for their staff on the other.[64] Forty years later, cases arising from the former type of confusion still arrive at the Constitutional Court, though the entering into force of the Administrative Procedure Act in 2001 has somewhat remedied the latter. It is also noteworthy that the Taiwanese Administrative Procedure Act (APA) itself was the product of neither the EY's LAC nor the Ministry of Justice, but the EY's Council for Economic Planning and Development (currently National Development Council).[65] The Council, which began as the Council for United States Aid (also known as CUSA) in 1948, has long

63 胡開誠 [Hu Kai-cheng], '我國現行法制之結構及行政法規之檢討整理' [The Structure of Our Country's Legal Institution in Force and the Critical Analysis and Systematization of Administrative Laws and Regulations], 臺大法學論叢 [*National Taiwan University Law Journal*] 6, no. 2 (June, 1977): 109–10. Hu was born in 1925, graduated from Jinan University in 1949, and chaired the EY's LAC from 1973 to 1987. He was credited for being in charge of the compilation of 36 volumes of laws and regulations and the creation of a search engine of rules.

64 Ibid., 116–17.

65 王泰升 [Wang Tay-sheng], 臺灣法律現代化歷程—從「內地延長」到「自主繼受」 [*The Process of Legal Modernization in Taiwan: From "Extending the Mainland" to "Independent Reception"*] (Taipei: NTU Press, 2015): 219–21.

been the primary policy coordinator in Taiwan's government, and it survived the party-state period.[66]

The Ministry of Justice and its dependence on prosecutors

A closer look into the Ministry of Justice is necessary to demonstrate the institutional deficiency of legal advice in government, because it, not the LAC, is in charge of litigating.

To begin with a recent event, Minister of Justice Chiu Tai-san presented an oral argument on behalf of the government on the morning of March 24, 2017 at the Constitutional Court. This case later led to Interpretation No. 748, which held that same-sex marriage is protected by the Constitution. As Minister, Chiu argued that there had never been same-sex marriage "for thousands of years in our country" without specifying to which country he referred, and that his ministry would support a "separate but equal" marriage law that categorized same-sex marriage in a specific act rather than the civil code. In the afternoon of the same day, Lin Chuan, then Premier (head of the EY), said that Chiu only represented the Ministry of Justice and that his argument was not the government's position.[67] Interestingly, there was no call for Chiu's resignation, to my knowledge, and he stayed in office until July 2018, after Lin's resignation in September 2017.

This event epitomizes the Ministry's weakness in government lawyering as well as litigating. It is intriguing that the Minister of Justice, himself a former prosecutor, failed in presenting his arguments with legal technicality. The same-sex marriage issue matters in constitutional law, but it is manageable in civil law vocabulary. Unlike constitutional law, which was of little use for the minister's generation, the civil law has always been a crucial subject for those who wanted to pass the judicial and the bar exams. It provides a system of concepts discussed in abstract and timeless terms. The minister himself and his staff should have been able to present arguments that sounded professional, technical, and almost value-free, whether for or against same-sex marriage.

There are two hypotheses that might explain this weakness, both related to the KMT regime's political tradition. One is the attempt in the 1930s to politicize judges and prosecutors while the other is the Jiangs' dictatorship since the 1950s, which tended to minimize the significance of legality in governance. The first explanation is that the KMT extended to post-war Taiwan the policy of so-called "party-izing the judiciary" (司法黨化, *sifa danghua*) adopted in the Chinese mainland, though with variations. The policy's underpinning idea

66 J.-R. Yeh, 'Experimenting with Independent Commissions in a New Democracy with a Civil Law Tradition: The Case of Taiwan,' in *Comparative Administrative Law*, eds, S. Rose-Ackerman, P. L. Lindseth, and B. Emerson, 2nd edn (Cheltenham: Edward Elgar, 2017): 199–200.

67 J. Pan, 'Same-Sex Marriage Hearing Commences,' *Taipei Times* (March 25, 2017): I. A. Hsiao, 'Lawmakers Pan Minister over Gay Marriage Stance,' *Taipei Times* (March 25, 2017): 3.

appeared in 1926. It consisted of revealing judges' party affiliations, advocating the appointment of KMT members to judicial positions, and indoctrinating non-members.[68] This experience led to the insertion of the phrase "above partisanship" in the judiciary-related Article 80 of the ROC Constitution at the insistence of opposition parties, though some KMT members admitted and criticized the Article's ineffectiveness in Taiwan.[69] The second explanation is that, as mentioned above, the KMT regime in Taiwan constructed a party-state structure in which the party monopolized the coordination of the state's many agencies after Jiang Jieshi successfully reformed his party in the early 1950s.[70] Thus providing legal advice for the coordination of rule-making, rule-drafting, and litigating may have become a secondary concern. However, these two hypotheses explain little about the non-KMT periods and still less of the aforementioned episode of Chiu's apparent ineptness in civil law.

The Ministry's twisted history is too complicated for this chapter. To simplify the story, its primary task has always been asserting political control over the justice system. It supervised trial judges, i.e., the high courts and the district courts, until 1980, and remains capable of influencing the public prosecutor. As mentioned earlier, Constitutional Interpretation No. 86 declared unconstitutional the Ministry's authority over the high courts and district courts. A reform in 1980 restored the courts to the Judicial Yuan. As the population of Republican Chinese legal professionals was too small to fill even the courts, the ministry has long been short of government lawyers and thus periodically transferred judges (until 1980) and prosecutors for lawyering. Though there are also civil servants recruited as agents for legal affairs, this career path is among the least attractive options for law degree holders because of its inferiority in "the four Ps" compared to other career paths: pay, prestige, power, and promotion opportunities.

Moreover, an ignored yet vital problem is the disuse of the public prosecutor's civil law duties, such as the protection of absentees' estates and the oversight of non-profit associations and foundations.[71] A more obscure issue is the government's representation in administrative justice, for which the prosecutor may be appointed in some cases. So far, discussions on this issue remain isolated. The narrow understanding of the prosecutor's competence has produced little if any pressure from civil society. Lei Zhen (Lei Chen) – a former bureaucrat of legal affairs, one of the Republican Chinese constitution's framers, and a leading liberal figure under Jiang Jieshi – argued that the "court" in the constitution included both judges and prosecutors and that judicial independence applied

68 X. Xu, *Trial of Modernity: Judicial Reform in Early Twentieth-Century China, 1901–1937* (Stanford, CA: Stanford University Press, 2008): 85–92.

69 雷震 [Lei Zhen], '各級法院應不應該隸屬於司法院？' [Should All Levels of Jurisdictions be under the Auspices of the Judicial Yuan?], 自由中國 [*Free China Review*] 20, no. 3 (February, 1959): 85–7.

70 Chu and Lin, Political Development, 113, 115.

71 See arts. 8, 14, 15–1, 36, 38, 58, 62, 64, 412, 1094, 1178, and 1178–1 of the Civil Code.

to prosecutorial activities in criminal justice.[72] Lei's view was that chapter 7 of the Republican Chinese Constitution referred to not merely the judiciary but the administration of justice, a mechanism involving prosecution and adjudication. This argument faded into oblivion after Lei's incarceration in 1960. Now, many take the separation of trial judges from the Ministry of Justice in 1980 as the KMT regime's belated concession to judicial independence and accept the Ministry's authority over, and even power to instruct, prosecutors.

Instead of providing well-rounded legal counsel, the KMT regime has compromised the integrity of the public prosecutor's office by offering them pecuniary incentives for prosecution. While prosecutors ought to be rule-based officials, it has become a long-standing practice that the Ministry of Justice orients them toward politically selected goals by means of bonus payments for what are often called "special tasks" (*zhuanan*). The Ministry coordinates prosecutors and the Investigation Bureau under its jurisdiction, sometimes along with other police agencies, to target specific types of offenses and people. At the end of their operations, the officials and officers involved receive a certain amount of money in accordance with their performance. An example of this practice is that prosecutors were entitled to anti-narcotics bonuses, like police officers or other field agents, until 2013.[73] This late reform, however, has yet to restore the rule-based character of the public prosecutor. Debates over whether prosecutors are to be declassed and stripped of their powers in criminal procedure keep dominating Taiwan's judicial reform discourse.

Any foreign influence?

A more general question may arise from Taiwan's case: is the centralization of legal advice and counsel the only solution possible to attain an operationally-consistent body of law? This question is particularly relevant to Taiwan because Germany, whose legislation and legal scholarship has substantially influenced Taiwan for more than a century, suggests a negative answer. So does the US model, which is constitutionally less similar than the German one to Taiwan's. As far as the Basic Law in force is concerned, the legislative process, according to Article 65, is the competent ministry's responsibility (so-called *Ressortprinzip*) as long as it follows the chancellor's guidelines. The Federal Ministry of Justice and Consumer Protection may only give legal advice to other ministries upon request or if it finds a draft bill or regulatory text incompatible with the law in force.[74] Unlike the US unitary judiciary, the German judiciary is segmented. It

72 雷震 [Lei Zhen], '各級法院應不應該隸屬於司法院？' [Should All Levels of Jurisdictions be under the Auspices of the Judicial Yuan?], 87–8.

73 See the past revisions of art. 20 of the Regulation regarding rewards and punishments in anti-drug efforts (防制毒品危害獎懲辦法 [*fangzhi dupin weihai jiangcheng banfa*]) enacted in 1955.

74 Geschäftsordnung der Bundesregierung [GOBReg, Rules of Procedure of the Federal Government], art. 26(2).

maintains the public–private law division, and assigns to the office of public prosecutor criminal affairs and a small number of tasks in civil law. The German institutional design seems to have much more in common with Taiwan's.

Questions about government lawyering in Germany belong elsewhere. This chapter contents itself with the argument that the well-known factual condition of *Juristenmonopol*, dominance or monopoly of jurists in German bureaucracy, which facilitates government lawyering in Germany, is nonexistent and seems unlikely to appear in Taiwan. The *Juristenmonopol* had been a legal rule until 1953. The preponderance of jurists in the bureaucracy is on the wane, yet it still characterizes the German bureaucracy among its European peers. Non-jurist civil servants still must learn how to operate the legal machinery of government built by past jurists. This traditional importance rests on a considerable population of jurists interested in public administration. This picture is far from the reality in Taiwan.

The departmentalism and the derivative demand for outside counsel which have marked Taiwan's government lawyering since 1945 are peculiar among neighboring jurisdictions and preceding Chinese regimes. Formally, there is a single agency vested with the authority to coordinate rule-drafting and rule-making in Japan, South Korea, Hong Kong, and Macau.[75] As to litigation other than criminal prosecution, Japan, Korea, Hong Kong, and the Philippines all have a specialized agency under their ministries of justice, and Macau's Prosecutor General is in charge of civil, criminal, and administrative proceedings at all instances. The KMT regime itself used to have an agency for legislation when it ran part of the Chinese mainland. The regime's National Government (*guomin zhengfu*) established a Legislation Bureau (法制局, *fazhiju*) in 1928, three years prior to the Provisional Constitution of 1931. The Bureau drafted parts of the major law codes still in force in Taiwan. Though the 1928 institution was dissolved that same year, the KMT decided that there would be another Legislation Bureau one month after the Constitution of 1947 was published. Republican China could have been inspired by, among other influences, the Japanese Cabinet Legislation Bureau, founded in 1885 as an imitation of the consultative sections of the French *Conseil d'Etat* and which survived the Allied occupation to become one of the country's longest-living institutions.[76] Establishing such an institution was not a matter of comparative law, but an urgent and universal issue of governance by legal rules. Obviously, both Japan and Republican China opted for centralized, unitary states like the French one and the Imperial Chinese predecessor, rather than German federalism. Hence,

75 Japan: the Cabinet Legislation Bureau; Republic of Korea: the Ministry of Government Legislation; Hong Kong: the Department of Justice; Macao: the Secretariat for Administration and Justice.

76 内閣法制局百年史編集委員会 [Board of Editors of the Centennial History of the Cabinet Legislation Bureau], 内閣法制局百年史 [*The Centennial History of the Cabinet Legislation Bureau*] (Tokyo: Cabinet Legislation Bureau, 1985): 3. Oppler, *Legal Reform*, 106–7.

the organizational defect in post-war Taiwan's government lawyering seems to be an unfinished reform of a state institution rather than a deliberate choice from a number of foreign models.

Nevertheless, the German and US models of rule-drafting may have contributed to the marginalizing of the issue of coordination of the executive branch's lawyering in Taiwan since 1945. Some Taiwanese scholars translated and commented on the US APA of 1946 and several drafts of its German counterpart of 1976 in the 1960s and 1970s. The Taiwanese APA of 2001 introduced the US rule-making process with the intent to foster democracy. On the other hand, reforms on administrative penalties and justice still draw inspiration from the German legislation. Thus, departmentalism still holds sway and the French or Japanese models of centralized legal advice remain unused. Scholars take part in law-related committees of government agencies or municipalities. Some complain about the lack of respect for legality that they witness. Few have proposed putting their expertise into an overarching institution.

Conclusion: the dragging of Taiwan toward a modern state amidst bloody backsliding

From a legal historical perspective, from 1895 to 1999 Taiwan's justice system abruptly dragged society towards a modern state in the first 50 years. Thereafter it slid back with bloodshed, and finally regained credibility at an uneven pace in civil, criminal, administrative, and constitutional jurisdictions. While the first 50 years of Taiwan's justice system drew upon Meiji Japan's state-building blueprint, subsequent decades were characterized by a party-state system that prioritized the survival of the KMT regime. And while judicial reform has been pursued since 1999, weakness in government lawyering and society's indifference to this issue have persisted.

Republican Chinese legal advisors serving in successive regimes could only envy the Japanese "era of legislative bureaucrats," as Yamamuro called it.[77] The career of someone like Inoue Kowashi (1843–95), who visited Europe with the Iwakura Mission, headed the Cabinet Legislation Bureau, and advised Itō Hirobumi in designing the Meiji State, was unfathomable in Republican China as well as in Taiwan under the KMT. The KMT regime since 1950 has been busy preserving a state temporarily transferred to Taiwan instead of creating a new one. Despite its intention to fix the state's legal and regulatory inconsistencies, it has maintained departmentalism while prescribing a set of common procedural requirements with its APA.

77 See 山室信一 [Yamamuro Shinichi], 法制官僚の時代：国家の設計と知の歴程 [The Era of the Legislative Bureaucracy: State-Planning and the Process of Intelligence] (Tokyo: 木鐸社 [Bokutakusha], 1984).

This legal historical account may imply some pessimism about future judicial reforms. The 2017 reform succeeded the 1999 attempt, and others are likely to follow. Without implying any linear view of history, Taiwan is behind in terms of state building. Reforming the judiciary from merely judicial points of view may allow the executive branch to substitute democracy for the rule of law, when they are supposed to coexist with one another.

3 The development and reform of Taiwan's prosecutorial system

1945–2014

Heng-da Hsu

Introduction

The principle of accusation (控訴原則; in German: *Akkusationsprinzip* or *Anklagegrundsatz*) plays an important role in modern criminal justice.[1] No one can be convicted without being accused by a public prosecutor in advance. In order to investigate possible crimes and file charges against suspects, the public prosecutor possesses several legal tools to collect evidence. Under Taiwan's Criminal Procedure Code, for example, a public prosecutor can directly summon a defendant or witness for questioning. In addition, he is also entitled to apply to a court for warrants to search, intercept communications, and detain a suspect. These regulations in the Criminal Procedure Code demonstrate the public prosecutor's important role in criminal investigations. Because the public prosecutor has such strong powers, his conduct must be closely controlled by law, or else prosecutorial powers can be abused or even infringe on human rights.

A representative example of public prosecutors' misuse of investigatory powers can be seen in the recent "Sunflower Movement" that took place in March and April 2014. Many students and civil society groups protested against the imminent passage of the Cross-Strait Service Trade Agreement (CSSTA; 海峽兩岸服務貿易協議) without a clause-by-clause review. They then occupied Taiwan's parliament, the "Legislative Yuan" (立法院) and attempted to enter the "Executive Yuan" (行政院). During the occupation of the Executive Yuan on March 23, riot police arrested a student leader named Wei Yang Wei, accusing him of committing five crimes including participation in an open assembly involving violence or threats (Article 150 of Taiwan's Criminal Code) without clear evidence. The public prosecutor took the unusual step of applying for

1 The "Principle of Accusation" comes mainly from German theories. German and Taiwanese scholars use this term to make clear that their criminal procedures are not inquisitorial ones, in which the same court prosecutes defendants and issues the final verdict. See Lin Yu-Hsiung (林鈺雄), CRIMINAL PROCEDURE LAW, Vol. 1, 50–4 (5th. edn, 2007); Werner Beulke, STRAFPROZESSRECHT, 11–12 (5th edn, 2001); Lutz Meyer-Goßner, STRAFPROZESSORDNUNG, 627 (50th edn, 2007).

detention immediately after arresting him, arguing Wei could destroy, forge, or alter evidence. This application was soon rejected by the Taipei District Court for insufficient evidence that Wei committed any crimes or intended to destroy evidence.[2] Wei was thereafter released. Although the court rejected the public prosecutor's application for detention and protected a leader of the student movement from losing his personal freedom, the prosecutor's actions caused great unease. The case raised the issue of whether public prosecutors can submit an application for detention without sufficient evidence justifying a long-term restriction on freedom of action.

This article reviews the historical development of Taiwan's prosecutorial system and discusses reforms that have come mainly during the democratic era. Because Taiwan was a Japanese colony prior to 1945 and then transferred to the Chinese Nationalist Government at the end of World War II, it is important to examine how these periods have influenced the present system. I will discuss developments during these times in the first and second sections. Then, I will analyze developments during the era of authoritarian Kuomintang party (KMT; 中國國民黨) governance between 1945 and 1980, clarifying reforms during this time. Finally, I will discuss the drastic reforms after the 1990s that came about because of political liberalization in Taiwan. In particular, I will explain how prosecutorial power became more independent from intervention, prosecutors' loss of decision-making authority in imposing coercive measures, and the switch from inquisitorial criminal justice to adversarial procedure in Taiwan. Lastly, I will mention a recent case from 2013 that concerned the professional integrity of Taiwan's chief prosecutor.

Taiwan's prosecutorial system prior to 1945

Public prosecutors under Japanese governance

After losing the First Sino-Japanese War between the Qing Dynasty and Japan in 1895, Taiwan was ceded to Japan as its colony under the Treaty of Shimonoseki (馬關條約).[3] Before the Japanese colonial era, there was no modern-style prosecutorial system in Taiwan under the Qing administration. The Japanese colonial administration in Taipei in 1895 initially established a court under the Office of the Governor-General for the resolution of criminal disputes.[4] A prosecutorial system was planned under the "Organization of the Court of the Office of the Governor-General Ordinance" promulgated on May 1, 1896, and detailed

2 See press bulletin released by Taipei District Court: www.judicial.gov.tw/tpnw/newsDetail.asp?SEQNO=153976.

3 For information on prosecutorial institutions before Japanese colonial era, see Wang Tay-Sheng (王泰升), Prosecutorial History in Taiwan – Institutional Change and Practice (台灣檢察史), 23–61 (1999).

4 See Wang, *supra* note 3, at 14–15.

provisions regarding the prosecutorial institution in colonial Taiwan were at last released in 1898.[5]

During the Japanese colonial era, public prosecutors were responsible for pre-trial criminal investigations, deciding whether to press a charge or drop it, representing the government in criminal courts, and supervising the execution of court judgments.[6] Because the Japanese government wanted to distinguish the colonial Taiwanese legal system from the mainland Japanese system, prosecutors in Taiwan were given more powers than their mainland colleagues, especially regarding pre-trial coercive measures.[7] In 1901, public prosecutors in mainland Japan were empowered to decide whether a defendant should be detained during pre-trial investigation. At the same time, like their colleagues in Japan, prosecutors in Taiwan had the same detention power. In 1905, the Office of the Governor-General Taiwan passed the "Ordinance on Special Criminal Procedure," pursuant to which public prosecutors in Taiwan were allowed to decide whether coercive measures could be taken to investigate crimes.[8] To some extent, criminal procedure in Taiwan was entirely inquisitorial, because it was set up primarily for Japanese rule in colonial Taiwan. Throughout proceedings, interrogation records and other documents played the most significant role. Instead of oral cross-examination of witnesses by the parties, prosecutors, defendants, and judges read from documents in the courtroom, and a verdict was then made.[9]

In spite of the situation described above, public prosecutors in the Japanese colonial administration in Taiwan projected an image of integrity among Taiwanese people. A key reason for this may be the differences between Japanese policemen and prosecutors. Japanese policemen mainly dealt with upholding social order, and they were notorious for their repression of the Taiwanese people. In contrast to policemen, Japanese public prosecutors were willing to protect Taiwanese people, especially when a criminal charge was deemed unnecessary. They often made a "non-prosecutorial disposition" (不起訴處分), a decision not to prosecute because of insufficient evidence, even when the suspect was Taiwanese. The rate of non-prosecutorial disposition reached more than 50 percent during the colonial era.[10]

In sum, an efficient prosecutorial system existed in Taiwan during the Japanese colonial period. Most public prosecutors recognized that they were obliged to abide by legal rules and work with integrity. However, since the entire system was founded to maintain colonial rule over the Taiwanese people, criminal justice lacked rights protections.[11]

5 See Wang, *supra* note 3, at 17.
6 See Wang, *supra* note 3, at 20.
7 See Wang, *supra* note 3, at 20–1.
8 See Wang, *supra* note 3, at 21–2.
9 See Wang, *supra* note 3, at 23.
10 See Wang, *supra* note 3, at 36–7.
11 See Wang Tay-Sheng (王泰升), Legal Reform in Taiwan under Japanese Colonial Rule, 225–302 (1999).

The mainland Chinese prosecutorial system prior to the KMT Government's evacuation to Taiwan

Developments in mainland China also influenced Taiwan's prosecutorial system after 1945. Late in the Qing Dynasty, the Dali Yuan Court Establishment Act (大理院審判編制法) of 1906 created a prosecutorial system influenced by the Continental European legal tradition.[12] But despite this institutionalization of a modern prosecutorial system, prosecutor training in the system was still extremely limited, resulting in an incomplete diffusion of the Continental system.[13]

The Qing Dynasty was then followed by the Republic of China in 1912. The Beiyang Government (北洋政府), which was internationally recognized as the legitimate government in the Republic of China from 1913 to 1928, promulgated the "Court Establishment Act" (法院編制法) in 1915. According to this law a prosecutorial office was set up to be responsible for deciding compulsory measures in pre-trial proceedings, filing public charges, representing the government in the courtroom,[14] and supervising the execution of judgments.[15] At that time, the "principle of prosecutorial integration" (檢察一體原則), under which all prosecutors have to abide by the orders of superior prosecutors, especially the Prosecutor General, was generally accepted.[16] In addition, prosecutors were also aware that they needed to execute their power independently from judges.[17]

The Beiyang Government was succeeded in 1928 by the Nanking Nationalist Government (南京國民政府), which ruled China until 1949. The main disputes concerning the prosecutorial system at that time involved the following two issues. First, since public prosecutors needed to work independently from the courts, particularly during this early time in the modernization process when unfamiliar Continental legal structures were being institutionalized, it seemed that the public prosecutor needed an equivalent status as judicial officer. But since prosecutors had to abide by legal instructions from the Prosecutor General, could they also be regarded as administrative officers?[18] This problem of the

12 See Huang Yuan-Sheng (黃源盛), Legal Changes and Jurisdiction in Early Republic: 1912–28, 301–3 (2000).

13 See Wang, *supra* note 3, at 40–5.

14 The Central Judicial Office released a decision (Decision No. 42, Shengtzu 42, 1913) that emphasized that criminal cases required accusation, meaning a public prosecutor needed to file a public charge for a case to move forward. This was an important milestone in the modernization of the prosecutorial system. See Huang, *supra* note 12, at 310.

15 See Wang, *supra* note 3, at 46–7.

16 The principle of prosecutorial integration was highly emphasized in Taiwan's criminal procedure theories. Because lower-ranking prosecutors might sometimes have different legal perspectives than their superiors (e.g., whether a suspect has "intentionally" committed a fraud), it is necessary to unify prosecutors' opinions. See Chen Wen-Chi（陳文琪）, Practice of Prosecutorial Integration（檢察一體之實踐）, 1 Taiwan Prosecutor Rev. 100 (2007).

17 See Wang, *supra* note 3, at 48–9.

18 See Wang, *supra* note 3, at 55–9.

legal status of public prosecutors was also connected to the supervision system for public prosecutors. There was a question over whether prosecutors ought to be administratively supervised by the Judicial Yuan, as "judicial officers" like judges, or by the Ministry of Justice under the executive branch. The issue was extremely controversial.[19] Second, a prosecutorial office was established to correspond to the Supreme Court and deal with cases at that level of the judiciary. However, there was a dispute over whether lower courts also needed corresponding prosecutorial offices to be responsible for criminal cases at the district or high court levels, since the supreme-level prosecutors' office was doing this work.[20] Neither of these disputes was resolved during the Nationalist period on the mainland, but they were finally settled after the Nationalist government retreated to Taiwan.

Taiwan's prosecutors under the KMT Government: 1945–80

Japanese colonial administration over Taiwan ended in 1945 after the surrender of Japan in World War II. The mainland Chinese government took control over Taiwan the same year and brought its legal system to the island. Although there were some differences between the Japanese and Chinese prosecutorial systems, both were adopted from the Continental European tradition, and it was not difficult to move from the Japanese to the Chinese legal system. Consequently, in view of the lack of personnel and financial support after Taiwan's retrocession to China, the Japanese legal system was not abandoned institutionally, although Chief Prosecutors in all prosecutor offices were replaced with staff from mainland China. As a whole, Taiwan's post-1945 prosecutorial system was marked by continuity with the Japanese Period.[21]

When the KMT Government was defeated by the Communists and lost control over mainland China, the political atmosphere in Taiwan was extremely tense. Fearing a repeat of the same errors that led to a loss of political control on the mainland, the Nationalist government did not tolerate any social disorder. The impact on the prosecutorial system was that lower-ranking prosecutors were ordered to obey the orders of senior colleagues in the name of the aforementioned principal of prosecutorial integration. The government thought that once senior prosecutors could be controlled and junior prosecutors were obliged to follow their orders, the prosecutorial system would be securely under political control. Then criminal prosecution could become an effective weapon against political opponents of the KMT.[22] Instructions to this end can be found in textbooks for law school students. In the *Court Organization Act*, an important

19 See Wang, *supra* note 3, at 60.

20 See Wang, *supra* note 3, at 62.

21 See Wang, *supra* note 3, at 72–4.

22 For relevant critique, see Lin Yu-Hsiung (林鈺雄), Treatise on Public Prosecutor, 113–47 (2000).

textbook on the judiciary, a famous scholar wrote that "The prosecutor, as he exercises his authority, is obliged to obey the orders of the Chief Prosecutor [of his office]."[23]

However, there were some brave prosecutors who stood out for fighting for their independence. An example of the principle of prosecutorial integration can be found in a very famous case known as the "no appeal on orders of higher officials" (奉令不上訴) case that occurred in Taichung in 1958. A prosecutor named Huang Hsiang-Chian (黃向堅) served the prosecutors' office attached to Taichung District Court. He was in charge of a corruption case in which the Governor of Nantou county, Lee Kuo-Chen (李國楨), was accused of bribery. At the first instance, the Taichung District Court found Governor Lee not guilty. However, Huang did not agree with the first instance court's decision and wanted to file an appeal to the Taichung High Court. In contrast to Huang, his superiors, namely the Chief Prosecutor of the Taichung Prosecutors' Office, Yen Jian-Liang (延憲諒), as well as the Chief Prosecutor of the Taichung High Court Prosecutors' Office, Hsia Wei-Shang (夏惟上), both asked him not to appeal. Chief Prosecutor Yen even wrote in the internal documents: "no appeal on orders of higher officials." Instead of yielding to the order of his superiors, Huang filed an appeal to the High Court without the approval of Chief Prosecutor Yen. This scandal was then reported by a political magazine, and members of the Control Yuan, who were in charge of supervising the integrity of officers, began to investigate Huang and Chief Prosecutor Yen. In the end, Chief Prosecutor Yen was dismissed from his position.[24]

In the case of "no appeal on orders of higher officials," it is quite clear that the prosecutorial system was not entirely free from political intervention. Politicians at that time could directly influence prosecutorial decisions during an investigation and even lobby over the filing of criminal charges. Nevertheless, there were still some public prosecutors who held to their consciences. As a consequence, scandals like this sometimes occurred.

In addition to the public prosecutor's pursuit of independence while working on specific cases, some reflections on the strength of prosecutorial power at the criminal investigation stage also triggered amendments to the Criminal Procedure Act in 1967. While the change did not turn the process from an inquisitorial to an adversarial system, the powers of prosecutors were to some extent restricted.

One key change was that prosecutorial participation in the courtroom was expanded from its hitherto minimal role. An amendment to article 161 of the Criminal Procedure Code provided: "The public prosecutor shall bear the burden of proof as to the facts of the crime charged against an accused and shall indicate

23 See Lee Kuang-Hsia (李光夏), Court Organization Act, 67–8 (1st. edn, 1963).

24 For the entire story, see Huang Hsiang-Chian (黃向堅), The Case of "no appeal on orders of higher officials," 80 The Kaleidoscope 34, 34–40 (2006).

the method of proof." Accordingly, the prosecutor was required make more of an effort to prove a charge and to participate in trial proceedings. Although this provision marked an improvement, and led to prosecutors orally debating with defendants, the implementation was still disappointing. Although the public prosecutor actually showed up, he usually read the charges word by word and did nothing more. The reality of court proceedings did not change, and the trial was still mainly a judicial investigation lacking any material participation by the prosecutor.

Although there were some cases in which junior prosecutors resisted orders of their superiors, and a few provisions were modified so that public prosecutors needed to prove the facts of defendants' crimes, it goes without saying that the most serious problem before the 1980s remained the organizational structure of the entire prosecutorial system. Prior to 1980, only the Supreme Court was under the administrative supervision of the Judicial Yuan. All high and district-level courts were still supervised by the Ministry of Justice, which was an executive agency. This strange structure gave most Taiwanese people an impression of the judiciary as the "judge and prosecutor working together to punish people."[25]

Early in the 1960s, Taiwan's Constitutional Court made Interpretation No. 86 regarding the organizational structure of the court and prosecutorial system. It held that:

> Article 77 of the Constitution stipulates that the Judicial Yuan is the highest judicial organ of the State and holds the judicial power over trials of civil and criminal litigation, of which trials shall include civil and criminal litigation at courts of all levels. In view of the fact that different levels of courts and subsidiary courts below the High Court inclusively hold the judicial power over trials of civil and criminal litigation, these courts shall be subordinate to the Judicial Yuan.

However, the KMT government, as it had just retreated from mainland China to Taiwan, never regarded judicial structure as an important issue. Consequently, it did not do anything to comply with Constitutional Court Interpretation No. 86.

By the 1980s, the Nationalist government had been settled in Taiwan for more than 30 years. With the passing of time, for the KMT, Taiwan became much more than a shelter or reserve camp for future battles against Communists, and it began to undertake more economic and even political reforms to respond to the social expectations of the Taiwanese people.[26] The Court Organization Act was thus amended in 1980, and the administrative structure of courts and prosecutors' offices were officially separated. District and high courts were

25 See e.g., Lee Mau-Sheng (李茂生), Power, Subject and Criminal Law, 157–60 (1998).
26 See Wang, *supra* note 3, at 83.

thereafter under the administrative supervision of the Judicial Yuan. In other words, they belonged to the judicial rather than the executive branch.[27]

Prosecutorial reform after the 1980s

Despite several changes in Taiwan's prosecutorial system, the entire criminal procedure remained quite authoritarian during the 1980s. At the investigation stage, by using coercive measures for example, the public prosecutor had enormous discretion, unchecked by the need for court approval for many actions. All kinds of warrants for coercive measures, such as for detention, searches, and wiretapping, needed only to be signed by the prosecutor. In addition, lower-ranking public prosecutors had to follow orders from superiors because the principle of prosecutorial integration was still the dominating rule. Prosecutors were also unwilling to play an active role in the courtroom. In court, a prosecutor would usually simply say that "The criminal charges are as indicated in the indictment," before sitting down without taking any further steps to prove his case.[28] The job of finding the facts of a crime as well as reaching the correct legal decision belonged solely to the judge.

However, with the growth of democratic movements starting from the middle of the 1980s, Taiwanese society gradually accepted the values of democracy and liberty. The authoritarian regime of KMT governance was coming to an end, as President Chiang Ching-Kuo (蔣經國) ended martial law and allowed family visits to China in 1987. President Lee Teng-Hui (李登輝) abolished the "Temporary Provisions Effective during the Period of Communist Rebellion" (動員戡亂時期臨時條款) in 1991. All these events made the 1990s an era of liberalization, and these social developments also changed the prosecutorial system. We can analyze developments in this period from three different perspectives: (1) the internal reform of the prosecutorial system; (2) the restriction of prosecutors' powers at the investigation stage; and (3) the switch from purely inquisitorial proceedings to the modified adversarial system in criminal trials.

Prosecutorial reforms from the 1990s onward

Internal reform of the system

Internal prosecutorial reform began in the 1980s, but it did not succeed. One reason for this failure might be the authoritarian regime at that time, which sought to punish its political enemies via criminal justice. The other reason for its failure was the insistence on the principle of prosecutorial integration. As a

27 See Wang, *supra* note 3, at 84–5.

28 See e.g., Chen Wen-Chi (陳文琪), Evaluation of the Project of Prosecutor's Attendance at Courtroom at Shihlin District Court, 66 The Taiwan L. Rev. 65, 69 (2000).

consequence, corrupt politicians always asked chief prosecutors to order their junior colleagues to prosecute their enemies. It was difficult for junior staff to refuse such orders from chief prosecutors. This situation changed with the democratization of Taiwan in the 1990s.[29] An event arousing widening social concern occurred in 1989 and raised people's expectations of prosecutorial reform.

A junior prosecutor of Hsinchu Prosecutors' Office named Kao Shin-Wu (高新武) refused to transfer his case to another prosecutor designated by the Office's Chief Prosecutor.[30] It was a criminal case of bribery, and the suspect was a Department Director at the Judicial Yuan – a very senior judge. Kao was deeply engaged in investigating this case, and it had the potential to create a scandal involving senior judicial officials. To avoid the eruption of a scandal, the government tried to transfer this case to another prosecutor, who would follow instructions from superiors. The Chief Prosecutor of the Hsinchu Office ordered Kao to hand over his case. Instead of obeying this order, Kao argued that such a case transfer order was illegal and refused to stop his investigation. Surprisingly, almost all his colleagues at the Hsinchu Office openly sided with his refusal. To resolve the dispute, an ad hoc group of three public prosecutors, including Kao, was assembled to continue the investigation.[31] This event provoked social concern about prosecutors' independence while conducting criminal investigations.[32]

Another similar scandal involved a golf course project in Taichung in 1994. A successful businessman, Yang Tian-Sheng (楊天生), was accused of bribing officials for a golf course construction project. Three public prosecutors in charge of this case, Chu Chao-Liang (朱朝亮), Wu Wen-Chung (吳文忠), and Lee Ching-Yi (李慶義), were responsible for investigating this, but they were subsequently ordered to relinquish control of the case. They refused to follow this order and gained social support. The governing KMT party at that time was involved in several scandals involving bribery, illegal profiteering, and misuse of official power. Due to junior public prosecutors' growing sense of integrity, it became harder to cover up scandals.

But because having too many scandals could influence the outcome of legislative or county governor elections, the KMT decided to propose an amendment to the Criminal Procedure Code requiring detention at the investigation stage be determined only by an office's chief prosecutor. If the chief prosecutor alone, instead of junior prosecutors, could issue detention warrants, politicians would

29 Regarding the concept of "democratization" and the prosecutorial system, see e.g., Tang Ching-Ping (湯京平) and Huang Hung-Sen (黃鴻森), Democratization and Judicial Independence: A Political Analysis of the Public Prosecutor Reforms in Taiwan, 12 The Taiwanese Political Science Rev. 82 (2008).

30 See Hsieh Chi-Ta (謝啟大), http://mag.chinatimes.com/mag-cnt.aspx?artid=4063&page=2.

31 After the investigation of this ad hoc group, a bribery charge against this judge was brought to court. However, the judge was acquitted of the crime. Prosecutor Kao resigned from Hsinchu Prosecutor Office. See http://catalog.digitalarchives.tw/item/00/5e/25/26.html.

32 Especially the opinions of lawyers, see Petitions of Some Lawyers, 43 Formosa L. Rev. 4 (1989).

find it easier to control chief prosecutors' decisions through their appointments, and scandals would not erupt. However, since the Taiwanese people in the 1990s were aware of the importance of judicial integrity and independence, this proposal triggered many critiques and indirectly led to the Constitutional Court's Interpretation No. 392. According to the Justices, a pre-trial detention warrant needed to be signed by a neutral and detached judge. The details of this significant Interpretation will be discussed in the following section.

After 1995, due to the preliminary achievements of democratization and liberalization movements, many junior public prosecutors were willing to refuse the unreasonable, and possibly illegal, orders to hand their cases over to other prosecutors. Scandalous events were also broadly reported by the media. For example, a 1995 scandal occurred in which the Chief Prosecutor at the Taipei District Prosecutors' Office manipulated the random case distribution process to prevent a young public prosecutor,[33] Liu Wei-Zong (劉維宗), from involvement in a certain case.[34] In 1997, the chief prosecutor of the Kaohsiung District Prosecutors' Office intervened in a corruption case being investigated by a prosecutor there named Lin Ying-Hua (林應華).[35] Eventually, the Minister of Justice, Liao Cheng-Hao (廖正豪), ordered a personnel transfer for Lin.[36] The intervention of superiors and even the Minister of Justice led to deep dissatisfaction among junior public prosecutors, and in June 1998 they created the "Prosecutor Reform Association" (檢察官改革協會) with five reform demands for the prosecutorial system:[37]

1 The drafting of concrete legal provisions defining the principle of prosecutorial integration and providing clear guidelines for case transfer;
2 The creation of an "Act on the Organization of a Prosecutors' Personnel Review Committee" before June 1998;
3 Non-binding elections for chief prosecutors should be held before July 1998;
4 An evaluation of all chief prosecutors regarding their integrity and professional performance had to be completed before October 1998;
5 A mechanism for prosecutors' complaints and for whistleblowers had to be established.

Because this association was assembled by junior prosecutors, their goals challenged the original authority of senior prosecutors. Consequently, and as

33 When a case is delivered by police to a prosecutors' office, the prosecutor who will be responsible for it is randomly determined so that political or personal influences on prosecutorial decisions can be eliminated.

34 See Chu Chao-Liang (朱朝亮), Prosecutorial Reform over 10 Years, 1 Taiwan Prosecutor Rev. 53, 67 (2007).

35 www.businessweekly.com.tw/KArticle.aspx?id=6018.

36 www.jrf.org.tw/newjrf/rte/myform_detail2.asp?id=1232.

37 See Chu, *supra* note 34, at 68.

expected, these demands were not realized as scheduled. These junior prosecutors' lack of recognition of their superior-level colleagues probably delayed the internal reforms they sought, but their demands were all gradually accepted after 2000.

Another major reform occurred after Chen Shui-Bian of the Democratic Progressive Party (DPP) won the Presidential election in March 2000. After his inauguration, President Chen founded the "Black Gold Investigation Center" (查緝黑金行動中心), at the Taiwan High Court Prosecutors' Office, to be responsible for investigating high-profile bribery or corruption cases. (Illegal profits or slush funds are known as "black gold" in Taiwan.) This special agency aimed at a centralizing authority over prosecutorial power in special cases in order to avoid improper political interventions and grant prosecutors greater freedom in investigating such cases. In 2006, during the second term of Chen's presidency, legislative amendments concerning the prosecutorial system structure were passed. The three main points of the 2006 amendments are as follows.

First, the appointment procedures and term of office of the prosecutor general were changed. Prior to 2006, the prosecutor general was appointed by the President without approval of the Legislative Yuan and even had life tenure. This could cause the possible misuse of power because he was under no-one's supervision. According to the new provision, the candidate for prosecutor general nominated by President needed to be approved by the Legislative Yuan. His term of office was limited to four years with no possible reappointment. The main idea was to guarantee the independence of the prosecutor general from political intervention through the four-year term.

Second, since the integrity and independence of the prosecutor general would be trusted more under the new system, the office was given greater authority and power in criminal investigations. The "Black Gold Investigation Center" was renamed the "Special Investigation Division" (特別偵查組), institutionalized into the Court Organization Act, moved as an agency at the Prosecutors' Office of the Supreme Court, and placed under the direct control of the prosecutor general. Members of the division would be designated by the prosecutor general, who would also supervise their investigation activities.

Third, personnel changes and promotions for prosecutors were to be determined by a newly created "Prosecutors' Personnel Review Committee" (檢察官人事審議委員會) under the Ministry of Justice. As mentioned above, senior prosecutors might influence junior colleagues in several ways. The power to determine personnel affairs was usually one of them. The goal of setting up such a committee was to make decisions concerning prosecutors' personnel affairs open and transparent so that prosecutors did not need to obey improper orders from superiors or politicians for promotion.

Additional changes could also be found in the enactment of the Judges Act in 2011. Although the name of the law suggests that it is not relevant to public prosecutors, some provisions regarding prosecutors were inserted into this statute. These included protections against demotion, reassignment, transfer of a case, the creation of clear disciplinary sanctions, and their procedures at a newly created Court of the Judiciary.

In sum, it goes without saying that the post-2000 changes mentioned above increased prosecutors' independence in carrying out criminal investigations.

Restrictions on public prosecutors' powers at the investigation stage

Another key point in Taiwan's prosecutorial reform process lies in the restriction of the public prosecutor's power at the investigation stage. As mentioned above, before the 1990s, Taiwan's public prosecutors had sweeping powers to undertake coercive measures such as detention, searches, and wiretapping. They were also often criticized for misusing their authority.

In 1995, the KMT made a legislative proposal to concentrate detention authority into the hands of chief prosecutors so that political intervention would be easier, and the Constitutional Court wrote Interpretation No. 392 in the same year. During the trial period at the Constitutional Court, many public prosecutors argued that they were also judicial officers and thus competent to reach decisions on detention at the investigation stage.[38] In contrast, most scholars objected to prosecutors' powers to detain because, they argued, prosecutors were just one party at trial and were in charge of deciding charges and investigation. They should not be placed in charge of determining whether the other party should be detained, otherwise the legal requirement of "due process" would be violated.[39] The Constitutional Court decided that the prosecutor should not solely decide whether to issue a detention warrant at investigation stage and the relevant provisions in Criminal Procedure Code would lose effect within two years.

A very interesting issue during the debate of Interpretation No. 392 concerned a public prosecutor's legal status. Justices did not deny that public prosecutors held judicial officer status. However, as the Constitutional Court reasoned:

> The notion of "judiciary" is relative to legislation and administration (in the constitutional framework of this state, relative to examination and control, too). Conceptually, this is a legal term that connotes multiple meanings. Distinctions can be made between judiciary of a substantive meaning v. judiciary of a formal meaning, and judiciary of a restrictive definition v. judiciary of an expansive definition. Judiciary of a substantive meaning refers to declarations made by a state for resolution of a controversy (i.e., a trial), as well as any state function auxiliary to this trial power (i.e., judicial administration). Judiciary of a formal meaning extends further to include any state function provided by law to the judicial power to further its purpose – for example, the "notary public" by its nature is not within the category of the judiciary, however, it was annexed to the judicial department

38 See e.g., Chu Nan (朱楠), Public Prosecutor Should Possess Detention Authority, 6 Taiwan L. J. 20 (1995).

39 See e.g., Lin Tzu-Yi (林子儀), Personal Freedom and Detention, 6 Taiwan L. J. 29 (1995).

> to further its purpose. Judiciary of a restrictive definition is the common meaning for the judiciary. It refers to state functions in civil and criminal trials, and the capacity to carry out this function is called judicial power or adjudicative power. Because it refers to the civil and criminal trials, it is also called trial power. Whereas in this state, the administrative litigation, the disciplinary measures against public functionaries, judicial interpretation, the trial for dissolution of unconstitutional political parties and any sort of "state functions of adjudication" shall also be included. That is to say, any of those state functions implicating a judicial independence are within this meaning of judiciary. Therefore, the position and duty of the Judicial Yuan provided by Chapter 7 of the Constitution, i.e., the Judicial Yuan shall be the highest "judicial organ" of the state provided by Article 77, the judicial interpretation provided by Article 78, and the trials for dissolution of unconstitutional political parties provided by Article 4, Paragraph 2, of the Amendment of the Constitution, shall be deemed the judiciary of a restrictive definition. As to those state functions to further the purpose of the judiciary of a restrictive definition (i.e., state functions with a judicial nature), they are included in the category of the judiciary of an expansive definition.[40]

As for public prosecutor's authority over detention at investigation stage, the Constitutional Court held that:

> The protection of the people's physical freedom provided by Article 8 of the Constitution is a fundamental right. It not only openly declares the importance it places on the protection of physical freedom, but also explicitly provides for the procedures in carrying out this protection. By tackling the aims and means simultaneously, it was indeed a refined constitutional provision. The custodial measure segregates a person from his or her family, society, and professional life, "detains" the person in a custodial ward, and restrains said person's movement for a long period of time. This deprivation of physical freedom will have a tremendous impact on the person, not only in terms of psychological effect, but also in terms of loss of reputation and credit standing – and a tremendous impact on personal rights. It is a coercive measure that has maximum impact on physical freedom. Therefore, it should be reserved as "the last measure in evidence preservation proceedings," and must be administered with extreme caution. Unless all legal requirements are met and there are necessities, it should not be invoked easily. To carry through this idea of protection for physical freedom, the assessment of legality and necessity of this measure should be made by an independent tribunal in accordance with the procedure prescribed by law.

40 Judicial Yuan Interpretation, No. 392 (1995).

> Only by doing so can it be said that the spirit of Article 8, Paragraph 2, of the Constitution is upheld. The current provisions of the Code of Criminal Procedure, Article 101, stating that an accused may be detained after examination if it is deemed necessary and it is discovered that one of the conditions specified in Article 76 exists, Article 102, Paragraph 3, applying mutatis mutandis to Article 71, Paragraph 4, for the order of detention issued by a prosecutor and Article 120 providing that after an accused has been examined ...; if one of the circumstances of Article 114 is present, the accused may not be detained unless it is impossible to release him on bail or to the custody of another or with a limitation on his residence, provide the prosecutors, besides the court, with a power to take an accused (criminal suspect) into custody. Article 105, Paragraph 3, of the same Code states: ... such restraint shall be ordered by the officer in charge of the detention house, and such order shall be referred immediately to the court or prosecutor concerned for approval provides the prosecutor with a power to approve a detention order submitted by the chief officer of the detention house. Article 121, Paragraph 1, of the Same Code: "The cancellation of detention specified in Article 107, ... the suspension of detention specified in Articles 115 and 116, and the resumption of detention specified in Article 117 ... shall be made by a court ruling or by a prosecutor's order," and Article 259, Paragraph 1: "A detained accused who received a ruling not to prosecute, ... if the circumstances warrant, may be ordered to remain in custody." These laws provide the prosecutor with the power to cancel, cease, resume, or continue detention, and the power to implement other measures in conjunction with the power to detain an accused (criminal suspect). These powers are incongruous with the spirit of the abovementioned Article 8, Paragraph 2, of the Constitution.[41]

Two years after the promulgation of Interpretation No. 392, relevant provisions in the Criminal Procedure Act were amended pursuant to the Justices' opinion. From then on, prosecutors' powers in criminal investigation have been more restricted.

Before the enactment of the Communication Security and Surveillance Act (CSSA; 通訊保障及監察法), public prosecutors, police, and even agents of the National Security Bureau (國家安全局) could wiretap crime suspects without any restrictions. In 1999, the Legislative Yuan passed a law which regulated the use of wiretapping in criminal investigations. According to Article 5 of the CSSA, an "interception warrant" could only be issued by a judge if it was necessary for the investigation of specified felonies. In other words, under the CSSA, the public prosecutor lost the discretion to decide on wiretapping at the investigation stage.

41 Judicial Yuan Interpretation, No. 392 (1995).

Despite the transfer of powers of detention and wiretapping to judges, the public prosecutor was still entitled to determine whether to search a person, property, electronic records, a dwelling, or other premises after 1999. This search and seizure power was transferred to judges as a consequence of a political event.

In 2001, an agent of the National Security Bureau named Liu Kuan-Chun (劉冠軍) was suspected of corruption. This scandal was soon reported by the *China Times Express* (中時晚報). Because it was actually a highly-sensitive case concerning national security, the chief prosecutor of the Taipei District Prosecutors' Office directly ordered the search of the offices of the *China Times Express* with warrants signed by himself. Since this was the first case in which a public prosecutor searched a news outlet's offices, some reporters, politicians, and even the general public criticized the search. In order to counter prosecutors' arbitrary use of their powers to search for evidence, some legislators proposed a bill depriving prosecutors of the authority to issue a search warrant at the investigation stage. This legislative proposal was soon passed. From then on, the public prosecutor has had to apply to the court for a search warrant if he deemed that a search at the investigation stage would be necessary for a criminal investigation.[42]

One of the most interesting points during the debate on who should have the authority to issue search warrants was that there were few voices opposing the amendment. The main idea that a warrant to infringe on peoples' rights had to be signed not by a public prosecutor but by a neutral and detached court had been generally accepted as a principle since the detention warrant debate in 1995. Because this idea was accepted at that point, it was inevitable that it would eventually be extended to cover search warrants.

In addition, Taiwan's Criminal Procedure Code adopted Germany's legislative example regarding coercive measures. The concept of a "search" (搜索), according to Article 122 of Taiwan's Criminal Procedure Code, denotes only the physical intrusion onto property, electronic records, dwellings, or other premises for the arrest of a suspect or evidence collection. "Bodily examination" (身體檢查處分) was not regarded as a "search" under the statutory definition and remained legally unregulated until 2003. In 2003, it was recognized as a coercive measure requiring written permission from prosecutor. However, the authority to obtain the written permission for a bodily examination was not in accord with the same principles that governed detention and search warrants. The legislature thus divided the bodily examination process into two different stages, one by the public prosecutor at the investigation stage and another by a judge during trial.[43]

42 However, at the trial stage, if the court deems that a search is necessary, it can issue a warrant by itself without approval of prosecutor or higher court. See Article 128, sub. 3 of Taiwan's Criminal Procedure Code.

43 See e.g. Lin Yu-Hsiung (林鈺雄), Consider Bodily Examination from the System of Basic Rights, 33 Nat'l Taiwan Univ. L. J. 149 (2004).

Since the debate on the required authority for detention warrants in 1995, public prosecutors gradually lost total control over many of their key tools of criminal investigation. Warrants for detention, wiretapping, and search must currently be issued by a neutral and detached court. It is unfortunate that a bodily examination at the investigation stage can be ordered by a public prosecutor. This situation may violate the principle of the separation of powers, as it may involve executive action in a judicial field. The issue involves the Taiwanese view of prosecutors as judicial officers, a view that is gradually coming under pressure. Coercive measures through which effective evidence can be gained should at any rate be decided by a neutral and detached authority unless there is an urgent circumstantial need. Further legislative amendments are needed on this issue in the future.

Introduction of a modified adversarial system and the public prosecutor's participation in the courtroom

Last but not least, we come to the issue of the change in a public prosecutor's role in the criminal trial. In July 1999, in response to the social expectation of judicial reform, a "National Judicial Reform Conference" (全國司法改革會議) was held to forge a consensus. One key conclusion of the discussion was to switch Taiwan's criminal trial style from the European inquisitorial model to a "modified adversarial system" like that in Japan. To realize the conclusions gained in the forum, several legislative amendments were made in the following years covering issues such as hearsay rules and cross-examination. These legislative amendments actually changed public prosecutors' behavior in criminal trials.

As mentioned above, prior to the 1980s, public prosecutors rarely came to the courtroom to represent the government in accusing defendants. After the 1980s, public prosecutors began to appear in the courtroom, but did not say much other than "the criminal charges are as indicated in the indictment" ("詳如起訴書所載").[44] What happened in the courtroom on the trial date was only an inquisitorial oral examination made by the judge. Judges' vast responsibilities, not only to deliver verdicts "neutrally and detachedly," but also to investigate the facts of the crime "inquisitorially and ex officio," has been severely criticized.[45] The key to rebalancing the judge's role as a detached adjudicator was to increase public prosecutors' participation in trials. Amendments to the Criminal Procedure Act since 1999 have been aimed at the prosecutor's actions in the courtroom. These legislative changes created a separation in the work of public prosecutors, meaning that all prosecutors were divided into two different sections: the

44 See e.g., Chen Wen-Chi (陳文琪), Evaluation of the Project of Prosecutor's Attendance at Courtroom at Shihlin District Court (士林地檢署實施檢察官專責到庭施行公訴情形及相關問題), 66 The Taiwan L. Rev. 65, 69 (2000).

45 See e.g., Wang Jaw-Perng (王兆鵬等), Criminal Procedure Law, Vol. 2, 11–15 (2012).

"prosecution section" (公訴組) and the "investigation section" (偵查組).[46] Those belonging to the prosecution section had to appear in the courtroom from the very beginning of the trial, cross-examine witnesses, and make a final statement representing the government.[47] The main reason why prosecutors were divided into two sections had to do with their workload. Prosecutors are extremely busy and have a lot of cases in their charge. A prosecutor responsible for investigation has to perform out-of-office duties, such as searching the defendant's house to collect evidence, and it is not possible for him to attend the courtroom to engage in debate. Hence, prosecutors were divided into two sections, one of which is mainly responsible for investigation, while the other one is in charge of courtroom attendance and debate with suspects and defense lawyers.[48]

To some extent, the switch in Taiwan's criminal trials from a pure European inquisitorial style to the modified adversarial system forced the prosecutor to become intensively involved in the criminal trial. This was definitely a step forward for a just and fair criminal justice.

The Prosecutor General controversy of 2013

The discussion in the last section introduced and reviewed the transition in Taiwan's prosecutorial system since 1990. It is not too much to say that currently prosecutors possess more freedom to work on criminal cases without the intervention of superiors and politicians. Even though the public prosecutor is no longer authorized to issue detention, search, or wiretapping warrants, their reputation in the eyes of the public has improved and their work against crime has won them more and more trust.

However, a criminal case involving the Prosecutor General's abuse of power occurred in September 2013 and deeply damaged the hard-gained social trust of all public prosecutors. The case led to a district court decision.[49] The Special Investigation Division investigated a corruption case concerning a judge at the Taipei High Court, and some telephone conversations between Wang Jin-Pyng (王金平), Speaker of the then-KMT-led Legislative Yuan, and Ker Chien-Ming (柯建銘), a senior legislator of the then-opposition party (DPP), were accidentally wiretapped. Ker requested that Wang lobby Tseng Yung-Fu, the Minister of Justice, to drop the prosecution's appeal in Ker's case, in which the first instance verdict was not guilty. The Special Investigation Division reported the conversation as soon as possible to Prosecutor General Huang Shih-Ming

46 See Tsai Bi-Yu (蔡碧玉), Public Prosecutor and Change of Criminal Justice, 1 Taiwan Prosecutor Rev. 43, 44 (2007).

47 As for the public prosecutor's actions in the courtroom, see Lin Jun-Yi (林俊益), Trilogy of Public Prosecutor's Court Actions, 35 Taiwan L. Rev. 171 (2008).

48 See Tsai Zong-Hsi (蔡宗熙), Evaluation on Project of Prosecutor's Attendance in Miau-Li District Court for Two Years, 91 The Taiwan L. Rev. 222 (2002).

49 See Decision of Taipei District Court, No. 1 of Zhuyizi, 2013.

(黃世銘), who subsequently reported it to President Ma Ying-Jeou (馬英九). President Ma called a press conference right away and expelled Wang from KMT party membership. This event was later called the "September Strife" (九月政爭). However, since the case was still under investigation, no-one other than public prosecutors, even President Ma, was entitled to be told of the conversation. As Prosecutor General Huang revealed the relevant facts to President Ma, the principle of non-disclosure of an investigation (偵查不公開), in accordance with Article 245, Section 1 of the Criminal Procedure Act, was breached. Prosecutor General Huang was thereafter charged with disclosing confidential information to outside persons. On March 21, 2014, the Taipei District Court gave Huang a guilty verdict and handed down a sentence of five months' imprisonment that could be commuted to a fine.

The most controversial issue in the affair involved Prosecutor General Huang's refusal to quit when he was charged by lower prosecutors. He did not resign from his position until he was found guilty by the first instance court. This guilty verdict was ultimately upheld on appeal.[50]

This guilty verdict at the first instance was undoubtedly the most important decision involving public prosecutors' independence ever in the history of the judicial system. The prosecutor general is the head of all public prosecutors, possessing significant powers, including transferring a case from one prosecutor to another as well as holding the final say in deciding whether or not to file a charge. To maintain his integrity, the prosecutor general has needed the legislature's approval and his term of office is only four years without any extension. Although Prosecutor General Huang was approved by Legislative Yuan, he still abused his power by revealing facts of a highly controversial case under criminal investigation to President Ma, who is absolutely not responsible for criminal investigations. This event tells us that once a public prosecutor cooperates with politicians and allows them to influence his discretion, he can be punished for abuse of prosecutorial power.

Concluding remarks

Since 1945, Taiwan's criminal justice has been influenced by Japanese colonial law, the authoritarian KMT government, and even the democratization movement of the 1990s. For some people, democratization in Taiwan has ended in success, but as a researcher of Taiwan's criminal justice, I feel compelled to argue that we still have much to do. Although prosecutors seem to work independently without direct interventions, as in the 1980s, they sometimes still face indirect influence coming from superior colleagues and even politicians. The case of Prosecutor General Huang might be a very good illustration.

50 Jason Pan, "Huang Shih-ming guilty verdict upheld by court," *Taipei Times*, July 6, 2017, www.taipeitimes.com/News/front/archives/2017/07/06/2003673985.

As representatives of the government in criminal prosecution, prosecutors must actively uncover the facts of a crime on the one hand, while on the other hand also respecting citizen's rights, as enshrined in the protective rules of the Criminal Procedure Code. This remains a very difficult job for Taiwan's public prosecutors. To balance the requirements from both sides in criminal prosecution is at any rate their ultimate mission and, undoubtedly, they still have a long way to go.

Part II

Institutional transformations

4 Separation of the judiciary and the public prosecution

The cornerstone of judicial reform in Taiwan

Yueh-Sheng Weng and Chien-Liang Lee

Introduction

In July 1999, responding to public opinion urging for reform, the Judicial Yuan (J.Y.) held the "National Judicial Reform Conference." It was the first time the Judicial Yuan responded to demands for judicial reform in a public way. The Conference came to a total of 49 conclusions,[1] reflecting to a considerable extent the social pressure for judicial reform, and in that sense, the conference has been a milestone in the history of judicial reform in Taiwan. Sixteen years have gone by since the Conference at the time of this writing, however the conclusions passed by the Conference have not yet all been put into law, and the work of judicial reform has not yet been finished. Over the years, criticisms and recommendations for reform from society have never ceased, and there remains much to do in terms of judicial reform.

Looking back at the course of judicial reform in Taiwan, establishing the independence of the judiciary has always been one of the main issues and goals. One crucial step toward that goal in the earlier stage was the realization of the separation of the administration of the judiciary and that of the public prosecution from July 1, 1980, which was not only a significant milestone for the judiciary in Taiwan, but also laid a key cornerstone for later reforms. Only after the organizational restructuring were the high and districts courts able to sever their organizational ties with the administrative agencies and cease to be part of the executive, thereby starting a new phase of judicial reform. On its surface, the severance of organizational ties with the executive is just a change in the administration of the courts. But in substance the move has significant implications for the status of the courts and the judges, for the different roles of the judiciary and the public prosecution, and for the establishment and consolidation of judicial independence. One can even say that this organizational separation has served as

1 Judicial Yuan, 司法院史實紀要 [Minutes of Judicial Yuan History], Vol. 5, Part I, 87 (September 2007).

the foundation for the reform measures put forward by the successive Presidents of the Judicial Yuan since 1980. Examples of such reforms include: the 1987 amendment of the "Rules of Review of the Documents and Archives by the Courts during Trials" (法院辦案書類及文卷審查實施要點) to abolish *ex ante* review of judgments of the courts composed of a collegiate panel of judges; the 1989 abolition of *ex ante* review of rulings made by courts composed of a single commissioned judge (實任法官), replacing it with review after the delivery of judgments; the ultimate abolition of review of decisions made by any court composed of commissioned judges (實任法官) or of judges in their probationary period (試署法官); and changing the review of rulings made by alternate judges (候補法官) into *ex post* review since November 1996.

Further, in February 1998, the Judicial Yuan consolidated the effort to separate the judiciary and prosecution by putting forward the draft "Judges Act," which provided the reform with a statutory foundation. Despite the entry into force of the Judges Act in 2011, the separation of the judiciary and prosecution, and its implications for the nature of the judicial power and the status of the judge, continue to be an important issue in judicial reform in Taiwan to this day.

The nature of judicial power and the status of judges

The nature of judicial power

In the development of contemporary states, state powers have gradually been divided into three fields: the legislature, the executive, and the judiciary. State patterns have moved from the authoritarian state, with its concentration of state powers, to the constitutional system, with the separation of powers. In this evolutionary process, people have been gradually recognizing the function of the judiciary and the necessity of its independence. Even Montesquieu, who first advocated the separation of three state powers, also found the judiciary in "some way insignificant" (*en quelque façon nulle*). From the perspective of separation of powers, the check and balance ideas put forward by Montesquieu primarily focused on the checks and balances between the executive and the legislature, not checks and balances that the judiciary could exercise against the legislature or the executive. Montesquieu was of the opinion that the judiciary would be impartial when judges were free from interference from the legislature or the executive in civil and criminal trials, but he also thought that the judiciary should exercise almost no checks and balances.[2]

Following Montesquieu's theory of separation of powers, the judiciary was endowed with no checks and balances against the legislature in the original design of the United States' Constitution. The judicial review of laws was not

2 See Charles de Secondat, Baron de Montesquieu, *The Spirit of Laws*, 173–5, 350 (1748, translated by Thomas Nugent 1752, reprinted 2001).

expressly stipulated in the Constitution but was established by case law,[3] so as to firmly establish the judiciary as one of the state powers alongside the executive and the legislature.

Comparable situations were found in states in other parts of the world, where the judiciary was conservative, weak, or was attached to or controlled by the executive. Nevertheless, as constitutional democracy evolves, the important role played by the judiciary in constraining tyranny or protecting human rights has gradually been realized, together with the awareness of the necessity of strengthening the judiciary on a par with other state powers. The trend of strengthening the judiciary continued after the end of World War II, with the judiciary playing an ever more important role in the balance of powers and protection of human rights in nations around the world. In this light, judicial reform has been a pivotal part in political development and the construction of the rule of law in every state, and in this trend Taiwan is no exception.

Among the core elements and basic issues in judicial reform are the nature of judicial power and the constitutional status of the judge. As one of the branches of state power, the most distinctive characteristics of judicial power are that judges passively accept concrete cases, exercise their powers as neutral arbiters, and deliver legally binding judgments after conducting proceedings in accordance with due process. In other words, the judiciary is by nature passive.[4] The court is engaged only when a case that falls within its jurisdiction arises. Judges may exercise their powers only in a way that is neutral, impartial, and objective. They identify facts, apply laws, and declare binding decisions on issues of law after conducting open hearings in which open debates are held according to applicable criminal and civil procedures. In terms of applying law, the functions carried out by judges might seem similar to those carried out by the executive, but there is one essential difference: the executive is active. Although the

3 *Marbury* v. *Madison*, 5 U.S. 137 (1803).

4 Alexander Hamilton, one of the framers of the Constitution of the United States of America, discusses the judiciary in Federalist no. 78:

> Whoever attentively considers the different departments of power must perceive, that, in a government in which they are separated from each other, the judiciary, from the nature of its functions, will always be the least dangerous to the political rights of the Constitution; because it will be least in a capacity to annoy or injure them. The Executive not only dispenses the honors, but holds the sword of the community. The legislature not only commands the purse, but prescribes the rules by which the duties and rights of every citizen are to be regulated. The judiciary, on the contrary, has no influence over either the sword or the purse; no direction either of the strength or of the wealth of the society; and can take no active resolution whatever.

Hamilton believed the judiciary to be the least dangerous part of the Constitution because of its "passiveness." On the other hand, the "counter-majoritarian difficulty" faced by the judiciary discussed by Alexander M. Bickel concerns legitimacy where the judiciary challenges the legislature. See generally, Alexander M. Bickel, *The Least Dangerous Branch: The Supreme Court at the Bar of Politics* (1962).

application of law by the executive is legally controlled, in general the executive applies law to pursue administrative purposes, and in this sense, legality is not the only consideration. It has to take into account whether the law suits administrative purposes. By contrast, the foremost aim of the judiciary is to make correct judgments of law. The only concern of judges should be making a declaration about the "law" they confirm and expressing the will of the law through their judgments. The difference between the competences and functions of the judiciary and the executive also applies to the different roles played by the judges and public prosecutors, although both of them are orientated towards the fulfillment of state power concerning criminal punishment.

In its organizational structure, the executive operates according to a principle of unity among the various offices it establishes.[5] In principle, public functionaries in the executive bear the duty to obey the orders of their superiors. By contrast, the judiciary exercises its power independently. There is a system of appeal, but there is no command and supervisory relationship between the appellate court and the lower court. A court is usually composed of a collegiate panel of judges to ensure the correctness of judgments and rulings. A court composed of one single judge is exceptional in Taiwan. The judiciary has the final say on matters of law. It enjoys the ultimate, highest authoritative power to interpret law.

To sum up, passiveness, independence, impartiality, correctness, and authoritativeness are the basic characteristics of the judiciary. Consequently, the judiciary often serves as the final safeguard of justice.

The status of judges

From the discussion above we see the essential differences between the judiciary and executive in their administration and exercise of power. However, the distinction between judges and public prosecutors is less clear, from the perspective that both exercise the state's power of punishment. Judges and public prosecutors are often categorically called "judicial officers," especially in Taiwan[6] and

5 See J.Y. Interpretation no. 613.

6 For example, Article 8 Paragraph 1 of the ROC Constitution stipulates that "Personal freedom shall be guaranteed to the people. Except in case of flagrante delicto as provided by law, no person shall be arrested or detained otherwise than by a judicial or a police organ in accordance with the procedure prescribed by law…." As for the term "judicial organ," references should be made to J.Y. Interpretation no. 392, which points out that:

> Criminal procedure, the judicial proceeding to try criminal cases, is one of the powers held by the judicial branch. It is a process with the purpose of carrying out the penal power of a state. A criminal trial begins with an indictment, which resulted from investigations. When a judgment is final, execution of punishment is necessary to realize the content of judgment. Therefore, these steps, namely, the process of investigation, indictment, trial, and execution of punishment, are closely related to trial and punishment – they are different stages of the process of criminal justice. In this process, the prosecutor's offices act on behalf of the state

in the German legal tradition to which it belongs. Used in this way, this "judicial officers" concept blurs the constitutional status of judges and public prosecutors, with the implication that judges are to be categorized as civil servants, a position which subtly deprives judges of their independence and prevents them from balancing other state powers. In the late period of the German Weimar Constitution, judges cooperated with the Nazi regime, "faithfully" obeying and enforcing laws that violated human rights.[7] This was related to the fact that judges' independence was not taken seriously.

Learning from the painful lesson of human rights violations under the Nazis, the framers of the Basic Law in (West) Germany after World War II chose to adopt a system in which the judiciary checks and balances other state powers. Article 19 Paragraph 4 of the Basic Law establishes a seamless system of remedies for rights, by which people may combat the exercise of state powers before the court by exercising their rights to litigate. The Basic Law paid special attention to delineating concepts such as "judge," "court," and "the judiciary," and it strictly differentiated the roles of the judge vis-à-vis public servants and those of the court vis-à-vis administrative organs. Further, the "German Judge Act" (*Deutsches Richtergesetz*, or DRiG) was promulgated on September 8, 1961 and came into force on July 1, 1962. The *Richtergesetz* guarantees the special status of judges. It stipulated the legal status of federal judges and judges of each Land (state). Judges were no longer civil servants who happened to adjudicate. In addition, different administrative litigation systems in each Land were unified

to investigate, indict, and punish. Since the duty and function of a prosecutor's office is to carry out its role in criminal justice, its conduct within this sphere of state action shall be deemed "judiciary" in an expansive sense. Therefore, the term "judicial organ" used in Article 8, Paragraph 1, of the Constitution would not have the same meaning as the term "judicial organ" used in Article 77 of the Constitution. Instead, the term is applied as an expansive definition in order that the prosecutor's offices may be included therein.

7 Gustav Radbruch, a German scholar of jurisprudence, published a newspaper article entitled "Five Minutes of Jurisprudence" (*Fünf Minuten Rechtsphilosophie*) on September 12, 1945, and its influence lasts until now. The first "minute" reads:

> "An order is an order," the soldier is told. "A law is a law," says the jurist. The soldier, however, is required neither by duty nor by law to obey an order whose object he knows to be a felony or a misdemeanor, while the jurist … recognizes no such exceptions to the validity of a law or to the requirement of obedience by those subject to it. A law is valid because it is a law, and it is a law if, in the general run of cases, it has the power to prevail. This view of a law and of its validity (we call it the positivistic theory) has rendered jurists and the people alike defenseless against arbitrary, cruel, or criminal laws, however extreme they might be.

This criticism was aimed at jurists, especially judges in the Nazi period. See the translation in Bonnie Litschewski Paulson and Stanley Paulson, *Oxford Journal of Legal Studies*, Vol. 26, no. 1 (2006), pp. 13–15.

and placed under the judiciary, which put beyond doubt that the jurisdiction of administrative law litigation belongs to the judiciary.[8]

At the same time, the German Basic Law established guarantees for human dignity and fundamental rights and set up the Federal Constitutional Court as the guardian of the constitution. Furthermore, there are also constitutional courts in every Land to safeguard the constitution and protect human rights. An important role of the new constitutional court system is to check and balance other state powers, especially the legislature. The constitutional courts are invested with the competence to be the final adjudicator over constitutional controversies. It not only stands equally alongside the executive and the legislature but also effectively checks the powers of other branches. This mechanism has played a key role in the development and consolidation of Germany's democracy. The achievements of the German Federal Constitutional Court are in general highly regarded, and it has a good reputation nationally and internationally. Its influence on other democratic countries can be seen in the global wave of the establishment of constitutional courts. By being the ultimate arbiter over constitutional matters, the judiciary can guard constitutional compliance by the executive and the legislature, which in turn gives the judiciary a new position that enables it to check other state powers and be balanced by them at the same time. Further, the facts that the judiciary safeguards the democratic state with the rule of law and extensively protects human rights enhance the legitimacy of strengthened judicial power.

The cornerstone of judicial reform in Taiwan: organizational separation between the judiciary and the public prosecution

The rendering of Judicial Yuan Interpretation no. 86

The starting point of judicial reform in Taiwan may be marked by the consolidation of the separation of the administration of the judiciary and that of the public prosecution. Prior to 1947, the Judicial Yuan's areas of responsibility were limited to the Supreme Court, the Administrative Court, and the Public Functionary Disciplinary Sanction Commission; apart from those, the high courts and their lower courts were under the Ministry of Judicial Administration (司法行政部) in the Executive Yuan. These lower courts were affiliated to the executive and there was no separation of the judiciary and the executive, a situation that continued even after the entry of the Constitution into force in 1947. On June 6, 1953, the Control Yuan petitioned the Grand Justices of Judicial Yuan for an interpretation on whether high courts and their lower courts should be affiliated

8 翁岳生 [Weng Yueh-Sheng], 行政訴訟制度現代化之研究 [On the Modernization of Administrative Litigation], in 行政法與現代法治國家 [Administrative Law and State under Modern Rule of Law], (3rd edn, October 1979) 381ff.

to the Judicial Yuan. About seven years later, on August 15, 1960, the Grand Justices rendered Judicial Yuan Interpretation (hereinafter referred to as J.Y. Interpretation) no. 86, which reads as follows:

> Article 77 of the Constitution stipulates that the Judicial Yuan is the highest judicial organ of the State and holds judicial power over trials of civil and criminal litigation, of which trials shall include civil and criminal litigation at courts of all levels. In view of the fact that different levels of courts and subsidiary courts below the High Court inclusively hold judicial power over trials of civil and criminal litigation, these courts shall be subordinate to the Judicial Yuan.

And its reasoning reads as follows:

> Article 82 of the Constitution, which stipulates that the structure of the Judicial Yuan and courts of all levels shall be organized by law and incorporated into the chapter of the Judiciary intending to establish the consistency of the judicial system, contributes as cross-evidence. Based on this reason, all levels of courts and subsidiary courts below the High Court shall be subordinate to the Judicial Yuan. All relevant acts and regulations shall respectively be amended to comply with the concept in Article 77 of the Constitution.

Prior to this decision, the key historical reason for the "non-separation of the judiciary and the public prosecution" lay in Section 87 of older versions of the Court Organization Act, which stipulated that "The supervision of the judicial administration shall be in conformity with the following provisions: ... II. The Minister of Judicial Administration supervises the Supreme Prosecutors Office and the High Court and its branches and their lower courts."

The implementation of Judicial Yuan Interpretation no. 86

Interpretation no. 86 was the first finding in the history of judicial review in Taiwan in which a legislative act was declared unconstitutional. After its rendering, the interpretation was not enforced because of the controversy over the personnel management of judges. The key issue was whether prosecutors should be considered "judicial officers," as mentioned above.

The authorities procrastinated over implementation of the Interpretation for several years, demonstrating their reluctance to reform. Only in 1978, when a momentous change of political and economic circumstances occurred alongside the severing of diplomatic relations between the Republic of China and the United States of America, did the authorities carry out several socio-economic reforms, among which was judicial reform. The essence of J.Y. Interpretation no. 86 was enforced on July 1, 1980. The high courts and their lower courts were moved to affiliation under the Judicial Yuan, while the name of the Ministry of

Judicial Administration (司法行政部) was changed into the Ministry of Justice (法務部). It took 20 years from the rendering of Interpretation no. 86 on August 15, 1960 for it to be implemented, which reveals the difficulties in improving the court system.[9]

After World War II, the development of the judiciary in Taiwan was fundamentally influenced by Western trends. This evolution included the increasing importance of public law litigation, judicial review, administrative litigation, proceedings at the special court for disciplining civil servants, and the interpretation of the Constitution by the Justices of the Judicial Yuan. Generally speaking, the change of the judiciary and litigation systems in Taiwan worked toward the protection of human rights and building a balance between the executive and legislature. Nevertheless, the development of true independence in the judicial system occurred at a later stage in Taiwan, where the judiciary was traditionally not well respected. Before the separation of the administration of the judiciary and the public prosecution, the high courts and their lower courts under the Ministry of Judicial Administration functioned according to the old civil law system in which the judiciary and the executive were not differentiated and the judiciary was affiliated with the executive. It was difficult for the judiciary to be independent under such a system. After the separation of the administration of judges and prosecutors, the former were freed from the supervision of the executive, laying the foundation of judicial independence in conducting trials and rendering judgments.

A key issue of judicial reform in Taiwan: functional separation of the judiciary and the public prosecution

After the separation of the administration of the judiciary and public prosecution, Presidents of the Judicial Yuan took successive follow-up measures and requested additional changes in judicial reform. The forums for pushing forward those measures were judicial reform conferences, including the "Nationwide Judicial Conference" (全國司法會議), held in 1980 and again 1988, the "Judicial Reform Committee" in 1994, and the "National Judicial Reform Conference" (全國司法改革會議) in 1999. Many people made great efforts over many years, resulting in improvements in the quality and impartiality of court rulings.[10]

9 The issue of the courts' subordination to the executive existed before the Constitution came into effect. Many scholars had different opinions on the issue, making it complicated and difficult. See further 阮毅成 [Ruan Yi-Cheng], 法院改隸案釋疑 [Questions on Reshuffling the Administration of the Courts], in 法語 [Thoughts on Legal Matters], Vol. II (1980), 438–61, for the development of the controversy over separating the administration of the judiciary and the public prosecution.

10 For example, Zain Taj Dean, a citizen of the United Kingdom, was sentenced to four years imprisonment on March 25, 2010, for drunken driving, negligently causing the death of another and fleeing after the vehicle he drove caused an accident resulting in a death. See 臺灣高等法院 100年度交上訴字 第49號刑事判決 [Criminal Judgment Jiao – Appeal no. 49, Taiwan High

While many issues relating to the statuses of judges and prosecutors, as well as the relations between judicial administration and adjudication, were resolved in the key decision of J.Y. Interpretation no. 86, tasks for judicial reform still remained. The enactment and enforcement of the Judges Act was one of the key outcomes of ongoing judicial reform efforts, which continued to carry the torch of reform.

Judicial independence and organizational separation of the judiciary and the public prosecution

Safeguarding judicial independence is a core issue of judicial reform. The key to success in judicial reform resides in securing the independence of adjudication. This means that judicial independence hinges on the status of judges. The influences that may affect judges come from two sources: external sources that exert institutional influences, and internal sources that exert influence on a judge's mindset, which is shaped in education and training. Whether a state is democratic and has the rule of law or not is closely related to the independence and quality of judges. That is why Article 80 of the Constitution guarantees the position and status of judges.[11]

In many civil law countries, the courts have traditionally been affiliated with the executive in their organization. Hence a significant issue concerns separating the judiciary from the executive to maintain the impartiality of courts and secure people's trust in judicial independence. Take Germany as an example: after World War II, the framers of the German Constitution used the term "law-interpreting power" (*rechtsprechende Gewalt*) instead of the original term "justice" (*Justiz*) to remove the image of the judiciary as dominated by a ruler and to enhance the judiciary's checking power against the executive and legislature. Some scholars called it the "third power" (*dritte Gewalt*) to distinguish the judiciary from other branches, differentiating administrative organs and

---

Court (2011)]. In August 2012, Zain Taj Dean fled Taiwan. In January 2013, the Taipei District Prosecutors Office negotiated Dean's extradition with the British government through the Ministries of Justice, Foreign Affairs, and Taipei Representative Office in the UK. On October 16 of the same year, the "Memorandum of Understanding Concerning the Extradition of Zain Taj Dean" signed with the UK came into force. The Scottish police arrested Dean on October 17. During the trial in Scotland, his defense lawyer repeatedly accused Taiwan of violating the European Convention on Human Rights provisions regarding fair trials. On June 11, 2014, the Scottish District Court ruled that Zain Taj Dean should be extradited to Taiwan to serve a prison sentence, thus rejecting his allegations that the judiciary in Taiwan was unfair. In addition, the family of Dean's victim sued him for civil compensation, and the Royal Courts of Justice recognized on May 23, 2014 that the Taiwanese civil judgment against him could be enforced. See 法務部新聞稿編號: 03–050 [Ministry of Justice Press Release no. 03–050] (June 11, 2014).

11 J.Y. Interpretation no. 13 states that "The Judge referred to in Article 81 of the Constitution means the Judge that Article 80 of the Constitution refers to and does not include the Prosecutor."

courts, public servants and judges. The aim of the "German Judges Act" in 1961, which explicitly stipulates the special status of judges and differentiates judges from public servants, was precisely this.

Traditionally, criminal procedure in Taiwan was dominated by an inquisitorial system, leading to limited participation of public prosecutors in trials, confusion between the roles of judges and that of public prosecutors, and to the fact that the human rights of the accused were often not fully respected. As dialogues with other legal systems progressed, together with greater emphasis on the protection of human rights, the adversarial system, which advocates the concept of equality between the defendant and prosecutor, was given more attention.

Making criminal procedure more adversarial became the main direction in criminal procedure reform, as seen in the conclusions of the National Judicial Reform Conference in 1999.[12] After the National Judicial Reform Conference, the Judicial Yuan worked toward amending the Criminal Procedure Act to construct a "modified adversarial system," in which evidential investigation was primarily conducted by the parties and secondarily by the court *ex officio*. The amendments were made complete step-by-step, ultimately coming into effect in 2004. In the procedural structure of the modified adversarial system, it is the parties who lead evidence production and examine witnesses. Now, public prosecutors, viewed as a party rather than quasi-judicial assistant to the judge, truly bear the burden of proof. Moreover, prosecutors engage with the defendant or his attorneys regarding evidence, fact, and law. These changes reflect the neutral status of judges. This clarification of the competencies of the court and public prosecutors has helped deepen people's trust in the court and prosecution, and it has aided the ideal of judicial impartiality.

The power to make legislative proposals and judicial reform

After World War II, the structure and functions of courts gradually consolidated around their adjudicative functions. Nevertheless, the concept of the "independence" of the judiciary from other powers (especially the executive) developed later and has been difficult to build because of the traditional cultural attitude of disregarding the judiciary. The separation of the administration of the judiciary and the prosecution did not solve the problem of the confused relationship between the judiciary and executive. There were still confusions between the

12 Before this, on March 23, 1998, the Judicial Yuan asked Taiwan Banqiao District Court to test the new criminal procedure from July 1 of the same year:

> This criminal procedure adopts the spirit of the adversary system, which strengthens the public prosecutors' activities in courts. Public prosecutors shall have the burden of proof, examine the witnesses, and debate the defendants or their attorneys in respect of evidence, fact and law.

See Judicial Yuan Order to Taiwan Banqiao District Court, March 23, 1998.

functions performed by the courts vis-à-vis those by the prosecution. Confusions also persisted with regard to whether prosecutors could retain their status as "judicial officers." What was at stake was the consolidation of the legal system under which the judiciary and the prosecution, separated in administration and in functions, the reform of court system, the improvement of administration of justice, the impartiality of judges, the independence of adjudication, and ultimately, peoples' trust in the judiciary.

As mentioned above, the enactment and coming into force of Germany's *Richtergesetz* (Judges Act) in 1961 was one of the key factors in the construction of an independent judicial system in Germany after World War II. Painful historical lessons from the Nazi era led the German authorities and legislature to make the policy decision to enact the Judge Act. But in Taiwan, following its transition from authoritarian rule, the executive faced great difficulty in drafting a legislation protecting judges' status to the exclusion of public prosecutors. A further difficulty in drafting a comparable Judges Act was that the Constitution stipulates that only the Executive Yuan and Examination Yuan may propose draft bills to the Legislative Yuan.[13]

Even the Judicial Yuan itself had reservations over whether it had been given the power to make legislative proposals, and this was reflected in the petition on that subject made by the Control Yuan in 1981.[14] In its petition, the Control Yuan stated that

> due to reservations held by the Judicial Yuan over its power to make legislative proposals, amendments of many acts that were important for judicial reform, such as the Discipline of Public Functionaries Act and the Grand Justices' Council Act, were put on hold.

On May 25, 1982, J.Y. Interpretation no. 175 was issued; it states:

> Because the Judicial Yuan is the supreme judicial agency of the country, it naturally has the authority to propose and present statutory bills to the Legislative Yuan with regard to matters within its authority based on the constitutional system of the "separation of powers" and "checks and balances" among the five branches of the Central Government.

13 Article 58 Paragraph 2 of the Constitution stipulates that

> Statutory … bills, … all of which are to be submitted to the Legislative Yuan … shall be presented by the President and various Ministers and Chairmen of Commissions of the Executive Yuan to the Executive Yuan Council for decision.

Article 87 of the Constitution stipulates that "The Examination Yuan may, with respect to matters under its charge, present statutory bills to the Legislative Yuan."

14 Before this, J.Y. Interpretation no. 3 (May 21, 1952) had ruled that the Control Yuan could propose drafts of acts to Legislative Yuan within its power.

And the reasoning of Interpretation no. 175 was, *inter alia*:

> Subsequent to the separation of power between adjudication and prosecution, the workload borne by the Judicial Yuan has become increasingly heavy. To facilitate judicial reform, to establish the Judicial Yuan, the Constitutional Court, and tribunals inferior to the Constitutional Court to adjudicate civil, criminal, and administrative cases and disciplinary actions against civil servants pursuant to Articles 77, 78, and 82 of the Constitution, and to exercise its authority to uniformly interpret provisions of the Constitution, the Judicial Yuan may propose and present statutory bills to the Legislative Yuan with regard to the organization of its subordinated judicial agencies and matters governed by its judicial authority.

J.Y. Interpretation no. 175 confirmed that the Judicial Yuan has the power to make legislative proposals, which allowed the Judicial Yuan to draft laws and effectively conduct judicial reform. The Justices explicitly cited the separation of the prosecution and judiciary as a reason for this decision. Interpretation no. 175 is one of the most significant interpretations in the history of judicial reform in Taiwan.

The deliberation and enactment of the "Judges Act"

From September 1988, the Judicial Yuan invited scholars, experts, and representatives of government agencies to join a committee that would meet regularly to draft a "Judges Act" for Taiwan. Through numerous meetings, the committee finished a draft Judges Act in April 1993. However, during the consultation process, the bill ran into obstacles involving the cooperation of the Executive Yuan and Examination Yuan – since the bill concerned their powers. The co-signatures of the Executive Yuan and Examination Yuan were necessary to formally present the bill to the Legislative Yuan. The Judicial Yuan actively advocated for the enactment of the Judges Act in order to assure the public that trials, judicial decisions, and judges' salaries were independent and fairly determined.

The July 1999 National Judicial Reform Conference revisited the sensitive question of judges' status in its panel discussion entitled "On the Public Servant Nature of Judges and Their Salary System." The Conference arrived at the conclusion that "judges belong to a special category of public servants" but reached no consensus about the salary system for judges. After this, the Judicial Yuan discussed the draft Judges Act with the Ministry of Justice, Prosecutors Reform Association, and the Judicial Reform Foundation. A new draft was sent to the Legislative Yuan on December 1, 1999. The Judicial Yuan set up the "Working Group Advocating the Enactment of the Judges Act" to push the bill. But it was not passed, and the bill languished in legislative limbo for years.

About ten years later, a series of scandals involving judges' behavior and public outrage at decisions involving lax punishments for rape and molestation changed the political situation. Facing serious public criticisms, President Ma Ying-Jeou felt pressured to undertake some reform, and he reached for a readily available reform measure to quell public discontent – the Judges Act. After numerous meetings and several changes of the draft, the Act was passed on June 14, 2011 and was promulgated by the President on July 6 of the same year. The Judges Act came into force one year after it was promulgated, except that Chapter 5 on Judges' Evaluations came into force half a year after the date of promulgation and Section 78 came into force three years and six months after the date of promulgation.

It took 24 years from the start of discussions over the drafting of the law in 1988 for the Judges Act to come into force in 2012. The reform was not easier than the implementation of the separation of the administration of the judiciary and prosecution. The key points of the Judges Act include: (1) it explicitly states that the Act is *lex specialis*, stipulating the rights and obligations of judges, and that the relationship between the judge and the state is an appointment relationship; (2) Justices of the Judicial Yuan, together with judges in ordinary courts, are judges under the Constitution; (3) it specifies the appointment process; (4) it specifies the supervision and assessment systems for judges as well as their autonomy; (5) it lays out the disciplinary system, an issue that was particularly important politically at the time of the law's enactment; (6) it specifies the removal process for judges unfit for office and the establishment of the Court of the Judiciary for that purpose; (7) it codifies judges' salaries; (8) it specifies training and continued education for judges; and (9) it guarantees the rights and benefits of judges currently in office.

The above-mentioned points are implementation of guarantees of the status of judges already provided in Articles 80 and 81 of the Constitution, in order to maintain judicial independence. These points should have been supported by the ruling party and opposition parties long ago but they were delayed for many years. Questions about the status and differences between "judges" and "public prosecutors" played a key role in the negotiations over the drafting of the law and its enactment.[15] In the legislative process, besides the Judicial Yuan's Draft Judges Act (co-signed by the Executive Yuan and Examination Yuan), there were eight other versions proposed by legislators, including a "Draft of the Judicial Officers Act," "Draft of Evaluation of Judges and Public Prosecutors Act," and "Draft of Supervision of Judges and Public Prosecutors Act." The drafts, which used the terms "judicial officers" or "judges and public prosecutors" in their titles, were written from the conceptual standpoint that judges and prosecutors have the same status and perform similar functions. They were inevitably controversial since they included judges and prosecutors in the same bill.

15 See 立法院第7屆第7會期第13次會議議案關係文書 [Legislative Yuan Agenda-Related Documents, 7th Appointment, 7th Session, 13th Sitting], Vol. 1, Yuan-General no. 445, Governmental and Member Proposal Nos. 12299, 7785, 7895, 8070, 9846, 9863, 9970, 10007, and 10108–1 (May 11, 2011).

The final version of the bill that passed did compromise on the symbolic issue of making references to prosecutors. The Judges Act contains a chapter titled "Public Prosecutors" (Chapter 10). It states that the stipulations for judges can be applied, *mutatis mutandis*, to prosecutors. The chapter also explicitly states the legal status of public prosecutors, their qualifications for appointment, rules on the transfer of positions, the system of personnel evaluations, and command and supervision structures. The Judges Act is therefore not fully a "Judges Act," in a strict sense.

Although the controversy over the legal status of judges and prosecutors was not completely settled, as Chapter 10 of the law shows, the Judges Act was passed with compromises by actors from various areas of society. To a great extent, the representatives of the Prosecutors Office in negotiations abandoned some of their stubborn opposition and made efforts to support many changes embodied in the law. To sum up, the establishment of the true separation of the judiciary and public prosecution and its implementation in the spirit of judicial independence requires a joint effort from both sides. And regarding the realization of judicial independence, there remains a long way to go in Taiwan.

Last but not least, from the perspective of the exercise of the state power of criminal justice, judges and prosecutors exercise their respective statutory powers. They are equally important. The differentiation of judges and public prosecutors is rather in their respective roles. Public prosecutors are not judges, but their different status and position should also be protected by the law to the same extent as judges. J.Y. Interpretation no. 13 calls for independence protections for prosecutors. It reads: "The guarantee of tenured prosecutors, according to Article 82 of the Constitution and Article 40, Paragraph 2, of the [Court Organization Act], apart from their transfer, is the same as that of tenured judges."[16]

Concluding remarks

The judiciary has traditionally been a tool of rulers, and because of that people have not had a favorable impression of it. However, in the contemporary democratic constitutional system, the judiciary as well as other state powers exists to serve the people. The courts should be the ultimate guardians in the protection of human rights. Judges should aim at achieving fairness and justice when judging in concrete cases. The judiciary must not be a tool for the ruler. The court is not merely another agency. The judicial system should keep pace with social change, meet the people's needs for justice in a timely way, and provide people with a judicial service of dignity, efficiency, and good quality. In recent years other countries have carried out judicial reforms and implemented measures to guarantee judicial independence. Taiwan should not be lagging behind on this issue.

16 See J.Y. Interpretation no. 13.

In addition to establishing institutions to protect judicial independence, judges' sense of responsibility and integrity, by which they are independent in their mindset and free from external interference when performing their functions, are key factors in the independence of trials and judgments. The maintenance of judicial independence takes courage. Judges should have the moral courage to safeguard judicial independence and even form a culture that protects it within the judiciary. But integrity and independence are merely the prerequisites for being a judge, not the aim. The point is that judges should make appropriate judgments in a timely fashion and of a high degree of quality. Therefore, judges should study continually, deepen their understanding of the law, amplify human virtue, and accumulate life experiences. Only when all of these conditions are achieved can the ideal that the judiciary exists for the people be realized.

The court system is not merely an administrative hierarchy. Courts are divided into instances, but the trials of cases has no hierarchy. Judges are different from civil servants. The power of judges does not come from the decisions of "superiors" but from the Constitution and the law. Judges exercise their power according to conscience and law. Only when we abandon the bureaucratic system for appointing judges can the spirit of judicial independence penetrate deeply into judges' minds. Then the people's confidence and trust in the judiciary will be established.

5 Regime *un*changed

The organization and failed reorganization of Taiwan's Judicial Yuan

Yen-tu Su

Introduction

On July 8, 2011, the Committee on Reassessing the Reorganization Reform of the Judicial Yuan (司法院定位改革成效評估委員會) finalized its policy recommendations on the very subject matter it was tasked to reassess. As part of a blue ribbon commission on judicial reform the Judicial Yuan initiated earlier that year, the Committee concluded, in essence, that the decade-long legislative campaign to transform the Judicial Yuan – from being principally the supreme judicial administrative agency into the highest court of the land – was a mistake. This campaign arose from one of the policy agreements reached in the National Judicial Reform Conference (全國司法改革會議) in 1999, but the subsequent two judicial administrations, under the leadership of Dr. Weng Yueh-sheng (翁岳生) and Dr. Lai In-jaw (賴英照), had sought in vain to push through the implementing legislation. Chaired by Justice-and-Vice-President of the Judicial Yuan Dr. Su Yeong-chin (蘇永欽), the Committee had since persuaded the Judicial Yuan to abandon such a regime-changing reorganization project and seek instead some moderate reforms of the status quo. To a large extent, the Committee's recommendations appear to be a replay of what Dr. Su, then a law professor and a member of a similar advisory committee, had proposed and persuaded the Judicial Yuan to do in 1997.[1]

The reorganization of the Judicial Yuan has been one of the most controversial issues of judicial reform in Taiwan since the late 1980s, when Taiwan began her transition to democracy. The case for reform began with an issue of constitutionality: The very existence of the Judicial Yuan as chiefly an agency of judicial

1 See 翁岳生 [Weng Yueh-Sheng], '司法院定位與大法官功能' [The *Ding Wei* of the Judicial Yuan and the Functions of the Grand Justices] in 司法院編, 司法院司法改革委員會會議實錄(上輯) [Conference Record of the Committee on Judicial Reform, Judicial Yuan.], ed. 司法院 [Judicial Yuan] (Taipei: 司法院 [Judicial Yuan], 1996): 1–15; 蘇永欽 [Su Yeong-Chin], '司法院重新定位–從司法院定位問題涉及的三個層面評估四個定位方案' [Re-positioning the Judicial Yuan – Three Dimensions and Four Plans for Resolving the *Ding Wei* Problem of the Judicial Yuan] in 司法改革的再改革 [Further Reform of the Judicial Reform] (Taipei: 元照 [Angle Publishing], 1998): 207–303.

administration was said to be inconsistent with the ROC Constitution (the Constitution) of 1947. In addition, the arrangement of letting the Judicial Yuan dominate the judicial branch is criticized for having adverse effects on judicial independence and the public's trust in the judiciary. To right this age-old constitutional wrong, reformers have called for the 'tribunalization' (審判機關化) of the Judicial Yuan.[2] These regime changers – i.e., those who sought this revolutionary reorganization of the Judicial Yuan – won a crucial battle in 1999, when the National Judicial Reform Conference went for their drastic reform proposal with an overwhelming vote of 99–10. The Justices of the Constitutional Court (also known as the Grand Justices of the Judicial Yuan) (司法院大法官) gave the reformers yet another victory in Judicial Yuan Interpretation No. 530 (2001), in which the Court held that the tribunalization of the Judicial Yuan is indeed a constitutional imperative and ordered the Legislative Yuan (立法院) to revise the relevant judicial organization laws within two years. All these victories, however, failed to secure the passage of laws needed to implement the proposed transformation. The failure could be attributed in no small part to the resilient resistance to the proposed regime change. Incrementalists – i.e., those who preferred reorganization reform at the margins – not only defend the constitutionality of the status quo, but also attack the far-reaching reorganization project as too reckless a move and a cure worse than the disease.[3] After being outvoted in 1999, the incrementalists continued to fight. Their sharp criticism of the Judicial Yuan Interpretation No. 530 as an unwarranted judicial power grab emboldened legislative obstruction of the reform agenda.[4] The regime-change

2 See e.g., 林子儀 [Lin Tzu-Yi], '司法護憲功能之檢討與改進—如何健全違憲審查制度' [Examining and Improving the Judicial Protection of the Constitution: On How to Enhance the Mechanism of Constitutional Review] in 權力分立與憲政發展 [The Separation of Power and the Development of Constitutionalism] (Taipei: 元照 [Angle Publishing], 1993): 5–82; 林明鏘 [Lin Ming-Chiang], '司法組織' [Judicial System.] in 黃宗樂主編, 民間司法改革白皮書 [The White Paper on Judicial Reform from the Civil Society] ed. 黃宗樂 [Huang Zong-Le] (Taipei: 業強 [Ye Qiang], 1997): 26–40; 黃昭元 [Hwang Jau-Yuan] '司法違憲審查的制度選擇與司法院定位' [Choosing a New System of Judicial Review for Taiwan: Some Reflections on the Status of Judicial Yuan], 臺大法學論叢 [National Taiwan University Law Journal], 32, no. 5 (2003): 55–64.

3 See e.g., 林三欽 [Lin San-Chin], '論司法改革會議「司法院定位」結論之可行性－以「大法官釋憲制度」所面臨的變革為中心' [The Feasibility of the Role of the Judicial Yuan as Determined at the National Judicial Reform Conference – Based on the Contingency in the Council of Grand Justices], 人文及社會科學集刊 [Journal of Social Sciences and Philosophy], 13, no. 1 (2001): 69–110; 蘇永欽 [Su Yeong-Chin], '金字塔的理念與迷思－何不以金字塔群來取代金字塔， 大幅降低無謂的改制成本？' [The Idea and Myth of a Judicial Pyramid: Why not Substitute the Pyramid with a Group of Pyramids to Lower the Cost of Institutional Change?] in 走入新世紀的憲政主義 [Constitutionalism: Towards the New Century] (Taipei: 元照 [Angle Publishing], 2002): 300–16; 蔡宗珍 [Tsai Tzung-Jen], '我國憲法審判制度之檢討' [On the System of Constitutional Adjudication in Taiwan] in 憲法與國家 [Constitution and Nation] (Taipei: 元照 [Angle Publishing], 2004): 101–34.

4 See 蘇永欽 [Su Yeong-Chin], '拾陸、憲法解釋方法上的錯誤示範－輕描淡寫改變了整個司法體制的第530號解釋' [16. A Bad Example for Method of Constitutional Interpretation: On the

campaign was long dead, one may argue, before the Judicial Yuan officially aborted the project in 2011.

The controversy over the place of the Judicial Yuan in Taiwan's judiciary cuts across a series of complicated and difficult issues of institutional engineering, as well as constitutional interpretation, that even the most able legal minds may find intimidating. As such, most Taiwanese (including most politicians) could not care less about the success or failure of the reorganization reform. Technically difficult as it may be, though, the controversy is *political* in every sense of the word. For those few who cared, the struggle was of utmost importance, for at stake was not just the future of the Judicial Yuan, but that of the judicial system in Taiwan.[5] The regime changers, on the one hand, envisioned a future in which the Judicial Yuan would reestablish itself as a Supreme Court primarily in the American or Japanese mold. The incrementalists, on the other hand, believed the proposed new regime would be worse than the status quo, and saw in the German judicial system a better model for Taiwan's court reforms. Needless to say, the struggle on the ground was as much about interests, power, and personalities, as about principles and ideas. The open conflict may now have receded into history, but contention over the interpretation of what the struggle was all about endures. For some, the story to be told is one of betrayal and opportunities missed.[6] For others, it is about redemption and crisis averted.[7]

This chapter reviews the legal-political history of the Judicial Yuan, and specifically, its failed reorganization reform over the past two decades. By focusing on the political dynamics rather than the proffered justifications for or against the reform, I especially hope to outline a process-based theory that better

---

J.Y. Interpretation No. 530 that Casually Restructured Taiwan's Judicial System] in 走入新世紀的憲政主義 [Constitutionalism: Towards the New Century] (Taipei: 元照 [Angle Publishing], 2002): 370–400; 陳愛娥 [Chen Ai-Er], '違憲審查與司法政策的關係－由程序法的觀點評論司法院大法官第530號解釋' [The Relationship between Judicial Review and Judicial Policy－A Review of J.Y. Interpretation No. 530 from a Procedural Law Perspective] in 法治與現代行政法學 [Rule of Law and Modern Administrative Law] (Taipei: 元照 [Angle Publishing], 2004): 145–63.

5 See e.g., 劉孔中 [Liu Kung-Chung], '儘速打破司法院定位爭議的僵局， 後續司改才能啟動' [Breaking the Gridlock on the *Ding Wei* Dispute of the Judicial Yuan for the Sake of Reenergizing Judicial Reform], 台灣法學雜誌 [Taiwan Law Journal], no. 130 (2009): 15–23; 湯德宗 [Tang Dennis Te-Chung] and 黃國昌 [Huang Kuo-Chang] (eds), '司法院定位（一）－一元多軌與一元單軌' [The Functions of the Judicial Yuan (1): Multiple Tracks v. Single Track] in 司法改革十週年的回顧與展望會議實錄 [The Tenth Anniversary of National Judicial Reform Conference: Retrospect and Prospect – Symposium Records] (Taipei: 中央研究院法律學研究所籌備處 [Institutum Iurisprudentiae (Preparatory Office), Academia Sinica], 2010): 13–84.

6 See 王泰升等 [Wang Tay-Sheng, ed.] '檢視現行司法改革系列座談會之三：司法院定位' [Symposium on the Current Judicial Reform (3): The *Ding Wei* of the Judicial Yuan], 台灣法學雜誌 [Taiwan Law Journal], no. 198 (2012): 52–74.

7 See 蘇永欽 [Su Yeong-Chin], '夏蟲語冰錄（十六)–歹戲拖棚' [Blind Man Can Judge No Color (16): That's Crap], 法令月刊 [The Law Monthly], 60, no. 4 (2009): 144–6.

accounts for the rise and fall of such a grand project as Taiwan's judicial regime change. Rather than to seek the return of the Constitution in exile or promote the restructuring of the power of judicial/constitutional review, I argue that the reorganization reform was driven more by the undercurrent pushing for the restructuring and downsizing (in terms of reducing the number of judges) of Taiwan's three final courts, i.e., the Supreme Court (最高法院), the Supreme Administrative Court (最高行政法院), and the Commission on the Disciplinary Sanctions of Functionaries (公務員懲戒委員會). In short, these final courts were perceived (at least in the reform community) to have too many judges, and the regime changers saw in the reorganization of the Judicial Yuan an opportunity to "pyramidize" Taiwan's judiciary from the top down. As to the project's demise, my main diagnosis is that the failure was largely a failure in political will. The moral of the story, in this regard, is that depoliticized/technocratic legal reform led by elite jurists – even with the help of constitutional law – cannot accomplish the heavy lifting of judicial regime change without sufficient support from the political actors.

The remainder of the chapter is organized as follows. Section 2 introduces the design and evolution of the Judicial Yuan. Section 3 recounts the ebbs and flows of the reorganization reform over the past two decades. Section 4 looks into the driving force behind the failed reorganization campaign and argues that the project was aimed at restructuring not just the Judicial Yuan, but Taiwan's top judicial authorities. Section 5 examines the structural causes of the failure of the proposed judicial regime change. The reform failed, it is argued, not because it was utterly ill-conceived or misguided, but because public support for the judicial transformation was simply not strong enough to overcome the hurdles of politics-as-usual. Section 6 is the conclusion.

The curious case of the Judicial Yuan

The place of the Judicial Yuan in the constitutional order of the Republic of China (ROC) is commonly referred to as its "*ding wei*" (定位) – meaning "status" or "position" – problem in Taiwan's legal-political discourse.[8] A one-of-its-kind institution that can be found nowhere except in China (1928–49) and Taiwan (1950–present), the Judicial Yuan commonly retraces its origins first to the legacy of Dr. Sun Yat-sen's idiosyncratic constitutional thought and then to the founding of the ROC Constitution in 1946–47.[9] These two origins, however,

8 See e.g., Weng Yueh-Sheng, *supra* note 1; Su Yeong-Chin, *supra* note 1; 李建良 [Lee Chien-Liang], '大法官的制度變革與司法院的憲法定位－從第四次憲法增修條文談起' [Reform of the Institution of the Grand Justices and Constitutional Status of the Judicial Yuan: An Analysis Based on the 1997 Constitutional Reform], 國立臺灣大學法學論叢 [National Taiwan University Law Review], 27, no. 2 (1998): 1–46; Hwang Jau-Yuan, *supra* note 2.

9 See Wang, Tay-Sheng. The Legal Development of Taiwan in the 20th Century: Toward A Liberal and Democratic Country, *Pacific Rim Law & Policy Journal*, 11, no. 3 (2002): 530–60;

have played limited roles in shaping the institutional identity of this unique judicial body, which is, after all, a product more of historical evolution than of coherent constitutional design.

The Nationalist Government of the Kuomintang (KMT) established the first version of the Judicial Yuan in 1928. Except for its name and its formal status in the so-called "five-power" constitutional order (五權憲法), however, Dr. Sun Yat-sen's constitutional ideas had limited influence on the making and workings of this pre-constitutional Judicial Yuan, which already had been at odds from time to time with the then existing Supreme Court, the Administrative Court, and the Ministry of Judicial Administration (司法行政部).[10] Having no fortune to rebuild the judiciary from scratch, the framers of the 1947 Constitution sought to transform the preexisting Judicial Yuan and judicial system into the judicial branch of a modern constitutional government. Whatever original intent they had, the final text of the Constitution regarding the basic organization and core functions of the Judicial Yuan obscures more than it clarifies[11] Consider the following provisions of the Constitution:

> **Article 77.** The Judicial Yuan shall be the highest judicial organ of the State. It shall be responsible for the trial of civil, criminal, and administrative cases and the disciplinary punishment of public employees.
>
> **Article 78.** The Judicial Yuan shall interpret the Constitution and shall have the power to unify the interpretation of laws and ordinances.
>
> **Article 79.** (I) The Judicial Yuan shall have a President and a Vice President. [...] (II) The Judicial Yuan shall have a number of Grand Justices to be responsible for the matters specified in Article 78 of this Constitution. [...]

By dividing the core functions of the Judicial Yuan into two separate articles (Articles 77 and 78) and specifying only one of the corresponding organizations (Article 79), the Constitution left what it means to be the "highest *judicial* organ of the State (國家最高司法機關)," in the words of Article 77, to be a matter of profound dispute. As a result, the difficult task of sorting out the *ding wei* problem fell to the later lawmakers of the Organization Act of the Judicial Yuan

王泰升 [Wang Tay-Sheng], '清末及民國時代中國與西式法院的初次接觸以法院制度及其設置為中心' [The Initial Encounter with Western-style Courts of Ch'ing and Republican China – A Discussion on the Institutions and Establishment of Courts], 中研院法學期刊 [Academia Sinica Law Journal], no. 1 (2007): 105–62.

10 It should also be noted that the pre-constitutional judicial systems in Republican China, overall, bore strong family resemblances to those of the late Qing Dynasty. See Wang Tay-Sheng, The Initial Encounter with Western-style Courts of Ch'ing and Republican China, *supra* note 9.

11 See Lin Tzu-Yi, *supra* note 2.

(司法院組織法). In March 1947, the Nationalist Government enacted the first post-constitutional Organization Act of the Judicial Yuan. The Act would have had the effect of merging all the final courts into the Judicial Yuan, making it essentially a mega-court of the highest instance for all sorts of cases. Before the Act was put into effect, however, it was substantively revised in December 1947 to appease opposition from the leadership of the final courts.[12] Under the revised Act, the Supreme Court, the Administrative Court (行政法院) and the Commission on the Disciplinary Sanctions of Functionaries remained as separate final courts and were subject only to the nominal administrative oversight of the Judicial Yuan.[13] The Judicial Yuan, in turn, was composed mainly of: (1) the Council of Grand Justices, in charge of the constitutional and legal interpretation specified in Article 78 of the Constitution, and (2) a small staff of judicial administration led by a President (with the assistance of a Vice President and a Secretary-General). The organization and functions of the Judicial Yuan have undergone significant changes in the following decades, but the two-part organizational structure built up by the revised Organization Act of 1947 has remained intact.

The institutional marriage of these two largely unrelated entities, in and of itself, has made the Judicial Yuan an odd family. Each of these two components of the Judicial Yuan, moreover, is an idiosyncratic establishment in its own right. Consider first the Justices of the Constitutional Court. Previously known as the Council of Grand Justices (大法官會議), the strangely-named Court is the only tribunal within the Judicial Yuan, and it has become a centralized constitutional court comparable to many of its peers around the world, at least in functional terms. Although the ROC Constitution arguably vests the power of constitutional review in the (Grand) Justices, the Justices' serving as the one and the only Constitutional Court of Taiwan is a development that cannot be taken for granted.[14]

12 See Weng Yueh-Sheng, *supra* note 1.

13 Before the structural overhaul of administrative litigation procedure in 1998–2000, the Administrative Court was the only court with jurisdiction over administrative litigation in Taiwan. Since 2000, the Administrative Court system in Taiwan has been reorganized into a Supreme Administrative Court and three High Administrative Courts.

14 See e.g., Fa, Jyh-Pin, Constitutional Development in Taiwan: The Role of the Council of Grand Justices, International and Comparative Law Quarterly, 40 (1991): 198–209; Liu, Lawrence Shao-Liang, Judicial Review and Emerging Constitutionalism: The Uneasy Case for the Republic of China on Taiwan, The American Journal of Comparative Law, 39, no. 3 (1991): 509–58; Ginsburg, Tom, Judicial Review in New Democracies: Constitutional Courts in Asian Cases (New York: Cambridge University Press, 2003); Chang, Wen-Chen, The Role of Judicial Review in Consolidating Democracies: The Case of Taiwan, Asia Law Review, 2, no. 2 (2005): 73–88; Tetzlaff, Thilo, Kelsen's Concept of Constitutional Review Accord in Europe and Asia: The Grand Justices in Taiwan, National Taiwan University Law Review, 1, no. 2 (2006): 77–107; 翁岳生 [Weng Yueh-Sheng], '憲法之維護者—省思與期許' [Guardian of Constitution: Introspection and Anticipation (Keynote Address)] in 憲法解釋之理論與實務第六輯 (上) [Constitutional Interpretation: Theory and Practice, Vol. 6, Part I] (Taipei: 中央研究院法律學研究所 [Institutum Iurisprudentiae, Academia Sinica], 2009): 1–169; Garoupa, Nuno, Grembi, Veronica,

In its early years, the Justices served more as legal counsel of the government than as the "guardian of the Constitution" (*Hüter der Verfassung*). Its first meaningful exercise of judicial review was Judicial Yuan Interpretation No. 86 (1960), which held that the arrangement of letting the high courts and district courts be administered not by the Judicial Yuan, but by the Ministry of Judicial Administration in the executive branch, was inconsistent with Article 77 of the Constitution. This Interpretation, however, was utterly ignored by the political branches for two decades. With some ups and downs, the Court nonetheless managed to survive authoritarian rule and has transformed itself into a powerful and active constitutional court armed with, among other things, a jurisprudence of "constitutional court supremacy" developed by the Court itself (Judicial Yuan Interpretation Nos. 185 and 405). This is often hailed as a success story, which is all the more impressive when viewed against institutional hurdles constraining the Court's decision making.[15] The hard-earned success of the Justices further complicated the reorganization reform of the Judicial Yuan in the past two decades, as many commentators worried that the proposed regime change would trade the proven for something unknown.[16]

The administrative section of the Judicial Yuan is a different story, however. Before the Organization Act of the Judicial Yuan was heavily revised in 1980 – to implement the separation of judicial and prosecutorial administration (審檢分隸), which was required by the long-ignored Judicial Yuan Interpretation No. 86

and Lin, Shirley Ching-Ping, Explaining Constitutional Review in New Democracies: The Case of Taiwan, Pacific Rim Law & Policy Journal, 20, no. 1 (2011): 1–40; Lin, Chien-Chih, The Birth and Rebirth of the Judicial Review in Taiwan－Its Establishment, Empowerment, and Evolvement, National Taiwan University Law Review, 7, no. 1 (2012): 167–222.

15 One notable hurdle is presented by the decision-making rules for Judicial Yuan Interpretation. Under the Governing Law of the Council of Grand Justices (司法院大法官會議法) of 1958, it took a 3/4 majority of Justices to form a quorum, and a 3/4 majority of attending Justices to vote on constitutional cases. Such strenuous requirements were made by the Legislative Yuan in retaliation to the holding of the Judicial Yuan Interpretation No. 76 (1957) that, in addition to the Legislative Yuan, the National Assembly (國民大會) and the Control Yuan (監察院) were equivalent to national parliaments as well. The Constitutional Interpretation Procedure Act (司法院大法官審理案件法) of 1993 has since relaxed the decision rules for the Justices of the Constitutional Court. But the current 2/3 majority rule for constitutional cases is still considered by some commentators in Taiwan to be a contributing factor to the Court's relatively low productivity. The method used for opinion writing is another institutional factor affecting the Court's performance, as both the Holding (解釋文) and the Reasoning (解釋理由) of a Judicial Yuan Interpretation are thoroughly deliberated and collectively written by the entire Court.

16 See e.g., Lin San-Chin, *supra* note 3; 蘇永欽 [Su Yeong-Chin], '反思台灣司法改革的經驗' [Reflections on Taiwan's Experience in Judicial Reform] in 走入新世紀的憲政主義 [Constitutionalism: Towards the New Century] (Taipei: 元照 [Angle Publishing], 2002): 318–41; 蘇永欽 [Su Yeong-Chin], '飄移在兩種司法理念間的司法改革－台灣司法改革的社經背景與法治基礎' [The Judicial Reform inbetween Two Visions of the Judiciary: On the Socioeconomic Background and the Rule-of-Law Foundation for the Judicial Reform in Taiwan] in 走入新世紀的憲政主義 [Constitutionalism: Towards the New Century] (Taipei: 元照 [Angle Publishing], 2002): 343–68.

and which also constituted the first major judicial reform in post-World War II Taiwan – the Judicial Yuan only had a relatively small staff (between 106 and 155 people) with which to handle the daily business of the Judicial Yuan and, to a lesser extent, coordinate the administration of the three final courts. Back then, the administration of the rest of the judiciary (i.e., the high courts and the district courts), along with that of the prosecutors, was discharged by the Ministry of Judicial Administration under the Executive Yuan.

Propelled by the legitimacy crisis facing the KMT regime at that time rather than by the toothless Judicial Yuan Interpretation No. 86 that the Justices issued 20 years earlier, the 1980 reform markedly expanded the administrative sector of the Judicial Yuan so as to enable it to carry out its newly acquired responsibility in coordinating and overseeing the administration of all the high courts and district courts.[17] From then on, this part of the Judicial Yuan has developed into an independent agency governing the whole judiciary, deciding matters such as where to build a courthouse and who gets appointed to particular judgeships. The reinvigorated Judicial Yuan further tasked itself to issue a variety of guidelines or rules regarding legal interpretation, which essentially instruct judges on how to adjudicate in different kinds of cases.[18] The specter of judicial administration overpowering judges and courts has been an issue of concern, and in 2001, the Justices of the Constitutional Court held that the Judicial Yuan could make such guidelines or rules only when it is doing so as a court, as opposed to an agency of judicial administration (Judicial Yuan Interpretation No. 530).[19] Even amid controversy, however, the Judicial Yuan's authority as the "highest judicial administration of the State" was strengthened, ironically at the urging of reform-minded judges and lawyers, by a 1997 constitutional amendment that minimized the Executive Yuan's influence on the annual budget of the judiciary as proposed by the Judicial Yuan (Article 5, Section VI of the Additional

17 See 翁岳生 [Weng Yueh-Sheng], '司法改革十週年的回顧與展望 (主題演說)' [The Tenth Anniversary of National Judicial Reform Conference: Retrospect and Prospect (Keynote speech)] in 湯德宗 [Tang Te-Chung] and 黃國昌 [Huang Kuo-Chang] (eds.), 司法改革十週年的回顧與展望會議實錄 [The Tenth Anniversary of National Judicial Reform Conference: Retrospect and Prospect – Symposium Records] (Taipei: 中央研究院法律學研究所籌備處 [Institutum Iurisprudentiae (Preparatory Office), Academia Sinica], 2010): 13–84.

18 Examples for the guidelines the Judicial Yuan issues include Precautionary Matters on Handling Civil Procedure (辦理民事訴訟事件應行注意事項), Precautionary Matters on Handling Compulsory Enforcement (辦理強制執行事件應行注意事項), and Precautionary Matters on Courts' Handling Criminal Procedure (法院辦理刑事訟訟案件應行注意事項).

19 See 李建良等 [Lee Chien-Liang, ed.] '「從釋字第530號解釋看司法院的規則發布權」研討會' [Symposium on the Rule-making Authority of Judicial Yuan as Viewed from the J.Y. Interpretation No. 530], 臺灣本土法學雜誌 [Taiwan Law Journal], 32 (2002): 43–147; Su Yeong-Chin, *supra* note 4; 法治斌 [Fa Zhi-Bin], '司法行政與司法審判之分與合—評司法院釋字第530號解釋之功與過' [The Separation and Integration of Judicial Administration and Judicial Adjudication – A Review of J.Y. Interpretation No. 530] in 當代公法新論 (上) [Modern Theories of Public Law Revisited (1)] (Taipei: 元照 [Angle Publishing], 2002): 773–93; Chen Ai-Er, *supra* note 4.

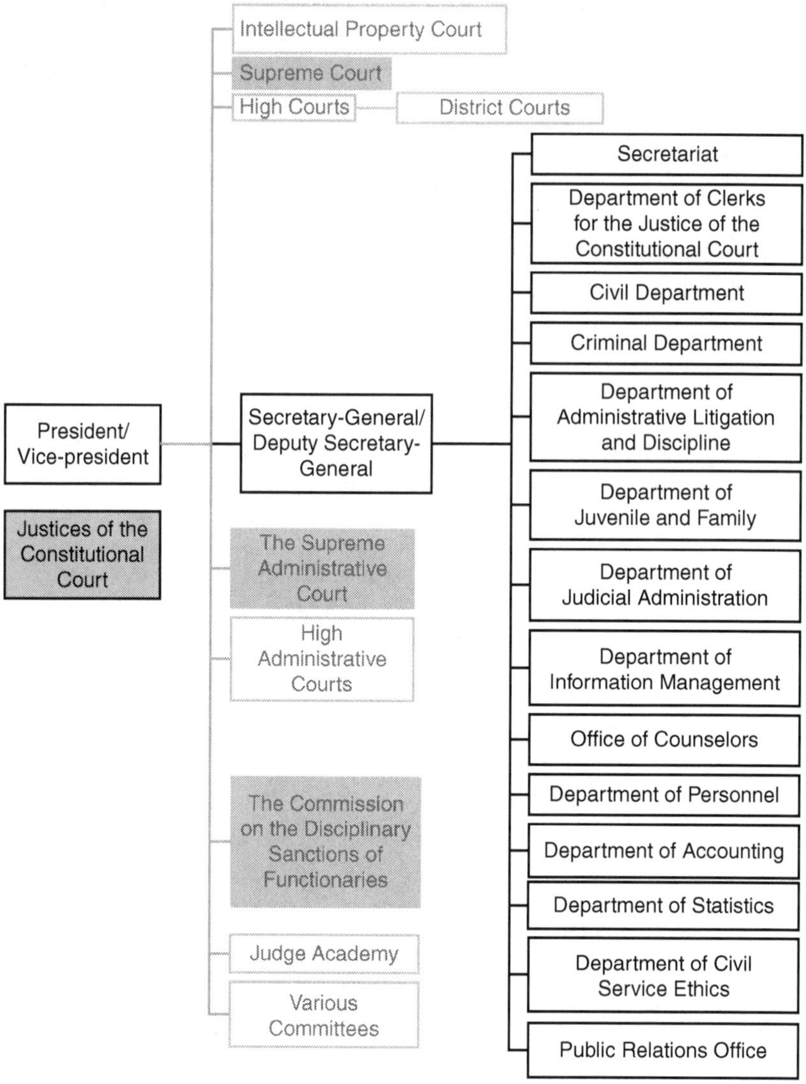

Figure 5.1 Organizational chart of the Judicial Yuan.

Articles of the Constitution). As of 2014, the Judicial Yuan has a staff of 438 employees, and its annual judicial budget is about 21 billion NT dollars.

The two sectors of the Judicial Yuan, as illustrated in Figure 5.1, are connected via the office of its President, who simultaneously serves as the head of the judicial administration and as the chair of the Justices of the Constitutional Court.

Before 1994 when Dr. Shih Chi-Yang (施啓揚) assumed office, most of his predecessors had served as members of the Central Standing Committee of the KMT while in office. It was not until 2003, when a 1997 constitutional amendment became operative, that the President and the Vice President of the Judicial Yuan were appointed, first and foremost, as two of the 15 Justices serving on the Constitutional Court (Article 5, Section I of the Additional Articles of the Constitution). Before this, the President (and sometimes the Vice President) was the non-voting chair of the Constitutional Court. According to some constitutional law scholars in Taiwan, the fact that the Judicial Yuan has been headed by a Justice-and-President may have already satisfied the central holding of Judicial Yuan Interpretation No. 530, that the Judicial Yuan be "tribunalized" as required by the Constitution.[20] Yet the inconvenient reality remains that there is a disjuncture between the two identities and capacities of this institution: the shared leadership notwithstanding, the Judicial Yuan serving as the Constitutional Court is simply not the Judicial Yuan when wearing the hat of judicial administration.

With or without the Justiceship, the President of the Judicial Yuan has long been held accountable for the success or failure of the judiciary. The President, should he choose, can play a prominent role in shaping judicial policies of the day by deciding, among other things, what bills the Judicial Yuan proposes to the Legislative Yuan.[21] Under the leadership of a reform-minded President, therefore, the Judicial Yuan may well function as the headquarters for judicial reform in Taiwan, and such reform may include reorganization of the Judicial Yuan itself.[22]

The derailed reorganization reform

Taiwan began her transition to democracy in the late 1980s, and a constitutional moment soon arrived in the 1990s. In those early days, reorganization reform aimed at the long-discussed *ding wei* problem of the Judicial Yuan and was often proposed as part of the comprehensive constitutional reform then under discussion. Even then, the question was no longer whether the "highest judicial organ of the State" was in need of reform, but how to tribunalize the judicial-administration-centered Judicial Yuan and in what mold. A general rule had since gradually emerged that constitutional lawyers trained in the US tended to embrace the idea of transforming the Judicial Yuan into an American or Japanese style Supreme Court, whereas constitutional jurists educated in Germany were inclined to envision the future Judicial Yuan as a Constitutional Court, which would coexist with other Supreme Courts, as in Germany. There were notable exceptions to this rule, to be sure, and some reform-minded jurists were willing to compromise so as to

20 See e.g., Tsai Tzung-Jen, *supra* note 3; Weng Yueh-Sheng, *supra* note 17.

21 Judicial Yuan Interpretation No. 175 (1982) affirms that the Judicial Yuan has the prerogative to make its own legislative proposals to the Legislative Yuan under the separation-of-powers system of the ROC Constitution.

22 See Weng Yueh-Sheng, *supra* note 17.

advance the cause of comprehensive constitutional reform.[23] But as the KMT government opted for the incremental and minimalist approach to constitutional reform, reform of the Judicial Yuan increasingly became a stand-alone project. As a result, the division between those who favored the American/Japanese model and those who preferred the German model became more and more difficult to bridge.

Judicial reform gained momentum following Taiwan's transition to democracy. In response to the various calls for reform, the Judicial Yuan, led by Dr. Shih Chi-Yang, first assembled a special committee (the Judicial Yuan Committee on Judicial Reform; 司法院司法改革委員會) in 1994 to brainstorm a myriad of reform policies, including those concerning the reform of the Judicial Yuan. One year later, the Committee devised three reorganization plans: the "One Court, Multiple Tribunals" (一元化多軌制) Plan, which would merge all the final courts into the Judicial Yuan; the "Bifurcated Judiciary" (二元化雙軌制) Plan, which proposed to create a bifurcated judicial system co-led by a Constitutional Court and a consolidated Supreme Court; and the "One Court, One Tribunal" (一元化單軌制) Plan, which aimed at transforming the Judicial Yuan into an American style Supreme Court. The Committee, however, stopped short of backing any of them, and another committee – the Committee on the *Ding Wei* of the Judicial Yuan (司法院定位委員會) – was called upon to further study the issue and make its policy recommendations.[24] The *Ding Wei* Committee reached a conclusion and thereby gave birth to the Judicial Yuan's first official policy in this respect in 1997. By a 16–5 vote, the *Ding Wei* Committee recommended, and the Judicial Yuan adopted, a fourth plan proposed by Professor Su Yeong-chin. According to this Plan for Improving the Existing Institution (現制改良方案), efforts would be made to upgrade the Council of Grand Justices into a fully fledged Constitutional Court. In addition, the Council of the Judicial Yuan (司法院會議) would assume the role of judicial council and take charge of major judicial policy-making,[25] while the existing judicial administration would be reassigned to handle such non-judicial tasks as research and development. The proposed reform, however, would not revamp the two-part structure of the Judicial Yuan. Nor would it alter the organization of the other three courts of final appeal.[26]

In so far as the institutional design of judicial review is concerned, the marginal reform proposed by Professor Su has been realized to a certain extent, even before it became the official policy of President Shih's Judicial Yuan. Since the 1993 Constitutional Interpretation Procedure Act (司法院大法官審理案件法)

23 See e.g., 許宗力 [Hsu Tzong-Li], 葉俊榮 [Yeh Jiunn-Ron], and 林子儀 [Lin Tzu-Yi] '憲改建言–「憲法時刻」的呼籲' [Policy Recommendations for Constitutional Reform: An Agenda for the "Constitutional Moment"], 律師通訊 [Taipei Bar Journal], 152 (1992): 50–62.

24 See Weng Yueh-Sheng, *supra* note 1.

25 On the function and design of judicial councils, *see generally* Garoupa, Nuno, and Ginsburg, Tom, Guarding the Guardians: Judicial Councils and Judicial Independence, The *American Journal of Comparative Law*, 57 (2009): 103–34.

26 See Su Yeong-Chin, *supra* note 1.

replaced the previous Governing Law of the Council of Grand Justices (司法院大法官會議法) as the main source of basic rules for the jurisdiction, procedures, and decision-making of the Constitutional Court, the Justices have embraced the Court's identity as a Constitutional Court. The Justices henceforth have downplayed not only the significance of its being organized as a Council rather than a Court, but also the fact that its merit decisions are issued in the format of "Interpretations" as opposed to court judgments. The later-abolished National Assembly re-engineered the number and tenure of the Justices in 1997 (Article 5, Sections I–III of the Additional Articles of the Constitution). In addition, the Court has been tasked to adjudicate the dissolution of unconstitutional political parties (since 1992) and the impeachment of the President or the Vice President of Taiwan (since 2004) (Article 1, Section X, Article 2, Section VII, and Article 5, Sections IV–V of the Additional Articles of the Constitution).

Regarding court administration, the 1997 reform plan arguably would not have made much difference. Major policies of the Judicial Yuan, after all, have usually been made in a collective manner by many of the would-be members of the proposed Council of the Judicial Yuan. The President and bureaucrats of the Judicial Yuan alone rarely dictate the making of major judicial policies. Professor Su's incrementalist proposal sailed through the *Ding Wei* Committee, the majority of whose members came from the judiciary or the government and thereby likely valued stability over change. It was a tough sale, however, in the larger reform community. Many reform advocates from civil society considered the three final courts to be as problematic as the judicial-administration-centered Judicial Yuan, and they certainly would not have been content with anything less than a comprehensive overhaul of the status quo.[27] During the 1997 campaign for enhancing the budgetary independence of the judiciary, reform activists from civil society secured President Lee Teng-hui's pledge to convene a National Judicial Reform Conference. In view of the gap between what the larger reform community wanted and what Dr. Shih's administration offered, it was not much of a surprise that the 1997 plan only lasted for two years.

In the wake of an inter-branch dispute over how the National Judicial Reform Conference should be administered, Dr. Shih resigned from office in December 1998 and was later succeeded by Dr. Weng Yueh-sheng, then the most senior Justice of the Constitutional Court. Like Dr. Shih, Dr. Weng received his doctoral degree in law from Germany. First appointed to the Constitutional Court at the age of 39, Dr. Weng has continued to teach law in the National Taiwan University and is widely revered as a public law guru in Taiwan's legal academia. Dr. Weng was also a member of the *Ding Wei* Committee, and, in 1997, he cast his vote for the "One Court, One Tribunal" Plan.

27 Prominent actors in Taiwan's judicial reform movement of the 1990s included, among others, the Taipei Bar Association (台北律師公會), the Judicial Reform Foundation (財團法人民間司法改革基金會), and the Taiwan Law Society (台灣法學會).

As the first major move of Dr. Weng's administration, the anticipated Conference took place in the summer of 1999. A total of 125 legal, governmental, political, and social elites attended the three-day Conference, which was divided into three committees that sought to deliberate and seek policy consensus over the 12 reform agenda themes and 57 reform proposals, as prepared and submitted by the Judicial Yuan.[28] The *ding wei* problem of the Judicial Yuan, along with five reorganization/tribunalization plans, was assigned to the First Committee chaired by Dr. Chiou Lian-Gong (邱聯恭). Dr. Chiou, who also served as one of the Conference's Vice-Presidents, received his doctoral degree from Japan and is a prominent law professor specializing in civil procedure.[29]

Over the dissent of Professor Su and several other public law jurists attending the Conference (including, among others, Professor Hsu Tzong-Li (許宗力), a leading public law scholar known for his liberal and progressive views and later an Associate Justice of the Constitutional Court from 2003 to 2011), the Conference finally approved, in an overwhelming vote that qualified it as a Conference Consensus, a regime-changing plan that came out of the Committee. According to the Conference Consensus, the short-term objective of reorganization reform was to implement the "One Court, Multiple Tribunals" (一元多軌) Plan by merging all the courts of final appeal into the Judicial Yuan as constituent tribunals that would exist alongside the Constitutional Court. The ultimate objective of the reform, however, was to realize the "One Court, One Tribunal" (一元單軌) Plan and thereby transform the Judicial Yuan into an American or Japanese-style Supreme Court, with 13–15 Justices hearing all kinds of cases before the Court. As for the judicial administration, the Conference resolved that, subject to the consultation of a Judicial Council, the President of the Judicial Yuan would continue as the chief executive of judicial administration, while judicial appointments to the High Courts and District Courts would be managed by a review board.[30]

Soon after the Conference, Dr. Weng's Judicial Yuan issued a detailed action plan for translating the Conference Consensuses into official policy. The reorganization reform, according to the Judicial Yuan's action plan and timetable, would be implemented in three stages as illustrated by Figure 5.2: By the end of 2003, all the final courts would be reorganized as (1) the Civil, (2) the Criminal, and (3) the Administrative and Disciplinary Divisions of the

28 The rule of order for the Conference stipulated that, in the absence of unanimity, the Conference could still reach a conclusion (policy recommendation) called a Conference Consensus (會議共識) by a 2/3 majority vote of the entire Conference. Otherwise the Conference could not take a position on a given policy issue.

29 See 司法院 [Judicial Yuan], '全國司法改革會議實錄 (上輯)' [Record of the National Judicial Reform Conference (I)] (Taipei: 司法院祕書處 [Secretariat, Judicial Yuan], 1999).

30 See 司法院 [Judicial Yuan], '全國司法改革會議實錄 (下輯)' [Record of the National Judicial Reform Conference (II)] (Taipei: 司法院祕書處 [Secretariat, Judicial Yuan], 1999).

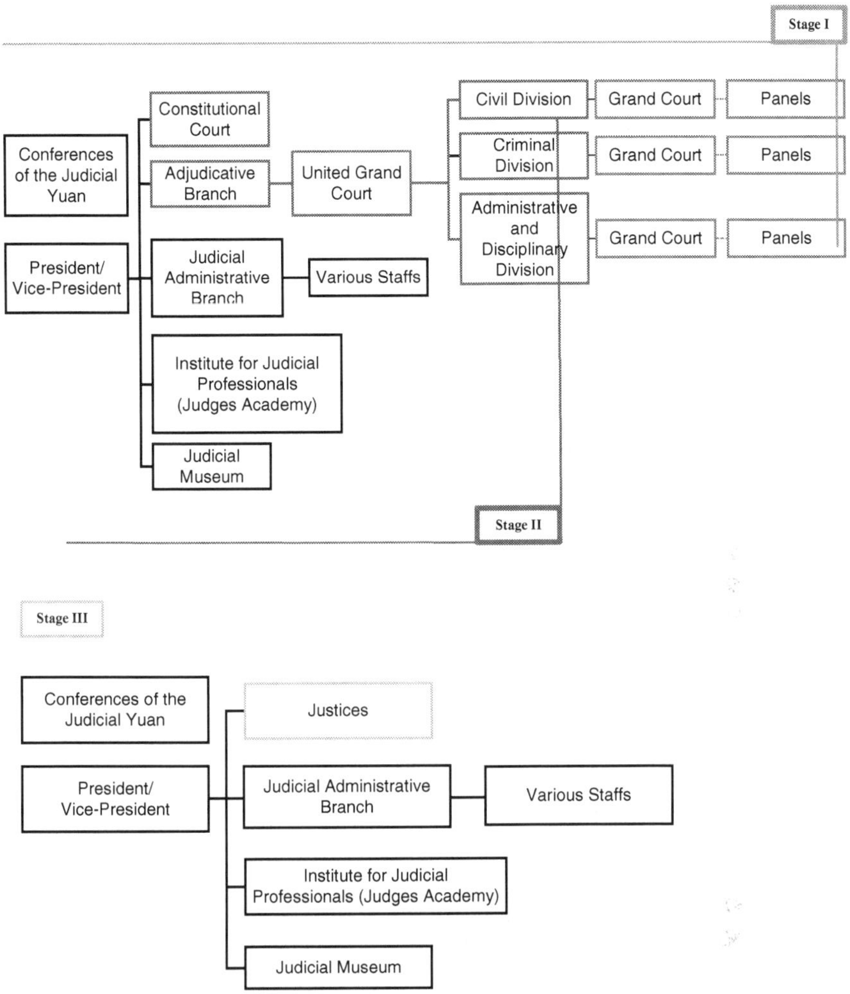

Figure 5.2 The 1999 plan for the reorganization of the Judicial Yuan.

Adjudicative Brach of the Judicial Yuan. Each Division would contain multiple panels of career judges, and the Judicial Yuan would also host a separate Constitutional Court composed of politically appointed Justices. This would constitute Stage I of the reform. By the end of 2007, Stage II would see the multiple panels in each of the three Divisions downsized and consolidated into a single Division tribunal. At Stage III, the Constitutional Court and the Adjudicative Branch would be merged into the Justices of the Judicial Yuan, thereby completing the ultimate reorganization reform by the end of 2010.[31] To draft the legislation necessary for implementing Stage I of the reform, in December 1999 the Judicial Yuan set up the Task Force for the *Ding Wei* of the Judicial Yuan (司法院定位推動小組), which compiled voluminous records as it completed its difficult assignments in 2002.[32] Notwithstanding their philosophical disagreements with the shift toward a unitary judiciary, both Professors Su and Hsu selflessly served on the 25-member Task Force.

With the assistance of the Task Force, the Judicial Yuan submitted a package of reform bills for Stage I of its reorganization to the Legislative Yuan in August 2002.[33] But President Weng and his deputies soon found themselves facing an indignant and uncooperative legislature, which was controlled by the KMT and its allies. The legislative indignation, ironically, was sparked by the Constitutional Court when it ruled, in Judicial Yuan Interpretation No. 530 (2001), that the Legislative Yuan needed to revise the relevant laws within two years to implement the constitutionally required tribunalization of the Judicial Yuan. The petition for the case came from the Control Yuan in 1996 and was buried in the Court's docket for almost five years.

By unearthing the case challenging the regulatory authority of the Judicial Yuan and using it to "command" the Legislative Yuan to overhaul the structure of the Judicial Yuan on a timetable, the Court might have intended to help the Judicial Yuan bring the Legislative Yuan on board and keep its reorganization reform on track. The Interpretation backfired, however. Professor Su Yeong-chin took the lead in sharply criticizing the Interpretation as an unwarranted judicial overreach.[34] By the time the Judicial Yuan's reform bills arrived at the Legislative Yuan, many legislators from the pan-Blue (泛藍) camp refused to cave in to what they considered undue pressure from the Court. The bills died with the end of the Fifth Legislative Yuan in 2005, even though they could have become laws at a certain point had the Judicial Yuan taken a deal negotiated by Speaker

31 司法院 [Judicial Yuan], '全國司法改革會議結論具體措施時間表' [The Action Plan and Timetable for Implementing the Conclusions of the National Judicial Reform Conference], www.judicial.gov.tw/aboutus/aboutus05/aboutus05-05-01.asp (accessed March 20, 2014).

32 See 司法院 [Judicial Yuan], '司法院定位推動小組會議實錄 (一)' [Conference Record of the Task Force for the *Ding Wei* of the Judicial Yuan (I)] (Taipei: 司法院 [Judicial Yuan], 2003). 司法院 [Judicial Yuan], '司法院定位推動小組會議實錄 (二)' [Conference Record of the Task Force for the *Ding Wei* of the Judicial Yuan (II)] (Taipei: 司法院 [Judicial Yuan], 2003). 司法院 [Judicial Yuan], '司法院定位推動小組會議實錄 (三)' [Conference Record of the Task Force for the *Ding Wei* of the Judicial Yuan (III)] (Taipei: 司法院 [Judicial Yuan], 2003).

33 The Judicial Yuan submitted six reform bills to the Legislative Yuan in 2002: (1) the Draft Amendment of the Organization Act of Judicial Yuan (司法院組織法修正草案), (2) the Draft Enforcement Act of Organization Act of Judicial Yuan (司法院組織法施行法草案), (3) the Draft Amendment of Constitutional Interpretation Procedure Act (司法院大法官審理案件法修正草案), (4) the Draft Amendment of Court Organization Act (法院組織法修正草案), (5) the Draft Amendment of Statute on Judicial Personnel (司法人員人事條例修正草案), and (6) the Draft Amendment of Public Functionaries Discipline Act (公務員懲戒法修正草案).

34 See Su Yeong-Chin, *supra* note 4.

Wang Jin-Pyng (王金平) that the laws be passed on the condition that they would not take effect until January 2006. Dr. Weng's administration declined the deal because it thought it had a moral duty to steer away from any politicking that would compromise the authority of Judicial Yuan Interpretation No. 530. It did not take long for this principled decision to become a source of deep regret.[35]

The Judicial Yuan resubmitted the revised reform bills in 2005 and 2008 to the Sixth and Seventh Legislative Yuan, respectively. Both times the bills were killed by legislative inertia. Dr. Weng's term expired in 2007, and while having advanced several landmark reforms concerning Taiwan's judicial system, he left the Judicial Yuan with the derailed reorganization reform being his biggest regret.[36] Dr. Lai In-jaw, the next Justice-and-President of the Judicial Yuan generally supported his predecessor's reform project. With two defeats in a row, however, any optimism for the judicial regime change had long dissipated, and the prospects of the 2008 reform bills were even bleaker, if not only because both the executive and the legislative branches were then firmly in the hands of the KMT, whose most influential legal brain was none other than Professor Su Yeong-Chin. Justice Lai resigned his presidency (and later his justiceship) in 2010 to take political responsibility for a corruption scandal involving a few High Court judges who took bribes. President Ma Ying-Jeou subsequently appointed Mr. Rai Hau-Min (賴浩敏) as Justice-and-President and Professor Su as Justice-and-Vice-President of the Judicial Yuan.

The only obstacle to the incrementalists' policy reversal, by then, appeared to be Judicial Yuan Interpretation No. 530. With the help of an agreeable advisory committee (as mentioned in the beginning of this chapter) and without asking in advance that Judicial Yuan Interpretation No. 530 be overruled, however, Mr. Rai's Judicial Yuan aborted the decade-long campaign for judicial regime change. It remains a matter of academic debate whether the embarrassment over Judicial Yuan Interpretation No. 530 becoming empty words is the fault of the KMT-controlled Legislative Yuan and Mr. Rai's Judicial Yuan that defied it, or of the Interpretation itself for overreaching.

What the reorganization reform was for

In a sense, Dr. Lin Tzu-Yi (林子儀), a prominent constitutional law scholar who served as an Associate Justice of the Constitutional Court from 2003 to 2011, was Professor Su's counterpart in the regime changers' camp. In 1989, Professor Lin authored an article which constituted part of a comprehensive constitutional reform proposal commissioned by the National Policy Resource Center (國家政策研究資料中心), then an influential non-governmental thinktank sympathetic

35 See Weng Yueh-Sheng, *supra* note 17.
36 Weng Yueh-Sheng, *supra* note 17.

to many reform causes.[37] This seminal article meticulously reviewed the problems of judicial review in Taiwan and proposed institutional reform towards a unitary judiciary and decentralized constitutional review. What Professor Lin did, one may argue, not only rekindled controversy over the *ding wei* of the Judicial Yuan, but also inspired the intellectual and political movement for the judicial regime change of the past two decades. Like the German-trained Professors Su Yeong-Chin and Hsu Tzong-Li, the American-trained Professor Lin attended the National Judicial Reform Conference and later served on the Task Force for the *Ding Wei* of the Judicial Yuan. Professor Lin arguably played a more prominent role in the pre-2000 struggle between the incrementalists and the regime changers, however, and it was not only because what he proposed in 1989 became the Judicial Yuan's long-term policy goal ten years later. By outlining the basic arguments for the regime-changing reorganization reform of the Judicial Yuan, Professor Lin's pioneering work also got to frame the issues and terms of the subsequent political-legal discourse.

In essence, Professor Lin and his fellow regime changers advanced three basic arguments for transforming the Judicial Yuan into an American or Japanese style Supreme Court. (1) The proposed judicial regime change would be much more faithful to the original meaning of the 1947 Constitution than the status quo. (2) In any event, the judiciary should be centered on judges, and the administrators of the Judicial Yuan must not compromise their independence. (3) A unitary judiciary with decentralized constitutional review would be a better institutional choice for Taiwan's new constitutional democracy than the existing fragmented judiciary and centralized judicial review. Professor Lin and others argued, for instance, that decentralized constitutional review could empower courts of all levels to protect constitutionalism and human rights while constraining the exercise of judicial power with the "case and controversy" requirement.[38] By the late 1990s, however, all of these three arguments had been heatedly contested. Originalism, to begin with, has limited appeal in Taiwan's constitutional discourse.[39] Opponents like Professor Su depicted the Japanese experience as a cautionary tale for letting the Supreme Court administer the whole judiciary.[40]

37 Lin Tzu-Yi, *supra* note 2.

38 See e.g., Lin Tzu-Yi, *supra* note 2; Hwang Jau-Yuan, *supra* note 2; 湯德宗 [Tang Dennis Te-Chung], 吳信華 [Wu Hsin-Hwa], and 陳淳文 [Chen Chwen-Wen], '論違憲審查制度的改進——由「多元多軌」到「一元單軌」的改制方案' [The Reform of Constitutional Review – On the Reorganization Plans from "Multiple Courts, Multiple Tribunals" to "One Court, One Tribunal"] in 憲法解釋之理論與實務第四輯 [Constitutional Interpretation: Theory and Practice, Vol. 4] (Taipei: 中央研究院法律學研究所籌備處 [Institutum Iurisprudentiae (Preparatory Office), Academia Sinica], 2005): 523–92.

39 See e.g., Lee Chien-Liang, *supra* note 8.

40 See 蘇永欽 [Su Yeong-Chin], '金字塔的理念與迷思－何不以金字塔群來取代金字塔，大幅降低無謂的改制成本？' [The Idea and Myth of a Judicial Pyramid: Why not Substitute the Pyramid with a Group of Pyramids to Lower the Cost of Institutional Change?] in 走入新世紀的憲政主義 [Constitutionalism: Towards the New Century] (Taipei: 元照 [Angle Publishing], 2002): 300–16).

And many commentators appreciated Taiwan's experience of a powerful Constitutional Court and considered as ill-advised the proposal for decentralized judicial review.[41] To the extent that the overall case for the regime-changing reorganization of the Judicial Yuan was grounded primarily on these three arguments, the case would be a plausible one at best, but hardly a compelling or a consensus-building one in public law circles in Taiwan. Why, then, did the 1999 National Judicial Reform Conference reach a Conference Consensus on the regime-changing project with such a resounding 99–10 vote?[42]

It surely matters who made the call. Unlike the two judicial-administration-based committees that chose the incrementalist approaches to reform in 1997 and 2011, the Conference had a clear majority of participants coming from outside the judiciary (who represented about 22 percent of the attendees) and prosecutors (accounting for about 17 percent of the attendees), and it thus could have been more receptive to reform options farther away from the status quo. That the Conference had many more attendees who had studied either in the United States or Japan than those who were educated in Germany probably also contributed to the vote for a Conference Consensus, considering that people usually tend to favor the regime model they are more familiar with. But given that a much larger proportion of the attendees did not study abroad, the comparative popularity of the American or Japanese model vis-à-vis the German model in the Conference was not assured. Moreover, constitutional jurists only accounted for a small fraction of the attendees, and this further casts doubts on the notion that the constitutional arguments as advanced by Professor Lin and others were the major motivations behind the Conference's endorsement of the regime-changing project.

Some commentators depicted the Conference as no more than a ceremonial gathering, whose sole function was to rubber stamp the predetermined reform agenda of Dr. Weng's Judicial Yuan.[43] While it is true that the Conference was asked to decide several policy issues in three days, most of the attendees simply could not be labeled as the loyalists to the then newly appointed Dr. Weng and his administration. Nor were they ignorant of the issues and proposals before them, which, after all, had been discussed for quite some time in legal circles as well as in the public sphere before the Conference took place. The fact that Dr. Weng was a known supporter of the unitary judiciary view might have, at best,

41 See e.g., 許宗力 [Hsu Tzong-Li], '普通法院各級法官及行政法院評事應否具有違憲審查權？' [Should Judges of All Levels of Ordinary Courts and Administrative Courts Exercise the Power of Judicial Review?] in 憲法與法治國行政 [Constitutional Law, and Administration in Rechtstaat] (Taipei: 元照 [Angle Publishing], 1999): 45–21; Lin San-Chin, *supra* note 3; Ginsburg, Tom. *Constitutional Choices in Taiwan: Implications of Global Trends*, Illinois Public Law Research Paper No. 06–01 (2006).

42 Judicial Yuan, *supra* note 30.

43 See Liu Kung-Chung, *supra* note 5.

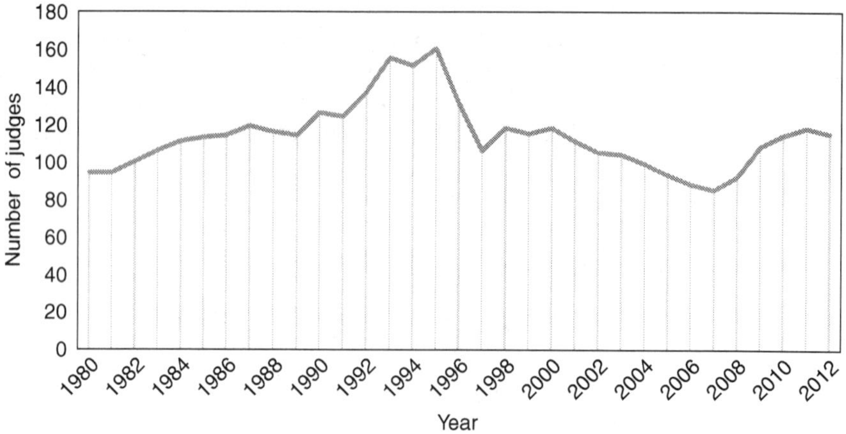

Figure 5.3 Total number of judges on the three courts of final appeal: 1980–2012.
Source: *Judicial Statistics Yearbook*, Department of Statistics, Judicial Yuan.

given the regime changers a fighting chance to succeed, but it did not render the Conference Consensus a foregone conclusion.

During the Conference, President Weng did not say a word on the record about what he personally thought of the *ding wei* problem of the Judicial Yuan. But Professor Chiou Lian-gong, who presided over the First Committee that drafted what later became the Conference Consensus, did make a few interesting remarks during the Committee sessions. Professor Chiou did not weigh in much on the tiresome debates over what the Constitution really means and which model of judicial review better suits Taiwan. Rather, his remarks centered on the peculiar situation that, in Taiwan, there were more than 100 judges sitting at the top of the judicial hierarchy (see Figure 5.3). As a leading authority on Taiwan's civil procedure, Professor Chiou made clear that he thought the membership of the Supreme Court was far too large (normally over 100) and that there should be no more than 37 judges serving on it.[44] During the Conference, Professor Chiou did not explain why he thought the Supreme Court in Taiwan had too many judges, nor did he explain how to calculate the optimal size of the Supreme Court. The total number of judges on the three final courts is outrageous when we take the comparable numbers in the United States (9), Japan (15), or South Korea (14) as our benchmarks. It appears less problematic when compared to its equivalent in Germany (127) or Italy (288).

But if we measure the size of the Supreme Court(s) in terms of the ratio of Supreme Court Judges to all judges in a given country, Taiwan stands out again

44 Judicial Yuan, *supra* note 30.

as an inexplicable outlier. For every 1,000 judges, Taiwan in 2013 had 56 Supreme Court judges, whereas Italy in 2008 had 27, and Germany in 2012 had 6 judges serving at the highest level. Moreover, it is one thing to have many Supreme Court judges who are outstanding and well-respected jurists. It is quite another if their credentials and job performance do not match their authority and prestige. Saying that the three final courts in Taiwan are overstaffed, therefore, could be a thinly veiled criticism of the dysfunctions or perceived incompetence at the top of Taiwan's judiciary.

Indeed, by taking issue with the size problem of the three final courts, Professor Chiou's remarks reflected a longstanding and prevailing discontent with Taiwan's top career judges. As such, his views arguably shed a somewhat different light on what the Conference's short-term and long-term plan to reorganize the Judicial Yuan was about. What Professor Chiou and many others saw in the reorganization reform of the Judicial Yuan was arguably, inter alia, an opportunity to downsize and reshuffle the three overcrowded final courts. To these reformers, the proposed regime change made sense, because it would address the root cause of many judicial problems in Taiwan. It may be argued, for instance, that the Supreme Courts in Taiwan have put too much emphasis on error correction at the expense of speedy trials. The panel splits within each of the final courts further take toll on the fairness and coherence of Taiwan's jurisprudence. Both of these problems can be linked to the size of Taiwan's Supreme Courts. Besides, it matters who occupy those top judgeships. Unlike the politically appointed Justices of the Constitutional Court, the composition of the three final courts has arguably had insufficient turnover after Taiwan's democratization. As a result, the top career judges in general have been trusted and respected much less than the Constitutional Court Justices, and even less than the younger judges sitting at the lower courts. Although the regime changers of the 1990s and 2000s had not developed a full account of the size problem, they did stress the need to "pyramidize" Taiwan's judiciary from the top down. In this regard, considerations behind Professor Chiou's comments may have boosted support for the regime-changing project at the Conference. The project was attractive because it held the potential to solve problems resulting from the top of Taiwan's judiciary, and it was even better that it could do so in the name of the Constitution.

The regime changers won big at the Conference, therefore, because they were able to build a coalition between those who loved decentralized judicial review and those who detested the numerous judicial old guard (i.e., judges trained and promoted to the Supreme Courts during the authoritarian period) occupying the three courts of final appeal. I also suspect that, at least at the 1999 Conference, the latter was a larger group than the former. Supporters of the German model were not as adept at coalition-building, and so they lost the vote. This process-based reinterpretation of what the reorganization reform was for is further evidenced by the fact that many Supreme Court Judges were among the most outspoken opponents to the Conference Consensus and the subsequent Judicial

Yuan Interpretation No. 530.[45] They were well aware that the reform would have taken away their prestigious positions at the commanding heights of the court system. The regime-changing project ultimately died. But even if it had survived, the Constitutional Court, the true love of many constitutional lawyers and jurists in Taiwan, would not have suffered collateral damage in the reorganization and downsizing of Taiwan's senior judiciary. Indeed, it was coalitional politics and not logic that drove the short-term plan of "One Court, Multiple Tribunals" (the two phases of reorganizing and downsizing the three final courts) as part of the long-term plan of "One Court, One Tribunal" (the final phase of merging the Adjudicative Branch and the Justices of the Constitutional Court). With the accomplishment of the short-term plan, supporters of the separate Constitutional Court might still have challenged the planned merger by reshifting the focus of reform back to the institutional design of constitutional review. By then, they might have stood a better chance because the size and composition of Taiwan's top judiciary would no longer be an issue.

Why the regime changers failed

The campaign for the structural reorganization of the Judicial Yuan over the 1990s and 2000s had failed. While the reasonableness and desirability of the proposed judicial regime change was not beyond doubt, its failure was not inevitable. If Taiwan had chosen comprehensive constitutional reform in the 1990s, the curious case of the Judicial Yuan might have been a case closed. If Dr. Weng's Judicial Yuan had accepted the legislative deal to let the reforms take effect at a later date in exchange for their passage, the Judicial Yuan and Taiwan's top judiciary might have already undergone Stage I and even Stage II of the reorganization project. Even after 2008, when the KMT controlled both the legislature and executive, the reorganization reform was not beyond saving. Had the later popular outcry – stirred by the White Rose Movement (白玫瑰運動) of 2010 – against "dinosaur judges" (恐龍法官) sitting on the Supreme Court been channeled to support structural reform of the judiciary, the reform bills submitted by the Judicial Yuan in 2008 might have seen daylight.[46] The entrenched structure of the Judicial Yuan as we know it, in short, is a result of historical contingency.

45 See 朱瓊華等 [Zhu Qiong-Hua], 周國龍 〔Zhou Guo-Long〕, 金經昌 〔Chin Jing-Chang〕, 柯慶賢 〔Ko Qing-Xian〕, 徐樹海 〔Zhu Shu-Hai〕, 高啟燦 〔Kao Qi-Can〕, and 郭仁和 〔Guo Ren-He〕, '透視司法院釋字第530號解釋的效力–正視司法改革的合憲性' [Seeing through the Effects of J.Y. Interpretation No. 530: Taking Seriously the Constitutionality of Judicial Reform], 法律評論 [Chas Yang Law Review], 69, nos. 10–12 (2003): 27–33.

46 The White Rose Movement of 2010 originated from the popular backlash against multiple lenient Supreme Court rulings on child molestation cases that many lay people found repugnant. The movement forced the Supreme Court to toughen the law against child molestation. It also prompted a Supreme Court Judge to withdraw from her nomination to serve on the Constitutional Court.

Failing to accept the terms of the legislative compromise was a strategic blunder on the part of Dr. Weng's judicial administration. But reasons for the failure of the reorganization reform arguably ran deeper, because, if the reform campaign were politically strong enough, it could have afforded some strategic mistakes like this along its way. To a significant extent, the regime changers failed because they had not garnered sufficient political will to see the job done. With only limited elite participation from outside the small confines of the legal community in Taiwan, the two-decade reorganization campaign attracted very little interest and attention from the public. Without strong backing of political and civil society at large, the regime changers simply stood little chance to overcome all sorts of barriers to structural reform, including, among others, strong opposition from vested interests. That the reform bills were killed in the legislative process without making much of a scene was but another indication of the campaign's political powerlessness.

Why then, did the regime changers place their bets on politics as usual, hoping or believing they could achieve the transformative reorganization of the Judicial Yuan through the ordinary legislative process without making serious efforts to mobilize public support? Maybe they thought the Conference Consensus they won in 1999 was strong enough to carry them through the subsequent legislative process. Maybe they believed that the constitutional mandate as affirmed by the Justices of the Constitutional Court was equally effective or even better than a hard-earned political mandate from the public. Perhaps they had misgivings about the wisdom of crowds. Or they may have thought the Judicial Yuan already had all the experts, competence, and resources needed to push through the implementation legislation. Whatever they thought beforehand, they should have learned the following lesson by now: For a structural reform to succeed, it is better to invest in transformative politics as epitomized and realized by a highly energized political campaign.

Conclusion

The *ding wei* problem of the Judicial Yuan was born at the founding of the ROC Constitution in 1946–47, as the framers of the Constitution struggled without much success to square a brainchild of Dr. Sun Yat-sen with the basic tenets of modern constitutionalism, as well as the then-existing judiciary. The ROC immigrated to Taiwan in 1949–50 and thereafter sustained a long period of authoritarian rule, during which time the Judicial Yuan slowly evolved into a curious combination of a constitutional court in all but name and an agency overseeing administration of the whole judiciary. The institutional evolution of the Judicial Yuan only aggravated concerns over the institutional design, or lack thereof, of Taiwan's judicial system.

By the 1990s when constitutional reform and judicial reform became salient issues in the wake of Taiwan's democratization, the *ding wei* problem of the Judicial Yuan was put on the reform agenda. "Tribunalization" was the code word for its reorganization reform, and this was later affirmed as a constitutional imperative by Taiwan's Constitutional Court. What soon followed, however, was a prolonged tug-of-war between the regime changers and the incrementalists. Two consecutive judicial administrations had, to no avail, campaigned for the legislation to implement the first stage of judicial regime change as endorsed by the 1999 National Judicial Reform Conference. The subsequently appointed incrementalist leadership of the Judicial Yuan officially abandoned the regime-changing project in 2011. As a result of the extended struggle, the regime has stayed essentially unchanged.

The coalition behind the regime-changing project, this chapter contends, was driven more by motivation to restructure and downsize the three courts of final appeal in Taiwan than by the major constitutional arguments advanced to justify the project. This chapter suggests that the failure of the regime-changing campaign resulted, to a significant extent, from the absence of sufficient political will. As difficult as it should be, sensible regime change is not a mission impossible, but it is just unlikely to be realized by reform-minded technocrats working through politics-as-usual.

6 Reform and resistance

Restructuring Taiwan's appeals process and the internal culture of Taiwan's Supreme Court

Puma Shen

Introduction

Since 1949, the Judicial Yuan, the Republic of China's judicial governance body in Taiwan, and the Supreme Court (SC), the terminus for all civil and criminal cases, have faced several challenges regarding the SC: a lack of consistency in legal opinions, an ossified precedent system, a controversial case allocation system, an overwhelming caseload, and the court's preference for remanding cases to lower courts rather than making final decisions. Although several judicial reforms have addressed these challenges, cultural factors, including ideologies, ingrained practices, and alternative reform plans, have hindered reform. In Bourdieu's words, the *habitus* of the judiciary largely determines the appearance of the Taiwanese appeal system.

This chapter examines the behavior of the five players critical to the distribution of intellectual and cultural capital in Taiwan's judiciary: the Judicial Yuan, the SC, legal workers (judges, prosecutors, and lawyers), scholars, and judicial reform groups. The conflicts between these individuals and institutions have created the existing system. In particular, I focus on the Supreme Court Reform Group (SCRG), which has been at the center of many reforms, including urging the legislature to abolish the confidential case allocation system in 2012.

Although scholars and lawyers have had greater access to the legislature and social movements, they have not been the strongest actors in processes of judicial reform. However, judicial reform groups, such as SCRG, have gained juridical capital and led the appeal system reform to a certain success. It is the *habitus* – which was transmitted from the pre-modern Chinese legal system and retained by the SC – that has resisted the appeal system reform.

The Judicial Yuan and the Supreme Court

The Judicial Yuan, the highest judicial body in Taiwan, was established in 1937. It supervises all courts in the nation, including the Supreme Court, high courts, district courts, administrative courts, and the Commission on the Disciplinary Sanctions of Public Functionaries, which is the highest appellate body for its matters. Simultaneously, the Judicial Yuan is able to interpret the Constitution through the Justices of the Constitutional Court, which consists of 15 Honorable Justices (Grand Justices). However, despite its powers of constitutional interpretation, the Judicial Yuan does not substantially adjudicate civil or criminal cases without a constitutional dimension, even though the Constitution empowers it to do so. In reality, the Supreme Court, under the supervision of the Judicial Yuan, serves as the highest appellate level for civil and criminal cases. Moreover, the SC holds its own personnel management power, without democratic supervision, contributing to the SC's role as an important player in the judicial system.

The appeal system in Taiwan, similar to its counterparts in other developed countries, has three levels and three corresponding legal instances. The judicial system consists of the Supreme Court, High Courts, and District Courts. There are roughly 85 to 100 judges in the SC assigned mainly to seven civil divisions and 12 criminal divisions. Each division has a Division Chief Justice and four Associate Justices deciding civil or criminal cases. Under the civil law system, it is common to have a large number of judges in the Supreme Court. For instance, the Supreme Courts of Germany and France have 131 and 201 judges, respectively, according to one recent count.[1] However, the imbalance in criminal and civil panels shows that the SC favors criminal cases.

Although the level of casework is overwhelming (in 2012, each district court judge faced around 40 cases per month), only a limited number of civil and criminal cases go through the SC (in 2012, each SC judge dealt with 16 new cases per month), since the SC decides only matters of law (Article 467 of Civil Procedure Code, Article 377 of Criminal Procedure). An appeal can be made to the SC only when the judgment of the High Court or District Court violates the law or precedents. Moreover, civil cases can be appealed only when the amount involved exceeds NT$1,500,000 (roughly US$50,000), and Article 376 of the Code of Criminal Procedure excludes misdemeanor offenses from appeal.

Structural and cultural challenges

The Taiwanese appeal system was inspired by civil law structure, but Chinese culture also influences it. Because of the complicated political relation between China and Taiwan, the current Taiwanese court's structure and culture are in part influenced by their counterparts in China. For example, since the current structure was directly transplanted from the long-standing Chinese Supreme Court, which was established in 1906 and renamed in 1927 in Nanjing, precedents that were established in China are still being used in Taiwan.

While outdated precedents established in China conflict with current case law in Taiwan, judges may provide different opinions to challenge precedents, and it is the SC's responsibility to unify legal opinions. However, in Taiwan, multiple

1 林孟皇 Lin Meng-Huang. 2013. 找回法官失落的審判靈魂 Finding Back the Lost Trial Soul of the Judge. 台北市 Taipei: 博雅書屋 Goodness Publishing House.

civil and criminal divisions in the SC structure make it hard to unify legal opinions. Although the divisions hold a regular conference every year that aims to make legal opinions uniform among the various divisions, the atmosphere in the SC renders the conference ineffective.[2] First, the chief justices of each division have been reluctant to switch to using local precedents since the SC relocated to Taiwan. Second, the structure within the SC hinders further reform. The structural issue can be observed in two ways. First, multiple divisions divide the SC judges, thereby hindering the formation of uniform legal opinions, which further increases the gap between divisions. Second, the SC selects its own judges through a process led by the division chief justices of each division, thereby making the SC vulnerable to cronyism. With its capture of the personnel system, a certain culture prevails without being challenged.

Although the nomination of the SC's Chief Justice on paper is controlled by the President, the true power exists within the SC itself, since the President will consider the Judicial Yuan's recommendation and the Judicial Yuan always ask the SC for its recommendation. The same scenario occurs with the selection of division chief justices. Despite this, there was one situation in the twentieth century where the Judicial Yuan nominated the SC's judges without the permission of the Division Chief Justices Conference, and the SC eventually claimed that there were "no seats available in the SC" to veto the nomination. This situation helps to explain why some Division Courts have less than five judges when there should be five. By wielding such power, which is not written into the law, the SC substantially controls its own personnel policy (appointment, promotion, and dismissal). In the end, the nomination of the Chief Justice and the selection of the SC judges also threaten democracy, due to the cronyism and lack of transparency present in the status quo.

Issues remain

Transparency problems can be observed in other ways as well. A case that is appealed to the SC is subject to the SC's initial review. If the Court finds the case improper in form or defective, it will send the case back to the original court. If the case is in proper form, it will be sent to the Case Allotment Subsection at the SC. However, before 2012, case allocation was manual and confidential, creating an opportunity for political control of the courts.[3] Even though the SC abolished confidential case allocation in 2012, other procedures remain secret. Deliberation is confidential, decisions are short in form and do not adequately explain reasoning, and oral arguments are seldom held. These SC

2 Ibid.

3 錢建榮 Chien Chien-Jumg. 2012. "秘密分案是助長關說文化、危害審判獨立的殺手 Secret Case Assignment is a Killer to Encourage the Illegal Lobby Culture and to Jeopardize the Judicial Independence." Edited by 財團法人民間司法改革基金會 Judicial Reform Foundation. 台北: 財團法人民間司法改革基金會 Taipei: Judicial Reform Foundation.

practices render the appeals system mysterious and deepen the gap between the people and the legal system. Consequently, this gap creates popular resentment, which has sparked judicial reform.[4]

Another strong criticism that the SC faces concerns the *legal oriented* precedent system (判例). Since legal opinions vary among civil and criminal divisions of the SC, the judgment (判決) is viewed in a way similar to *stare decisis* only when it is adopted as a precedent (判例). According to the Article 57 of Organic Law of Courts, the SC may call a joint meeting to select judgments (判決) to turn into precedent (判例). This joint conference between all civil or criminal judges is the only forum to adopt, amend, or abolish precedents. However, the joint conference never adjudicates cases; it merely amends the judgment, extracts the legal opinion, and then turns the judgment into an abstract rule *without facts*.[5] Accordingly, district court judges have no basic facts to compare to their own cases when using precedents for reference.

This joint conference system again resembles the pre-modern Chinese legal system in which the Qing judicial system collected cases and used them to create binding decrees for lower-ranking magistrates.[6] Accordingly, precedent is as powerful as law in Taiwan, if not more binding, and the SC enjoys legislative power in a disguised form. As a result, the SC can exert its power to create and amend precedents, thus controlling inferior courts' opinions without stating facts.

The SC's primary challenge is the caseload as it is so vast. After a case is filed, the SC can dismiss it on procedural grounds, reverse and remand the case to the inferior court, or render final judgment. In order to ease its workload, the SC frequently remands cases on the basis of erroneous fact-finding.[7] Otherwise, the SC often simply dismisses the case. In 2012, the dismissal rate was 80.9 percent, while 15.5 percent of cases were reversed, and the SC adjudicated only 3.6 percent of cases. This institutional behavior irritates other players in the legal system and infuriates the public, since the main goal of the SC – uniformity of legal opinion – cannot be met if the SC does not render judgment itself. The SC appears to many observers to be abdicating its responsibility.

In addition to structural, cultural, and efficiency issues, the last challenge the SC has is populism.[8] When some major cases attract public attention, the SC

4 Similar situations can be observed in Italy. On February 10, 1999, a controversial decision by the Italian Supreme Court on a rape case triggered a wave of protest, which led to judicial reform (Calavita 2001).

5 林孟皇 Lin Meng-Huang. 2012. "提升最高法院審判效能芻議： 以統一法律見解的組織變革為中心（上）Debate on Promotion of Supreme Court Trial Performance: Focus on Organizational Change of Unified Legal Opinion — Part 1." 司法周刊 Judicial Weekly 1617: 2–3.

6 Ibid.

7 Chen, Kong-Pin, Kuo-Chang Huang, and Chang-Ching Lin. 2015. "Party Capability Versus Court Preference: Why Do the 'Haves' Come Out Ahead?" *Journal of Law, Economics and Organizations* 31.

8 In China, judicial opinions are often subject to populism (Michelle Miao. 2013. "The Politics of

usually issues new so-called "rulings" (決議) through the joint conference, and they are as powerful as precedent (判例); both enjoy *stare decisis*-like status. These rulings become one of the tools that the SC utilizes to ease public anger, but whether this systematic response facilitates democracy remains a question.

Judicial reforms: the failures

The start of the reform process

The first non-KMT president of the Judicial Yuan, Weng Yueh-Sheng, was eager to change the SC's behavior and tackle many other issues. He organized the 1999 Judicial Reform Conference, inviting 125 individuals, including scholars, judges, and NGO activists. These attendees reached a consensus on numerous critical issues, including the reform of the whole appeal system, especially the SC's institutional behavior.[9] Even though an agreement formally existed between these attendees, disagreement surfaced because different styles of knowledge collided. There were many disagreements between German- and American-educated scholars because they had different visions of the future of the Supreme Court and appellate system.

Scholars gain their legal knowledge from different developed countries such as the US, Germany, or Japan, which are all popular destinations for Taiwanese masters and doctoral students. Judges are usually trained in an exclusively local way. While several SC judges can speak Japanese because of colonial history, junior judges are typically more familiar with academic works in English because of Taiwan's general school training. Cause lawyers, often marginalized, often possess the same knowledge as scholars, and they often work with scholars who share their views.

Although different players provide different knowledge based on their language skills, the most important question here is how the debate about judicial reform is *set*. We already observe numerous problems that our appeal system faces, but we need to know how these problems are perceived by those who have the voice to establish the discourse about it. Originally, it was the Judicial Yuan that raised the issue of the court's overwhelming caseload, saying that the main problem of our appeal system was related to the debate between an inquisitorial system and an adversarial system. Since the debate was simplified and narrowed

---

China's Death Penalty Reform in the Context of Global Abolitionism." *British Journal of Criminology* 53(3): 500–19). Also, in Southern Africa, the judicial review power was designed to assuage worries and anger (Ran Hirschl. 2004. *Towards Juristocracy: The Origins and Consequences of the New Constitutionalism*. Cambridge, Mass.: Harvard University Press).

9 湯德宗 Tang Dennis Te-Chung and 黃國昌 Huang Kuo-Chang. 2010. 《司法改革十週年的回顧與展望》會議實錄 Tenth Anniversary of the National Conference on Judicial Reform: Retrospect and Prospect (Symposium Records). 台北 Taipei: 中央研究院法律學研究所籌備處 Institutum Iurisprudentiae (Preparatory Office), Academia Sinica.

down to questions about which legal system Taiwan should adopt, scholars could only passively discuss their knowledge.

Although different styles of knowledge were brought into the conference, allowing for the diffusion of law, the ideologies that underlie procedural reform were basically divided into two categories: an adversarial system (America and Japan) and an inquisitorial system (Germany). Although attendees agreed to reform the appeal system, they did not reach a consensus about which litigation ideology would dominate the courts. In 1999, the Judicial Yuan chose the adversarial system to serve its own interests. Generally speaking, the judiciary's caseload issue took precedence over the problems citizens perceived – especially the SC's reluctance to issue final decisions.

The Judicial Yuan was motivated to adopt the adversarial system – the American system – by its tension with prosecutors, who are supervised under the Ministry of Justice, which is a governmental body under the Executive Yuan. Tensions between the Judicial Yuan and Ministry of Justice predate the reform events of 1999. Before 1999, prosecutors were seldom present during trials. When they appeared, they merely stated something standard to the judge (e.g., "I have no comment, your honor"), and they were notably inactive in trials. Although the inquisitorial system requires prosecutors' active participation in proceedings, the Taiwanese inquisitorial tradition emphasizes the supremacy of the judge. Due to this cultural interpretation of the inquisitorial system, the Ministry of Justice was reluctant to urge prosecutors to be more active. Prosecutors tend to believe that it is the court's responsibility to search for the truth, not prosecutors'. The Judicial Yuan wished to enhance prosecutors' roles to reduce the workload of judges, believing the adversarial system to be a panacea of sorts, and it subsequently established a goal to create a "redefined" adversarial system.[10]

In other words, the Judicial Yuan believed that once its workload was reduced, judges would be more motivated to adjudicate cases instead of dismissing them. However, the Judicial Yuan ignored the possibility that the problem could also be solved using the inquisitorial system. Scholars who studied in Germany provided the solution: we could urge the Ministry of Justice to enact regulations that force prosecutors to participate in trials, then reduce the caseload by emphasizing prosecutorial roles under the inquisitorial system. However, due to tension between the Judicial Yuan and the Ministry of Justice, the Judicial Yuan firmly believed that the adversarial system was the cure, without considering that the inquisitorial and adversarial systems both deal with appeals differently.

In 2002, Taiwan's Code of Criminal Procedure accepted the adversarial proceedings ideology by revising Articles 161 and 163, which partially shifted the investigative responsibility from judges to prosecutors during the trial. Simultaneously,

10 Retrieved from interviews with two district judges. Date: August 3, 2013.

the Code of Civil Procedure stipulated that all appeals to the SC needed to obtain SC permission, with the exception of certain cases outlined in Article 469 that relate to situations where judicial opinions violate laws and regulations.

The 2002 reforms were a milestone marking the transition from the American-style system to a Taiwanese-American hybrid system.[11] However, the diffusion of law is a long process, and Taiwanese inquisitorial ideology still persists.[12] Although the American legal system did influence the revision of criminal procedure and civil procedure, there is still a gap between hope and reality. However, the reforms are clearly shifting Taiwan away from the Continental style of appeals to the SC, which are almost automatic, toward a more US-style, where they are rare and require special permission.

Institutional resistance

The organization – the main player of the legal system – that can foster or impede legal change in Taiwan is the SC, not the Judicial Yuan, due to the SC's remarkable power. The SC can overrule, block, or fight reforms proposed by the Judicial Yuan because the SC controls its own personnel system. Thus, the Judicial Yuan has formed a culture of respect for the SC.

The American criminal system demands substantial participation on the part of prosecutors, and its judge is not required to investigate evidence during the trial, as is now the case in Taiwan (Criminal Procedure Article 163). However, in keeping with the SC's resistance to change, the criminal divisions of the SC immediately established a ruling (決議) in 2002 stating that the judge still possesses investigative powers despite the revision of Article 163. The ruling created by the SC division has all the force of the law. In other words, even though the Judicial Yuan proposed the adversarial system and the Legislative Yuan put it into effect, the SC was able to effectively nullify the legislative change. The SC's informal rule-making power is thus able to overturn the decisions of the democratic legislative process. The Judicial Yuan and other political branches accept the SC's behavior because of institutional *habitus* driven by the SC's self-appointment of its personnel.

The SC finally accepted the adversarial system at the end of 2012. The Chief Justice Yang Ren-Shou was going to retire in 2012, and during the 2002 reform, Yang worked as General Secretary in the Judicial Yuan, the highest office in the judicial administration that bureaucratically supervises the courts, and it supported the adversarial system at that time.[13] After Yang took office in the SC in

11 王兆鵬 Wang Jaw-Perng. 2010. 刑事救濟程序之新思維 *New Thinking in Criminal Remedy Procedure*. 台北 Taipei: 元照 Angle Publishing.

12 Margaret K. Lewis. 2009. "Taiwan's New Adversarial System and the Overlooked Challenge of Efficiency-Driven Reforms." *Va. J. Int'l L.* 49: 651–726.

13 林孟皇 Lin Meng-Huang. 2013. 找回法官失落的審判靈魂 *Finding Back the Lost Trial Soul of the Judge*. 台北市 Taipei: 博雅書屋 Goodness Publishing House.

2007, he attempted to fulfill his goal of instituting the adversarial system before his retirement. He tried to persuade the SC to apply the new law substantially, but he was unsuccessful. But the 2012 reform was a kind of retirement "gift" for him.[14] Interestingly, in order to convene a meeting to reverse the aforementioned anti-adversarial ruling in 2002, one of the SC divisions deliberately rendered a judgment against the previous ruling and "proposed" that Yang reexamine the ruling through a joint division conference. He decided that a judge could no longer investigate evidence against a defendant.[15] This shows how the SC can manipulate its decisions almost flippantly in order to engage in informal policy-making that inferior courts deem to have the same effect as law. However, in the same year, some judges and prosecutors protested against this new ruling.[16] They desired to keep the old investigative power because they think the inquisitorial system better fits Taiwanese culture and that the adversarial system is not the solution to existing issues. Their protests failed.

Another reason the SC decided to switch to supporting the adversarial system was selfish – it wanted to stop prosecutors from appealing on grounds of "insufficient investigation by judges" and reduce the SC's workload.

Effects on the appeal system

The SC's nearly omnipotent power renders the appeals system a nightmare for lawyers, and it even raises constitutional questions.[17] Its power controls not only cases filed to the SC, but also cases filed at the High Court (HC) level. In 2007, to reduce the SC's caseload, the legislature amended Article 361 of Taiwan's Code of Criminal Procedure to say that a written petition of appeal needed to set forth *specific grounds of reason* at the second legal instance. This meant that appeals would need to specify what went wrong in the district court. Even though the law did not give details of what *specific grounds of reason* would be acceptable, the SC convened a meeting to urge all divisions to adopt a ruling restricting the right to appeal (97 Tai Shang No. 892). This ruling stated that appeals to the High Court should be as strict as those to the SC. That is, the SC made rules for the HC. To enforce this restraint on the law, the SC disseminated

14 王文玲 Wang Wen-Ling. 2012. "觀察站／法官角色變革 楊仁壽的退休禮 Observatory — the Judge Role Change, the Retirement Gift of Jen-Shou Yang," in 聯合報 *United Daily News*.

15 Similar things happen in civil procedure. At inferior courts judges, even though civil procedure law stipulates that the judge may not investigate unless both parties agree, the judge often asks for permission and subsequently investigates the case. This reflects the deep-rootedness of inquisitorial ideology in Taiwan.

16 法庭中心 Court Center. 2012. "百檢「集體散步」變相規避《集遊法》 Hundreds of Prosecutors 'Took a Walk Collectively' to Avoid Assembly and Parade Act in Disguised Form," in 蘋果日報 *Apple Daily*.

17 許宗力 Hsu Tzong-Li. 2011. "釋字六八七：許宗力法官部分不同意見書 Judicial Yuan Interpretation No. 687: The Partial Dissenting Opinion of the Honorable Justice Tzong-Li Hsu," edited by 司法院 Judicial Yuan.

the ruling and suggested that inferior courts dismiss appeals unless a written petition set forth specific grounds that the SC would allow.[18] According to a Control Yuan's report, the number of cases dismissed through procedural rulings by high courts increased from 133 before 2007 to 3,464 after 2007 (representing 5,214 percent growth).[19]

Simultaneously, pro-judicial reform lawyers and scholars who supported appellate reform in 1999 withdrew their support for the changes that would further implement adversarial ideologies.[20] Some scholars thought that the legal system was not ready for fundamental change, as the American SC takes only a few cases per year while the Taiwanese SC takes many cases.[21] After 1999, the appeal rate to the SC did not decrease significantly,[22] but the percentage of dismissals on procedural grounds increased from 54 to 73 percent.[23] Although the SC adjudicates fewer cases on merit than before, and its rate of remanding cases to inferior courts has decreased, these figures conceal the fact that the SC has shifted to using dismissals instead of remands. Dismissal closes a case, but remand does not. For example, in a case with erroneous findings, a proper judgment involves reversing and remanding the case, sending it to the inferior court; however, the SC instead dismisses the case in order to close it, thereby causing the increase in dismissals shown above.[24] Without rendering judgment, the SC improperly ends appeals.

Some scholars believe that allowing for a stricter, US-style appeal system, similar to *certiorari*, could ultimately improve the SC's behavior. However, German-oriented scholars, who were partially excluded from the 2002 reform,

18 In short, the de facto grounds of appeal turned into *de jure* grounds of appeal due to the tremendous power of the SC (Eisenberg and Huang 2012)

19 張熙懷 Chang Hsi-Huai. 2011. "從實務角度談上訴審之改造 Debate the Reform of Appeals from the Practical Point of View." 檢察新論 *Taiwan Prosecutor Review* 9: 36–64.

20 林鈺雄 Lin Yu-Hsiung, 吳巡龍 Wu Hsun-Lung, 何賴傑 Her Lai-Jier, 林麗瑩 Lin Li-Ying, 陳瑞仁 Chen Jui-Jen, 楊雲驊 Yang Yun-Hua, and 趙彥清 Chao Yen-Ching. 2005. "刑事訴訟上訴制度學術座談會 Colloquium on Appeal Systems of Criminal Procedure." 臺灣本土法學雜誌 *Taiwan Law Journal* 67: 121–60.

21 吳巡龍 Wu Hsun-Lung. 2005. "從美國上訴制度檢討我國刑事訴訟上訴審修正草案 Review the Draft Amendments of Appeals in the Code of Criminal Procedure from the View of the United States System of Appeals." 臺灣本土法學雜誌 *Taiwan Law Journal* 67: 121–42.

22 湯德宗 Tang Dennis Te-Chung and 黃國昌 Huang Kuo-Chang. 2010. 《司法改革十週年的回顧與展望》會議實錄 *Tenth Anniversary of the National Conference on Judicial Reform: Retrospect and Prospect (Symposium Records)*. 台北 Taipei: 中央研究院法律學研究所籌備處 Institutum Iurisprudentiae (Preparatory Office), Academia Sinica; 黃國昌 Huang Kuo-Chang. 2012. "引燃司法改革再出發的意外火苗 Accidental Ignition of the Small Flame of Judicial Reform Re-Start." 臺灣法學雜誌 *Taiwan Law Journal* 197: 48–51.

23 張熙懷 Chang Hsi-Huai. 2011. "從實務角度談上訴審之改造 Debate the Reform of Appeals from the Practical Point of View." 檢察新論 *Taiwan Prosecutor Review* 9: 36–64.

24 林鈺雄 Lin Yu-Hsiung, 吳巡龍 Wu Hsun-Lung, 何賴傑 Her Lai-Jier, 林麗瑩 Lin Li-Ying, 陳瑞仁 Chen Jui-Jen, 楊雲驊 Yang Yun-Hua, and 趙彥清 Chao Yen-Ching. 2005. "刑事訴訟上訴制度學術座談會 Colloquium on Appeal Systems of Criminal Procedure." 臺灣本土法學雜誌 *Taiwan Law Journal* 67: 121–60.

generally oppose this strategy. These scholars believe that the SC appeals problem would be better addressed by limiting the appealing cases, not by selecting cases based on the SC's preferences. They also challenge the exclusionary rule for evidence that the Judicial Yuan introduced after 1999.[25]

There is a considerable difference between the German-style SC and the American-style SC, and it is possible that German scholars have interests in common with the SC, which prefers the inquisitorial system.[26] The key differences between the German and US styles of SC are: the latter requires fewer judges on the SC to adjudicate fewer cases, while the former necessitates more judges in the SC. Additionally, since several SC judges speak Japanese, they invite Japan-oriented scholars into the informal SC conferences (研修會), and these scholars, allying with the Taiwan Bar Association and judicial reform groups, oppose a further revision to the 2002 appeal system.[27] Pro-Japanese SC judges believe in the inquisitorial system, and so they favor a reform that would not reduce the number of the SC's judges.

In passing, it is worth noting that some scholars believe the Taiwan Bar Association opposed reducing appeals because it would reduce their work.[28] Also, it is interesting that some pro-American scholars were excluded from SC conferences because of personal issues.

Civil procedure as an example of a failure in judicial reform

In order to reduce the SC's caseload, the amount of money required to be involved in order to appeal a civil case to the SC was raised three times within the last decade, from NT$450,000 (roughly US$15,000) in 1999 to $1,500,000 (about US$50,000) in 2002, creating a significant barrier to appeals. Additionally, the SC routinely dismisses civil cases on procedural grounds, as in criminal cases. In such situations, the SC does not have to adjudicate an appeal based on merit. Ninety percent of the dismissals are written in a standard format of less

25 林鈺雄 Lin Yu-Hsiung. 2000. "直接審理則與證人審判外之陳述-最高法院相關裁判之綜合評釋 Comprehensive Comment of Related Supreme Court Judgments on the Principle of Direct Trial and Oral or Written Statements Made out of Trial by a Witness." 臺灣本土法學雜誌 *Taiwan Law Journal* 6: 60–83.

26 However, the SC adopted the exclusionary rule quickly after 2003. The SC appears to have accepted this change because the exclusionary rule does not substantially challenge the SC's power.

27 林鈺雄 Lin Yu-Hsiung, 吳巡龍 Wu Hsun-Lung, 何賴傑 Her Lai-Jier, 林麗瑩 Lin Li-Ying, 陳瑞仁 Chen Jui-Jen, 楊雲驊 Yang Yun-Hua, and 趙彥清 Chao Yen-Ching. 2005. "刑事訴訟上訴制度學術座談會 Colloquium on Appeal Systems of Criminal Procedure." 臺灣本土法學雜誌 *Taiwan Law Journal* 67: 121–60.

28 Lawyers contend that lawyers do not represent the parties who experience most dismissed cases. In short, a stricter appeal system does not affect lawyers, some claim. (林永謀 Lin Young-Mou. 2010. 刑事訴訟法釋論 *Code of Criminal Procedure*. 台北市 Taipei: 三民 San Min Book Co).

than one page.[29] The problem worsened when Chief Justice Yang encouraged dismissal by establishing an informal rule (內部規則) that one case can be deducted from a judge's workload by the Case Allocation System if he dismisses one case per month. As a result, judges were given an incentive for procedural dismissals, again demonstrating the SC's preference for lowering its workload over substantive adjudication.[30]

In civil procedure, three fundamental changes in the appeal system were made in the 2002 reform. First, except for the six serious procedural problems that can arise during trials (enumerated in Article 469), civil appeals to the SC can only be heard if the SC permits (Article 469–1).[31] This represents the formal legalization of the SC's discretionary power to control its civil dockets. Second, the new civil procedure requires that the SC hear cases on merit, except for situations where hearings are "unnecessary" (Article 474), an extremely vague legal term. This unclear requirement demonstrates how the vagueness of the law allows organizational behavior to determine its impact.[32] Third, with both parties' consent, they can directly appeal to the SC from a district court if no error is present in the findings (Article 466–4), which can save time for the HC.

A leap-appeal from the district court level to the SC can save judicial resources,[33] but giving the SC statutory discretionary power would probably not do so.[34] It is common to let the SC choose its own cases in common law systems, and the SC in this system can utilize this power to focus on resolving inconsistent legal decisions and questions of principal importance.[35] In this respect, the SC may turn the appeal system from a case-oriented system to an issue-oriented one, as the Legislative Yuan would like. However, according to recent empirical

29 Theodore Eisenberg and Kuo-Chang Huang. 2012. "The Effect of Rules Shifting Supreme Court Jurisdiction from Mandatory to Discretionary: An Empirical Lesson from Taiwan." *International Review of Law and Economics* 32(1): 3–18

30 Anonymous interviews with two district court judges, date: 8–1–2013.

31 The Taiwan Code of Civil Procedure (TCCP) explicitly specifies that such permission shall be granted only if one of the following three conditions is met: (1) the appeal is necessary for the continuous development of the law; (2) the appeal is necessary for resolving inconsistent decisions; or (3) the appeal involves legal questions of principal importance.

32 Ryken Grattet and Valerie Jenness. 2005. "The Reconstitution of Law in Local Settings: Agency Discretion, Ambiguity, and a Surplus of Law in the Policing of Hate Crime." *Law and Society Review* 39(4): 893–942.

33 吳明軒 Wu Ming-Hsung. 2003. "民事訴訟法修正後關於第三審程序之規定 After Amending Taiwan Code of Civil Procedure, the Articles of Appellate Procedure in the Third Instance." 月旦法學雜誌 *The Taiwan Law Review* 99: 10–28; 姜世明 Chiang Shyh-Ming. 2003. "民事訴訟法修正—上訴審及其他程序部分 Amendment of Taiwan Code of Civil Procedure: Appellate Procedure and Other Procedures." 月旦法學教室 *Taiwan Jurist* 6: 104–20.

34 黃國昌 Huang Kuo-Chang. 2010. 民事訴訟理論之新開展 *New Developments of Civil Litigation Theory*. 台北 Taipei: 元照 Angle Publishing Co.

35 Theodore Eisenberg and Kuo-Chang Huang. 2012. "The Effect of Rules Shifting Supreme Court Jurisdiction from Mandatory to Discretionary: An Empirical Lesson from Taiwan." *International Review of Law and Economics* 32(1): 3–18.

research, the 2003 reform did not change the SC's institutional behavior.[36] The dismissal rate stayed the same after 2003, reversal rates also remained similar, and the length of the SC's written opinions increased to a limited extent. Eisenberg and Huang have concluded that the low degree of change in behavior at the SC is attributable to its institutional character and the political environment in which the SC functions.

The SC also appears to shirk its legal responsibility to hold oral arguments under the 2002 reform. Even though the law stipulates that hearings should be held, only two cases have had oral arguments in ten years, demonstrating the SC's lack of respect for complying with the reform. The absence of hearings and high dismissal rate have irritated the Taiwan Bar Association, which has been attacked by its clients who believe their lawyers did not write acceptable appeal briefs.[37] Although the Taiwan Bar Association has produced expert opinions to prove lawyers' innocence and even held a nationwide conference to condemn the SC's arguably unconstitutional behavior, the SC has continued to resist holding oral arguments.

However, the dismissal rate did stop rising after the reform. Institutional culture alone does not fully account for the SC's resistance to follow reforms.[38] According to Eisenberg and Huang's research, the SC is unwilling to dismiss a case with too many fundamental fact-finding errors, as a dismissal will close the case. In such situations, the SC prefers to reverse and remand the case to the inferior court.[39] Nowadays, as it balances its heavy caseload and responsibility to harmonize legal interpretations, the current dismissal rate of 60 percent is optimal for the SC. The SC thus has kept its Continental-style error-correcting role rather than become a US-style issue-oriented adjudicator.

The Supreme Court habitus *and foreign knowledge*

As mentioned in the previous section, even though civil procedure has changed fundamentally, the Court's output remains unchanged. The substantial remodeling of criminal procedure to be more adversarial was resisted by the SC from 2002 until 2012. Taiwanese judicial culture has hindered the reform, and in Bourdieu's terms, the *habitus* in this legal field determines the appearance of our

36 Ibid.

37 林鈺雄 Lin Yu-Hsiung, 吳巡龍 Wu Hsun-Lung, 何賴傑 Her Lai-Jier, 林麗瑩 Lin Li-Ying, 陳瑞仁 Chen Jui-Jen, 楊雲驊 Yang Yun-Hua, and 趙彥清 Chao Yen-Ching. 2005. "刑事訴訟上訴制度學術座談會 Colloquium on Appeal Systems of Criminal Procedure." 臺灣本土法學雜誌 *Taiwan Law Journal* 67: 121–60.

38 Theodore Eisenberg and Kuo-Chang Huang. 2012. "The Effect of Rules Shifting Supreme Court Jurisdiction from Mandatory to Discretionary: An Empirical Lesson from Taiwan." *International Review of Law and Economics* 32(1): 3–18

39 黃國昌 Huang Kuo-Chang. 2012. 程序法學的實證研究 *Empirical Research on Procedure Law*. 台北 Taipei: 元照 Angle Publishing Co.

appeal system.[40] The questions is, how does foreign knowledge flow into this field, and connect to the reform and its resistance? Indeed, the social capital brought into the Taiwanese legal field by scholars that studied abroad has produced a number of legal arguments and many initiated discussions. In each episode of reform, relevant institutions (the Judicial Yuan or the SC) have chosen foreign-derived legal arguments that fit their interests, and this has led to the amendment of laws. In this scenario, scholars' participation is somewhat passive – they are invited when institutions need them, and their knowledge is adopted upon request. In the end, the institutional interests (e.g., caseload concerns and conflicts between the Ministry of Justice and Judicial Yuan) surpass imparted knowledge, which may well explain the current hybrid version of our appeal system (partially adversarial and partially inquisitorial).

Law-on-the-books differs from the law-in-action in Taiwan's appeals and procedural law. In closing or narrowing the gap between them, changing the existing *habitus* is needed and further empirical study is necessary to guide reforms. To avoid marginalization, scholars have begun to involve themselves with judicial reform groups to accumulate juridical capital, enhance their role in the field, and question the *habitus* that hinders reform. In the next section, I will introduce the second wave of appeal reforms that occurred in 2012.

Successful reforms

The Supreme Court Reform Group (SCRG)

While Taiwanese judicial culture may stand in the way of judicial reform generally, some appeal system reform efforts take cultural considerations into account. As mentioned above, SC case allocation to its five-judge divisions was confidential before 2012, but resistance to reform was overcome by efforts led by the Supreme Court Reform Group (SCRG) (法官籲請改革最高法院行動聯盟). This group has been comprised of only nine members, and all of them are district court judges. How did such a small group change the confidential allocation process, one of the SC's longstanding traditions?

Most reformist judges at lower courts seek to comply with the SC's authority. Judges do not dare challenge the SC's precedents in making decisions, since the correction of an "erroneous decision" would influence the judge's annual performance evaluation, possibly decreasing his year-end bonus, and preventing promotion to higher courts.[41] (This situation may have changed somewhat recently with the passage of the Judges Act that has de-emphasized evaluation

40 Pierre Bourdieu. 2001. *Practical Reason: On the Theory of Action*. Cambridge: Polity.

41 林孟皇 Lin Meng-Huang. 2013. 找回法官失落的審判靈魂 *Finding Back the Lost Trial Soul of the Judge*. 台北市 Taipei: 博雅書屋 Goodness Publishing House; 錢建榮 Chien Chien-Jumg. 2011. "Review on the Issues of Judge Personnel and the Cultures of Precedent Application Currently." 全國律師 *Taiwan Bar Journal* 15(4): 30–71.

reports). Even the Judicial Yuan, with its supervisory powers, has historically rarely challenged the SC's internal rules, informal practices, and adjudicative process.[42] However, in the 2012 judicial reform, the District Court's judges directly challenged the SC by using the media to make reform a populist issue. In 2012, more than 500 judges signed a petition calling for the devolution of the SC into the District Court, which also appealed to the idea of democratization in the judicial system, by requesting that the Chief Justice be elected by lower-level judges. The SCRG formed during the petition in order to reach the goal of devolution.

The nine-member SCRG issued a statement requesting ten reforms; this agenda also included the abolition of confidential case allocation. Subsequently, the SCRG chose the reform of confidential allocation as its primary goal because ordinary people would find it understandable. The public would never recognize the problems of the inquisitorial system, but they could understand the issue of making decisions behind closed doors. The SCRG successfully attacked the confidential allocation system through newspaper pieces, TV shows, and broadcasts, and they did it at the right time, when the legal system was a political issue due to numerous social events occurring at the time.[43] Distrust of the courts was rising, and President Ma Ying-Jeou wanted to address the situation. In a meeting with the President, the SCRG successfully encouraged Ma to call for reform on February 9, 2012.[44]

Ma's request for judicial transparency was powerful and stated in plain language. The SCRG transformed reform discourse from a conversation among elites to a populist "people vs. bureaucracy" public debate. When the SC rejected the SCRG's demands, they had to face public outrage, not the SCRG. Indeed, the SC said that confidential case allocation was designed to protect its judges from lobbying or bribery, but their statement irritated people because they believed that it just wanted to preserve its power. However, the day after the SC's statement, the opinion section of a newspaper detailed a case where litigants tried to bribe the Chief Justice to know which judges received a case.[45] This

42 Traditionally, the Judicial Yuan has declined to challenge SC's internal rules and informal customs, although it has legally-granted administrative authority to do so. (劉志原 Liu Zhi-Yuan, 楊國文 Yang Quo-Wen, 項程鎮 Xiang Cheng-Zhen, 謝文華 Xie Wen-Hua, and 胡健森 Hu Jian-Sen. 2011. "違失法官懲處過輕／宜蘭地院長請辭槓司院 Yilan District Court Chief Judge Resigned the Commission of Judicial Administration Affairs to Protest Judicial Yuan, because the Punishment of the Offending Judge Was Too Light." P. A1 in 自由時報 *The Liberty Times*: 自由時報).

43 林孟皇 Lin Meng-Huang. 2013. 找回法官失落的審判靈魂 *Finding Back the Lost Trial Soul of the Judge*. 台北市 Taipei: 博雅書屋 Goodness Publishing House.

44 謝莉慧 Hsieh Li-Hui. 2012. "總統見基層法官，承諾廢秘密分案 President Met with the Judges, and Promised to Abolish Secret Case Assignment," in 新頭殼 *New Talk*.

45 錢建榮 Chien Chien-Jumg. 2012. "秘密分案是助長關說文化、危害審判獨立的殺手 Secret Case Assignment Is a Killer to Encourage the Illegal Lobby Culture and to Jeopardize the Judicial Independence," edited by 財團法人民間司法改革基金會 Judicial Reform Foundation. 台北 Taipei: 財團法人民間司法改革基金會 Judicial Reform Foundation.

revelation stirred public outrage over transparency in case allocation, and the SCRG requested that the Judicial Yuan again urge the SC to abolish the rule.

The final nail in the coffin was Yang's retirement speech. In an attempt to defend the SC's allocation system, Yang admitted that, "someone tried to bribe me, but I rejected [the bribe]," and, he added, "all the bribery evidence was destroyed".[46] While Yang tried to state his innocence, the media asked, "who was it?" and "why do they have opportunities to bribe?".[47] Yang also emphasized the independence of judges, saying that SCRG and President Ma interfered with the SC by demanding reform.[48] However, the new Chief Justice abolished the confidential allocation system to restore public confidence. The reform also attracted international attention and was also described as "the District Court's protest against the SC in Taiwan" (村上太揮夫).

While the confidential allocation system had some merit, few scholars – who possess social capital in the legal system – stood on the SC's side primarily because the SCRG grasped the cultural argument and controlled moral capital. Given Taiwan's gradual democratic development, transparency and anti-corruption have become top concerns. The SCRG brought public scrutiny and pressure on the SC's traditional practices. Furthermore, in addition to creating a bottom-up reform process, SCRG successfully persuaded the President to care about the overall appeals problems at the SC. His inclination to change the confidential allocation system proved timely and politically beneficial.

The SC's defense

As aforementioned, the new civil procedure already requires the SC to hear oral argument cases on the merits unless the hearing is unnecessary (Article 474). In contrast, criminal procedure stipulates that oral arguments shall not be entertained, as a matter of principle, unless the hearing is considered necessary (Article 389). Although the rules for civil procedure and criminal procedure differ, it is clear that the SC enjoys discretionary power to publicize cases it encounters through hearings. A simple revision of the law cannot fix the problem.

Therefore, in order to push the SC to hold oral arguments on principally important issues, the SCRG solicited the Legislative Yuan's help. Legislators froze the SC's budget in 2012 until the SC could hold hearings regularly.[49] This

46 黃意涵 Huang Yi-Han. 2012. "楊仁壽籲總統勿侵犯審判權 Former Supreme Court President Jen-Shou Yang Appealed to the President Not to Infringe on the Power of Jurisdiction." 中央社 Central News Agency.

47 林孟皇 Lin Meng-Huang. 2013. 找回法官失落的審判靈魂 *Finding Back the Lost Trial Soul of the Judge*. 台北市 Taipei: 博雅書屋 Goodness Publishing House.

48 黃意涵 Huang Yi-Han. 2012. "楊仁壽籲總統勿侵犯審判權 Former Supreme Court President Jen-Shou Yang Appealed to the President Not to Infringe on the Power of Jurisdiction." 中央社 Central News Agency.

49 中華民國 102 年度中央政府總預算案審查總報告 Republic of China. 2013. Central Government General Budget Review Report, 559, 560, 562, 563.

move scared the SC to the extent that the criminal divisions held six hearings shortly thereafter (2012.4 to 2013.7). The SC's budget was restored afterwards, and this seems to have been another success for SCRG, although hearings are still rare.

However, civil divisions have still ignored the oral arguments requirement. In the fight against the SC's institutional behavior, the SCRG seemed to overlook the legislature's character – its short attention span. The legislature required a "report" from the SC to restore the budget, and if a proper report were sent to the legislature in correct form, the budget would be released automatically. Public attention on the SC decreased after few months of debate, and the legislature failed to oversee deep reform, thereby allowing the SC to retain its institutional culture. In the end, the SC's limited additional hearings were only symbolic, representing a start to reform. A thorough, democratically led reform process is necessary to rigorously implement changes. Sadly, moral arguments do not lead public emotions in this direction, and a democratic overhaul currently seems improbable in Taiwan.

Additionally, of the six hearings that the SC held since 2012, five were death penalty cases.[50] While holding hearings for death penalty cases, the SC prohibited the defendant on death row to attend the hearings because the SC insists that the third legal instance only examine issues of law.[51] This approach to appeals reflects an old Chinese style of inquisitorial adjudication that has not been completely displaced, even by formal legal changes.[52]

Democratization of the judiciary: a victory?

The Personnel Review Conference

In order to press for the devolution of judicial administrative power, the SCRG focused on reform of the personnel management system. The SCRG believed that an internal democratic process in the courts, as opposed to current bureaucratized decision-making, would be beneficial. Internal reforms have occurred, but their effects are still subject to debate. Examining the history of the SC's control on its own personnel system further illustrates the difficulty in reallocating moral capital.

The Judicial Yuan does not supervise the SC's personnel policy (appointment, promotion, and dismissal) although the law enables it to do so.[53] The Personnel Review Conference (PRC) (人事審議委員會) in the Judicial Yuan could

50 謝煜偉 Hsieh Yu-Wei. 2013. "簡評近來有關死刑案件之最高法院判決 Short Comment on Recent Death Penalty Judgments of Supreme Court." 全國律師 *Taiwan Bar Journal* 7: 5–21.

51 Ibid.

52 林孟皇 Lin Meng-Huang. 2013. 找回法官失落的審判靈魂 *Finding Back the Lost Trial Soul of the Judge*. 台北市 Taipei: 博雅書屋 Goodness Publishing House.

53 錢建榮 Chien Chien-Jumg. 2011. "Review on the Issues of Judge Personnel and the Cultures of Precedent Application Currently." 全國律師 *Taiwan Bar Journal* 15(4): 30–71.

easily review, approve, and reject personnel transfers and promotions involving the SC, but it has become a rubber stamp. Before 2011, the PRC consisted only of judges, and promotion to the SC required the SC's approval.[54] Any promotion to the SC without the SC's support would be blocked because the SC controlled the make-up of the PRC, and an informal rule held that all promotions to the SC would be by its own recommendation.[55] In the event of a promotion lacking the SC's recommendation, it would reject the promotion by claiming that there were "no seats available," nullifying the nomination power of the Judicial Yuan.

In practice, the SC alone determines its judges,[56] and from a democratic perspective, citizens have no power to choose their own SC judges, even indirectly through elected legislative officials. The Judicial Yuan only nominates candidates for the SC after receiving recommendations from the SC's Division Chief Justices, and the SC selects only judges who comply with their precedents that establish abstract rules without facts.[57] For example, in 2008, the Judicial Yuan nominated 12 HC judges to serve on the SC, but three of them were rejected by the PRC because they were not recommended by the SC. The unspoken rule is that if a judge challenges precedents often, he will not be promoted. The SC substantially controls its own personnel policy and its self-selected community influences the adjudicative atmosphere throughout the court system.

After passing a national examination, would-be judges have needed to complete two-years of training at the Judge and Prosecutor Training Institute (JPTI) under the Ministry of Justice. The convener of the training committee, who is in charge of training future judges, is the Chief Justice of the Supreme Court. Therefore the SC, instead of the Ministry of Justice, holds the real power over the judge training process.[58] Every year, the SC assigns a Division Chief Justice, and he is in charge of appointing lecturers to teach would-be judges the appropriate way to write legal documents. Judges are told to be compliant with the SC's rules, whether they are ethical or not, during the training process. Accordingly, judges are educated to comply with the SC from the beginning of their careers. After passing an examination at the end of the two-year training, one becomes a probationary judge.[59] A probationary judge can adjudicate all cases alongside other so-called lifetime judges, and after five years of adjudicative

54 「法院庭長、法官、委員遴選要點」 Chief Judge, Judge Selection Key Points, 第4條第1項第1款 Article 4, Item 1, Para. 1.

55 Ibid.

56 黃錦嵐 Huang Jin-Lan and 劉鳳琴 Liu Feng-Qin. 2008. "賴英照提人事案，再遭否決 Personnel Nominations from Judicial Yuan President in-Jaw Lai were Rejected Again," in 中國時報 *China Times*.

57 林孟皇 Lin Meng-Huang. 2011. "法官人事審議制度改革芻議 Humble Opinion of Judge Personnel Review System Reform." 司法新聲 *Judicial Aspiration* 97: 30–48.

58 林孟皇 Lin Meng-Huang. 2013. 找回法官失落的審判靈魂 *Finding Back the Lost Trial Soul of the Judge*. 台北市 Taipei: 博雅書屋 Goodness Publishing House.

59 司法人員人事條例 Judicial Personnel Regulatons, 第10條第1項 Article 10, Item 1.

experience and one more additional probationary year, the judge becomes a permanent judge with tenure.

During this six-year-period, judges learn how to write proper decisions, but a judge's opinion is subject to SC censorship. A committee consisting of current and former SC judges reviews 20 of each judge's decisions annually during the six-year period. Importantly, if an issued decision challenges a precedent, no matter how sound the decision is, the judge who wrote the opinion is considered to have failed.[60] As a result of this training system, judges become compliant and do not dare to criticize SC precedents. After the six-year-period, the SC's authority still looms over judges, as a judge needs to be compliant to receive favorable annual personnel evaluations in order to be promoted.

The Judges Act reform

Things changed somewhat after enactment of the Judges Act in 2011. Requests for the Judges Act surfaced in 1988, but activists failed to persuade the legislature to enact it, since no consensus had been reached on the sensitive question of whether the law should include prosecutors, who have jealously guarded their quasi-judicial status and wanted to be covered by the law. Another controversy concerned the composition of the committee that would review incompetent judges.

From 2010 onward, a series of scandals at the High Court and Supreme Court became a source of public irritation. A number of the High Court judges accepted bribes, and one SC judge even lobbied a district court judge to acquit his son, who was responsible for a hit-and-run car accident.[61] These scandals exacerbated the public's distrust of the legal system, and interest in the Judges Act was revived.[62] The Judges Act aimed to provide a review process for incompetent or disgraced judges through a Judge Review Committee (JRC) (法官評鑑委員會) under the Judicial Yuan. The JRC did not replace the PRC since the JRC only reviews incompetent judges, while the PRC reviews personnel transfers and promotions. Judicial reform groups saw this as an opportunity to improve the problematic PRC, suggested that PRC reform be included in the new Judges Act, and further recommended that the composition of the PRC include outsiders, social representatives, and scholars in order to fight favoritism and institutional inertia within the PRC.

60 錢建榮 Chien Chien-Jumg. 2011. "Review on the Issues of Judge Personnel and the Cultures of Precedent Application Currently." 全國律師 *Taiwan Bar Journal* 15(4): 30–71.

61 中時電子報, *China Times Electronics News*. 2010. "肇逃關說案牽連 女法官哭罵審判長「鬼扯」 The Female Judge Cried and Denounced 'Nonsense' to the Presiding Judge in the Hit-and-Run Case of Illegal Lobby." 中國時報.

62 Lin has listed ten high-profile cases that triggered public resentment (林孟皇 Lin Meng-Huang. 2013. 找回法官失落的審判靈魂 *Finding Back the Lost Trial Soul of the Judge*. 台北市 Taipei: 博雅書屋 Goodness Publishing House).

However, some judges and prosecutors strongly opposed the PRC reform, fearing interference from politicians as a result of including outsiders. The worry was that politicians might control personnel transfers and promotions if they could become the members of the PRC. The impasse was broken after another scandal in 2011, when one district court judge was accused of professional misconduct; he received only a minor penalty from the PRC (there was no JRC at the time, and the PRC did the JRC's job). The legislature believed that favoritism resulted in the minor penalty, and it then passed the Judges Act. The JRC was created and included some non-judges from other fields. The PRC also benefited from this reform as it was restructured to have three academic experts who can vote on certain personnel issues.

These reforms passed because of scandals, resulting in three new features of the PRC that reflect a partial democratization. First, the new PRC has 26 members, including 11 members designated by the Judicial Yuan, 12 judge representatives selected by judges, and three scholars chosen by the Judicial Yuan. In France's equivalent of the PRC, five out of 12 of its members come from the legislative and executive branches, and in Spain, the legislature assigns eight out of 21 members of its PRC.[63] By contrast, such democratic accountability does not exist in the Taiwanese PRC.[64] Second, scholars may not represent the public to show informal democratic accountability, and they can only vote on certain issues (e.g., promotions are excluded). Third, there are 1,321 judges in district courts and 579 judges in the High Court and Supreme Court, but only seven out of 12 judge representatives work at the district level. Superior judges in the judicial hierarchy are disproportionately represented.[65]

In essence, although the Judges Act appoints the JRC to supervise judicial misconduct, the PRC remains dominated by individuals likely to preserve the status quo. Although the personnel of the SC are still partially controlled by the SC, most other personnel transfers are arranged by the Judicial Yuan, since it now dominates the selection of PRC members according to the Judges Act. Additionally, the six-year training continues to affect judges' behavior, and the inadequate precedent system remains influential. As long as the Judicial Yuan controls the PRC, and the SC controls judges' behavior, judges are incentivized to comply with the hierarchical judicial culture instead of confronting it.

In 2011, the SCRG challenged the personnel system again and demanded that the President of the SC be selected by Legislative Yuan, but the High Court and

63 Carlo Guarnieri. 2001. "Judicial Independence in Latin Countries of Western Europe." *Judicial Independence in the Age of Democracy: Critical Perspectives from around the World*: 111–30.

64 王金壽 Wang Chin-Shou. 2008. "司法獨立與民主可問責性：論台灣的司法人事權 Judicial Independence and Democratic Accountability." 臺灣政治學刊 *Taiwanese Political Science Review* 12(2): 115–64.

65 林孟皇 Lin Meng-Huang. 2013. "司法院人審會的組成結構該調整了 It Is the Time to Adjust the Membership Structure of Judge Personnel Review Commission of Judicial Yuan." 司法改革雜誌 *Judicial Reform Magazine* 95: 17.

the Supreme Court rejected their petition.[66] The SCRG's petition had collected 518 signatures from among 1,321 district court judges and moved the argument to the media, which eventually drew the President's attention. However, the SCRG decided to focus on confidential case allocation and oral arguments as their main subjects for appeal in 2012, as these issues were directly connected to the people's requests for transparency. Therefore, further reform of the personnel system that would allow judges to confront the SC's institutional culture was put aside at that time. Attempts at reform now lack an internal force challenging the institutional culture or *habitus* of the SC.

The SC's internal culture is a key factor in the problems reformers seek to address, and it has proven difficult to fix. The Court's lack of hearings, high rate of procedural dismissals, and its problematic precedents persist because the SC's culture is not changing substantially. On the other hand, the current PRC and JRC reforms are intended to change institutional behavior, but they have not produced deep change so far. Because reforms occur in the wake of populist anger, efforts become ineffective once there are no longer scandals in the headlines. Additionally, reforms have failed to establish democratic accountability.[67] Moreover, without internal democratization, external democratic supervision might degenerate into populism, which is often seen as a negative consequence of Taiwanese democratization.[68]

Conclusion

Since 1949, the SC has faced several challenges, including a lack of consistency in legal opinions, a problematic precedent system, a controversial case allocation system, an overwhelming caseload, and the court's preference for remanding cases to lower courts rather than making final decisions. This chapter has discussed two important reforms: those of 2002 and 2012.

First, the 2002 reform was a *top-down* reform that was led by the Judicial Yuan. The Judicial Yuan established a discourse on choosing between the adversarial system and inquisitorial system in order to solve the problem of the judicial workload. However, institutional resistance by the SC stymied further reform. Since the SC strongly influences personnel management, a culture of respecting the SC already formed before the reform took place. It was not until 2012 that the SC substantially adopted the adversarial system that was required by law.

66 林孟皇 Lin Meng-Huang. 2013. 找回法官失落的審判靈魂 *Finding Back the Lost Trial Soul of the Judge*. 台北市 Taipei: 博雅書屋 Goodness Publishing House.

67 王金壽 Wang Chin-Shou. 2008. "司法獨立與民主可問責性：論台灣的司法人事權 Judicial Independence and Democratic Accountability." 臺灣政治學刊 *Taiwanese Political Science Review* 12(2): 115–64.

68 謝煜偉 Hsieh Yu-Wei. 2013. "簡評近來有關死刑案件之最高法院判決 Short Comment on Recent Death Penalty Judgments of Supreme Court." 全國律師 *Taiwan Bar Journal* 7: 5–21.

During this reform, Taiwanese scholars were roughly divided into two groups based on preferences for the adversarial system and inquisitorial system, and each group contributed to reform and resistance. In the end, the American-style appeal system seemed to win in reform efforts, but in practice, the SC's institutional behavior continued to shape the contours of the appeal system.

The 2012 reform, which can be viewed as a *bottom-up* reform, was initiated by the SCRG. Instead of focusing on caseload, the SCRG transformed public anger against the SC into the reform that targeted the case allocation system and personnel management. They successfully abolished the confidential case allocation system and urged the SC to hold hearings on certain issues. However, the victory resulting from changing the personnel management is still doubtful.

The SC's power has been somewhat weakened after the successful reform to the case allocation system, but power has shifted to the Judicial Yuan. While the SC still controls the promotion of judges within the SC, other personnel affairs, including judges' appointments, dismissals, and job transfers, are now substantially managed by the Judicial Yuan through a new internal personnel management rule, established by the Judicial Yuan in 2012. As a result, through the new rule and domination of the PRC, the Judicial Yuan has become the new enemy of democratic reforms.

During the 2012 reform, an understanding of English, the leading international language of scholarship, among judges, scholars, and activists may have contributed to academic debates. Although numerous law professors were trained in Germany, bottom-up reformist actors, not limited to scholars, often championed American solutions to Taiwan's problems, such as reducing caseloads, introducing exclusionary rules, etc. Another reason they preferred US-style reforms is that they emphasize democratic accountability. Also, the SCRG's ideas are based on American-style thought, since they prefer a smaller Supreme Court, rather than maintaining the current German-sized model. Overall, since the partial adoption of the adversarial system in criminal procedure, the current Taiwanese legal system has been increasingly influenced by American legal structures and ideas.

This does not mean that the German or Japanese legal solutions are inappropriate for Taiwan. As mentioned above, the SC's problematic behavior is related more to its institutional *habitus* than German or Japanese legal structures. The German inquisitorial system bears little resemblance to the old Chinese inquisitorial system, in which there were no prosecutors, that still influences Taiwanese judicial behavior. When attacking the SC's behavior, reformers seldom differentiate between the SC's stubborn attitude to change and the German inquisitorial system. Thus, German-style reforms were not used not because of their defects, but because the SC's *problematic implementation* of the inquisitorial system damaged its reputation, and made reformers desire more radical reform. The SC's institutional behavior seems to be rooted in traditional Chinese judicial culture, with its high expectations for judge involvement and mysterious procedures.

The enhancement of democratic governance in the judicial system is still ongoing, and challenging inner culture is imperative. To address this issue, new reforms should target culture, which shapes the law-in-action. Some reforms successfully challenge the institutional behavior, such as the abolition of the confidential case allocation system, but still fail to alter institutional culture significantly.[69] The improper precedent system continues to exist, and the PRC lacks democratic legitimacy.[70] The training committee prohibits judges' decisions from citing any academic work, and the abstract rules in precedents are binding for lower court judges. Failure to follow precedents disadvantages judges seeking promotion, which is still tightly controlled by the undemocratic PRC.

Article 80 of the Constitution states that "judges shall be above partisanship and shall, in accordance with law, hold trials independently, free from any interference." In order to keep this constitutional promise, challenging the SC's power is essential. First, the SC should be encouraged to take a more open stance toward scholars. Although the SC holds a conference every year, most attendees are scholars who prefer the Japanese system. The top-down reform led by the Judicial Yuan and the bottom-up reform triggered by the SCRG were both influenced by American thoughts, but a dialogue between American ideas and Japanese/German theories has not really taken place during reform efforts. Second, since judges are prohibited from citing academic works in their decisions, the barrier between scholars and judges is currently too firm. To achieve independence for judges, dissenting opinions should be allowed in all adjudication. Third, precedents without facts and SC's rulings should be abolished and replaced by precedents with facts, which can resolve conflicting division decisions. Fourth, and most importantly, reform in personnel policy, especially as it is governed by the PRC, is required to inject new blood into the currently self-reproducing SC. New ways of thinking at the SC could then trigger reform in the Court and lead to further judicial reform.

69 The SCRG and scholars recently suggested the idea of a "Grand Court Room," which may replace the SC's annual conference and help the SC to unify legal opinion (林孟皇 Lin Meng-Huang. 2013. "愼選大格局、學養俱優的大法庭法官 Carefully Elect the Judges of Grand Court Room with Broad Mind and Excellent Character and Learning." 司法改革雜誌 *Judicial Reform Magazine* 94: 40–6). But if the SC's institutional culture were left in place, the Grand Court Room may symbolically select one case per year to adjudicate and further refuse to unify legal opinions by remanding cases to the inferior courts. The problem could worsen since the SC is reluctant to adjudicate high-profile cases (張升星 Chang Sheng-Hsin. 2013. "程序扭曲與正義失衡—妥速審判法之實證觀點 The Distortion of Procedure and the Imbalance of Justice: The Empirical Point of View of the Criminal Speedy Trial Act." 臺灣法學雜誌 *Taiwan Law Journal* 216: 72–86).

70 王金壽 Wang Chin-Shou. 2008. "司法獨立與民主可問責性：論台灣的司法人事權 Judicial Independence and Democratic Accountability." 臺灣政治學刊 *Taiwanese Political Science Review* 12(2): 115–64.

7 Adopting a lay participation system in Taiwan

The trial observer reform attempt

Mong-Hwa Chin

Introduction

Allowing lay people to participate in the judicial process is perhaps the most vivid example of the fusion between democracy and judicial reform in Taiwan. Not long ago, Taiwanese people were oppressed by an authoritarian regime and threatened by court-martial trials, but now earning trust from the people has become a priority for judicial authorities. Under a possible new lay participation system, average citizens would be invited into courts to become adjudicators involved in the criminal judicial process.

The goal of this chapter is to provide a basic description of the past and present of the lay participation system in Taiwan. It will be divided into three sections. The first section surveys the discussions and proposals of different forms of lay participation in the past. It aims to provide a simple historical and social context to the development process. The second section is an introduction to the new lay participation system, the trial observer system, proposed by the Judicial Yuan.[1] Important features, including the basic design, the selection process of trial observers, the trial itself, and the deliberation process, will be explained. The third section will provide critiques of the trial observer system. The discussion will focus on the key problem of the interaction between judges and lay participants, namely how judges try to influence the decisions of lay participants. This section argues that a more radical reform is needed before the trial observer system can truly be seen as the democratization of the Taiwanese judicial system.

1 It should be noted that, as of July 2014, when this chapter was first written, the Trial Observers Bill proposed by the Judicial Yuan was not yet passed into law. As it turned out, the proposal ultimately stalled in the Legislative Yuan and was dropped after the election of the new President, Tsai Ing-wen.

A brief history of the lay participation system in Taiwan

From a historical perspective, the idea of a lay participation system is not new in the history of the Republic of China. From 1929 to 1931, when the government of the Republic of China still had control over mainland China, the "Temporary Jury System for Anti-revolution Cases" required the court to assemble juries for crimes that involved attempts at revolution. In 1956, the "Code of the Proceedings for Martial Law" required courts to assemble officers to preside in trials when the case at issue involved military expertise.[2]

However, these early forms of lay participation hardly had anything to do with democratizing the judicial system. The temporary jury system was aimed at suppressing political dissidents. According to the law, only members of the ruling political party, the Nationalists (or Kuomintang), were eligible to become jurors. As for martial law proceedings, requiring military officers to sit in trials was considered to be a way to maintain the independence of military judicial power and to avoid intrusion from the ordinary jurisdiction.[3] Both systems were supported by an authoritarian political agenda.

In 1949, the Nationalists lost the Chinese Civil War to the Communist Party. The party and the government retreated to Taiwan and began a period of martial law. It lasted for 38 years, and thousands of people were arrested and imprisoned under it for political reasons. It was later known as the "White Terror Era." The White Terror Era made many Taiwanese people believe that the law enforcement authorities and the courts were in the service of those in power. In 1987, martial law was lifted, the authoritarian state period was ended, and a new era of democracy finally began. The economy was soaring and the people were expecting a more liberalized political environment. Between 1991 and 2000, six amendments were made to the Constitution. One highlight of the changes was that people were allowed to vote directly in presidential elections.[4]

In the wake of the political reforms, judicial reform was triggered. A draft of the first lay participation bill – the Criminal Lay Participation Trials Bill – was proposed by the Judicial Yuan in 1994. According to the bill, lay participation trials would be conducted only when criminal defendants requested to be tried by lay participants. Defendants would have been able to submit such request in three kinds of cases: juvenile delinquency, crimes punishable by a sentence of ten or more years, and cases involving professional knowledge or technology. To become a lay participant, the following requirements had to be fulfilled: (1) the candidate had to be more than 30 years old; (2) he/she must be registered to

2 孫健智 [Jian-Zhi Sun], 人民參與審判法制之研究 [A Study on Lay Participation], 臺灣澎湖地方法院101年度研究發展報告 [Peng Hu District Court Research and Development Report] (2012), Chapter 4 (unpublished Peng Hu District Court research paper).

3 Ibid.

4 Tay-sheng Wang, "The Legal Development of Taiwan in the 20th Century: Toward a Liberal and Democratic Country," *Pac. Rim L. and Pol'y J.* 11 (2002): 536–9.

a specific court's jurisdiction for more than six months; (3) he/she must possess a high school or higher degree. Furthermore, people who were deprived of civil rights, declared bankrupt, sentenced to prison due to deliberate criminal conduct, suspected to be involved in criminal conduct and currently under investigation, mentally impaired, or more than 70 years old were excluded from the pool of lay participants. A committee in each county had to be formed to select eligible lay participants. A committee would have consisted of nine to 17 members. Possible sources of committee members included judges, prosecutors, representatives of the bar association, principles of local schools, representatives of the local administration and legislature, and others who were deemed fair by the local community. Once selected, lay participants would remain eligible to serve for three years. A lay participation trial would have been presided over by three professional judges and two lay participants. A case would be decided by the majority among the five votes, but the fact of the criminal conduct had to be approved by at least one of the lay participants. The written verdict would have been prepared by professional judges but signed by all the members of the panel. The design of the system proposed in the bill was very similar to that existing in Germany.[5]

However, after dozens of meetings, people within the judicial bureaucracy failed to reconcile their different opinions, and the bill was never formally introduced to the Legislative Yuan.[6] The most apparent problem for adopting a lay participation system was that people found it difficult to incorporate it into the criminal procedure at that time.[7] In 1994, criminal cases in Taiwan were usually being tried on paper. That is, in most cases, judges, prosecutors, and defense attorneys would communicate with each other by exchanging legal documents. The trial itself played a relatively insignificant role during the whole process. Judges would rely largely on the files in the dossier to make decisions. Although the new bill requested lay participants to read the files before trials just like their professional colleagues, however, it was believed that this would create an unreasonable burden on lay participants. Not only would lay participants be overburdened by the amount of files in the dossier, it was also unrealistic to think that lay participants would be able to fully understand the files even when they were given the chance to read the dossier in advance. If lay participants were not able to process the files, obviously, it would be unlikely for them to make a meaningful contribution to the judicial decision-making process. During one of the meetings, a representative of the Taipei District Court, for example, came to the conclusion that the new lay participation system was destined to fail unless there was going to be a fundamental change to the principles that governed

5 孫健智 [Jian-Zhi Sun], 人民參與審判法制之研究 [A Study on Lay Participation], 臺灣澎湖地方法院101年度研究發展報告 [Peng Hu District Court Research and Development Report], Chapter 4.

6 Ibid.

7 Ibid.

criminal trials. The representatives of Taipei and Taoyuan District Courts further recommended that adversarial features be incorporated into the current system.[8] Since the bill failed to provide answers to these issues, most practitioners at that time rejected the idea of adopting a lay participation system.

In 1997, representatives of reformist groups, including the Taipei Bar Association, the Taiwan Law Society, the Judges Association, and the Taiwan Bar Association requested a meeting with the then-President Lee Deng-Hui to push for comprehensive judicial reform. After the meeting, President Lee approved their proposal and requested related government authorities hold the National Judicial Reform Conference to provide a platform for further discussion on issues of judicial reform.

The meeting was finally held in July 1999. However, the problems that haunted judicial authorities in 1994 continued to exist in 1999. This meant that to earn the support of practitioners, changes had to be made to the first draft of the lay participation proposal. After the meeting, a joint resolution was made by the participants. Article 5 of the resolution provided that the Judicial Yuan (the highest judicial authority in Taiwan) should acknowledge the importance of earning the public's trust, respect the diversity of social values, and strengthen judges' expertise in non-legal areas. To achieve these goals, the Judicial Yuan was asked to introduce "expert participants" to cases involving juvenile law, family law, employment law, intellectual property law, medical disputes, administration disputes, and high-profile criminal cases.[9] Thereafter, the discussion on lay participation deviated from the main issue and came to be limited to "expert participation."

Limiting lay participation to expert participation was perhaps the most reasonable solution to accommodate the existing criminal procedure at that time. As mentioned earlier, most of the critiques of the earlier draft were related to the dossier and lay participants' ability to process it. To avoid colliding with the same problems, the new draft limited its subject to a small group of non-legal experts. In this way, these experts could focus their energy on the limited issues related to their expertise without going through the whole dossier.

To learn more about the system that allowed experts to act as lay participants, the Judicial Yuan sent representatives to Germany and Denmark to learn about their experiences on the non-legal expert participation system. The Judicial Yuan also assembled a committee to revise the original draft. This process took six years to complete.[10] It was not until 2005 that the committee produced a revised

8 Ibid.

9 司法院 [The Judicial Yuan], 全國司法改革會議結論具體措施時間表 [Timetable for realizing the conclusions of National Judicial Reform Conference], www.judicial.gov.tw/aboutus/aboutus05/aboutus05-05-03.asp.

10 孫健智 [Jian-Zhi Sun], 人民參與審判法制之研究 [A Study on Lay Participation], 臺灣澎湖地方法院101年度研究發展報告 [Peng Hu District Court Research and Development Report], Chapter 4.

version of the bill. According to the new bill, non-legal expert participation trials would not be used exclusively on criminal cases. The two parties could also apply for experts to participate in civil and administrative trials. The qualifications for expert participants were largely the same as lay participants, except that the committee that was responsible for choosing expert participants should include experts in related fields. Surprisingly, the non-legal expert participation bill was soon rejected by the then-President of the Judicial Yuan because he saw lay participation rather than expert participation as a worldwide trend, and that Taiwan should not exclude itself from it.[11] The Judicial Yuan soon refocused on lay participation and came up with a new version of the lay participation bill in 2006.

The new bill was based on the original draft proposed in 1994. A large portion of it was identical to the original draft, except for a few differences. First, the new bill focused more on earning legitimacy from the people. According to the bill, only four kinds of cases were eligible for a lay participation trial: crimes punishable by death or life imprisonment, public corruption, crimes jeopardizing the validity of presidential elections, and other high profile cases or cases with major effect on public order. The reason for specifying cases of public corruption and crimes related to presidential elections was because these crimes have traditionally been sources of public distrust toward the judicial system. Under the authoritarian regime, there was a common belief among Taiwanese people that the judicial system had close ties with the political party in power. Inviting lay participants to join trials in these kinds of cases could be seen as an effort to cure the distrust between the people and the judicial system.

A second difference was an attempt to resolve the dossier problem. The new rules simply forbade lay participants to access the dossier. It further forbade professional judges from telling their lay colleagues what they had read in the dossier. In this way, it was believed that judges would be forced to shift the core of the judicial process from documentation to trial activity. Essentially, the new rules required judges to spend more time in the courtroom, displaying all evidence through live oral presentations and arguments. The discussion of the new bill lasted from 2006 through 2007, but it never drew sufficient attention in the Legislative Yuan.

Things began to change after 2010.[12] A lay participation system started to gain support from the public not because of judicial independence concerns, but rather because of dissatisfaction with the integrity and competence of judges. In 2011, three High Court judges were found guilty of accepting a bribe of NT$3,500,000 (approximately US$125,000) from a former legislator who was involved in political corruption. The legislator was sentenced to 15 years by the district court. However, he was acquitted on appeal. The judges involved were

11 Ibid.
12 Ibid.

all sentenced to more than ten years in prison,[13] but damage was already done to the reputation of the judicial system.

Besides the problem of judges' integrity, the last straw that finally raised a massive social outrage against the judicial system was a series of sex crime trials. In 2010, a district court judge sentenced a sex crime recidivist to three years and two months in prison, while the prosecutor recommended a sentence of seven years and ten months. The defendant was accused of raping a six-year-old child by force, but the judges found that there was no proof showing force was used during the crime, and therefore he could only be convicted of statutory rape.[14] Later, a high court judge acquitted a person who was accused of molesting a three-year-old child because, "the evidence did not show that the girl had cried or made any noise after she left the defendant."[15] In another case, a judge found a person who was accused of raping a two-year-old child not guilty simply because "there was slight discrepancy between the time of rape" recalled by witnesses.[16] In 2011, a district court judge granted NT$50,000 (approximately US$1,700) bail to a taxi driver who was accused of sexually assaulting a Japanese college student. The authorities found the accused after he failed to show up to a later hearing.[17] As these incidents drew more and more attention, the media started to portray judges as "dinosaur" or "fossil" judges, meaning that they are outdated and their opinions are against public sentiments and expectations.[18]

In response to the social outcry urging the judicial system to reform, the Judicial Yuan, decided to push through a new system called "Guan Shen Zhi" (trial observer system). The sole purpose of this new model was to restore the public's faith in the judicial system.

The trial observer system

Allowing laypeople to participate in trials is not an innovation for Continental countries. Different types of lay participation systems have been adopted by European countries such as Germany, France, Poland, Italy, and Croatia, as well

13 Staff Writer, Corrupt Judges Handed Lengthy Prison Sentences, *Taipei Times*, July 1, 2011, www.taipeitimes.com/News/taiwan/archives/2011/07/01/2003507146.

14 News Staff, Judges Incur Fury over Pedophile Sentencing, *China Post*, August 26, 2010, www.chinapost.com.tw/taiwan/national/national-news/2010/08/26/270104/Judges-incur.htm.

15 Pao Chien-hsin, Not Guilty Verdict in Assault Case, *Taipei Times*, April 2, 2011, www.taipeitimes.com/News/taiwan/archives/2011/04/02/2003499732.

16 News Staff, Gov't to Toughen Child Sex Law, *China Post*, September 4, 2010, www.chinapost.com.tw/taiwan/national/national-news/2010/09/04/271334/Govt-to.htm.

17 Wang Ji-you, "Dinosaur Judge" Protests Resurface as Rapist is Freed on Bail, *China Times*, July 18, 2011, www.wantchinatimes.com/news-subclass-cnt.aspx?id=20110718000002&cid=1503&MainCatID=0.

18 News Staff, Public Sentiment an Issue for Lawmakers, not Judges, *China Post*, April 5, 2011, www.chinapost.com.tw/editorial/taiwan-issues/2011/04/05/297278/Public-sentiment.htm.

as by Asian countries such as Japan and South Korea.[19] Although these countries have different forms of lay participation, the idea is the same: the judicial decision-making process should not be monopolized by professionals.

The goal of the Taiwanese new model is simple: to promote legitimacy of legal authorities and to incorporate public opinion into the judicial decision-making process. The legislative note on Article 1 of the Trial Observers Bill said that the lack of communication and interaction between the judicial system and public opinion is the key reason why the public distrusts judges.[20] The drafters assumed that if the public understood more about how the law works and if people realized that most judges work diligently on their cases, the public would have more faith in the judicial system. Similarly, if judges understood the concerns of public opinion, they would be able to adjust their decisions accordingly.

Before looking into the statute's provisions, it should be emphasized that there is a major difference between the jury system in the United States and the new observer system in Taiwan. Jury trials in the United States are considered to be the right of the accused and can waived by the accused. However, the Judicial Yuan says that the accused will not be able to refuse being tried by observers, because promoting public trust and improving the judicial system is not in conflict with the rights of the accused.[21] Only under certain circumstances may a judge exclude observers from trials. For example, when the court reasonably believes that trial observers will be biased, when a case is too complicated for a layperson to understand, or when the defendant has confessed.[22] It should also be emphasized that, as of February 2014, the bill proposed by the Judicial Yuan has not been passed into law, passed into law, and therefore the rules illustrated in the following paragraphs are still subject to change.

The following section will begin to introduce some of the rules of the proposed trial observer system. For the purpose of making them easier to understand, the rules will be divided into three categories: rules governing procedure before trial, the trial itself, and rules related to deliberation. It is important to keep in mind that the purpose of this proposed system is to respond to public dissatisfaction toward legal professionals. However, whether these rules truly recognize the value of introducing public opinion into the courtroom remains debatable in Taiwan. The rules governing interaction between judges and observers are most salient on this point.

19 Daniel Senger, "The Japanese Quasi-Jury and the American Jury: A Comparative Assessment of Juror Questioning and Sentencing Procedures and Cultural Elements in Lay Judicial Participation," *U. Ill. L. Rev.* 741 (2011): 748–9.

20 Legislature note, art. 1.

21 司法院 [Judicial Yuan], 司法院構思中人民觀審制度Q&A進階版 [A Proposal on the Trial Observers – Q&A Advanced Version], Question 6, www.judicial.gov.tw/revolution/司法院構思中人民觀審制度Q&A進階版.doc.

22 人民觀審試行條例草案 [Trial Observers Bill], art. 6.

Before trial

According to the bill, except for drug-related crimes or cases of juvenile delinquency, a group of five laypeople will act as trial observers in crimes punishable by death, life imprisonment, or a sentence of more than seven years.[23] The Judicial Yuan says that the reason for excluding drug crimes is that offenders of these crimes are often isolated from society, and therefore it would be hard to expect trial observers to make meaningful contributions in these kinds of cases. As for juvenile delinquency cases, they are excluded because they are governed by a special court system and a different set of rules.

Like the United States, a *voir dire* process is proposed to select trial observers. Any citizen 23-years old or more who has been living in the jurisdiction of the court for more than four months is eligible to become a potential observer.[24] A potential observer may be disqualified for many reasons. Some of the most important reasons include: a prior criminal conviction, incompetence, kinship toward a party, or expertise in law.[25] A potential observer may be exempted from the obligation if he or she is 70-years or older, a school teacher or student, or due to illness, a conflict with family obligations, or prior service as an observer.[26] A special administrative committee in each district would be formed to make an initial list of qualified observers.[27] After this, judges would be responsible for randomly choosing a number of potential observers and verifying their qualifications.[28] Before trial, judges and the two parties would be allowed to question the potential observers.[29] The two parties each have three preemptory challenges.[30] Finally, the court would choose five people from the pool of qualified potential observers.[31]

In order to make cases more understandable to lay people and to increase the efficiency of trials, a commissioned judge would be appointed by the court to conduct a preparatory proceeding. During the proceeding, the rule mandates that the judge and the two parties confirm the scope of the facts and the charges and whether there is a guilty plea from the accused. They should also sort out the facts and issues crucial to the case, argue on the admissibility of evidence, request the investigation of evidence, hear the two parties comment on court-investigated evidence, decide the sequence, scope, and methodology of the investigation, produce a list of evidence that will be used in trial, and order expert witness testimony or schedule an inspection. After the preparatory

23 Ibid. art. 3; art. 5.
24 Ibid. art. 12.
25 Ibid. art. 13–15.
26 Ibid. art. 16.
27 Ibid. art. 19.
28 Ibid. art. 21.
29 Ibid. art. 26.
30 Ibid. art. 27.
31 Ibid. art. 28.

proceeding, the commissioned judge should produce a "trial plan" that includes the decisions on the issues discussed during the preparatory proceeding.[32] However, it should not be misunderstood that the commissioned judge has the exclusive power to determine the admissibility of evidence. The commissioned judge should bring admissibility issues to the other two judges so they can be decided by the whole panel.

The significance of the trial plan is that it requires judges to fundamentally change their decision-making process on the admissibility of evidence. In the past, judges usually decided admissibility issues during deliberations. But now, to accommodate lay participants, they would be required to determine the admissibility of evidence before the trial to ensure that lay participants would not be exposed to inadmissible information.

During the trial

Under the proposal, judges retain the central role in a trial. Judges would have to explain the facts, law, and procedure to lay observers at the start of the trial[33] and during the "intermediate discussion."[34] An intermediate discussion may be held whenever observers have questions about the facts or procedure.[35] Observers generally have the same investigative power of a judge, therefore, during the trial observers may question a witness.[36] It is also implied that an observer may request the court conduct an investigation a piece of evidence.[37] However, observers will not be able to determine the admissibility of evidence or seek explanation of law.[38]

To expedite the process and to prevent bias, neither the judges nor observers would have access to the dossier, except for the commissioned judge who conducts the preparatory proceeding.[39] Therefore, judges and observers would have to rely on the two parties to construct the case. However, as mentioned above, the admissibility of evidence is to be determined by the whole panel, therefore, although the other two judges are not allowed access to the dossier, they are still exposed to all questionable evidence. To ensure that the procedure runs smoothly, the defense is required to be represented by a lawyer. If the defendant fails to hire a lawyer, a lawyer will be appointed by the court.[40] Finally, to ensure

32 Ibid. art. 39.
33 Ibid. art. 47.
34 Ibid.
35 Ibid.
36 Ibid. art. 52.
37 Legislature note, art. 50.
38 Ibid. art. 50.
39 Ibid. art. 45.
40 Ibid. art. 5.

that observers fully understand the case, observers are obliged to be present during the whole trial.[41]

Deliberations

At the end of the trial, observers are required to deliberate along with the panel of professional judges on the final verdict.[42] The deliberation process is divided into six steps. First, the rule requires the judges and observers to have a joint discussion on the case. To preserve the original opinions of the observers, during the initial joint discussion, professional judges are not allowed to express their opinion on the issues of the case first.[43] Observers must express their opinions to the judges first. After this, a meeting should be held among judges. If the majority of judges determines that the defendant is guilty, then the judges and observers should discuss sentencing. In this, observers express their opinions to the judges on issues of sentencing. Finally, the judges should deliberate on the sentence.[44]

During the process, observers may give opinions on factual questions, the application of the law, and sentencing.[45] However, unlike American juries that are allowed to determine the facts on their own or European lay judges that allow lay participants to decide a case with a judge or a panel of judges, trial observers are only allowed to give advice to the judges. This is a crucial point. Judges are not bound by the opinions of the observers, but they must provide a written statement of explanation in their verdict if they disagree with the majority opinion of the observers.[46]

Critiques of the trial observation system

After the Judicial Yuan proposed the new lay participation system, there were discussions within the legislature on whether a more radical change was needed. As the name of the new system implies, trial observers would be there only to watch the process, not to decide. Trial observers may give opinions to professional judges, but judges are not bound by their opinion. In legislative hearings, several participants expressed their opinion that Taiwan should move toward an American-style jury system. A representative from the People First Party made a statement that the proposed trial observer system is a system that reflected professional judges' distrust toward the people instead of people's distrust

41 Ibid. art. 8.
42 Ibid. art. 56.
43 Ibid. art. 57.
44 Ibid. art. 56.
45 Ibid.
46 Ibid. art. 59; art. 64.

toward professional judges.[47] In other words, the system would not take social outcry seriously. Instead it is a system that aimed to resolve the "misunderstanding" between professional judges and the people. In the representative's view, the trial observer system denies progress and distorts the public's opinion.

The same problem was also pointed out by an attorney who participated in the hearing. In his opinion, the problem of the judicial system is not transparency, but democracy. Asking people to observe trials would not prevent professional judges from taking bribes nor would it deter judges from being affected by political power. He believes that the lay participation system is merely using lay participants to endorse the existing system dominated by professional judges.[48] However, these critiques did not have a substantial effect on the bill proposed by the Judicial Yuan.

Here, we will focus more on opinions of scholars and practitioners who accepted the basic ideas of the proposed system and who pointed out its internal inconsistencies.

The most common criticism of the joint decision-making process between judges and lay people is that judges would dominate the process, and that the importance of the lay participants would be diminished. For example, Professor Sanja K. Ivković reported that most lay judges in Poland, Hungary, and Croatia did not actively or meaningfully participate during the process.[49] Most judges in Croatia believed that the biggest problem for lay judges was their lack of legal knowledge.[50] It has also been reported that in Croatia, Sweden, and Germany, lay judges rarely express different opinions. Therefore, professional judges would normally dominate deliberations.[51] The contribution of lay judges on cases was considered to be minor.[52]

Ivković suggested that the imbalance between professional and lay participant can be explained from the perspective of status characteristic theory. Essentially, status characteristic theory suggests that status differences between group members may have a great influence on group dynamics.[53] In a judicial decision-making environment, it is the legal knowledge and trial experience that gives professional judges a higher status. Studies have shown that high-status group members will not only be given more opportunities to contribute, their opinions

47 張靜 [Jin Zhang], 陪審制是我國司法改革的新契機 – 我為什麼力主陪審制 [The Jury System is an Opportunity for Future Judicial Reform – Reasons Why I Support the Jury System], 人民參與審判制度公聽會 [Hearing on the Lay Participation System], 8th Congress, 2013: 81.

48 鄭文龍 [Wen-Long Zhang], 陪審團 – 人民當家做主的審判制度 [The Jury System – A System that Allows the People to Make Decisions]: Hearing on the Lay Participation System, 8th Congress, 2013: 115–16.

49 Sanja Kutnjak Ivković, "Exploring Lay Participation in Legal Decision-making: Lessons from Mixed Tribunals," *Cornell Int'l L. J. 40* (2007): 440–1.

50 Ibid. at 441.

51 Ibid.

52 Ibid. at 441–3.

53 Ibid. at 437.

are also more likely to be welcomed by other group members.[54] Therefore, members with higher status are usually more influential in group decision-making processes.

The Trial Observers Bill takes into account the criticism of European lay judges. For example, to balance the status difference between judges and observers, the bill provides multiple opportunities for judges to explain the factual and legal issues of a case. Under the bill, the two groups would be able to exchange opinions before the trial starts, during the intermediate discussion and during deliberation. Also, traditionally judges are expected to review the files in the dossier before trial, while in the lay observers system, in order to avoid an imbalance of familiarity toward the case, the rule forbids judges and lay participants altogether from accessing the dossier, except for the commissioned judge. Finally, during deliberations, the rule requires judges not to express their opinions on the issues of the case before the observers express theirs.

The following section introduces several incompatibilities between the trial observer system and inquisitorial culture. These problems were reported by attorneys who participated in the nine mock trials held by the Judicial Yuan from 2012 to 2013. These problems show that the efforts made by the Judicial Yuan to improve the trial observer system were far from enough.

Lack of awareness of the need to prevent observers' exposure to inadmissible evidence

In one mock trial, at the pre-trial preparatory stage, the defense attorney filed a motion to argue that the police interview record should be excluded from trial. The judge approved the motion (according to the rules of hearsay), and excluded the interview record from the "trial plan." However, at trial, the contents of the interview were still mentioned in the prosecutor's opening statement and in the slideshow presentation that he used. The defense attorney objected. But the court not only refused to exclude the record, instead, the judges ruled that the record was allowed at trial.[55]

An American lawyer would probably think that the way the court handled the piece of inadmissible evidence was absurd. How can evidence be inadmissible and yet be allowed to be presented at trial? There are two possible explanations: one is that the judges were unmindful of the fact that they were conducting a trial with lay participants. Therefore, they were simply following the traditional rules of evidence that allowed all proof to be presented to the court regardless of admissibility issues. Under the traditional rules of evidence, a piece of inadmissible evidence could only be excluded during final deliberation.

54 Ibid. at 439.

55 陳芬芬 [Fen-Fen Chen], 律師在觀審法庭活動的角色與功能 [The Role and Function of Lawyers in Lay Participation Trials] (2013): 2–3 (unpublished conference paper, Seminar on the Mock Lay Participation Trials, Taipei Bar Association).

The second explanation is more cynical. It can be argued that the judges purposefully wanted that piece of inadmissible evidence to be presented to the lay participants. It should be noted again that despite the bill's forbidding two of the three judges from accessing the dossier, all three judges are still exposed to the evidence when its admissibility is argued by the parties, because admissibility of evidence is to be determined by all three members of the panel. It is therefore possible that the judges wanted the observers to be exposed to all the evidence that they were exposed to, so that the possibility of differentiation in the final decision could be minimized.

No matter which explanation best explains the mentality of the judges, the experience of the attorney showed that the judges were trying to influence the decisions of trial observers. The goal of such influence was to prevent disagreement between judges and lay participants. But what is the legal effect when judges disobey the rules in the bill? The bill does not provide an answer. Does it mean that the rules in the bill are only for reference, and that judges may choose to follow them voluntarily? Does it mean that the new system does not appreciate the ideal of preserving the untainted opinions of the lay observers?

Furthermore, in Taiwan, most criminal cases can be appealed to the High Court. Unlike the United States, the High Court will make a second determination on both factual and legal issues. However, the trial observer system does not apply to the High Courts. Therefore, facts would be decided by professional judges alone on appeal. This design further diminishes the incentive for judges to follow the proposed rules and to exclude inadmissible evidence. From the perspective of District Court trial judges, is it possible that they would rather disobey rules that have no consequences than produce a decision that conflicts with what the High Court judges will later decide? The latter will have full access to all the evidence available.

The misuse of trial plans

Another defense attorney reported that in the mock trial that he participated in, the judge interfered with the defense argument strategy through the trial plan. In that case, the accused was charged with attempting to murder his neighbor with a fruit knife. The defense's strategy was to present the accused's lack of motive, the slightness of the injury the victim suffered, and the victim's reaction after the incident to prove that the accused was trying to threaten the victim instead of attempting to murder him and that the injury was caused by accident.[56]

However, the judge refused the notion that the incident was caused by a threat that went wrong. To him, the difference was only between whether the accused

56 尤伯祥 [Bo-Xiang You], 第四次觀審模擬審判心得報告 [Reflections on the Fourth Mock Lay Participation Trial] (2013): 10–12 (unpublished conference paper, Seminar on Mock Lay Participation Trials, Taipei Bar Association.)

acted with the intent to murder or injure the victim. Regardless of the opinion of the defense attorney, the judges decided not to put the option of "negligently causing injury to another" into the trial plan. The judge even refused to consider the possibility of negligence during the first stage of deliberation. As a result, during the independent deliberation process among the trial observers, the possibility of negligence never came into the observers' discussion agenda. In fact, the record shows that one of the observers actually proposed to other observers that perhaps there was a possibility that the injury was caused by negligence. But the foreman replied to him that they should follow the agenda that was provided by the judge. Thus, the proposal was ignored by the other observers.[57]

Besides the problem with the deliberation process, the attorney was also dissatisfied with other aspects of the trial plan. According to the bill, the trial plan would virtually script the trial. It should have a detailed list of the evidence presented to the court, the names of the witnesses, and even the facts that the witnesses would testify to. Before the mock trial, the defense attorney noticed that in the trial plan the judge allowed the prosecutor to present the files in the dossier, including records of police interviews, medical examinations, and other documents in the file. The attorney argued to the court that not only were some of the files inadmissible, but that the presentation would also defeat the design of the rule forbidding judges and observers to access the dossier. However, the commissioned judge refused to revise the plan. The judge replied that an introduction to the files in the dossier would allow observers to have a basic understanding of the case. It would also expedite the process, he said.[58]

The report of this mock trial also demonstrates that judges would try to influence lay participants. Judges not only used the trial plan as an instrument to limit the scope of discussion during the deliberation process, but also allowed inadmissible information in the dossier to be presented to observers before the parties started to examine the witnesses. Again, this shows that judges are unable to acknowledge the importance of new rules of evidence and how they keep lay participants untainted.

Efforts to personally connect with the observers

A third attorney who participated in the mock trials reported that judges strenuously tried to make personal connections with the observers. For example, before trial, one judge would hold a meeting with all the observers. According to the description of the attorney, the judge treated them as friends during the meeting. Yet the bill provides that the purpose of the pre-trial meeting is for the judges to describe the basic principles of law and the core issues of the case to the

57 Ibid.

58 Ibid. at 13–15.

observers. But in the pre-trial meeting at the mock trial, the defense attorney reported that the judge essentially made his own "opening statement." Not only that, but he briefed them on the factual and legal issues of the case, and further told them what he thought the conclusion should be.[59] Again, this observation provides an obvious example of judges trying to influence lay observers.

The problems mentioned above should not be attributed to individual judges. These judges are just doing what the system expects of them. Unlike juries, which receive information passively from the parties, inquisitorial judges are expected to gather information actively. Regardless of the performances of the two parties, judges are mandated by law to search for the truth. Therefore, inquisitorial judges are trained to become investigators and to develop their own theories on cases. To search for the truth, the system allows judges to be exposed to all the investigative information in the dossier, regardless of admissibility issues. Psychologically speaking, because judges are expected to solve cases on their own, their mentality is more similar to an investigator; this means they are less likely to digest what other people have to say. And they are more likely to neglect or discredit information that does not conform to their original hypothesis.

Also, because judges are the sole decider for both legal and factual issues, as far as they are concerned, the rules of evidence can be no more than a reminder or a recommendation of what kind of evidence is less reliable or which piece of evidence should be excluded during deliberation. As briefly mentioned above, the meaning of "admissibility" in the inquisitorial system is different from the common understanding in the United States. In the inquisitorial system, evidence is "always" allowed to come into trial. If a piece of evidence is inadmissible, it means that judges are not allowed to use it as a basis of their decision.

As Mirjan Damaška puts it, inquisitorial judges, during deliberation, "are expected to switch to a third person's viewpoint and attempt to arrive at a decision by hypothesizing what outcome another adjudicator would reach who was uncontaminated by the forbidden information."[60] In reality, issues regulated in the rules of evidence would go to weight rather than admissibility. After all, it may not be reasonable to expect judges to first exclude a piece of evidence and then pretend it does not exist while making the final decisions. All they can do is to diminish the value of that inadmissible evidence. Unsurprisingly, when judges are asked to decide a case along with lay participants, without a clear legal sanction for a violation of the rule that requires judges to perform a gatekeeping duty, most of them would not change their routine practices or appreciate the significance of the rules of evidence.

59 林俊宏 [Jun-Hong Lin], 從跆拳計分新制看觀審－士林地院試行觀審評析 [Commenting on the Lay Participation Mock Trials held in Shulin District Court], 司法改革雜誌 [Judicial Reform Magazine] 91 (2012): 22–3.

60 Mirjan Damaška, "The Jury and the Law of Evidence: Real and Imagined Interconnections," *Law, Probability and Risk* 5 (2007): 255.

These problems indicate that a new issue should be added to the judicial training process. The ideology behind the current training process is elitism. The judicial test and judicial training process are what distinguish judges from lay people, or even lawyers. The process emphasizes professionalism, independence, and integrity.[61] Combining the three aspects together, it also creates a special social identity among judges. It makes professional judges different from lay people, not only in that they possess an expertise that no one else has, but that they are also trained specifically to make decisions without interference from outside sources. Judicial training thus engenders an attitude that creates a wide gap between judges and lay participants.

This can be inferred from the fierce competition and the training they received before becoming judges. To become a Taiwanese judge, law students have to pass an extremely competitive judicial exam and then go through an intense process of training. The judicial exam in Taiwan is held once a year. In 2011, the passage rate was less than 1 percent (only 71 among 7,982 people passed the exam). The test is divided into three stages: the passage rate for the first test is 33 percent; the passage rate for the second exam is 3 percent; and the pass rate for the third exam is 91 percent.[62] After the exam, those selected go through a training process for 1.5 to two years.[63]

According to the curriculum announced in May 2013,[64] the training courses are divided into five categories: basic courses, practical legal courses, theoretical legal courses, supplementary courses, and general courses. Basic courses include, for example, the introduction to the judicial system, judicial ethics, introduction to human rights protection, computerized legal research, and legal research on foreign laws. Practical legal classes include, for example, trial experience, legal writing, legal research, and techniques of cross-examination. Theoretical legal courses include advanced and specialized topics in the law. For example, seminars on financial law, intellectual property law, public construction law, internet law, international law, and medical law. Supplementary

61 Charles H. Koch, Jr., "The Advantages of the Civil Law Judicial Design as the Model for Emerging Legal Systems," *Ind. J. Global Legal Stud.* 11 (2004): 143–8.

62 考試院 [Ministry of Examination], 100年司法官特考第一試定於9月15日放榜 [The result of 2011 judicial exam first test is published on September 15], wwwc.moex.gov.tw/main/news/wfrmNews.aspx?kind=3&menu_id=42&news_id=847; 考試院 [Ministry of Examination], 100年司法官特考第二試定於11月25日放榜 [The result of 2011 judicial exam-second test is published on November 25], wwwc.moex.gov.tw/main/news/wfrmNews.aspx?kind=3&menu_id=42&news_id=932; 考試院[Ministry of Examination], 100年司法官特考第三試定於12月20日放榜 [The result of 2011 judicial exam-second test is published on December 20], wwwc.moex.gov.tw/main/news/wfrmNews.aspx?kind=3&menu_id=42&news_id=957.

63 法務部司法官訓練所司法官訓練規則 [The Ministry of Justice Training Regulations for the Training Institute of Judges and Prosecutors], art. 10.

64 法務部司法官訓練所, Judges and Prosecutor's Institute, Ministry of Justice, 法務部司法官訓司法官第54期訓練計畫 [Training Plan for the 54th Training Section for Judges and Prosecutors], www.tpi.moj.gov.tw/public/Attachment/35231704689.doc.

courses include classes on, for example, foreign language, legal theory, law and economics, legal philosophy, criminal psychology, negotiations, international treaties, gender and law, forensic science, and issues in environmental protection. General courses include, for example, social activities, judicial ethics, interaction with the media, and sport activities. This curriculum covers a huge range of subjects and professional knowledge, and it provides the foundation for the unique legal expertise of judges.

Not only does the system require trainees to know the law, they are also purposefully isolated from the general public. During the training period, they are given a salary that matches a mid-level government employee along with benefits and health insurance.[65] The training institute functions as a boarding school, and future judges and prosecutors live in the institute during weekdays. They attend a packed schedule of classes five days a week under the instruction of presiding judges and prosecutors.[66] They are not allowed to have a part-time job elsewhere.[67] The idea is that isolation leads to independence, and independence is a praiseworthy quality for judges. Indeed, independence is considered to be a strength of inquisitorial judges, but, obviously, it may decrease the willingness of judges to listen to what lay participants have to say, or lower judges' capacity to appreciate their insights on cases.

Ironically, independence has its internal limits. On one hand, the system asks judges to be independent from external interference, on the other hand, it requires judges to defer to the organization's internal discipline and culture. In a normal criminal trial in Taiwan, a case is decided by a panel of three judges. There is a presiding judge who oversees the whole process and acts as a commanding officer. The presiding judge appoints one of his staff judges to act as a commissioned judge. The commissioned judge is responsible for preparing the case for trial. His work normally includes presiding over preliminary proceedings and resolving pre-trial motions raised by the parties. The commissioned judge is also responsible for writing the final verdict once the panel reaches a conclusion. In practice, the commissioned judge is usually the only judge who reviews the dossier carefully from beginning to end. Finally, there is a third requisitioned judge who is required to sit through the whole trial and to vote along with other two judges during deliberation. Cases are decided by the majority opinion among the three.

According to the Code of Court Organization, the presiding judge is the chair of the deliberation meeting.[68] Except for the duty to coordinate the meeting, the law does not give the chair any privileges during the deliberation. The chair's

65 法務部司法官訓練所司法官訓練規則 [The Ministry of Justice Training Regulations for the Training Institute of Judges and Prosecutors], art 9.

66 Ibid. art. 3. (Since 2012, judicial trainees are not required to live in the institute anymore. Nevertheless, the extensive training schedule remains the same.)

67 Ibid. art. 2.

68 法院組織法 [Code of Court Organization], art. 102.

vote will be counted as equal to the other two votes. However, in reality, the opinion of the presiding judge weighs much more than the other two judges. According to the qualitative studies conducted by scholars Chin-Shou Wang and Hung-Ru Wei, the "atmosphere" of the deliberation meetings is determined by all three judges, but the "style" of the presiding judge plays a crucial role.[69] According to their analysis, there are three kinds of leadership among presiding judges: the first kind of presiding judges tend to authorize the commissioned judge to play a leading role throughout the whole trial. Unless the commissioned judge lacks the ability to make certain decisions or makes an error, the senior does not interfere. For this kind of presiding judges, deliberation is merely a process required by the law. The other judges usually defer to the decision of the commissioned judge. The second kind of presiding judges tends to carefully review the dossier, and conduct a substantive discussion with the other two judges. The third kind of presiding judge decides the case on the basis of his opinion, and he forces the others to accept his view.[70]

The most common type of leadership is the first type. However, the study pointed out that most presiding judges choose to defer to the opinion of the commissioned judge for practical reasons. Since commissioned judges are the first judges to examine the case and prepare for trial, the commissioned judge is usually the only one who has reviewed the whole dossier in the three-judge panel. Therefore, compared to the other two judges, the commissioned judge is almost always the one who is most familiar with the case. Therefore, unsurprisingly, the other two judges normally defer to the opinion of the commissioned judge.[71]

It is important to clarify that the presiding judge is not required defer to the commissioned judge. The power of the commissioned judge should be understood as a power authorized by presiding judges. Therefore, when the commissioned judge wins the vote of the requisitioned judge but the presiding judge has a different opinion, the results may vary with the different styles of presiding judges. It is possible for the presiding judge to overrule the other two votes, though that rarely happens. What happens more often is that when the presiding judge and the commissioned judge have different opinion and the former manages to win the vote of the requisitioned judge, the commissioned judge would have to deliver the written verdict on behalf of the other two judges.[72] It should be noted that the law requires the most junior judge to be the first to speak out his opinion during deliberation. The reason for this rule is to allow the most junior judge to speak freely before presiding judges express their opinion.

69 王金壽 [Chin-Shou Wang] and 魏宏儒 [Hung-Ru Wei], 台灣地方法院裁判評議制度之實證研究 [An Empirical Study of Judicial Deliberation in District Courts in Taiwan], 台灣社會研究季刊 [Taiwan: A Radical Quarterly in Social Studies], 88 (2012): 139.

70 Ibid. at 140–1.

71 Ibid. at 144.

72 Ibid. at 155.

However, in practice, regardless of seniority, the commissioned judge normally speaks first, and then the requisitioned judge speaks, and finally the presiding judge.[73]

The third judge who is neither a presiding judge nor a commissioned judge normally remains silent and defers to the opinions of the other two judges. One judge even pointed out that many requisitioned judges work on other things regardless of what is happening in the courtroom.[74] The presiding judge would normally choose not to interfere because, to ease the case load, there is an unspoken understanding between judges that allows the requisitioned judge to work on his/her own case.[75]

The above discussion on judicial deliberations provides a possible reason for why a joint deliberation process between professional judges and lay observers seems impractical. Despite how the law that requires judges to be independent and mandates every vote be equal among judges, in reality, judges usually defer to either power or information. Presiding judges are usually considered to be more influential than the other two judges in the panel. When a presiding judge refrains from exercising his influence, the panel usually defers to the opinion of the commissioned judge simply because he is more familiar with the case. If judges themselves are accustomed to defer to authority or the person who is most familiar with the case, how can we expect judges to listen to lay people, who neither have authority nor familiarity with the facts of cases? Adding a bottom layer to the deliberation hierarchy is not going to change how the people on top make decisions.

In summary, the above discussion shows that the nature of the inquisitorial criminal procedure, the training of judges, and the organizational culture of the judicial system are problems for a potential Taiwanese trial observer system. Simply asking lay participants to sit through trials may not make much difference to the judicial decision-making process after all.

Conclusion

The Judicial Yuan's attempt to adopt the trial observer system is worth praising. After all, introducing lay participants into the courtroom is a huge step forward for the Taiwanese judicial system. It shows that the leading officials of the Judicial Yuan realize Taiwan has transformed into a democratic country, and it is important for the court system to earn the trust of its people.

However, the experience of the lawyers who have participated in the moot trials shows that many judges simply have no interest in preserving the untainted opinion of the people. To achieve a coherent decision, judges tend to do all they

73 Ibid. at 144.
74 Ibid. at 153.
75 Ibid.

can to influence the decisions of trial observers. This casts doubts on the legitimacy of the trial observer system. The purpose of a lay participation system is to undermine the monopoly of elites in the legal arena, and to democratize the judicial system. If the Judicial Yuan is more interested in using the new system as a political measure to soothe the social outcry or as a tool of legal education than a reform that would help to improve the judicial decision-making process, then the core values of lay participation are defeated.

For the new system to succeed, this chapter suggests that the new bill should take the judicial culture and the nature of the inquisitorial system into consideration. In a traditional inquisitorial system, judges have always been the only authority in the courtroom. They have developed a unique culture that encourages judges to be aggressive, to make decisions independently, and to be in charge of the process. But the new lay participation system brings in another group of people to participate in the decision-making process. The new system provides a set of non-compulsory rules asking judges to accommodate the needs of that group of people, and to respect what they have to say. This requires a fundamental change to the mentality of judges. It is foreseeable that there will be large discrepancies among lay participation trials conducted by different judges, due to the loosely designed regulations. Therefore, the judicial authorities should direct their attention to revising rules to restrain the discretion and power of judges and to encourage them to recognize the contributions that lay participants may bring to the process.

8 Transformation from the top-down or bottom-up?

Legal education reform as a microcosm of Taiwan's inconclusive judicial reform process

Neil Chisholm and Hwei-Syin Chen

Taiwanese reforms in East Asian context: why was Taiwan different?

Taiwan's abrupt abandonment of plans to introduce an American-inspired law school system in 2007 suggests two questions in light of regional developments. First, why was the US graduate-level legal education model that was adopted, and modified, in Japan and Korea rejected in Taiwan? Second, why was legal educational reform hardly even on the agenda in Taiwan's judicial reform process? Given what occurred in neighboring countries with similar legal systems and moments of reform, we would have expected the opposite. The answers to these two questions help to address a third, more important issue: what were the features of Taiwan's judicial reform process that caused it to turn out so differently from the judicial reforms in Japan and Korea?

An outline of the law school reforms in Japan and Korea

Legal education was at the center of judicial reform in Japan and South Korea. In those countries, reformers were primarily concerned with expanding the number of lawyers from their relatively low numbers.[1] Postwar Japan, Korea, and Taiwan qualified comparatively low numbers of new lawyers each year, and this was widely believed to be a deliberate policy to maintain the strength of the government and its bureaucracy in economic and social life, the latter more

1 Prior to the law school reforms, it was well-known that there were very few lawyers in Korea and Japan. Dohyun Kim and Seung Heum Hwang, "Career Patterns of the Korean Legal Profession," in Dai-Kwon Choi and Kahei Rokumoto, eds., *Korea and Japan: Judicial System Transformation in the Globalizing World* (Seoul: Seoul National University Press, 2007), 141–55.

clearly important in authoritarian Korea and Taiwan.[2] However, various factors in each place led policymakers and legal system stakeholders to believe it to be necessary to increase the number of lawyers. Economic related motivations included a desire for a major reform to end the long-running slump in Japan and in Korea the fear of the local legal market falling under the domination of British and American law firms following the conclusion of free trade agreements with the US and EU.

To increase the numbers of lawyers, judicial reform negotiators needed to address the judicial examination. The examination was the means through which entry to the legal profession was restricted, with annual pass rates of around 5 percent or lower in the postwar era. Raising the pass rate of the examination meant not only a numerical adjustment to a quota, but an ideological shift from a German-derived "judicial examination," aimed at qualifying judges and prosecutors, to the more American-style "bar examination" designed primarily to certify practicing lawyers. In Korea, this shift involved renaming the exam the "Lawyer Examination" (*pyŏnhosa sihŏm*). Additionally, it was believed that merely raising the judicial exam's pass rate would remove all quality control and that improving undergraduate legal education was not a feasible replacement for the quality control mechanism embodied in the old exam.[3] The establishment of graduate-level law schools came to be seen as the best solution to the problem of quality assurance.

Reformers in Japan and Korea, often law professors themselves, desired to seize the opportunity to improve legal educational pedagogy. They had at least two reasons for this. First, they desired to improve their relative standing in the legal system. Law professors' role in educating lawyers had hitherto been, to some degree, usurped by cram schools – roughly analogous to bar preparation courses in the US. Low judicial exam pass rates meant that law students with any serious hope of being among the few who succeeded on the test attended cram schools outside of, and sometimes entirely as a replacement for, their university studies. A formal law degree course was widely viewed as insufficient preparation for the judicial exam, the gateway to the legal profession. Many students thus focused their energies on cram school rather than university law classes. To add insult to injury, law professors were sometimes looked down upon in the legal world as failed candidates for the judicial exam who had opted to obtain doctorates when they could not pass the test. These status-related considerations were more important in Korea.

Second, many reformist law professors sincerely believed that transforming the legal education system would improve the quality of lawyers and therefore

2 Tom Ginsburg, "Law and the Liberal Transformation of the Northeast Asian Legal Complex in Korea and Taiwan," in Terence Halliday, Lucien Karpik, and Malcolm Feeley, eds., *Fighting for Political Freedom: Comparative Studies of the Legal Complex and Political Liberalism* (Portland: Hart, 2007).

3 Mayumi Saegusa, "Why the Japanese Law School System was Established: Co-optation as a Defensive Tactic in the Face of Global Pressures," *Law and Social Inquiry* 34 (2009): 379–80.

benefit society and the economy. They were inspired by the example of America, with its graduate-level law schools and internationally successful law firms. The secret to its success seemed, to some, to lie in its legal education model. Students at the graduate level, many professors believed, approached the study of law with greater maturity and knowledge of social reality than East Asia's undergraduate law students. US legal education's lack of preoccupation with the bar examination also liberated students to learn law with intellectual interest rather than foreboding over a coming examination that would decide their career. The evidence of the American model's success seemed to be in its vibrant economy, in which its lawyers played a major role. This stood in contrast to the bureaucratic guidance of the East Asian economic model, whose prestige in Japan was damaged by a lengthy recession.

Judicial reform and legal education reform

Meanwhile, democratization loomed large in the decisions to expand the legal profession and reform legal education. This was especially true in Korea, where reformers believed that increasing the size of the bar would expand access to justice and result in a net benefit to society. Korean reformers thought that more lawyers would essentially mean more social problem-solvers for citizens, who had long been deprived of redress against government and big business by the rarity, high cost, and elite ethos among lawyers. A surprisingly similar line of thought existed in the already-democratic Japan. There, reformists believed that increasing the number of lawyers would shift the nation from relying on administrative guidance to the "rule of law," and the role of government in directing society would be transferred to citizens, lawyers, and courts. Japan's Justice System Reform Council directly stated this.[4] The adoption of US-style law schools was thus connected to democratic deepening or quality of democracy concerns that motivated judicial reform overall, although more so in Korea.

Democratization also played an important role in judicial reforms in Taiwan, although its judicial reform experience has differed greatly from that of Japan and Korea. In Taiwan, as elsewhere, the executive, President Lee Teng-Hui, pushed for an overhaul of the legal system. However, there was no one- or two-year-long deliberative committee, as in Japan and Korea respectively. In 1999, a three-day conference was initiated by Weng Yueh-Sheng, Lee's appointee as President of the Judicial Yuan, the institution charged with overseeing the judicial branch. Participants in the National Judicial Reform Conference (NJRC) discussed various issues for the first two days and spent the final day voting on several resolutions, seeking consensus on reform. Reform of the legal educational system was only

4 "This 'rule of law' constitutes an essential base for promoting deregulation, aiming at abolishing unclear advance administrative control and converting to an after-the-fact review/remedy type society …" The Justice System Reform Council, *Recommendations of the Justice System Reform Council*, 12 June 2001, https://japan.kantei.go.jp/policy/sihou/singikai/990612_e.html.

addressed in one of the items, and it failed to make it to the final agenda, demonstrating the issue's lack of urgency.[5] The Judicial Reform Foundation, the leading NGO advocating judicial reform, called for expanding postgraduate legal education six months before the Conference, but it did not ask for the abolition of existing undergraduate institutions.[6]

By contrast, in Japan legal education reform was at the heart of judicial reform discussions. Increasing the number of lawyers was a key goal of the reforms. The body that created the roadmap for judicial reform, the Justice System Reform Council, was staffed by law professors from elite universities along with representatives from the judiciary, legal profession, business world, and leading social groups. The Committee's 13 members largely deferred to the elite law professors in designing the new law school system. They promised more emphasis on practical training to keep the quality of lawyers high, and new guidelines required that over 20 percent of professors have practical experience.[7] The elite law professors also initially desired to open a small number of graduate-level schools and abolish the undergraduate law departments. But compromises led to a large number of law schools being allowed to open and undergraduate law departments being left open. After the 74 law schools opened in 2004, the qualifying exam's pass rate rose to around 50 percent,[8] although it has since fallen, and the legal profession expanded significantly.

Korea's judicial reform process was very similar to Japan's. A 21-member, consensus-seeking body composed of representatives from various legal and social sectors, the Judicial Reform Committee deliberated from 2004 to 2005 over various proposals for reform. The expansion of the legal profession was a leading issue in the discussions. Pro-reform NGOs and professors wanted to increase citizens' access to justice, while the judicial establishment (lawyers, judges, and prosecutors) was on the defensive owing to widespread public distrust of the court system. Unlike in Japan, the judiciary, prosecutors, and lawyers' association representatives put up significant resistance to the idea of establishing graduate-level law schools, but the professors were eventually able to gain the support of senior judges. Many high-ranking judges had obtained LLM degrees in US law schools thanks to a judiciary-sponsored "overseas training" program, and their experiences gave them positive views of the American system. Other factors contributed to the victory of the professors' position, and these included strong executive support from President Roh Moo-Hyun, Japan's

5 司法院 [Judicial Yuan], 全國司法改革會議, 下輯 [National Judicial Reform Conference Proceedings, Volume 2] (臺北 [Taipei]: 司法院 [Judicial Yuan], 1999): 1569.

6 民間司法改革基金會 [Judicial Reform Foundation], 司法改革藍皮書 [Judicial Reform Blueprint] (Taipei: Judicial Reform Foundation Press, 1999): 48.

7 Hisashi Aizawa, "Japanese Legal Education in Transition," *Wisconsin International Law Journal* 24 (2006): 142.

8 This paragraph draws from information in Saegusa, "Why the Japanese Law School System Was Established," 385–93.

recent example, and the growing perception of a need to strengthen the legal profession ahead of a future opening to competition from Anglo-American firms. Reformist professors, long dissatisfied with Korean legal education, had wanted the law school reform since at least 1995, when they lost the argument in President Kim Young-Sam's Presidential Committee on Globalization. But following the 2004–05 judicial reform process, law professors were granted much autonomy in designing the new system, and they eventually succeeded in drastically limiting the number of law schools to 25, which opened in 2009. Furthermore, only law school graduates would be allowed to sit the exam, unlike in Japan where non-law school students could take the exam if they first passed a preliminary test. Korea's limits on the number of law schools and exam takers are significant points of difference with the Japanese situation. But as in Japan, the schools would hire at least 20 percent of new professors from among practitioners.[9] The law professors who designed Korea's new law school system paid close attention and numerable visits to Japan during the planning process in order to learn from Japan's perceived failures and successes.

In 2005, Taiwan eventually followed the Japanese and Korean examples in debating a law school reform. In fact, Taiwan's law school reform process was in some ways similar to its East Asian neighbors' processes – although it occurred later and as a reaction to these processes – but the results were strikingly different in Taiwan: the graduate-level law school model was rejected and a bottom-up legal pedagogical reform movement was initiated. This chapter examines why Taiwan rejected the US model and compares its reform process with those of Japan and Korea. It highlights the special factors in Taiwanese law and politics that led to its very different outcomes in legal educational reform and judicial reform more generally. Assessing legal educational reform in light of judicial reform reveals recurring themes in the politics of systemic legal reform in Taiwan. Although the Taiwanese law school proposal was not fully attached to judicial reform, the fundamental reasons why it collapsed and was reborn in a new form are closely related to the similarly uneven progress in Taiwan's still-unfinished judicial reforms.

This chapter first analyzes the situation in Taiwan leading up to the law school proposal, covering the history of legal education, the low number of lawyers, and why legal educational reform was absent from the 1999 National Judicial Reform Conference. Next the chapter recounts the story of the law school reform process and its ultimate failure while also examining the perspectives of participants and observers of the reform attempt. Third, the chapter explains the rebirth of legal educational reform as a "bottom-up" effort addressing pedagogy. The chapter concludes by evaluating Taiwan's reforms in East Asian context and their significance in judicial reform.

9 Youngjoon Kwon, "Recent Reform in Korean Legal Education," *Journal of Korean Law* 13 (2013): 21.

Taiwan's legal education tradition and early reforms

Modern legal education in Taiwan began during the Japanese colonial period (1895–1945). To become a lawyer, one needed to travel to Japan for training. While the precursor to National Taiwan University (NTU) had no law department, it had a Department of Government that taught legal subjects such as criminal law, civil law, and administrative law, among others. Under the Japanese conception of legal education, law was treated as a social science subject akin to politics. Even though Japan lost control of Taiwan and its educational institutions after World War II, the Japanese conception of legal training was maintained because the new government of Taiwan, the Republic of China, had followed Japanese models in its drive for modernization. Legal education in Taiwan formally commenced in 1946 when the first College of Law was founded at NTU, and this department was also home to the political science faculty.[10] National Chengchi University's (NCCU) law college, traditionally viewed as the second best in Taiwan, was established in 1961 and it also included social science departments alongside law.

The first major structural break with Taiwan's tradition of legal education came with the creation of an American-style, graduate-level program at Soochow University. Hitherto, graduate-level legal education began to appear in Taiwan gradually, with NTU, for example, creating a master's program in 1955 and a Ph.D. course in 1974. These degrees complemented undergraduate legal training. But in the late 1980s, Li Mo (李模), a well-connected law professor and government advisor, urged Soochow to create an American-inspired, Juris Doctor-like program. Li had obtained an LL.M. degree from Harvard Law School in 1956, and his experience had given him a positive impression of US legal education.[11] He envisioned a three-year master's course that, unlike existing graduate programs, taught law to students who had not studied it as undergraduates. Additionally, the course would provide a more diverse curriculum and include some US-style pedagogy, such as classroom discussion. Li's proposal was considered radical, and it faced much opposition. Professor Lin Tzu-Yi said in an interview that it was Li's good relationship with the then-head of the Executive Yuan, Premier Hau Pei-Tsun, a senior military officer turned KMT politician, that enabled him to receive government permission to create the program. Soochow University, for its part, was willing to experiment and potentially boost its standing among Taiwanese law departments. The program opened in 1990 as the "Group B Master's Course"

10 Tay-Sheng Wang, trans. Sean Cooney, "The Development of Legal Education in Taiwan: An Analysis of the History of Law and Society," in Stacey Steele and Kathryn Taylor, eds., *Legal Education in Asia: Globalization, Change and Contexts* (New York: Routledge, 2010), 135–40.

11 李模先生簡歷 [Mr. Li Mo's Resume], http://ktli.sinica.edu.tw/people/%A7%F5%BC%D2.html.

(碩乙班).[12] Its students often came from government, and after graduating most returned to their former work rather than become lawyers. This led some professors to question whether the famous program truly represented the introduction of US-style legal education.[13] In any case, its example would inspire other law departments.

The relatively low passage rate on the judicial and bar examinations has been an important feature of Taiwanese legal education. The Judicial Examination (司法官考試) that has qualified judges and prosecutors has had a pass rate of around 4 percent since the 1960s. The Lawyer Examination (律師考試) had a pass rate of around 17.5 percent in the 1950s, but it fell to about 2 percent on average during the 1960s, 1970s, and 1980s. In the 1990s, the passage rate rose to about 9 percent on average.[14] Taiwan's 1960–80s' success ratios were thus comparable to those of the Japanese and Korean judicial examinations over the same era. In some years, Taiwan's Lawyer Examination had extremely low pass rates, such as for example 0.81 percent in 1970, 0.87 percent in 1973, 0.75 percent in 1978, 0.34 percent in 1980, and 0.75 percent in 1988.[15]

The following year, however, there was a remarkable change. In 1989 the Examination Yuan – the branch of Taiwan's unique, five-power constitutional order that administers state examinations – unexpectedly raised the pass rate of the Lawyer Examination to about 14 percent. This abrupt increase suggests two questions: why were bar exam pass rates kept so low historically, and why did the rate jump in 1989? The Examination Yuan has never publicly explained its reasons regarding the bar examination passage rate, and neither have historians of the legal profession uncovered any direct evidence on these issues. The most reasonable conjectures on these questions relate to Taiwan's then-unfolding democratization and perceived economic pressures. Prior to 1989 and the turn to democracy, Taiwan's authoritarian government did not desire a vibrant civil society or bar. This authoritarian apprehension stemmed from the anti-government activities of dissent lawyers. For example, several lawyers were arrested in the 1979 Formosa Magazine Incident protest against the government, and their defense team included Chen Shui-Bian, who was later elected President in 2000. Starting in the late 1980s, however, Taiwan's government began to liberalize, partially lifting martial law in 1987 and holding fair elections in 1991. It was in these transitional years that the Examination Yuan seemed to respond to criticism from law professors and lawyers

12 A comprehensive English-language account of the creation of Soochow University's program can be found at: Joseph L. Pratt, "The Two Gates of National Taiwan University School of Law," *UCLA Pacific Basin Law Journal* 19 (2001): 163–7.

13 Tay-Sheng Wang, "The Development of Legal Education in Taiwan," 142.

14 Ibid., 140.

15 陳惠馨 [Chen Hwei-Syin], "百年來台灣的法學教育與法曹的養成制度" [100 Years of Taiwan' Legal Education and Legal Professional Training Systems], in 陳惠馨 [Chen Hwei-Syin], ed., 法學專業教育制度比較: 以法學教育改革為核心 [Legal Professional Education System Comparisons: Focusing on Legal Education Reform] (臺北 [Taipei]: 元照 [Angle Press], 2010), 78.

by raising the passage rate so highly that the 288 passers of the 1989 Lawyer Examination represented about 36 percent of all 782 lawyers qualified by the test over the 1950–88 period.[16] Economic concerns about liberalization and future WTO membership may also have played a role in the Examination Yuan's decision, as many believed these goals required a strengthening of the legal profession.

Another important change to the legal education environment has been the substantial increase in the number of law departments over the past two decades. In 1990, there were only eight law-teaching departments in Taiwan. But from the 1990s onwards, many new universities opened, and the number of legal education institutions mushroomed. By 2006 there were 109 undergraduate and graduate legal departments at 37 universities.[17] The rise in the number of universities and law-teaching institutions seems to have been part of the global trend toward the expansion of higher education. The increase was also aided by the Taiwanese government's more laissez-faire approach to accreditation since the 1990s. Another reason for the creation of the new law programs was their appeal to university administrators seeking low-cost means of raising student enrollment and tuition revenue.[18]

The gradual spread of Li Mo's Soochow model of graduate-level legal education was another cause for the expansion of legal education. The model was quickly adopted by National Taiwan Ocean University (1991), National Defense Management College (1992), and other universities later. These programs sometimes positioned themselves as offering specialist legal training – for example National Taiwan Ocean University's course concentrated on maritime law. In 2000, National Chiao Tung University and National Tsing Hua University established a joint law and technology graduate program, which has since split, that drew synergy from the universities' location in Hsinchu, a city known for its technology industry. Taiwan's two leading schools, NTU and NCCU, followed the trend in 2004 and 1997 respectively.[19] Currently, it is estimated that there are 17 graduate-level law programs for non-law undergraduate majors and 300–500 students enrolled in these courses.

Professors and deans view the new programs as problematic for several reasons. They say that students commonly drop out after about a year, because they only desired to obtain the 20 credits required to take the bar exam; they want to study for the examination at a cram school (補習班, *buxiban*);[20] the

16 Jane Kaufman Winn and Tang-chi Yeh, "Advocating Democracy: The Role of Lawyers in Taiwan's Political Transformation," *Law and Social Inquiry* 20 (1995): 573.

17 Tay-Sheng Wang, "The Development of Legal Education in Taiwan," 141.

18 Ibid.

19 The definitive English-language account of the debate on the opening of the program at NTU is Joseph L. Pratt, "The Two Gates of National Taiwan University School of Law," 169–81.

20 The influence of *buxiban* cram schools on Taiwan's legal profession is comprehensively explained in Grace Shu-chin Kuo, "Another Form of Legal Education: Examining the Cramming Culture and Legal Professional Identity in Taiwan," *Dong-A Law Review* 39 (2006): 1–29.

course was harder than they expected; or, because of pressure from their parents and the wider culture, to begin to support themselves after undergraduate studies. Another problem is that at most schools besides Soochow, graduates simply sit in on undergraduate courses, despite their different learning needs. Teachers report that graduate law students are more creative while undergraduates are analytically superior – an assessment commonly made in Japan and Korea as well.

An important effect of the expansion of legal education has been the perceived problem that many institutions, especially at the new and private universities, produce no graduates who pass the annual Lawyer Examination. Many professors at elite law programs are alarmed by this and view it as a negative consequence of the enlargement of legal education. The Ministry of Education reportedly takes a similar view but is concerned from the perspective of wasted state subsidies and student time. This anxiety is intensified by the issue of declining birth rates and student enrollment in universities. Officials in the Ministry have worried that the number of law programs is unsustainably large. However, other professors argue that the increased availability of a legal education makes knowledge of law more widespread in society and benefits non-lawyers who will deal with law in their careers.

A final reform of note has been the separation of law departments from other social science subjects, which had been housed together since the Japanese era. At NTU, for example, the College of Law contained the departments of law, political science, and economics. Law professors who obtained doctoral degrees in the US felt that this was improper, and their numbers grew over time. In 1993, Fa Zhi-Bin (法治斌), an American-educated law professor who headed NCCU's law department, pushed through a separation of the law and social science departments, of which there were about ten. Thereafter the law program stood apart within its own College of Law. This reform later spread throughout Taiwan, with NTU adopting a similar change in 1999.

The reform effort at NTU was led by then-department head, Lin Tzu-Yi, who said in an interview that the process was complicated by symbolic considerations of whether the law department or the other departments were to be seen as leaving their shared College. The separation was ultimately amicable in that regard, but the discussion also came to involve the issue of graduate-level legal education. In the late 1990s and during Lin's term as department head, NTU professors debated whether they should create a Soochow-style graduate program and whether that program ought to be the only law course at all. In other words, the faculty considered following the American J.D. system. The scholars split according to where they had obtained their doctorates, with US-educated professors mainly supporting such a move while German- and Japanese-trained faculty members were opposed. The American-educated professors, concerned about the growing complexity of Taiwanese society and its lawyers' competitiveness vis-à-vis international law firms, argued that it was clear that lawyers needed knowledge of non-law subjects, whether scientific or social-scientific, and they elicited sympathy from opponents on this point. Lin and his allies contended that it would be easier to teach law at the graduate level to students already trained in other subjects than vice versa – teaching lawyers scientific or social-scientific subjects at the graduate level. The outlines of the debate are explained in greater detail elsewhere,[21] but the conclusions of the discussions were that the law department would become an independent College of Law and a graduate-level program would be introduced without abolishing the undergraduate program. The Soochow-style course opened in 2004. This debate was important because as the leading law school in Taiwan, if NTU had opted to shift all education to the graduate level, it would have set an authoritative example for the rest of Taiwanese legal academia, akin to the gradual beginnings of the American J.D. course.

The discussions at NTU in the late 1990s can be seen as the embryo of the later 2005–07 law school reform effort. Although they lost the debate, many of NTU's US-trained law professors continued to support the adoption of the main elements of American legal education, including its graduate nature, classroom dialogue, and the use of casebooks. According to interviewees, many professors favoring varying degrees of reform were disappointed by the 1999 National Conference on Judicial Reform, because it did not recommend significant legal educational reform measures. The Conference did pass an "interim proposal" that suggested that the Ministry of Education should consider changing law departments into independent law colleges.[22] This was an anti-climactic development for US-trained, reform-minded professors, because the judicial reform conference was meant to be a transformative moment of change following democratization.

Why was legal education reform, which was at the heart of the Japanese and Korean judicial reform processes, not a major issue in Taiwan? One answer, some Taiwanese law professors suggest, is that the NJRC was held under the aegis of the Judicial Yuan, which does not actually control legal education institutions. Legal education is governed more by the Ministry of Education, under the Executive Yuan, and the Examination Yuan, which sets the qualification examinations. Thus the NJRC would not have been the appropriate authority to recommend changes to legal education, some say.

Another explanation is that the pressure for legal education reform was removed by the Examination Yuan's 1989 decision to raise the Lawyer Examination's passage rate. In Japan and Korea, no such change occurred, and the issue of expanding the practicing bar retained its urgency until their judicial reform processes occurred. The Japanese and Korean law school reforms were adopted mainly because of their connection with the more important agenda item of increasing the number of lawyers. But in Taiwan, the problem of the low bar

21 Joseph L. Pratt, "The Two Gates of National Taiwan University School of Law," 169–81.

22 司法院 [Judicial Yuan], 全國司法改革會議, 下輯 [National Judicial Reform Conference Proceedings, Volume 2], 1569.

exam pass rate was already solved, making legal education a relatively less pressing issue in its judicial reform process.

By about 2000, Taiwan's postwar legal education tradition had been transformed by various reforms, but no wholesale adoption of the US law school model had been undertaken. The Lawyer Examination passage rate had been raised, a new graduate-level course for students with no legal background was adopted, the new course had diffused to several law schools across the island, and law faculties were declaring independence from the social science departments under which they had existed since the Japanese colonial era. During the late 1990s, discussion of further legal education reform had been ongoing but was inconclusive. In December 1999, the Taiwan Law Society held a conference on legal education, but no consensus on reforms emerged. About five years later, the professors who favored adoption of the American-style law school system would re-emerge to push for change.

Too "top-down?" The movement to adopt American-style law schools

While the story of Taiwan's law school reform has been recounted in English by Wang Tay-Sheng and also by Thomas Chih-Hsiung Chen, this section presents new information gathered through interviews with Taiwanese professors as well as new interpretations of the facts.[23]

The course of events

The opening of Japan's new law school system in 2004 and Korea's decision to adopt a similar system in 2005 spurred action in Taiwan. In 2004, the Ministry of Justice held a conference that discussed recent changes in Japan as well as Germany. In March 2005, Vice President Annette Lu (呂秀蓮), in her capacity as head of the Presidential Human Rights Advisory Commission, created the "Taiwan Legal Personnel Training System Reform Committee" (台灣法律人養成制度改革委員會), which set out to establish a law school system in Taiwan. Interviewees suggested that Lu's motive for creating the Committee was to gain a policy victory that would help position her as a candidate in the upcoming 2008 presidential election. The practical reason for such a committee was to bridge the divides between the various state agencies in charge of legal training and qualification: the Examination Yuan governs testing, the Judicial Yuan selects judges, the Ministry of Justice selects prosecutors, and the Ministry of Education oversees universities.

The Committee delegated the task of researching and planning reform to Professor Lo Chang-Fa (羅昌發), the Dean of National Taiwan University's College

23 This section relies on interviews conducted by the co-author, Neil Chisholm.

of Law (2003–07). He organized three conferences to discuss legal educational reform. An international conference that included participants from America, Japan, and Korea was held in September 2005 to hear their advice. In October, a conference with the Examination Yuan convened to discuss the practicalities of changes to the legal practitioner examination and the examination for "judicial officials" (i.e., judges and prosecutors). The final conference in November elicited domestic opinions on the changes.[24] After these three forums, and about a year of research and deliberation, in April 2006 the Committee completed its work and produced a white paper on recommendations for reform. The white paper indicated that three-year graduate-level law schools should be established and that their degrees would serve as the main qualification for entry to the legal profession. It also suggested that the lawyer examination passage rate should be raised to 70 percent, that teacher to student ratios be 12 : 1, and that 20 percent of teachers at the schools be drawn from practitioners – all points that demonstrate a high degree of policy diffusion from the Japanese and Korean experiences. The question of whether and how long undergraduate law departments would operate was left open to further discussion, but the reformers leaned toward shifting the focus of legal education to the graduate-level institutes. Importantly, the report not only called for structural changes, but the introduction of new teaching methodologies involving greater classroom discussion and the American "Socratic Method."

In the same month of April 2006 Vice President Lu's Presidential Human Rights Advisory Commission moved swiftly to the planning stage for the creation of the law schools, which were termed "Legal Professional Graduate Schools" (alternatively, "Institutes;" 法律專業研究所), with Lo continuing to head the effort. By October 2006, he finished drawing up law school accreditation guidelines for the Ministry of Education.[25] In interviews, critics and proponents of the plans indicated that only six or seven law schools would be permitted to operate. One opponent worried about the geographic distribution of the schools:

> Professor Lo … tried to adopt the South Korean system [of closing most law departments]. The government thought there should only be six or seven law schools, so many professors thought that they would be NTU, NCCU … one in the South, one in Central Taiwan, and perhaps two or three left for North Taiwan.

24 王泰升 [Wang Tay-Sheng], "台灣法學教育的發展與省思：一個法律社會史的分析" [The Development of and Reflections on Taiwan's Legal Education: A Legal Sociological Analysis], 臺北大學法學論叢 [Taipei University Law Review] 68 (2008): 27–8. This article is the basis for Wang's aforementioned book chapter that was translated and abridged by Sean Cooney.

25 Thomas Chih-hsiung Chen, "Legal Education Reform in Taiwan: Are Japan and Korea the Models?" *Journal of Legal Education* 62 (2012): 49–50.

This design alarmed many law departments, especially at the dozens of young private schools that seemed to be facing closure. As planning for the law schools proceeded, professors began to gather in informal meetings to discuss their disagreements with the reform that was taking shape.[26] In early April 2007, Chen Ming-Zhen (陳明真) a Member of the Legislative Yuan, introduced a bill that would have moved their opening up to 2013. Acting separately from Lo, Chen's proposal settled the question of maintaining undergraduate legal training by making it clear that only students who studied at the graduate-level schools would be permitted to take qualifying examinations.

In April 2007, Chen Hwei-Syin (陳惠馨), then-head of NCCU's graduate law department and the co-author of this chapter, wrote a press release petition voicing opposition to Chen's bill. As organizer of many of the opposition meetings, she arranged this statement signed by 39 professors. Among other issues, the press release drew attention to the low number of students that would be permitted to enroll in the law schools annually – 650 total per year.[27] Such a low number would have represented a major decline for law schools since at that time NTU alone had around twice as many students in total in its graduate and undergraduate law department. Under the reform plan, NTU's law school would have shrunk to about 300 students, or about 100 per annual cohort. In addition, the concerned professors saw no problem in principle with undergraduate law departments and thought that they should at least be permitted to operate alongside new law schools.

Professor Lo indicated in an interview that he was amenable to a compromise on the question of the future of undergraduate law departments. He believed that undergraduate students could be permitted to study law if they first completed two years of another major, thus obtaining the non-legal knowledge base many reformists desired lawyers to have. Under Lo's vision, these undergraduates would then be permitted to transfer into graduate level-law schools and even continue their undergraduate work as a double major. According to Lo, other law professors declined to accept such a compromise, as they believed law required students' full attention.

In June 2007 a delegation of ten law school administrators met with President Chen Shui-Bian to ask for an end to the reforms. Two similar delegations had earlier visited the Ministry of Education and Examination Yuan. President Chen acceded to the law professors' requests and withdrew executive-branch

26 Additional information on these meetings can be found in the appendices of the following report: 陳惠馨 [Chen Hwei-Syin], "化危機為轉機 – 談法學界如何因應法學教育改革的呼聲" [Turning a Crisis into a Turning Point – Discussion on Legal Educators' Response to Legal Education Reform], June 23, 2007.

27 陳惠馨 and 王晨桓 [Chen Hwei-Syin and Wang Chen-Huan], "台灣各大學法律相關系所主管針對 '國內法學教育變革' 公聽會發表新聞稿" [Taiwanese Universities' Law-Related Department Heads' "Domestic Legal Education Reform" Public Hearing Press Release], April 18, 2007, http://fuldali.blogspot.tw/2007/04/blog-post_18.html.

involvement in the reform process. This petition was made in the political context of the latter half of Chen's second term. During this period, Chen's political capital was dwindling amidst accusations of financial scandals involving him and his family. Perhaps more importantly, the failed assassination attempt on the eve of Chen's 2004 re-election triggered public suspicions that he arranged the shooting to boost his popularity. All this led to partisan warfare that lasted throughout his second term. As one opponent of the law school reforms said of the timing, "it was not hard to say no to the government."

Yet this was not the end of the law school reform process. It should be noted that by this point Lo Chang-Fa had finished his term as Dean of NTU's College of Law and been replaced by reform opponent Tsai Ming-Cheng. With the transfer of power, Lo had relinquished a position that conferred moral authority to enact reform. But as the prospects for the law school reform looked bleak, on August 14, 2007 legislator Chen Ming-Zhen reintroduced his earlier bill requiring the establishment of law schools.[28] His proposal left only about six years for the schools to be planned, established, and for the unselected programs to be closed. By this point opponents of the reforms were alarmed but also tired of the issue, and for a time it seemed as if Chen's bill would be passed by the legislature. However, some law students approached Chen Hwei-Syin and requested that she act again to block the reform. She told them that they needed to lead the charge and suggested they contact key legislators to urge them to halt the bill. The students did so, and the law school proposal was finally abandoned. (Additionally, it has been said that medical departments feared that their undergraduate programs might be next in line for reform, and therefore they pressured the Ministry of Education to lobby legislators to reject the bill).[29] Officially, the bill failed following the absence of consensus after two committee sessions and 12 party caucus negotiations.[30]

The perspectives and motivations of actors in the law school reform process

The views of participants in the reform effort are crucial for understanding why the process unfolded as it did. It is first of all important to note that many professors and observers were dissatisfied with the structure of the undergraduate law curriculum and the way law has traditionally been taught in Taiwan.[31] One

28 陳明真 [Chen Ming-Zhen], 高等考試法官檢察官律師考試條例草案 [Higher Examination Judge, Prosecutor, and Lawyer Examination Regulation Draft], August 14, 2007, www.ly.gov.tw/03_leg/0301_main/leg_bill/billList.action?lgno=00132&stage=6.

29 Tzung-Mou Wu informed the author of this "slippery slope" concern, which was also shared by business departments.

30 立法院 [Legislative Yuan], 委員會紀錄 [Committee Records], March 5, 2008, 258, https://lci.ly.gov.tw/LyLCEW/communique/final/pdf/97/03/LCIDC01_970301_00007.pdf. The author thanks Tzung-Mou Wu for notifying him of this document and these details.

31 Tay-Sheng Wang, "The Development of Legal Education in Taiwan," 143–46, 149.

activist at the Judicial Reform Foundation explained that the low pass rates of the qualifying examinations cause students to avoid elective courses in favor of doctrinal classes that lead them to become narrow-minded and unaware of law's social context. He bluntly stated that "the exam leads education, and students don't care about education." The activist also mentioned concerns about students' passivity and independence of thought:

> Lectures do not have debate or use the Socratic Method. But lecturing is the traditional way because of Chinese culture's authoritarianism. Professors enjoy their authority and being respected as teachers.... Students are too young to study law from high school ... a graduate degree course would make them more independent.

A judge agreed with these arguments, saying, "When I learned civil law, I just learned what the law is and how you explain it. I didn't know what the connection was between law and real life."

One professor indicated that the key problem of legal education has been that students are required to memorize set interpretations of the law and repeat them on the bar exam, while practical skills are neglected:

> We always emphasize the interpretation of statutes, the meaning of legal provisions. We use cases to show this. We do not teach students to find facts or arguments from real cases. The bar examination comes from interpretations, the memorization of official reasoning.... The German style [prevalent in Taiwan] is this: professors tell students the details of a theory, they illustrate it with an imaginary case, and students learn to understand how to apply legal provisions to circumstances. [Students] don't need to worry about finding facts. In the final exam, the professor gives facts and the student gives the answer.

This professor also said that in academic discussions on how to improve legal education, "professors often advocate reforms according to foreign systems, based on where he or she studied." The professor, who received a degree in the US, added that, "I welcome American legal educational methodology. I use it in my class. But I don't think we need to introduce a graduate-level-only system." On the conclusions of the scholarly discussions, he said, "My colleagues have no incentive [to change how they teach]. We've discussed it for over ten years, but there is no result. Professors have the freedom to teach how they want."

Generally, key criticisms of legal education often include students' narrow-mindedness and lack of social awareness, and the causes of these problems are identified as their youth as undergraduate students, the centrality of memorization of official legal interpretations, and the lawyer and judicial examinations' testing of memorized material. An additional concern is that most students' efforts are wasted as they will never pass either of the examinations. The lawyer exam's pass rate currently hovers around 10 percent. No satisfactory answer to this problem has been agreed upon, since raising the passage rate would worsen the oversupply of lawyers and harm the legal profession's prestige, while reducing numbers of law students would harm schools' budgets.

Regarding reforms that would raise the quality of legal training, a seminal article on the issue was published by Professor Tzu-Yi Lin in 2000.[32] In the article, which he said in an interview that he wrote because of the NJRC's failure to address legal education in-depth, the US-trained professor advocated for the adoption of America's J.D. model. The problems he identified with Taiwanese legal education included: a need for better lawyers for society in the post-democratization era; that legal training needed to respond to changing technologies; the necessity for internationally minded lawyers to improve the foreign investment climate and compete with the Anglo-American international firms that would be allowed to practice in Taiwan; and gaps between theory and practice that would need to be addressed through reformed teaching materials and clinical education. These challenges, Lin argued, had to be addressed through the adoption of the J.D. model and legal curriculum reforms based on American legal educational practices. Although Lin's vision was not implemented, it influenced academic discourse. Eventually, his call for clinical education on the US model was realized at his university, NTU, through the efforts of Lo Chang-Fa and Serge A. Martinez, an American visiting professor in 2011–13.[33]

During the 2005–07 period, while Lo was Dean of NTU's College of Law, he sought to realize the implementation of the system Lin advocated. Lo said in an interview that his background as a specialist in trade law and WTO issues deeply affected his outlook. Working in a highly internationalized field of law, he had many opportunities to interact with foreign professors, hear about legal education in their countries, and compare overseas developments with the situation in Taiwan. Lo was particularly impressed with China:

> I observed the development of China. Peking University has the School of Transnational Law in Shenzhen.... I'm not sure if it's a success, but what highly impacted me was their ambition, willingness to change, and creativity.... I personally saw ambitions in a number of areas. It shocked me. Because in the past, we considered ourselves ahead of China, but they're catching up or have surpassed us in many areas like international law, international business, and UN instruments for transactions.

32 林子儀 [Lin Tzu-Yi], "法學基礎教育的課程內容" [The Curricular Content of Foundational Legal Education], 台灣法學會學報 [Taiwan Law Society Journal] 21 (2000).

33 For additional information on Martinez' views on clinical legal education in Taiwan, see Serge A. Martinez, "Law Clinics in Taiwan: Can Clinical Legal Education Succeed in This Civil Law Jurisdiction with an Undergraduate Legal Education System?" *National Taiwan University Law Review* 7 (2012).

He also elaborated on how seeing this gave him a sense of urgency about reform:

> Thcy have ambition, resources, and young scholars active at international conferences. This is not common in Taiwan. So this gave me an urgent feeling that we needed to do something, that it was urgent to make students and professors more active in international activities.

Lo initially focused his efforts on training a small group of students to participate in international WTO moot events while encouraging others to go to the US to obtain doctoral degrees. After he became Dean of NTU, his interest in legal education intensified:

> My concern for legal education came from my NTU deanship. Previously, I did research and didn't care much about other things. I just thought my work was more important. After I assumed the deanship, I observed closely the content of legal education in other schools and countries. The only thing in my mind was "we are good enough in Asia!" … I exchanged views with colleagues from Japan; I have a lot of international friends, and I chatted with them about legal education. I started to look at the situation in NTU, though it is not easy to reform from inside the college.… First, it's too personal, we meet on a daily basis, and second, if only NTU changes, that doesn't change the bar exam and then not much changes [overall]. So we need a nationwide reform.

Lo thus came to view Taiwanese legal academia as declining relative to other Asian countries, and this served as his main motivation during the reform process. Indeed, the title of one of the two English-language articles he wrote on reform demonstrates the comparative mentality that inspired Lo: "Driving an Ox Cart to Catch up with the Space Shuttle."[34]

The other English-language article Lo published made clear his views on the specific items of his reform proposal.

> 1. One of the positive elements of the US J.D. system is that graduates have the choice of whether to study law immediately after graduation or after several years of work, perhaps when they realise that the study of law would help them in their existing profession or because they would like to become lawyers.… These students will have richer social experiences and wider knowledge in some other fields. They will enrich the legal community as students, academics or practitioners. This

34 Chang-Fa Lo, "Driving an Ox Cart to Catch up with the Space Shuttle: The Need for and Prospects of Legal Education Reform in Taiwan," *Wisconsin International Law Journal* 24 (2006).

ameliorates the problem now faced of students being too young and unable to appreciate the complexities of law and society.

2. The proposed system would also allow students who have completed two years of undergraduate studies (in other fields) to take law as part of their double major, or to transfer to the J.D. programme. This is the second source of students. In other words, law schools will not admit students directly from high schools. Students must first enter into other (undergraduate) departments to complete at least two years of (non-legal) education before they can be admitted into law schools. If they decide to do a double major, they can maintain their original major with their (undergraduate) department while they study law.... Compared to students entering law school immediately after high school, these students will be more mature and have more general knowledge when they start studying law.[35]

The first two points of Lo's plan address the complaint of students' immaturity and lack of wider social and academic knowledge to aid their understanding of law. He clearly viewed graduate-level legal education as the solution to these issues. The remaining points of the plan dealt with other problems:

3. The proposed system must introduce more interactive teaching methods and clinical legal training.... We need to train students to "think like a lawyer" and to be more adept at dealing with real disputes.
4. There must be an accreditation system established to ensure that the law schools have sufficient teaching staff and resources.... This will help to ensure that legal education in any law school in Taiwan will be of a certain acceptable quality.
5. There must be a reform of the professional examination system. Currently, those in charge of professional examinations are not comfortable with increasing the passing rate.... If we are able to improve the quality of university legal education, those responsible for the professional examinations can be persuaded to increase the passing rate significantly. Only then will law students not be unduly distracted from their academic legal education by the need to pass the professional examinations.[36]

The third point indicated curricular reforms to accompany the structural reforms. Here Lo suggested that the adoption of the Socratic Method and clinical education would be desirable. These proposals proved to be controversial as the more

35 Chang-Fa Lo, "Possible Reform for Legal Education in Taiwan: A Refined 'J.D. System'?" *Asian Journal of Comparative Law* 1 (2006): 6–7.

36 Ibid., 7.

traditionalist and Continentally inclined law professors believed them to be too alien to legal education as they knew it. Interactive learning would also challenge the traditional Confucian cultural image of the student-teacher relationship as that of a humble disciple learning from a learned master. Lo's fourth and fifth points related to closing down most law schools in order to reduce the number of takers for the bar examination, which would make it politically possible to maintain a high passage rate. This would solve one of the classic perceived problems of legal education in East Asia – students' focus on cramming to pass the examination over intellectual enrichment.

Professor Lo believed there were several reasons for the collapse for the reform effort. In an interview, he cited a "lack of leadership" politically and the absence of "consensus" among law professors. Regarding leadership, he indicated that the Ministry of Education and Vice President Lu were insufficiently determined to see reform through, while President Chen was not strongly supportive enough. As to the opposition of legal academics, it existed for various reasons. First, Lo believed they mainly liked the fact that students were college-aged, either because they wanted to "inculcate values in the young" or because they felt that while graduate-level students were more creative, undergraduate-taught law students had better analytical skills. Second, small, private law departments, long believed to be of inferior quality and whose graduates rarely passed the bar or judicial exams, did not want to "shut down and focus on paralegals," legal clerical training, or teaching real estate agent courses. Third, professors did not want to hire practitioners, because, unlike in Korea and Japan, this was thought to be improper. According to Lo, NTU professors feared lawyers would use teaching positions to "advertise or improve their law firms' [reputations]. They didn't see that 'they're helping us,' but 'we're giving them the name of NTU!' " This attitude could be related to the Confucian cultural preference for teachers over commercial agents or the fact that Taiwan's expansion of the quota for bar exam passage diminished the prestige of the profession relative to law professors by the time the law school reform was considered, which was not the case in Japan and Korea.

A fourth reason for professors' opposition to the introduction of a law school system was the widespread perception among Taiwanese law professors that Japan's reform failed. The professors believed that the changes in Japan had various negative effects, including the loss of the best students as the study of law declined in prestige and competition to pass the qualifying examination remained. These impressions were conveyed to legal academics in Taiwan by their frequent contact with Japanese law professors. For example, as one Taiwanese professor recounted, "The Dean of Tokyo University Law School [Masahito Inoue] was here in 2010. I asked him about how the law schools were doing. He said, 'I might be judged in Japan as a war criminal.' " This was a joking reference to the unpopularity among legal academics of the system he advocated as a member of the Justice System Reform Council. However, Lo interpreted the Japanese case differently:

> My observation is that there was too much compromise among the planners [of reform].... In the beginning, they only wanted a handful of law schools, but they turned off track and created a large number. In the beginning, the pass rate was very high, but after establishing so many law schools, the passage rate dropped, and it caused an abnormal kind of competition. The law schools became cram schools, teaching law to pass the bar exam. One reason Japan's reform didn't work was this compromise [to raise the number of law schools].

A similar situation emerged in Korea, although more slowly, owing to the higher bar exam passage rate (originally set at over 75 percent) and law graduates' limited number of chances to take the test.[37] A fifth reason Lo gave for professors' opposition to reform was that there was insufficient communication with other legal academics, a concern they echoed. Another professor attributed this to a lack of time since Vice President Lu, the political patron of reform, wanted an achievement quickly.

Who were Lo's allies in his reform effort? It is notable that he did not coordinate his work with the Judicial Reform Foundation, the leading activist group for legal systemic reform issues. Lo did not believe that the JRF was interested in legal education reforms, but an operative from the group said in an interview that "civil society felt left out" of the issue, and they would have welcomed such a reform. This suggests a lack of communication or miscommunications among those who wanted the law school reform to succeed. Additionally, although Lo saw eye-to-eye with the legislator who proposed the law school bill, Chen Ming-Zhen, he said he did not work with Chen to draft his bill, suggesting a degree of disconnection in the push for the reform.

Most observers believe that Chen enthusiastically favored the adoption of American-style law schools. Chen was a legislator representing the overseas community and had lived in America for 30 years, where he was a successful businessman. His experience in the US seems to have made him view the skills of American lawyers very positively. According to a law professor who met with Chen to discuss legal educational reform, Chen made clear that he believed Taiwanese lawyers were incapable in law and technology issues compared to US lawyers. The professor recalled that Chen "believed that American legal education made US lawyers good, so Taiwan should adopt the US system," although the professor disagreed with this assessment and felt that it was training in law firms that accounted for American lawyers' skills. Professor Chen Hwei-Syin also met him and wrote of her impression of him:

> Legislator Chen Ming-Zhen publicly stated that Taiwan's university law departments were all very lacking, that students' level of ability was very bad, and in addition he mentioned that he lived in America for over thirty

37 Youngjoon Kwon, "Recent Reform in Korean Legal Education," 26.

> years. He believed the US was the strongest country in the world, and so America's system must be good. Thus he personally definitely wanted to implement this system in Taiwan.... [He] despised Taiwan's legal education ... and overly trusted his own personal judgement.[38]

In the early stages of the reform, Chen Hwei-Syin, a co-author of this article, supported it. Chen was a member of Vice President Lu's Presidential Human Rights Advisory Commission, and in that capacity she mentioned to Lu that she believed the low passage rate on the bar examination was a violation of human rights. The idea of legal education reform originated with Chen, but Lu then took Chen's suggestion and commissioned Lo Chang-Fa to undertake research leading to reform. When she believed this turned into an effort to adopt the Japanese-Korean interpretation of the American law school system, Chen emerged as a leading voice opposing the proposed reform. Skeptical deans met once per month as the changes loomed. The opposition was based on fear of departments being closed or a loss of quantity or quality of students, as occurred in Japan. The skeptical deans and department chairs had contact with Japanese and Korean law professors. The Japanese professors conveyed to them their view that enrollment declined in quality and often quantity as lawyer salaries fell. They also generally believed that undergraduates were better law students than graduates. This latter view matched the feeling among many in academia that having graduate-level law students meant teaching learners who elected to study law as a second choice, rather than their first choice. Professors felt they would be teaching students who failed at their first choice subject. Another professor from Soochow University concurred with these views, and added that he was afraid his department would have too few students allocated. He wished that more law schools would have been planned, perhaps 50 to 60, but this was far off from Lo's vision of six or seven.

Chen Hwei-Syin believed that a key problem with the law school reform was an overemphasis on changing the structure of legal education rather than its inner workings, which she felt were the main problem. Although Chen possessed a German doctorate, she did not oppose American influences outright, but rather took a different inspiration from the US. She said in an interview that, "I won't say American influence failed in Taiwan, but there was another form of influence – on dialogue between students and professors, combining practice and theory, and strengthening legal ethics." She also opposed the reformists' strategy of imposing changes in a "top-down" manner.

> We reject the law schools also because it's a centralized system. Government control over law schools is not good for the democratic process.... I

38 陳惠馨 [Chen Hwei-Syin], "化危機為轉機 – 談法學界如何因應法學教育改革的呼聲" [Turning a Crisis into a Turning Point – Discussion on Legal Educators' Response to Legal Education Reform], 5.

> am against presidential-level reform.... We need more discussion in society, so once society agrees, we can do it ... the most important thing is the decentralization of discussion.

This preference for "bottom-up" reform would come to characterize the next legal educational reform movement, which Chen would lead.

Regarding the possibility of future progress, Lo was pessimistic, believing that professors were exhausted after discussing the issue for almost two decades. He suggested that it could take 10 to 20 years for another reform effort to appear. Another professor agreed, saying that the debate over reform has "stopped, even academic debate. All of us feel tired. We don't want to discuss this continually." A few scholars expressed the opinion that the issue ought to be reopened. Huang Kuo-Chang, a young US-educated scholar (now a prominent legislator) was not a part of the legal education debate but has been active in other reform movements in recent years. He stated in an interview that he believed legal education was still problematic.

> Grades don't matter. Students try to memorize everything because of the bar exam.... I tried to have a discussion with my students. I asked them to read some material. In a class of fifty, maybe three students read it.... They are not serious; they are not adults.

He strongly believed that graduate-level students would be more suited for the study of law.

Why did the law school reform fail? Proximate causes

To summarize, the law school reform effort failed for reasons centering on political viability. The causes for the failure of the reform can be divided into proximate reasons that are immediately apparent and deeper reasons that can be seen when the process in Taiwan is compared those of Japan and Korea. The many causes and their logical relationships can be untangled as follows.

Regarding proximate causes, first, as Lo explained, there was insufficient political will from the Ministry of Education, Vice President Lu, or the then-politically embattled President Chen, who eventually cancelled the reform at the behest of several opposing deans and department heads. And the perception that Lu's motive for pushing the reform, albeit gently, was political self-interest probably weakened the reform's legitimacy in the eyes of some professors.

Second, as Lo noted, not enough professors and deans were convinced. Indeed, the majority of deans and department heads opposed the plan. Many scholars saw no inherent problem with teaching young students at the undergraduate level, the normal mode of Continental European legal education. Also, some prestige-conscious professors, including many at NTU, did not wish to hire practitioners. Legal academics also perceived the Japanese law school reorganization to be a failure – an assessment Japanese scholars often conveyed directly to Taiwanese professors. But, most importantly, Taiwanese professors opposed the plan on grounds that an insufficient number of schools would be protected from closure. As some opponents stated, Taiwan's law school reform seemed to move in the Korean direction of closing most institutions so the bar exam pass rate could rise. Professors, even at the remaining elite schools, were unhappy with this. As Lo put it, "opposition was about jobs and revenues for many schools." Opponents also believed that closing many non-Taipei-based schools would contradict the tendency toward educational decentralization that was behind the opening of such institutions.

The third proximate reason for the failure of the reform was the rise of a well-organized countermovement. The anti-law school movement connected law professors opposed to the impending reforms and met once per month. Opposition to reform became a grave matter for these teachers, deans, and department heads, as some feared a decline in the quality or quantity of students and others the outright closure of their institution. The anti-law school movement was further emboldened by the anti-government political atmosphere.

Fourth, Lo was politically isolated because of the lack of agreement from law professors and the rise of the vocal anti-law school movement. In interviews, professors described this as a lack of communication. Lo might have been able to succeed had he compromised on the number of law schools, but he believed doing so would have undermined the success of the reform, as it had in Japan. Alternatively, success could still have been achieved had the President or Vice President supported the effort more strongly. Thus, the isolation of the reform's leadership harmed its prospects for success.

Fifth, it was important that, in Taiwan, legal scholars who have obtained doctorates in Continental-style jurisdictions (especially Germany, but also Japan and France) outnumber those educated in America. To the civilian-oriented professors, undergraduate legal training is unobjectionable, while the US legal tradition vehemently rejects such an approach. Thus, the radical, Americanizing plan was unlikely to have found favor with most of Taiwan's legal academic community. This analysis is complicated, however, by the fact that some US-trained professors did not support the reform, indicating that the conflict was not purely based on participants' biases toward their countries of education. Educational divides of similar proportions existed in Japan and Korea, but the often-US-trained reformists in those places succeeded because they benefitted from strong political support.

Deeper reasons for failure: comparisons to Japan and Korea

There were also more profound reasons for the collapse of Taiwan's law school reform effort. First, there was no urgency over expanding the number of lawyers, because in Taiwan this perceived problem was already resolved when in 1989 the Examination Yuan raised the Lawyer Examination passage rate to about 14 percent and maintained similarly high rates ever since. The low number of lawyers was a key factor in the success of law schools reforms in Japan and Korea. By the time Taiwan's law school reform was considered in 2006–07, many lawyers and professors in Taiwan believed there were already too many lawyers. Taiwan thus lacked the Japanese and Korean too-small legal professional problem that aided the adoption of law schools in those nations.

Second, Taiwan's law school reform took place mainly within the ordinary political process, unlike the special reform committees in Japan and Korea that were forums for consensus-building discussions and the drafting of legislation to implement the results of agreements. In Taiwan, the preparatory research and discussion of reform was carried out by Lo Chang-Fa under the aegis of Vice President Lu's Presidential Human Rights Advisory Commission. At first glance this appears similar to the executive-launched reform processes in Japan and Korea, but there are key differences. In particular, there was little consensus-building and compromise. Lo's compromise on allowing some undergraduates to transfer into the law schools after two years was not enough for most professors who feared the loss of their institutions or a significant number of their students. Indeed, reaching a consensus may well have been impossible owing to entrenched opposition to the abolition of undergraduate legal education. Additionally, the implementation of Taiwan's law school reform was split between Lo and Chen Ming-Zhen, the Legislative Yuan Member who proposed law school bills twice in 2007. This differs from what occurred in Japan and Korea, where special "implementation committees" were established under the prime ministerial offices in order to draft laws carrying out the recommendations of the judicial reform committees. Reformers in Japan and Korea feared that leaving the law-drafting up to legislators would politicize the issues and alter the agreements reached in their judicial reform committees. In Taiwan however, a legislator drafted a bill largely independently. Left to the ordinary political process, reform lacked support from stakeholders and a legislative process that would have sheltered it from political controversy.

Third, the reform processes in Japan, Korea, and Taiwan all shared in common a top-down ethos. In each place, changes were to be agreed upon by opinion leaders and imposed across the system. Discontented members of legal educational community would be forced to accept new national policies creating graduate-level law schools. This top-down imposition of uniform policies succeeded in Japan and Korea as opposing groups capitulated to the reforms. But in Taiwan, the top-down style did not work. Dissidents did not abandon their opposition, as occurred in the other two countries. There are cultural differences in leadership and decision-making styles in the three places. Centralized decision-making, deliberative consensus-building among stakeholders, and the top-down imposition of transformative change may be more acceptable in Japanese and Korean cultural contexts than in Taiwan. This is also evident in Taiwan's turbulent judicial reform process in which dissenters to the decisions reached at the 1999 National Conference on Judicial Reform were able to delay or impede reform.[39] Lo did not believe it was possible to both compromise and produce viable reform. As he said in an interview:

> When reform was initiated, a committee was important. But for me, the ideal situation is not change from the bottom-up because there would never be consensus. Reform from the top-down is better for achieving results. There has been no progress ever since this [attempted law school reform].

Yet after the end of the top-down reform effort, a new legal educational reform process began that attempted to produce change from the bottom-up. On this point, Japan and Korea have no parallel history.

From the "bottom-up:" the next wave of legal education reform

After Vice President Lu's Presidential Human Rights Advisory Commission produced its white paper on the law school reform in 2006, the network of dissenting professors, deans, and department heads coalesced into an informal organization with its own vision for reform. Chen Hwei-Syin coordinated the activities of the "Legal Education and National Examination Reform Forum" (法學教育與國家考試改革論壇), which gathered monthly at different law colleges or departments in turn.[40] In early 2007, Professor Lo Chang-Fa resigned from the Ministry of Education Office he headed that worked on the law school reform, the "Legal Education Innovation Project Office" (法學教育教學研究創新計劃辦公室).[41] Chen replaced him and changed the direction of the reform program. When Chen took office, its five existing official goals were to: "establish legal ethics studies, experiment with the Socratic Method, integrate the discipline of law [by teaching courses crossing traditional subject boundaries], revise case materials, and accredit new law schools."[42] Except for the fifth item, these objectives were essentially maintained.

39 See the chapter by Neil Chisholm in this volume.

40 For a collection of documents related to the group, see: www.law.nccu.edu.tw/change/archive.php?class=401&y=2010&m=01&d=1.

41 陳惠馨 [Chen Hwei-Syin], "創新與實踐 – 臺灣法學教育的改變嘗試 (2007年至 2011年)" [Innovation and Practice: The Attempt to Reform Taiwan's Legal Education], in 陳惠馨 [Chen Hwei-Syin], ed., 創新與實踐: 臺灣法學教育 [Innovation and Practice: Legal Education in Taiwan] (台北 [Taipei]: 教育部 [Ministry of Education], 2011), 5. It should also be noted that from 2005 the Ministry of Education Advisory Office began to develop a four-year program to improve pedagogy and curricula in social science and humanities departments. There were many sub-programs under this project, and the Legal Education Innovation Project Office was one. For further information, see: "教育部99年度補助辦理法學教育教學研究創新計畫" [Ministry of Education 2010 Subsidy Management Legal Education Pedagogy Research Innovation Plan], www3.nccu.edu.tw/~hschen/PDF/law%20and%20ethik%20course.pdf.

42 陳惠馨 [Chen Hwei-Syin], "創新與實踐 – 臺灣法學教育的改變嘗試 (2007 年至 2011 年)"

As the academics opposed to the law school reform exchanged views about the problems of legal education, they came to view them as primarily pedagogical issues that would be best solved by a bottom-up movement that engaged professors one-by-one. This bottom-up approach was a deliberate decision by the Legal Education Innovation Project Office, a reaction against the top-down nature of the unsuccessful law school reform. Professors would be encouraged by ministerial subsidies to participate in the reform, but they would not be compelled to join.[43] The effort was especially well-received at private universities and southern schools, which were more welcoming of subsidies and open to experimentation than relatively prestigious northern institutions such as NTU. Leaders of the previous law school reform effort considered such private and southern schools to be failures that needed to be closed for graduating few passers of the bar and judicial examinations. The professors in the next wave of reform had a different perspective; they believed that these schools were training students who would take an understanding of law into the private sector, government, and civil society. According to this theory, non-lawyer graduates would diffuse useful legal knowledge into society, enhance legal consciousness, and promote the rule of law environment in Taiwan. Passing the professional examinations should not be the only goal of legal education, the bottom-up reformers thought.

To do their work, the organizers set broad objectives for reform and then invited professors from around Taiwan to realize the goals with financial support from the Legal Education Innovation Project Office. This involved funding participants to write casebooks, create new courses, and test new teaching methodologies. To promote the reforms and instruct applicants for the subsidies, the Office held workshops and public hearings around the island. The grant projects the Office funded were designed by law professors hailing from different areas of Taiwan, which the Office divided into North, Central, South, and East as it promoted geographical diversity among the reform participants. The legal academics who were awarded grants came not only from law faculties but also from General Studies departments that teach classes such as Introduction to Law, Law and Life, or Constitutional Law. The Ministry of Education funded the Office for four years, until October 2011. By the time the program ended, about 600 professors had received grant funding.

The course of reform was as follows.[44] From 2007 to 2008 the Legal Education Innovation Project Office focused on supporting the development of "local

[Innovation and Practice: The Attempt to Reform Taiwan's Legal Education], 6. See also, Thomas Chih-hsiung Chen, "Legal Education Reform in Taiwan," 58–9.

43 For more details about this program, see: Hwei-Syin Chen and Chia-Chen Lee, "Innovative Teaching Program of Legal Science in Taiwan," 2007–2010, February 12, 2010, www3.nccu.edu.tw/~hschen/PDF/Projedt%20of%20leagl%20educationsreform%201003.pdf.

44 The ensuing details on the project are described in: 陳惠馨 [Chen Hwei-Syin], "創新與實踐 – 臺灣法學教育的改變嘗試 (2007年至 2011年)" [Innovation and Practice: The Attempt to Reform Taiwan's Legal Education], 8–24.

case studies" (本土案例) for classroom instruction. This effort was aimed at changing professors' ingrained habit of teaching law through the use of foreign cases. For example, Taiwanese law professors would teach freedom of speech using American Supreme Court cases or substantive criminal law using German cases. The jurisdiction whose cases would be used depended on where the teacher had studied, which nation's law was more influential in the area, and the foreign educational experience of the author of the textbook used in class. Fictitious cases have also often been used. But the reformers believed that it would be preferable to teach Taiwanese law using real Taiwanese cases, even if the principles or theories being illustrated originated abroad. The Office funded dozens of professors to compile actual, local cases, and 53 casebooks were ultimately published.

During 2008–09, the reformers encouraged law professors to use "dialogue-style pedagogy" (對話式教學). The goal was to steer Taiwanese professors away from using the so-called "monologue style" and toward class discussion. The reformers desired to involve students more in the education process because they believed students were too passive and professors were overly respected. In traditional East Asian education, students have been silent before teachers because speaking with the teacher was viewed as challenging the authority of a highly esteemed person. But reformers believed it was important to cultivate students' confidence and abilities to critique ideas in the modern world. The Legal Education Innovation Project Office thus maintained the essence of Lo Chang-Fa's idea of introducing the Socratic Method but changed it into the more general concept of class discussion and teacher-student dialogue. The Project Office subsidized professors to develop new methods and courses along these lines and also encouraged the incorporation of local cases into the dialogue process.

From 2009–10, the reform program focused on the development of "combined theory and practice teaching" and incorporating in this the local case materials and dialogue pedagogy. The reformers believed, like legal educators elsewhere, that there was a gulf between law as taught in universities and the reality of practice. To take steps toward expanding practice-oriented teaching, the Legal Education Innovation Project Office provided subsidies for legal academics to invite guest lectures from people employed in practice areas. Participants in this program included judges, lawyers, prosecutors, civil servants working with law and regulations, members of the business community, and workers in non-profit organizations. About 94 professors participated in this project over the course of the year, and in total over 100 people from various practice areas participated in classes.

In the fourth year of the reform, from 2010–11, the Office focused on enhancing "specialized law and professional ethics" teaching. It was hoped at the time that schools could extend the specialization of students beyond the traditional judicial, generalist lawyer, and civil servant roles. The reformers desired to expand the number of law classes relating to medical issues, engineering, business, education, media, data science, social movements, religion, social work, and other areas. Out of 40 project applications, 16 were subsidized. The funded projects developed new types of courses, class sessions for existing courses, and teaching methods. About four to five law professors participated in each project, and besides these, 39 subsidies were given to individual professors. This was another area where reformers built on the vision proposed by Lo Chang-Fa that was itself influenced by changes in Japan. Additionally, the reformers sought to enhance legal ethics, which they believed was a neglected area of education in legal education curricula.

Over the four years of its operations, the Legal Education Innovation Project Office created various materials related to its aims as well as an alliance of professors across disciplines and schools through its hosting of various teaching workshops, interdisciplinary workshops, symposia, and informational meetings on how to write books. Many professors who were previously isolated came to have increased contact with others.

Regarding the evaluation of the 2007–11 bottom-up reform, some professors not associated with it stated in interviews that the changes were insufficiently lasting, harmed academic freedom, and that the bottom-up nature of the changes proved ineffective. Critics claimed the reforms only held while financial support flowed from the Ministry of Education and that when this ended in 2011, progress ceased. Supporters of the reform stated that many professors' minds were opened to new ways of teaching and many of the new casebooks are still in use. On the issue of subsidies, the Ministry of Education typically funds projects for only four years, and thus this kind of support could only last for a limited time. With respect to a charge that trying to alter how teachers educate infringes upon academic freedom, which was also suggested about Lo Chang-Fa's attempted reform, it is questionable whether this is a valid concern. Universities can reasonably set requirements for a course's subject matter and style of instruction without encroaching upon academic freedom.

Regarding the claimed ineffectiveness of the bottom-up approach, there is an unavoidable philosophical difference on this issue. Top-down reforms may be more effective by nature since they rely on compulsion to change established patterns and practices. The bottom-up effort by its nature depends more on cooperation and agreement among a larger number of people. The earlier top-down reform attempt to create the law school system resulted in the Taiwanese legal educational community pushing back against the plans with petitions, protest, and lobbying. The proposal was not able to overcome this resistance, demonstrating the difficulty of successfully executing a top-down reform in Taiwan. In the Taiwanese legal community, achieving consensus for transformative top-down reforms was not as successful as in Japan and Korea.

The second reform effort did not depend on consensus, but rather tried to nudge professors toward reform with subsidies that eventually ran out. Many professors have continued to use the casebooks and teaching styles created by the program, but many have not. Additionally, the fact that some elite northern schools declined to join in the Project Office's effort illustrates a shortcoming of the bottom-up style: participation is optional. But this fact also illustrates a dilemma of Taiwanese legal educational reform objectives – whether to cultivate a legal elite or train large numbers of students. Lo Chang-Fa's law school reform aimed to improve the quality of legal professionals, especially lawyers, and shift their training to a few elite institutions. Chen Hwei-Syin's effort sought to improve the quality of legal training by encouraging reform at many institutions, even if their graduates would never become lawyers. Where the first reform regarded most such institutions as problematic, the second viewed them as helpfully producing non-lawyer legal technicians. If the goal of legal educational reform is to create an elite group of lawyers capable of competing with international law firms, then the bottom-up reforms certainly did not succeed. But if the goal of reform ought to be to enhance the quality of classroom education for a large number of students, most of whom will never be lawyers, then the bottom-up effort could be considered more successful. There is no consensus on the appropriate goal of reform however.[45] Thus, the status quo of the past decade and a half has remained.

Examination reform

As a postscript to the story of this latter wave of reform, deans and department heads succeeded at lobbying for changes to the qualifying examinations after they were invited by the Examination Yuan for consultations about reform. Starting in 2010, the judicial and lawyer examinations were divided into two phases, similar to Japan's examination. The first phase is a mainly multiple choice test, a new development in Taiwan, while the second phase is a traditional essay-based examination. In the first phase, "Comprehensive Law I" is composed of constitutional law, administrative law, criminal law, criminal procedure, public international law, private international law, and lawyer ethics. In the second stage, "Comprehensive Law II" includes civil law, civil procedure law, company law, insurance law, negotiable instruments, maritime law, securities law, and legal English. Effective from 2015, the second part of the examination contains five elective subjects, and the test taker selects one out of intellectual property law, labor and social law, tax law, maritime law, and law of the sea. Of the takers of the first test, 33 percent can proceed to the second part of the test. Additionally, the passage rate in recent years has been about 10 percent.[46] There were about 963 people who passed the lawyer exam in 2011, 915 in 2012, and 892 in 2013.

Finally, since 2015, the first part of the examination will no longer distinguish between judges, prosecutors, and lawyers – they will all take the same exam for

45 Some observers from National Chiao Tung University Law School have recently argued that the bottom-up reforms have had lasting beneficial effects at their institution. Chih-Chieh Lin, Mong-Hwa Chin, and Shang-Jyh Liu, "Legal Education in Taiwan: Evolution and Innovation," *Asian Journal of Law and Society* 3 (2016).

46 Thomas Chih-hsiung Chen, "Legal Education Reform in Taiwan," 59–60.

the first stage.[47] This is a major change and represents a rationalization of the examinations because they have historically been almost identical. The second parts of the examinations, although largely similar, will remain separately administered for lawyers and for "judicial officers."

Conclusion: legal educational reform as a microcosm of judicial reform

Legal education in Taiwan has undergone significant changes since World War II, although the extent of change has often been more incremental than reformists have desired. Japan's influence on both colonial Taiwan and the Republic of China left the legacy of a very small bar and legal training at the undergraduate level that was viewed as related to political and social science education. In 1989, the Examination Yuan raised the Lawyer Examination passage rate to 14 from 0.75 percent in the previous year, marking the start of an expansion of the legal profession. A new system of graduate-level legal education, for learners who had not studied law at the undergraduate level, began at Soochow University in 1990. This model soon spread to dozens of schools around Taiwan. In the 1990s, colleges of law became independent from social science colleges, representing a break from the Japanese conception of legal training.

While the 1999 National Conference on Judicial Reform could have dealt more seriously with legal education, as judicial reform committees in Japan and Korea had, it opted to suggest that the Ministry of Education consider a symbolic change to the status of law departments – that they become independent "colleges." Leaders at the Judicial Yuan, host of the NJRC, felt legal education reform was more the responsibility of the Executive Yuan's Ministry of Education.

These changes were not enough for some professors, who desired that lawyers possess greater levels of social experience, maturity, and non-legal education. The hopes of these academics coincided with the political aspirations of Vice President Annette Lu, who wanted a reform accomplishment in preparation for the next presidential election. The domestic debate over adopting a graduate-level system was also given new urgency by similar reforms in Japan and Korea. Lo Chang-Fa led a committee to establish a new law school system, and his ultimate plan drew heavily from the Japanese experience but aimed to improve upon it by closing the law departments not selected to host a limited number of law schools. The goal of the reform seemed to be to shift legal education toward producing a higher quality of elite lawyer. Lo's blueprint for reform attracted vocal opposition and ultimately failed. Most law professors opposed the plan because

47 More detailed information can be found at: 考選部 [Ministry of Examination], 104年專門職業及技術人員高等考試律師考試 (第一試) [2005 Professional and Technical Personnel Higher Examination Lawyer Examination (First Test)], April 24, 2015, wwwc.moex.gov.tw/main/news/wfrmNews.aspx?kind=3&menu_id=42&news_id=2108.

only six or seven law schools would be permitted to open for around 650 students, meaning that most departments would close and enrollment would be limited across the board. For perspective, roughly 900 or so lawyers are currently qualified each year. A determined anti-law school movement sprang up, and publicly advocated for the rejection of the reform. Political support for Lo was lacking, as the President, Vice President, and Ministry of Education declined to firmly support him against the opponents of the law school plan.

Deeper reasons for the failure of the reform can be seen in light of the Japanese and Korean reform processes. The law school reforms there were attached to the perceived problem of increasing the number of lawyers. Reformers in those countries wanted to expand the legal profession but maintain its high quality by enhancing legal training through the adoption of graduate-level law schools. But in Taiwan, the problem of the low number of legal professionals had been solved since the 1989 rise in the Lawyer Examination passage rate. The law school reform thus had less urgency in Taiwan. Second, Taiwan's reform was debated largely in the ordinary political process. The Japanese and Korean judicial reform committees were extraordinary, consensus-seeking bodies shielded from ordinary political pressures and supported by the executive. Lo Chang-Fa's committee did not contain opposing voices with which he had to compromise, nor did he have unwavering presidential support. His vision was contested by an external anti-reform movement that lobbied against him. A legislator, not coordinating closely with Lo, proposed a similar law school system in the Legislative Yuan, but lobbying again defeated the plan.

There was an aversion to the pursuit of top-down transformation in Taiwan that paralleled what occurred in its wider judicial reform process. In Japan and Korea, the judicial reform committees sought to achieve a consensus that would then be imposed upon the system, resulting in comprehensive change to address a national challenge. In Japan, this was the economy's long-running slump, while in Korea more and better lawyers would fix the public loss of trust in the judiciary by enhancing access to justice. Compromises were reached in both places: in Japan, a large number of law schools were opened and undergraduate law departments were maintained, and in Korea the number of designated law schools was expanded from 15 to 25. In Taiwan, however, the top-down reform process was viewed as unwelcome and even undemocratic by many professors. Opponents aimed at ending the reform rather than compromise. Whereas majorities of legal academics in Japan and Korea did not want reform, but grudgingly accepted it as necessary, law professors in Taiwan did not acquiesce to the changes. Indeed, Taiwanese professors are aware of how their reform process was handled differently than Japan's. As one law school opponent said,

> Some Japanese say they have a lot of problems [with the current law school system]. But they are an interesting people. They collectively adopt one way. Many individuals criticize it, but because they made a collective decision, they'll follow it. Lots of Japanese law professors dislike the law schools, but they still follow the system.

Was the American model was truly rejected? Opponents of the law school reform maintain that Taiwan has already adopted, at least partially, the US model through the establishment of graduate-level law courses modelled on Soochow University's 1990 experiment. They would also say that the "American model" adopted in Japan and Korea is actually a Japanese reinterpretation of US-style law schools. Although law schools in America can open fairly easily and admit as many students as they would like, under the Japanese reinterpretation, the number of law schools was limited and the number of admitted students was regulated by the government.

The deliberative style in Taiwan's legal education reform process in some ways mirrored that of its judicial reforms. Taiwan's 1999 judicial reform process took the form of a three-day conference at which 125 attendees discussed and decided reforms. The voting rules were such that for a reform policy to be adopted, either the sub-panel considering the proposal had to unanimously agree to it, or else the whole Conference's four vice presidents had to agree to it before it could be submitted for a majority vote.[48] Collective decision making in this process thus emphasized the views of dissenters and gave them veto power over final decisions. However, in Japan and Korea, the judicial reform discussions aimed at reaching decisions collectively. Opponents of the policy goals were pressured to accept them by strong executive support and the collective sense of a national challenge. There were no formal rules giving a single dissenter the power to veto a reform policy. Dissenters were pressed to yield to reform and offered compromises rather than vetoes.

Taiwan's legal educational reform can be seen as a microcosm of its judicial reforms. There, the top-down imposition of change was viewed as mistreating dissenters and was perceived as "authoritarian" for not listening to their views. Ultimately, dissenting voices were able to stop, stall, or change the direction of the NJRC's reforms entirely. Likewise, the majority of professors were able to stop the law school reform process, and even take it in an entirely new direction later. Similarly, Taiwan's judicial reforms were taken in a very different direction when new leaders were appointed to the Judicial Yuan in 2010. This style of deliberation can also be seen in Taiwan's relatively slow democratization process. In the 1980s and 1990s, internal KMT discussions over political liberalization issues – such as the legalization of opposition parties, reforms making elections fair, and the issue of whether there would be a presidential or parliamentary system – took years of negotiations to reach decisions on gradual changes.[49] Meanwhile, in Korea, political liberalization decisions were reached in 1987 and implemented in 1988 after the authoritarian executive decided to permit a transition to democracy. In sum, while Japanese and Korean judicial

48 See the chapter by Neil Chisholm in this volume.

49 Denny Roy, *Taiwan: A Political History* (Ithaca: Cornell University Press, 2003), 176–7, 194–5.

and legal educational reformers created a transformative moment of change, in Taiwan, reform occurred more slowly.

As a side note, in Taiwan, symbolic questions about bureaucratic responsibility assumed considerable importance. Not only did this arise in relation to the NJRC's competence to discuss legal education, but law school reform opponents similarly claimed that Lo Chang-Fa's reform committee had no constitutional right to suggest educational policies. By comparison, such "bureaucratic turf" issues had little importance in Japan and Korea because the judicial reform committees were recognized as extraordinary bodies making suggestions that would be formally codified into law in the appropriate way at a later time.

The course of legal educational reform shifted in 2007, when Chen Hwei-Syin was appointed to head the Ministry of Education's Legal Education Innovation Project Office after it was vacated by Lo's departure. Essentially, the informal organization dedicated to opposing law schools took over the Office. Chen and her allies consciously rejected the top-down imposition of change and replaced it with a bottom-up reform process. The Office subsidized professors to develop casebooks using real Taiwanese legal cases, teacher-student dialogue pedagogy, classes combining theory and practice, interdisciplinary courses, and legal ethics teaching materials. Funding for the reform effort ended after four years in 2011, and it was hoped that many of the newly-developed casebooks, teaching methods, courses, and curricula would remain in use.

The two reform efforts were both inspired by the American legal education system and the examples of Japan and Korea in following it. However, these models of legal education have come under criticism. In Japan, the new law schools are regarded as a failure because the judicial examination passage rate has fallen to around 25 percent. This is because undergraduates were allowed to take the exam if they first passed a preliminary test. Students feel pressure to attend cram schools and eschew the humanistic legal education the system's planners intended. Professors are also reportedly alarmed that the traditional law B.A.-to-Ph.D. pathway has been disrupted by the new J.D. system, unsettling the training of the next generation of scholars. In Korea, similar phenomena have occurred. After years of gradual decline, the Lawyer Examination's pass rate fell below 50 percent in 2018.[50] Law schools have opened on-campus bar preparation courses to keep their students from fleeing to cram schools. Observers are also troubled by the sharp rise in law school tuition costs.

Tuition costs have become an issue in the home of the law school model, the United States. Virtually all law schools have raised degree prices above the rate of inflation for years, such that many students now borrow $100,000 to $200,000 to obtain J.D. degrees. Controversies over high tuition and often poor employment

50 유영철 [Yu Yŏng-ch'ŏl], 변호사시험 합격률 절반 밑으로 뚝 [The Lawyer Examination's Pass Rate Crashes Below Half], 자유일보 [Liberty Daily], February 19, 2019, www.jayoo.co.kr/news/articleView.html?idxno=6700.

outcomes for indebted graduates are raising questions about the very nature of law schools. For example, in 2013 President Obama publicly suggested that law school should last only two years, not three.[51] In retrospect, it is possible that Japan and Korea may have copied the US model at its peak, before certain problematic aspects were more apparent.[52]

While Taiwan's legal education system has problems, they are not the same as those in Japan, Korea, or America. The debate over legal education has ended, as participants have grown tired of inconclusive discussions. The political window for reform seems to have already closed as the era of post-democratization reform ends. At the present, major reforms, whether from the top-down or bottom-up, appear unlikely.

51 Peter Lattman, "Obama Says Law School should be Two, Not Three, Years," *New York Times*, August 23, 2013, http://dealbook.nytimes.com/2013/08/23/obama-says-law-school-should-be-two-years-not-three.

52 More detailed criticisms can be found at: Paul Campos, "The Crisis of the American Law School," *University of Michigan Journal of Law Reform* 46 (2012).

Part III

The procedural revolution

9 Conscience and convenience

Taiwan's rocky road to adopting the adversarial system in criminal procedure

Chia-Wen Lee

Introduction: a debate that had gone into overtime

On June 4, 2012, there was an unusual protest in Taiwan. Wu Hsun-lung (吳巡龍), a district prosecutor, staged a sit-in in front of the Supreme Court building to protest against a court resolution (最高法院101年第2次刑庭決議) made a few months earlier. In this resolution, the Supreme Court limited the obligation of the district courts and high courts to investigate evidence in criminal cases.[1] Trial courts were told to no longer initiate the investigation of evidence unfavorable to the defendant, meaning that prosecutors would shoulder 100 percent of the burden of proof. If the prosecutor fails to present solid evidence proving a defendant's guilt, the court will acquit the defendant of the unproven charges. This resolution immediately aroused a backlash from prosecutors. In order to pressure the Supreme Court, Prosecutor Wu launched the "June 4 Prosecutors Movement" (檢察官六四運動), and later staged a one-man sit-in. At the same time, 1,078 prosecutors, 27 law professors and 23 crime victims jointly signed a letter of protest initiated by the Prosecutors' Association.[2] However, the Supreme Court showed no intention to make concessions.

In fact, the "June 4 Prosecutors Movement" was not the only action against the Supreme Court in recent years. The Supreme Court has long been attacked as

1 According to the internal regulations of the Supreme Court (最高法院處務規程 Art. 32~33 最高法院民刑事庭庭長會議、民刑事庭會議及民刑事庭總會議議事要點), if judges have different opinions on one legal issue, the President of the Supreme Court can call a meeting of its judges. If two-thirds of criminal panel judges attend this meeting, and over half of the attending judges support one particular opinion, an official "resolution" can be made. The resolution does not have the same binding effect as *Pan Li* (判例) – the official precedents of the Supreme Court. But since the resolution is supported by the majority of judges in the Supreme Court, in reality it binds lower-court judges. If lower-court judges refuse to follow the resolution, their judgments are very likely to be vacated and remanded by the Supreme Court. As to 最高法院101年第2次刑庭決議, some Supreme Court judgments (see, for example, 100, 台上, 6259) in 2011 had varying opinions regarding judges' obligation of evidence investigation at trial. Therefore, the President of the Supreme Court called a meeting among criminal division judges to solve this issue.

2 Rich Chang, Prosecutor Begins One-man Protest, *Taipei Times* (June 5, 2012): 1.

irresponsible, mainly for its reluctance to render final conclusions to criminal cases by itself, instead frequently ordering lower courts to stage retrials because of trivial issues.[3] In addition, many of the Supreme Court's long-time practices, such as its confidential case assignment, have been attacked.[4] Moreover, quite a few Supreme Court opinions have aroused harsh criticisms. For example, in September 2010, the Supreme Court's resolution on child rape (最高法院99年第7次刑庭決議) was criticized as unconstitutional.[5] In May 2012, a Supreme Court judgment on the exclusionary rule (最高法院101台上2165號刑事判決) was condemned as impractical and illogical.[6] A few lower-court judges even organized a group – the Alliance of Judges to Call for the Reform of the Supreme Court (法官籲請改革最高法院行動聯盟) – to urge radical reform of the Supreme Court. The "June 4 Prosecutors Movement" was just another action against the Supreme Court.

Nevertheless, when we look closer at the controversy set off by the Supreme Court resolution that caused the "June 4 Prosecutors Movement," we see similarities between the debate in 2012 and the debate in the 1999 National Judicial Reform Conference (NJRC, 全國司法改革會議) over whether Taiwan's criminal procedure should be transformed from the inquisitorial system to the adversarial system. Both debates centered on the roles that the criminal court judge and prosecutor should play in the investigation of evidence.[7] Both witnessed a sharp opposition between courts and prosecutors.[8] In both debates, lawyers stood

3 See, for example, 張升星 [Sheng-hsin Chang], 最高法院的救援投手？ [The Closer Pitcher for the Supreme Court?], *China Times* (August 30, 2012): a14; 張升星 [Sheng-hsin Chang], 最高法院 才真令人火大 [It is the Supreme Court that Upsets People Most], *China Times* (January 15, 2013): a14.

4 See, for example, 王泰升等 [Tay-sheng Wang, ed.], '最高法院改革圓桌論壇系列之一：訴訟程序' [Roundtable for the Reform of the Supreme Court I: The Trial Process], 臺灣法學雜誌 [Taiwan Law Journal] 197 (April, 2012): 52–81.

5 See, for example, 李佳玟 [Chia-wen Lee], '違反罪刑法定主義的正義' [Justice That Violates the Doctrine of 'Nullum Crimen Sine Lege'], 臺灣法學雜誌 [Taiwan Law Journal] 160 (September, 2010): 1–3.

6 In 101台上2165, the defendant was not interrogated by the prosecutor immediately after he arrived for questioning. There was a 90-minute delay. The Supreme Court suspected that the prosecutor intentionally delayed the interrogation in the hope that the defendant would be anxious about being arrested and confess his guilt. The Supreme Court thus excluded the defendant's confession. Prosecutor Eric Chen attacked the Supreme Court for being ignorant of common prosecutorial practices. He argued that the delay was to give the defendant a rest period, and it was meant to protect the defendants' rights. See 王文玲、蕭白雪 [Wen-ling Wang and Pai-hsueh Shaw], 檢方遲延訊問 … 自白不能當證據 [The Confession from a Delayed Interrogation by the Prosecutor Must Be Excluded], *United Daily News* (May 3, 2012): a09.

7 See, for example, 林山田 [Shan-tien Lin], '別迷失在主義的叢林中 – 為職權原則與調查原則喊冤' [Do Not Get Lost in Jungles of Systems: A Defense for the Principle of Duty and the Principle of Investigation], 臺灣本土法學雜誌 [Taiwan Law Journal] 1 (April, 1999): 9; 李復甸 [Ful-dien Lee], 法官更超然 司改春雷 [The Judge Will Be More Neutral: (The Adoption of the Adversarial System) Is Like a Spring Thunder], *United Daily News* (January 19, 2012): a15.

8 陳志賢 [Chi-hsien Chen], 爭議提案表決 法部寡不敵眾 [When the Controversial Proposals Were Put to Vote, the MOJ Was Hopelessly Outnumbered], *China Times* (July 8, 1999): 3; 蕭白

with courts, whatever the disagreements they had on other issues,[9] while prosecutors received support from law professors, especially those who obtained their doctoral degrees in Germany.[10] In addition, similar accusations were used by opponents to attack each other: both judges and prosecutors claimed the other side "cared more about workload than the fairness of the trial."[11] The similarities strongly suggest that the debate over 最高法院101年第2次刑庭決議 in 2012 was a continuation of the debate in 1999 that had gone into overtime. The controversy in 2012 showed that the 1999 dispute over the inquisitorial versus adversarial system has never been settled, despite Taiwan's criminal procedural code being revised in 2002 to formally shift Taiwan's criminal justice system toward the adversarial system.

This chapter examines the transformation of criminal procedure in Taiwan from the inquisitorial system to the so-called "improved adversarial system" (改良式當事人進行主義). While all modern criminal legal systems are to some extent hybrids, the role of the judge in the investigation of evidence at trial varies between systems. In the adversarial system, the judge is passive at trial. The trial is rather dominated by the prosecutor and the defendant, who generally has an attorney. The prosecutor and defense attorney present their sides' evidence, arguments, and versions of the truth to the court or jury. Comparatively, in the inquisitorial system, the judge dominates the investigation of evidence. The judge is given broad discretion to uncover the truth in the case. The prosecutor in the inquisitorial system is considered to be the judge's assistant. The role of judge at trial is at the center of debates over Taiwan's transformation in criminal procedure.[12]

雪、許玉娟 [Pai-hsueh Shaw and Yu-chunag Hsu], 批最高法院「踐踏」 檢察官六四靜坐 [The Prosecutor Sat-in to Protest the Humiliation by the Supreme Court], *China Times* (May 9, 2012): a11.

9 鍾沛東 [Pei-tong Chong], 支持當事人進行主義 七律師學者上書總統 [Seven Lawyers and Scholars Petitioned the President to Support the Adoption of the Adversarial System], *United Daily News* (August 8, 1999): 8; 林峯正 [Feng-cheng Lin], 檢座善盡舉證責任才是要務 [The Primary Task for the Prosecutor is to Carry the Burden of Proof at Trial], *Apple Daily News* (June 5, 2012): a17.

10 See, for example, 林鈺雄 [Yu-hsiung Lin], 袖手旁觀是法官的天職？ [Is 'Look on and Do Nothing' What the Judge Is Supposed to Do at Trial?], *China Times* (July 7, 1999): 15; 許澤天 [Tze-tien Hsu], '法院調查證據之弊病檢討–再評最高法院101年度第2次刑事庭會議決議' [The Re-Examinations of the Problems in the Evidence Investigation by the Court: Re-evaluating 最高法院101年度第2次刑事庭會議決議], 台灣法學雜誌 [Taiwan Law Journal] 197 (April, 2012): 89–97.

11 See, for example, 陳恆寬 [Heng-kuan Chen], 人力國情 不是不改革的理由 [Short of Staff and Traditional Culture are No Excuse for Rejecting Reform], *United Daily News* (April 1, 1999): 15; 蕭博文、林偉信 [Pao-wen Shaw and Wei-hsin Lin], 檢察官靜坐嗆最高院 百檢聲援 [Over One Hundred Prosecutors Expressed Support for the Prosecutor Who Sat-in to Protest the Supreme Court], *China Times* (June 5, 2012): a05.

12 Brian Kennedy, LA Law in Taiwan? (May 1, 2002) Retrieved on April 10, 2014 from http://taiwantoday.tw/fp.asp?xItem=722&CtNode=124.

In retrospect, the transformation of the criminal procedure has had a deep impact on Taiwan's criminal justice system. Many procedural issues in practice and jurisprudence today have much to do with this transformation. It is thus important to understand why Taiwan pursued such a drastic reform at the turn of the twenty-first century, why an "improved" version of the adversarial system was adopted, and why debates over the two modes of criminal procedure still persist today. Since the transformation was initiated in the early 1990s and finalized in 2002, this chapter will begin by exploring the social context that led to the revolution in criminal procedure.

The discussion of these issues will proceed in chronological order. A set of concepts – "conscience" and "convenience," originally developed by historian David Rothman to study penal reform from the late nineteenth century into the second half of the twentieth century[13] – will be used to frame the discussion. I will first analyze how democratization reforms since the 1980s encouraged judicial reform in the 1990s (the call for conscience). I will then discuss how judges' heavy workload made the Judicial Yuan (JY, Taiwan's court administrative body and constitutional court) the number-one supporter of the adversarial system after the 1990s (the pressure of convenience). While acknowledging conscience and convenience as two driving forces behind the transformation of Taiwan's criminal procedure, I will study the backlash from the Ministry of Justice (MOJ), and explain how their resistance affected the outcome of the NJRC and led to the final version of reform. After looking into the NJRC, I will explore how the subsequent negotiations led to the reform. In the last section, I will show how the new system worked in reality after the adversarial transformation, and why there was a similar debate in 2012 in the last section.

The call of conscience: the demand for radical reform

Before criminal procedure was formally altered in 2002, Taiwan's criminal procedural code used the inquisitorial system. The old code was originally enacted in mainland China in 1928. In order to promote national unity and eliminate Western extraterritoriality, the Chinese Nationalist government (Kuomintang, KMT) of the ROC in mainland China followed the example of Meiji Japan to enact Western-style, and more specifically, pre-war German-style, codes[14] from

13 David Rothman, *Conscience and Convenience: The Asylum and Its Alternatives in Progressive America*, Boston: Little. Brown and Co. (1980).

14 In order to modernize Japan, the Meiji government pursued reforms that first followed the French Code of Criminal Procedure in 1880. In revisions in 1922, German inspiration was dominant, although the original French influences were not completely eliminated. Tay-sheng Wang, *Legal Reform in Taiwan under Japanese Colonial Rule, 1895–1945: The Reception of Western Law*, Seattle: University of Washington Press (2000): 551–2.

the late 1920s to mid-1930s.[15] After the ROC acquired Taiwan from Japan, these ROC codes, including the criminal procedural code, were brought to Taiwan,[16] along with the liberalism in these Western-style codes.[17]

In fact, it was not the first time a German-style criminal procedural code had been implemented in Taiwan. In 1924, the Japanese government directly implemented its pre-war German-style criminal procedural code in Taiwan under its new colonial policy.[18] Interestingly, when the KMT government enacted the criminal procedural code in mainland China, the Japanese criminal procedural code of 1922 was an important reference.[19] Both codes therefore drew inspiration from the German-style inquisitorial system, as it existed before post-World War II reforms. The judge in both the colonial system and in ROC system played a dominant role in investigating the truth of the case at trial, including questioning witnesses and extracting confessions from the defendant.[20] The prosecutor and the defense lawyer generally played small roles at trial. Even though the prosecutor was not active at trial, the prosecutor enjoyed broad pre-trial powers that generally belong to the preliminary judge in other systems, including powers to summon, interrogate, search, and detain persons not in flagrante delicto.[21]

15 Tay-sheng Wang. *The Legal Development of Taiwan in the 20th Century: Toward a Liberal and Democratic Country*. Pacific Rim Law & Policy Journal 11 (2002): 535–6.

16 In October 1945, the KMT government promulgated a special legal ordinance (*Shufazi* No. 36) to extend the application of the criminal procedural code to Taiwan. 郭威廷 [Wei-ting Guo], 台灣刑事訴訟法朝向當事人主義修正的歷史動因 [Historical Causes of the Adversarial Reform in Taiwanese Criminal Procedure] (台灣大學法律學研究所碩士論文 [Master's Thesis, Department of Law, National Taiwan University], 2004): 71.

17 Even though neither the Japanese colonial government or the KMT government respected liberalism, the liberalism rooted in these codes still influenced Taiwanese society and contributed to subsequent demands for reforms.

18 Both the French- and the German-influenced Japanese criminal procedural codes were applied in Taiwan, but in different ways. In 1898, the French-style code was put into effect in Taiwan for exceptional cases. But later, when the Japanese government decided to pursue assimilation in 1923, it took up the policy of "extension of the homeland." Under this policy, Japan extended the application of its laws in the colonies to the greatest extent possible. The German-style code was thus directly applied in Taiwan. Tay-sheng Wang, *Legal Reform in Taiwan under Japanese Colonial Rule, 1895–1945*, 551–2.

19 郭威廷 [Wei-ting Guo], 台灣刑事訴訟法朝向當事人主義修正的歷史動因 [Historical Causes of the Adversarial Reform in Taiwanese Criminal Procedure], 54. Japanese laws and jurisprudence had been influential for reformers since the late Qing Dynasty. The Qing Dynasty and the ROC learned much of Western law through Japanese laws. 黃東熊 [Dong-xiong Huang], 中外檢察制度之比較 [A Comparison of Foreign Prosecution Systems] (Taipei: 中央文物供應社 [Central Literature Publisher], 1986): 17–21.

20 In 1967, Taiwanese legislators revised the criminal procedural code comprehensively. The new code gave the prosecutor the burden of proof at trial (Art. 161). But according to the bill, the prosecutor was only required to provide evidence sufficient to create a reasonable suspicion. This code expressly gave the judge the obligation of evidence investigation at trial (Art. 163). Therefore, the revision did not transform the criminal procedure into the adversarial mode.

21 Tay-sheng Wang, *Legal Reform in Taiwan under Japanese Colonial Rule, 1895–1945*, 129–30. Prosecutors in Taiwan under the Japanese colonial government and the KMT government

Moreover, the prosecutor in pre- and post-war Taiwan sat alongside the judge in the elevated, central position in the courtroom, symbolizing the superiority of his status relative to the defendant and defense lawyer.[22] Therefore, even though the judge and the prosecutor were functionally different in formal law, there was no clear distinction between the judge and the prosecutor in the eyes of defendants.[23] When the ROC criminal procedure replaced the Japanese code after World War II, Taiwanese people felt few differences, if any, between the two systems.[24]

Nevertheless, the adoption of the inquisitorial system was not the only reason these two criminal procedures were similar. Both governments – the Japanese colonial government and the KMT government during the martial law era (1949–87) – supplemented the codes with a number of special laws to increase their control of Taiwanese society. The Bandit Punishment Law (匪徒刑罰令) was enacted by the Japanese government in Taiwan in 1898 to suppress any possible political threat. Likewise, the KMT government instituted martial law and enacted draconian statutes, such as the Statute for the Punishment of Rebellion (懲治叛亂條例) in 1949, to prevent any challenge to the regime. Both governments instituted separate systems to bypass due process. The Japanese government created a summary judgment system to allow the police to summarily decide both police offenses (after 1896) as well as certain misdemeanors (after 1904), while the KMT government abused military trials to control civilians.[25]

similarly enjoyed more power than prosecutors in mainland Japan, but for different reasons. Even though the ROC criminal procedural code modeled the Japanese code, ROC legislators gave prosecutors more powers to summon, interrogate, search, and detain suspects. 黃東熊 [Dong-xiong Huang], 中外檢察制度之比較 [A Comparison of Foreign Prosecution Systems], 19–20. Similarly, even though Japanese criminal procedural code was directly applied in Taiwan in 1924, the Japanese colonial government promulgated special legal ordinances to give prosecutors in Taiwan broader powers. 郭威廷 [Wei-ting Guo], 台灣刑事訴訟法朝向當事人主義修正的歷史動因 [Historical Causes of the Adversarial Reform in Taiwanese Criminal Procedure], 44.

22 郭威廷 [Wei-ting Guo], 台灣刑事訴訟法朝向當事人主義修正的歷史動因 [Historical Causes of the Adversarial Reform in Taiwanese Criminal Procedure], 46 and 100. In order to maintain traditional social hierarchy, the Meiji government adopted the inquisitorial system that had given the prosecutor a higher status than the defendant. It even gave the prosecutors a privileged physical position in the courtroom, seating them next to the judge. This arrangement was later adopted by the ROC government. Ibid., 100.

23 陳鈺雄 [Chih-hsiung Chen], 日治時期的台灣法曹－以國家為中心之歷史考察 [Taiwanese Jurists in the Colonial Period: A State-Centered and Historical Study] (台灣大學法律學研究所碩士論文 [Master's Thesis, Department of Law, National Taiwan University], 2004): 170.

24 郭威廷 [Wei-ting Guo], 台灣刑事訴訟法朝向當事人主義修正的歷史動因 [Historical Causes of the Adversarial Reform in Taiwanese Criminal Procedure], 87.

25 王泰升 [Tay-sheng Wang], 台灣檢察史：制度變遷史與運作實況 [The History of Taiwan's Prosecution System: The Changes of the Institution and Its Practices] (Taipei: 法務部 [Taipei: MOJ], 2008): 1–79. During the martial law era, the defendant's procedural rights were limited. Article 8 of the Martial Law, which gave military tribunals jurisdiction over various offenses, including muggings and robberies, further worsened the situation. Many civilian defendants were

These special laws were a very important reason why the liberalism in the Western-style criminal law and procedure in Taiwan was largely compromised.

During the martial law era, the KMT's interference with judicial independence was another reason why the Western-style criminal procedural code did not protect the rights of defendants as it was supposed to. By controlling the promotion, demotion, and transfer of judges and prosecutors, promoting party loyalists to higher positions in the judicial system, and manipulating certain procedural rules,[26] the KMT government was able to influence decisions of judges and prosecutors. Criminal procedure thus became an important mechanism for the KMT to suppress political dissent, punish disloyal politicians, and spare loyal politicians from convictions, either of vote-buying or corruption.[27] Several notorious incidents – such as one in 1958 in which a prosecutor was instructed by his superior prosecutor not to appeal the not-guilty verdict of a KMT politician, and the prosecutions against political dissents in the Formosa Magazine Incident in 1980 – showed Taiwanese society how the judicial system as a whole served the interests of the KMT government.[28]

In addition to political manipulation, incessant judicial scandals involving illegal lobbying and corruption greatly undermined faith in the judicial system in Taiwan.[29] News coverage about coerced confession and testimony from the

forced to stand trial in military tribunals and faced a much higher possibility of receiving death sentences.

26 Before the reform in the 1990s, junior judges were required to send their judgments to superior judges for review before announcing their decisions, and superior judges were thus able to influence the outcomes of cases. Also, court presidents had the power to assign cases. By assigning the case to the judge he favored, presidents were able to manipulate decisions. 王金壽 [Chin-shou Wang], '台灣司法改革二十年：邁向獨立之路' [Taiwan's Judicial Reform for Twenty Years: The Road to Independence], 思與言 [Thought and Words] 46, no. 2 (2008): 138–41. As to prosecutors, higher-ranking prosecutors could give instructions to their junior colleagues according to the principle of prosecutorial integration (檢察一體). Unlike the case assignment rule and the judgment review rule, the principle of prosecutorial integration was not by itself problematic. But because instructions by the superior prosecutors are mostly oral, and cannot be reviewed independently, the principle of prosecutorial integration lends itself to abuse by senior prosecutors to manipulate decisions.

27 王金壽 [Chin-shou Wang], '從邊緣到風暴中心的司法體制' [The Judicial System Has Moved from the Edge to the Center of Storm], in 王金壽等 [Chin-shou Wang, ed.], 秩序繽紛的年代：走向下一輪民主盛世（1990–2010） [The Years of Flowering Order 1990–2010: Towards the Next Heyday of Democracy] (Taipei: 左岸文化 [Left Bank], 2010): 230.

28 王泰升 [Tay-sheng Wang], 台灣檢察史：制度變遷史與運作實況 [The History of Taiwan's Prosecution System: The Changes of the Institution and its Practices], 1–78.

29 瞿海源、鄭宏文 [Hei-yuan Chiu and Hung-wen Cheng], '司法信賴的調查分析' [Investigation and Analysis of Trust on the Judicial System], in 澄社、民間司法改革基金會編, 司法的重塑－民間司法改革研討會論文集（一） [The Reconstruction of the Judicial System: Essays on the Civilian Conference of the Judicial Reform I], eds. 澄社、民間司法改革基金會 [Taipei Society and JRF] (Taipei: 桂冠 [Lauréat Publications], 2000): 100–1; 蘇永欽 [Yeong-chin Su], 當前司法問題的癥結 [The Key Issue of the Contemporary Judicial System], 司法改革的再改革 [A Second Judicial Reform] (Taipei: 元照出版公司 [Yuanzhao Publishers], 1998): 11–64.

police or even prosecutors undermined people's respect for the system.[30] Even though there was popular dissatisfaction with the administration of justice, it was not until several high-profile judicial scandals between 1989 and 1991 strongly suggested the judicial system was seriously corrupted that the collective call for the judicial reform emerged from various segments of Taiwanese society.[31] With an aggressive push by political dissents, reform-minded lawyers, and liberal scholars in the 1990s,[32] judicial reform gradually became a political issue that the KMT government could not ignore.

After the lifting of martial law in 1987, Taiwan entered an age of liberal-democratic reform. Press restrictions were lifted in 1988. The Temporary Provisions Effective During the Period of National Mobilization for Suppression of the Communist Rebellion (動員戡亂時期臨時條款), which had given the KMT government during the martial law era unchecked political power, were abolished in May 1991. In the same month, the statute for the Punishment of Rebellion, which was used to suppress political dissents, was also nullified. The Council of Grand Justices (司法院大法官會議), more commonly known today as the Constitutional Court, in Interpretation No. 261 in 1990 forced the KMT government to hold nation-wide elections. Fresh elections for all seats of the Legislative Yuan (LY) were held in 1992, which put more political dissidents into the LY. With the help of the Constitutional Court,[33] laws that were excessively harsh or unreasonably undermined basic civil liberties in Taiwanese society were repealed or revised by the LY in the years that followed.[34] Since the judicial system in general, and the criminal justice system in particular, had been

30 See, for example, 李作平 [Zuo-ping Lee], 秘密勸誘吐實、已屬違法 最高法院判例、蓋有年矣 [Old Supreme Court Precedent Indicates that Persuading the Defendant to Confess Secretly Violates the Law], *China Times* (January 11, 1987): 5.

31 For example, in 1989, one high-ranking official in the Judicial Yuan, Tien-hui Wu (吳天惠), and his lawyer wife were accused of attempting to bribe a prosecutor. The investigation of this case was allegedly obstructed by the President of Hsinchu District Court. Wu was acquitted by the District Court. Four district court judges, one prosecutor and three investigators resigned in protest. Three months later, the prosecutor who indicted the case was forced to resign. 王金壽 [Chin-shou Wang], '台灣司法改革二十年： 邁向獨立之路' [Taiwan's Judicial Reform for Twenty Years: The Road to Independence], 139.

32 羊憶蓉 [Yi-rong Yang], '司法改革作為社會變遷的機制' [Judicial Reform Serves as the Mechanism of Social Changes], in 澄社、民間司法改革基金會編, 司法的重塑－民間司法改革研討會論文集（一） [The Reconstruction of the Judicial System: Essays on the Civilian Conference of the Judicial Reform I], eds. 澄社、民間司法改革基金會 [Taipei Society and JRF] (Taipei: 桂冠 [Lauréat Publications], 2000): 109–27.

33 In addition to Interpretation No. 261 in 1990, the Constitutional Court made several interpretations that declared unconstitutional many laws and regulations that had given the government too much discretion (e.g., Nos. 384 and 392). These interpretations helped to speed up reform.

34 For example, the Regulation on Wartime Communicative Electronic Equipment and Device Protection (戰時交通電業設備及器材防護條例), which contained many provisions that prescribed the death penalty, was annulled in 1997. The pretrial detention system prescribed in the Criminal Procedural Code was reformed as well. Since then, only the court, not the prosecutor, has had the authority to detain the defendants before trial.

abused to suppress political dissidents, and since due process was largely disrespected by the judicial system during the martial law era, judicial reform naturally became part of collective efforts to transform Taiwan into a liberal, democratic country.

In retrospect, judicial reform was closely linked to the liberal-democratic reforms of that time. The political opposition movement that had been active since the 1970s and other social protests that proliferated in the 1980s had created a liberalized political atmosphere.[35] It was in this liberalized atmosphere that people became more willing to openly express their discontent with the justice system. During this time, some junior judges and prosecutors rebelled against political manipulation and illegal lobbying in the court system.[36] Even though some of the whistleblowers were later either forced to resign or administratively disciplined by the JY, some years later a small group of reform-minded judges and prosecutors pushed judicial reform from within the system.[37]

It was in this same atmosphere that reform-minded lawyers launched collective actions to take control of the Taipei Bar Association (TBA) in 1986 and 1990 and the National Bar Association in 1993.[38] Indeed, lawyers had risen up to challenge the KMT government much earlier. In the 1970s and the early 1980s, some lawyers actively participated in political opposition movements and human rights movements individually. But it was not until the mid-1980s that lawyers took collective action to demand professional independence and reforms. In 1990, the TBA and other liberal scholars organized an alliance to push radical judicial reform.[39] Out of concern that the scale and the areas of judicial reform would be narrowed by the government, in 1995 lawyers again joined with liberal scholars to establish a non-governmental organization – the Judicial Reform Foundation (JRF) (民間司法改革基金會), which aimed at providing bottom-up perspectives on how the judicial system should be reformed.[40]

After it was established, the JRF was quite vocal on legal issues relating to judicial reform. In 1996, it energetically joined a collective action to rescue the Hsih-Chi Trio from execution. The case of the "Hsih-Chi Trio" (蘇建和案)

35 Ming-sho Ho, Taiwan's State and Social Movements under the DPP Government (2000–2004), *Journal of East Asian Studies* 5 (2005): 401–2.

36 王金壽 [Chin-shou Wang], '台灣司法改革二十年：邁向獨立之路' [Taiwan's Judicial Reform for Twenty Years: The Road to Independence], 138–41.

37 Ibid., 138–50.

38 羊憶蓉 [Yi-rong Yang], '司法改革作為社會變遷的機制' [Judicial Reform Serves as the Mechanism of Social Changes], 113.

39 張春華 [Chun-hua Chang], 律師公會掀起司法改革熱潮 [The Bar Association Initiates an Upsurge of Judicial Reform], *China Times* (September 4, 1990): 4.

40 民間司法改革基金會 [JRF], '民間司法改革基金會簡介' [The Overview of the Judicial Reform Foundation], in 澄社、民間司法改革基金會編, 司法的重塑－民間司法改革研討會論文集（一） [The Reconstruction of the Judicial System: Essays on the Civilian Conference of the Judicial Reform I], eds. 澄社、民間司法改革基金會 [Taipei Society and JRF] (Taipei: 桂冠 [Lauréat Publications], 2000): v–viii.

involved a brutal double homicide.[41] Before they were to be executed, evidence strongly suggested their case had serious due process violations and that they were likely wrongfully convicted. The JRF worked hard to explain to Taiwanese society how problematic this case was.[42] For the JRF and other reformers, the case of the Hsih-Chi Trio showed that there were serious, deeply rooted problems in Taiwan's criminal justice system, and nullifying draconian codes enacted during the martial law era or eradiating illegal lobbies was not enough. Because evidence strongly suggested that the Hsih-Chi Trio were wrongful convicted and sentenced to death, reform of Taiwan's criminal procedure became not only a must-do in the age of democratic reform, but also a moral imperative. The case of the Hsih-Chi Trio and other problematic criminal cases in the 1990s put the reform of criminal procedure at the center of the judicial reform agenda.[43] It was against this backdrop that the JY aggressively offered the adversarial system as a solution to the problems of criminal justice.[44]

41 In fact, there were four defendants in this case. Evidence strongly linked Wang Wen-Shiau (王文孝) to the crime. But during the police interrogation, he claimed that three others, the Hsih-Chi Trio, also took part of the crime. Wang, who was in the army, was executed after his conviction by the military courts was finalized. The Hsih-Chi Trio were civilians and were tried by civilian courts. There was little evidence against them. There were also indications that the Hsih-Chi Trio were tortured during their police interrogation. Local activists quickly launched a large-scale rescue action, in which Amnesty International in Germany also took part. Under intensive local and international pressure, the executions of the Hsih-Chi Trio were unofficially postponed by the Minister of Justice. The case was later retried and their not-guilty verdicts were finalized in 2012.

42 李茂生等、蔡墩銘、許志雄、許玉秀 [Mao-sheng Lee, Dun-ming Tsai, Zhi-xiong Xu, and Yu-xiu Xu], 蘇建和、莊林勳、劉秉郎案 判決評鑑 [The Judgment Review of the Case of Hsih-Chi Trio] (1996) Retrieved on April 10, 2014 from www.jrf.org.tw/newjrf/index_new2014.asp?id=918.

43 The widespread belief that Taiwan's judicial system was deeply corrupt had invited a variety of proposals to reform the judicial system. People had different opinions as to what aspects of the judicial system needed to be reformed, which issues were most urgent, and what measures needed to be taken. See, for example, 黃宗樂主編 [Zong-le Huang, ed.], 民間司法改革白皮書 [The Civilian White Paper for Judicial Reform] (Taipei: 財團法人張榮發基金會、國家政策研究中心授權出版，業強出版社 [Chung Yung-Fa Foundation, National Policy Foundation, Yejiang Publisher Co.], 1997); 蘇永欽 [Yeong-chin Su], 當前司法問題的癥結，司法改革的再改革 [The Key Issue of the Contemporary Judicial System: Re-reforming the Judicial System] (Taipei: 元照出版公司 [Yuanzhao Publishers], 1998). But there was undoubtedly a consensus in Taiwan that radical reform was necessary to increase public confidence in the judicial system, and the reform of the criminal justice system was an indispensable part.

44 In fact, the social atmosphere of the late 1990s did not lend itself to demands for greater protection of human rights. In 1996 and 1997, there were three high-profile crimes. These cases had aroused a fear of crime in Taiwanese society and created public demand for crime control. Preventive detention was adopted in 1997. The criteria for parole were tightened. But overall, these events did not stop the JY from promoting judicial reform and the adoption of the adversarial system.

The pressure of convenience: the judiciary's high caseload burden

The JY showed an interest in the adversarial system before the Hsih-Chi Trio case revealed problems. After JY President Lin Yang-kang (林洋港) visited Japan in 1990 and learned of how the adversarial system had worked in Japan since 1948,[45] the JY began to promote the adversarial system in Taiwan.[46]

The first step the JY took was to include "the principle of the simple bill of indictment" (起訴狀一本主義) in its official report on judicial reform. This was a crucial practice in the Japanese-style adversarial system, and it meant that only the bill of indictment would need to be submitted to court prior to trial. The prosecutor would no longer need to transfer all evidence to the court before the trial but would only present evidence to the judge(s) at trial. The JY claimed that a more adversarial system would make trials fairer and would thus to increase defendants' confidence in the judicial system.[47] In 1991, the JY authorized a pilot experiment of the adversarial system in two high-profile cases in the Taipei District Court.[48] In 1993, the Taipei District Court and Prosecution Office agreed to experiment with the adversarial system on serious or controversial cases – i.e., the prosecutor would play a more active role at trial.[49] In 1994, the JY organized a "Judicial Reform Committee" (司法改革委員會). Issues that were discussed included prosecutors' inactivity or even absence at trial and judges' overactive role at trial to the extent that criminal procedure resembled the traditional

45 In 1948, Japan enacted a new Criminal Procedural Code under the US occupation. While this new code retained quite a few characteristics of the Continental European legal system, it adopted some features of Anglo-American law, including greater emphasis on protection of rights of the accused, hearsay rules, and the adversarial trial. Carl F. Goodman, *The Rule of Law in Japan: A Comparative Analysis*, Alphen aan den Rijn, The Netherlands: Kluwer Law International (2012): 277.

46 郭威廷 [Wei-ting Guo], 台灣刑事訴訟法朝向當事人主義修正的歷史動因 [Historical Causes of the Adversarial Reform in Taiwanese Criminal Procedure], 107.

47 汪士淳 [Shi-chun Wang], 林洋港：訴訟獨立比預算獨立更重要 [The Independence of the Trial is More Important than the Independence of the Budget], *United Daily News* (September 1, 1990): 4; 汪士淳 [Shi-chun Wang], 司法革新方向 符合社會期待 [The Direction of Judicial Reform Corresponds to the Expectation of the Society], *United Daily News* (September 1, 1990): 4.

48 汪士淳 [Shi-chun Wang], 三光案 華隆案 將採當事人進行主義審理 [The Court Will Adopt the Adversarial System to Handle the Sankuan Case and the Hwalong Case], *United Daily News* (May 15, 1991): 6. It is not unusual for the JY to authorize pilot experiments of new reform plans in district courts. A recent example can be seen in lay participation in criminal trials. The JY authorized pilot experiments of lay participation in Shilin and Chiayi district courts. But the pilot experiments were done on simulated cases. The goal of these experiments was to see whether the JY's plans would be feasible in practice, and what problems the plans might create. But it is unclear whether these pilot experiments have been carefully evaluated and the extent to which their results have affected the JY's plans.

49 楊肅民 [Su-ming Yang], 接獲紅字通知書 檢方需蒞庭論告 [If the Prosecutor Receives a Red Notice, the Prosecutor Must Argue the Case at Trial], *China Times* (January 11, 1993): 7.

Chinese inquisitorial-style system.[50] The adoption of the adversarial system was suggested at the conclusion of this committee, which further strengthened the JY's determination to promote this new system.

When the Hsih-Chi Trio case put more pressure on the JY to reform criminal procedure, the adoption of the adversarial system was still the answer for the JY and many other judges. In 1998, the JY authorized another pilot experiment of the adversarial system in the Banqiao District Court.[51] In 1999, Taiwan's High Court asked the Shilin District Court and its Prosecution Office to have prosecutors more actively participate at trials.[52] A few months before the 1999 NJRC, the JY released its official Blue Paper Report (司法改革藍皮書), formally including the adversarial system in its blueprint for judicial reform.[53] Since the resolutions of the NJRC would become the blueprint for subsequent legislation, the JY's decade-long efforts to promote the adversarial system seemed to be nearing their conclusion.

While it was undeniable that the adversarial system would improve the fairness of trials, some researchers believe that the increasing workloads judges faced were a more important factor for the JY.[54] Wei-ting Guo points out that the overall case burden on the judicial system had long been troubling the JY. Even though the JY adopted various strategies, including implementing expedited procedures in the criminal justice system and setting up procedural constraints on appeals to the Supreme Court, caseloads still grew every year.[55] In 1975, the total number of cases that district criminal courts handled was 164,374. The average number of cases each district criminal court judge had to resolve every month was 86.62. In 1984, the total number of cases that district criminal courts handled was 303,776. The average number of cases per district criminal court

50 司法院大法官書記處編 [Department of Clerks for the Justices of the Constitutional Court, ed.], 司法改革委員會會議實錄 [Meeting Minutes of the Committee for Judicial Reform] (Taipei: 司法院 [Judicial Yuan], 1996): 581–3.

51 雷鳴 [Ming Lei], 八項司法改革 板橋地院昨起試辦 [Yesterday Banqiao District Court Started to Experiment with Eight Measures for Judicial Reform], *United Daily News* (July 2, 1998): 8.

52 王兆鵬 [Jaw-perng Wang], 檢察官專責全程到庭實行公訴之實證問卷調查研究 [The Empirical Survey of the System of the Participation of the Prosecutor at Trial] (Taipei: 法務部 [Ministry of Justice], 2002); 王梅英 [May-ing Wang], 臺灣士林地方法院實行「檢察官專責全程到庭實行公訴」法庭活動之研究 [The Study of Courtroom Activities of the Shilin District Court] (Taipei: 司法院 [Judicial Yuan], 2002): 2.

53 張瓈文 [Li-wen Chang], 司法再造 五大改革五年完成 [Five Major Measures to Rebuild the Judicial System will be Completed within Five Years], *China Times* (March 30, 1999): 1.

54 See, for example, 郭威廷 [Wei-ting Guo], 台灣刑事訴訟法朝向當事人主義修正的歷史動因 [Historical Causes of the Adversarial Reform in Taiwanese Criminal Procedure]; 何賴傑 [Lai-jier Her], '論刑事訴訟法之傳承與變革–從我國與德國晚近刑事訴訟法修法談起' [On the Tradition and Reforms of the Criminal Procedural Law: An Analysis Starting from the Latest Revisions of Taiwanese and German Criminal Procedural Laws], 月旦法學教室 [Taiwan Jurist] 100 (February, 2011): 172–83.

55 郭威廷 [Wei-ting Guo], 台灣刑事訴訟法朝向當事人主義修正的歷史動因 [Historical Causes of the Adversarial Reform in Taiwanese Criminal Procedure], 104–5.

judge per month was 139.48.[56] This heavy caseload was harming the health of judges and jeopardizing the quality of court decisions,[57] and the caseload issue thus frequently arose in most discussions about judicial reform.[58] Guo's argument about the decisive influence of caseloads on the JY is quite plausible.

The efficiency-driven reforms which the JY has often pursued made other researchers wonder whether its real concern was judges' workloads.[59] In the conclusion of the 1994 Judicial Reform Committee's report, the JY listed several efficiency-driven measures, such as deferred prosecution (緩起訴),[60] simplified trials (簡式審判程序),[61] and restrictions on appeal to the Supreme Court (限制上訴第三審) along with its proposal to adopt the adversarial system.[62] In 2004, the JY endorsed the adoption of the sentence bargaining system (協商制度). The JY's relentless pursuit of efficiency-driven reforms strongly suggested that these reforms were not merely supplementary to the adversarial system. It is quite possible that many reforms, including the adoption of the adversarial system, were largely efficiency-driven. All things considered, under the pressure of high caseloads, the JY chose the adversarial system to respond to the call of reforming the criminal justice system.

After 1990, the JY had become the number-one supporter of the adversarial system in Taiwan. American and Japanese scholars were invited to Taiwan to

56 Ibid., 103.

57 江元慶 [Yuan-chin Jiang], 流浪法庭30年! 台灣三名老人的真實故事 [Drifting between Courts for Thirty Years! A True Story of Three Old Men] (Taipei: 報導文學 [Reportage], 2008): 88–96.

58 See, for example, 吳美凝 [Mei-nin Wu], 司法革新大醇小疵 高院合議精神不足 [The Lack of Spirit of Deliberation in the High Court as One Small Flaw in Judicial Reform], *China Times* (March 14, 1974): 4.

59 See, for example, Margaret K. Lewis, *Taiwan's New Adversarial System and the Overlooked Challenge of Efficiency-Driven Reforms. Virginia Journal of International Law* 49(3) (2009): 651–726.

60 Deferred prosecution is a measure the prosecutor could adopt as an alternative to formal indictment against the defendant in non-serious cases. The prosecutor could decide not to indict the defendant, if the defendant is willing to comply with prosecutor's orders, such as complying with the necessary order for the prevention of recommitting the offense, or to perform certain obligations within a limited period of time, such as community services or donating a certain sum to government or a designated non-profit organization. If the defendant complies with the orders, fulfills all obligations, and does not intentionally commit another crime within a period of time, the decision not to indict will be finalized. If the defendant fails to fulfill his obligations, the decision of deferred prosecution will be dropped, and the defendant will be indicted immediately. Deferred prosecution thus gives prosecutors more discretion and reduces caseloads for prosecutors and judges.

61 Simplified trials are special trials in which certain procedural rules, such as hearsay rules, are not applied. They are used in cases involving crimes that are not serious and when evidence against the defendants is strong. Because there are no cross-examinations at simplified trials, they save courts and prosecutors time in dealing with a case.

62 司法院大法官書記處編 [Department of Clerks for the Justices of the Constitutional Court, ed.], 司法改革委員會會議實錄 [Meeting Minutes of the Committee for the Judicial Reform], 290–4, 1259–62, 1363–81.

explain how the adversarial system worked. Law professors who received their doctoral degrees in the US and Japan became important consultants for the JY as it worked on reforms.

Sharp opposition and chaotic debate

The calls for judicial reform and caseload pressures explained why the JY aggressively promoted the adversarial system in the 1990s. But the story of how Taiwan adopted an "improved adversarial system" is far more complicated. It can be helpful here to examine how the adversarial and inquisitorial systems were perceived around the time of reform.

The JY's announcements and its official report were undoubtedly important sources of information for Taiwanese society to learn what the two systems were about. It should not be forgotten that before the 1990s, news coverage of the adversarial system in Taiwan's newspapers was generally released together with news about the progress of judicial reform.[63] It was thus possible that Taiwanese society already had a positive, if vague, impression of the adversarial system before the JY implemented this system.

Other kinds of media representations were probably more meaningful for Taiwanese society around the time of reform. Since the late 1980s, many US courtroom movies and dramas, such as *L.A. Law* (1986–94), were shown in movie theaters and broadcast on TV in Taiwan. These dramas and movies showed Taiwanese people how the adversarial system worked and how exciting courtroom cross-examinations could be.[64] More importantly, these media presentations inevitably connected the adversarial system to the US, its criminal procedure, and most of all, its democracy.[65] In a country where people have constantly

63 Media coverage has usually reported that judicial authorities announced that they would adopt some measure from adversarial criminal procedural to improve due process protections for the defendant. See, for example, 新法兼採當事人進行主義　拘提審訊均重視事實 防止濫押定期間限制 [New Law Adopts Some Measures from the Adversarial System; Arrest and Interrogation Will Emphasize the Facts of the Cases; Restrictions on the Time Limit Will Be Added to Avoid Abuse of Pretrial Detention], *China Times* (January 14, 1967): 2; 司法院完成刑訴法修正原則加強當事人進行主義 事實審中心移至一審 [The JY Completed the Revision of the Criminal Procedural Code; The New Law Will Adopt More Measures from the Adversarial System; The District Court Will Become the Focus of the Trial of Fact], *China Times* (January 21, 1985): 5.

64 郭威廷 [Wei-ting Guo], 台灣刑事訴訟法朝向當事人主義修正的歷史動因 [Historical Causes of the Adversarial Reform in Taiwanese Criminal Procedure], 90–1. Opponents of the adversarial system were fully aware of the positive influence of *L.A. Law*. Therefore, they had to specifically explain negative aspects of the adversarial system. See, for example, 「當事人進行主義」不是司法改革萬靈丹 [The Adversarial System is Not a Magic Cure for Judicial Reform], *United Daily News* (July 6, 1999): 2; 司法院 [Judicial Yuan], 全國司法改革會議實錄 [National Judicial Conference Minutes] (Taipei: 司法院 [Judicial Yuan], 1999): 1113, 1120, 1430.

65 Because most people in Taiwan learned of the adversarial system from American movies and TV dramas, it was quite possible that people had a strong assumption that this system would fit well

looked up to the US as a model in almost all areas,[66] it is reasonable to assume that Taiwanese society received a positive impression of the adversarial system through these media representations.

While the positive image of the American-style adversarial system helped the JY to promote the new system, dissatisfaction with Taiwan's criminal justice system was also helpful. After all, the criminal justice system in Taiwan needed to be reformed and the JY wished to give up on the inquisitorial mode. It was undeniable that the prosecutor was generally inactive at trial, and the defendant was thus forced to stand against the judge, who may have been biased by the evidence submitted by the prosecutor prior to trial. Anyone who wished to defend the inquisitorial system had to explain that the preference was not merely out of the selfish concern for the light courtroom workload for prosecutors, or the position of prosecutors in the criminal procedure.[67] Especially as most supporters of the inquisitorial system were prosecutors and the MOJ (prosecutors are subordinate to the MOJ), they had to show that they were not acting self-interestedly but cared about justice.

The MOJ had been reluctant to accept the JY's plan since the early 1990s. When the JY attempted to use the adversarial system in the trials of two specific cases in the Taipei District Court,[68] the Minister of Justice Lu You-wen (呂有文) disagreed, and insisted the criminal procedural code should be revised before the court tried any new practice. He admitted that the adoption of the adversarial system was inevitable in the future. But he emphasized that the new system should be adopted on the condition that prosecutors be given more discretion to drop and to defer prosecutions, since the new system would increase prosecutors' workloads.[69] Prosecutors also raised concerns about whether the adoption of the adversarial system would "degrade" prosecutors' status in criminal procedure (which they believed was equivalent to judges' status)[70] and contravene

---

with democracy. This assumption forced opponents to the JY's plan to emphasize the fact that the country that had pioneered the inquisitorial system – Germany – was also a democratic country. Selecting the adversarial system was not inevitable for Taiwan. 何賴傑 [Lai-jier Her], '正當法律程序原則－刑事訴訟法上一個新的法律原則?' [The Principle of Due Process: A New Rule in the Criminal Procedural Law?], 憲政時代 [The Constitutional Review] 25, no. 4 (April, 2000): 42–3.

66 Death Penalty Issue Research Group, *Taiwan Human Rights Report 2000: The Taiwan Death Penalty Issue in International Perspective* (2000), cited from David Johnson and Franklin E. Zimring, *The Next Frontier: National Development, Political Change, and the Death Penalty in Asia*. New York: Oxford University Press (2009): 192.

67 彭芸芳 [Yun-fang Peng], 有錢判生 沒錢判死？[Live if Bribing Judges, Die if Unable to], *United Daily News* (March 31, 1999): 8; 司法為民 檢察機關應該放下身段 [The Prosecutors Should Learn to Humble Themselves to Serve People], *China Times* (April 5, 1999): 3.

68 楊肅民 [Su-ming Yang], 三光案首度開庭「法官職權調查主義」為主 「當事人進行主義」為輔 過程嚴謹 [The Case of Sankuan], *China Times* (May 24, 1991): 6.

69 陳永富 [Yung-fu Chen], 當事人進行主義審案 尚不能試辦 [The Adversarial System is yet to be Experimented with at Trial], *United Daily News* (July 14, 1991): 7.

70 Prosecutors have fought for their position in criminal procedure since 1960. That year, the

Taiwan's traditional culture.[71] What prosecutors referred to was very likely a culture that celebrated the stories of Judge Bao (Bao Qing-tian, 包青天) – an iconic Chinese judge who aggressively pursued justice rather than acting as a neutral referee in a contest between two parties.[72] Furthermore, in the Judicial Reform Committee of 1994, the representative from the MOJ claimed that fairness at trial in the inquisitorial system could be achieved if the judge was friendlier to the defendant.[73]

Constitutional Court wrote Interpretation 86, holding that all civil and criminal courts should be subordinate to the JY. Prosecutors argued that prosecution offices should be subordinate to the JY as well because prosecutors also enjoyed judicial powers. They opposed the separation of prosecution offices and courts. 審檢一家系統嚴整 歷史編制不應割裂 [Courts and Prosecution are Derived from the Same System. This Historical Institutional Arrangement Should Not Be Broken], *United Daily News* (October 14, 1960): 3. Because of the opposition of prosecutors, the KMT government did not respond to Interpretation 86 until 1980, when the government decided to move all courts to the JY's control, despite prosecutors' complaints. A similar concern was raised in 1989, when prosecutors were asked to move their seats from the judges' position to a place equal to the defendant's at trial. 檢察官 該坐那? [Where Should the Prosecutor Sit at Trial?], *China Times* (March 21, 1989): 5. Under the leadership of the JY, this old practice was abandoned over prosecutors' protests. 汪士淳 [Shi-chun Wang], 檢察官席 置於審判台下右側 [The Seat of the Prosecutor will be Placed on the Lower Right-hand Side of the Judge's Bench], *United Daily News* (January 8, 1990): 1. In 1995, several legislators filed a petition with the Constitutional Court on the constitutionality of criminal procedural provisions that empowered prosecutors to detain suspects prior to trial. By the end of that year, the Court wrote Interpretation 392 and held that pre-trial detention, as prescribed in the criminal procedural code, was incongruous with the spirit of the Constitution. The Justices pointed out that the "court" provided in Article 8 of the Constitution did not include the "prosecutor's office." Therefore empowering the prosecutor to detain a person beyond the 24-hour period as authorized by criminal procedural code was unconstitutional. In the eyes of prosecutors, their status was steadily declining, and the adoption of the adversarial system would have been a large step further away from their quasi-judge status.

71 陳永富 [Yung-fu Chen], 當事人進行主義 應以職權主義為基礎 [The Adoption of the Adversarial System should be Based on the Inquisitorial System], *United Daily News* (July 15, 1991): 7.

72 Bao Qing-Tian (literally, "Clear Sky Bao") was the nickname of Bao Zheng, a government officer in ancient China (AD 999–1062). When he served, Bao consistently demonstrated extreme honesty and uprightness. He aggressively pursued justice, even if defendants were from powerful families. 翁文靜 [Wen-jing Weng], 包拯故事研究 [Study of the Stories of Bao Zheng], (輔仁大學中國文學研究所碩士論文 [Master's Thesis, Department of Chinese Literature, Fu Jen Catholic University], 1989). His largely fictionalized stories have appeared in a variety of literature and TV dramas and thus have had a deep impact on the public perception of justice in culturally Chinese societies. Even though from today's perspective Bao's style of justice had serious due process issues, he is still the cultural symbol of justice for many cultural Chinese societies. When prosecutors argued that the adversarial system contradicted the traditional culture of Taiwan, what they meant was that Taiwanese people expected that judges would aggressively lead the investigation of evidence at trial.

73 司法院大法官書記處編 [Department of Clerks for the Justices of the Constitutional Court, ed.], 司法改革委員會會議實錄 [Meeting Minutes of the Committee for the Judicial Reform] (Taipei: 司法院 [Judicial Yuan], 1996): 805–6.

Because the JY's Blue Paper Report on reform made the adoption of the adversarial system imminent, it instantly aroused strong opposition from the MOJ and prosecutors. Some worried that the workload would make it impossible for prosecutors to have meaningful cross-examinations at trial.[74] Some complained that the JY's plan unfairly put the judge in a superior position at trial relative to the prosecutor.[75] Prosecutors in Taiwan have tended to believe that they are "judicial officers" and should be equal in status with judges. Some warned that the adoption of the adversarial system would discriminate against the poor. Only the rich would be able to afford to hire lawyers and obtain justice in the adversarial system, the critics suggested. Others protested that the JY unfairly held prosecutors responsible for all the problems in criminal procedure. Some questioned whether it was legitimate for a judge to be passive at trial. But the MOJ denied being anti-reform.[76] It quickly released its own White Paper Report (檢察改革白皮書), which provided an alternative plan for judicial reform, a few days after the JY unveiled its plan in 1999. The MOJ's White Paper Report proposed an improved inquisitorial system, in which the prosecutor would carry the burden of proof at trial, but the judge was still required to actively participate in the investigation of evidence. It also proposed adopting the US jury system, a move that aimed at holding the courts at least partially responsible for the problems of the criminal justice system.[77]

While the debate over the criminal procedure resulted in sharp opposition between two "self-interested" governmental organizations, in the eyes of the public, lawyers, criminal law scholars, and even the press entered the debate, making it more chaotic. In general, lawyers favored the JY's proposals, because the adversarial system would put lawyers on equal footing with prosecutors,[78] a status they were generally denied in Taiwan's inquisitorial system. In early 1999, the JRF released its Blueprint for Judicial Reform (司法改革藍圖), formally supporting the adoption of the adversarial system. Its argument was about fairness at trial. For the same reason, it also favored the adoption of "the principle of

74 孟令士 [Ling-si Meng], 當「當事人進行主義」 碰到分身乏術的檢察官 [When the Adversarial System Meets an Overwhelmed Prosecutor], *United Daily News* (March 31, 1999): 15; 郭吉助 [Chi-chu Guo], 負荷過重 蒞庭流於形式化 [Because the Prosecutor's Responsibility is Too Heavy, the Prosecutor's Participation at Trial May Become Formalistic], *United Daily News* (April 1, 1999): 15.

75 越方如 [Feng-ru Yue], 惟有法官高高在上? [Only the Judge Sits Higher Up at Trial?], *United Daily News* (March 31, 1999): 15.

76 林益民 [Yi-ming Lin], 不是反改革, 是為人民 [The MOJ is Not Anti-Reform. What it has done is for People], *United Daily News* (July 9, 1999): 4.

77 楊肅民 [Su-ming Yang], 法部建議引進類似「陪審團」制度 [The MOJ Suggested that the Jury System or Similar Systems Should Be Introduced to Taiwan], *China Times* (April 1, 1999): 3.

78 See, for example, 顧立雄 [Wellington Ku], '挽救刑事審判, 取得人民信賴唯一的出路－採行「起訴狀一本主義」之刑事訴訟制度' [The Only Road to Save the Criminal Trial and to Win the Trust of People: The Adoption of "the Principle of the Simple Bill of Indictment"], 律師雜誌 [Taipei Bar Journal] 232 (January, 1999): 2–5.

the simple bill of indictment."[79] Despite this, there were still lawyers who joined the alliance against JY's plan, because they believed that the adversarial system favored the rich, who would be able to hire the best defense lawyers.[80] Thus, there was no consensus among lawyers.

As for law scholars, the debates over two systems started much earlier.[81] In the early phase of debate, scholars could not even agree with what Chinese translations should be used to connote these two systems,[82] let alone what these two systems really were. Even though the core differences between the two systems gradually became clear in the late 1990s, scholars still could not agree on which system was better for Taiwan.

Generally speaking, scholars who received their doctoral degrees in Germany opposed the JY's plan.[83] Opposition scholars were led by Lin Shan-tien (林山田),

79 民間司法改革基金會 [JRF], '民間司法改革基金會簡介' [The Overview of the Judicial Reform Foundation], in 澄社、民間司法改革基金會編, 司法的重塑－民間司法改革研討會論文集（一） [The Reconstruction of the Judicial System: Essays on the Civilian Conference of the Judicial Reform I], eds. 澄社、民間司法改革基金會 [Taipei Society and JRF], 9–10.

80 蔡兆誠 [Chao-chen Tsai], 最好與最壞的時代-當代司法與人權評論 [The Best and Worst of Times: Commentaries on Contemporary Judicial System and Human Rights] (Taipei: 元照出版公司 [Yuanzhao Publishers], 2000): 39–41.

81 The earliest debate was initiated by Professor Huang Dong-xiong (黃東熊). In 1981, Professor Huang candidly criticized several prominent scholars for misunderstanding the adversarial system. He discussed the bright and dark sides of the system. More importantly, he connected the adversarial system to due process. 黃東熊 [Dong-xiong Huang], 中外檢察制度之比較 [A Comparison of Foreign Prosecution Systems] (Taipei: 中央文物供應社 [Central Literature Publisher], 1986): 143–76. During the same period of time, Professor Lin Shan-tien redefined the two systems. He used civil procedure to explain what the US adversarial system was, and used modern German criminal procedure to explain what the inquisitorial system was. 林山田 [Shan-tien Lin], 刑事訴訟法 [Criminal Procedure Law] (Taipei: 劉幸一 [Hsin-yi Liu], 1981): 13–18, 22–3. Both of their theories, including their misunderstandings of the two systems, had great impact on subsequent discussions. 郭威廷 [Wei-ting Guo], 台灣刑事訴訟法朝向當事人主義修正的歷史動因 [Historical Causes of the Adversarial Reform in Taiwanese Criminal Procedure], (台灣大學法律學研究所碩士論文 [Master's Thesis, Department of Law, National Taiwan University], 2004): 121–6.

82 The current popular Chinese translations of these two systems came from Japan. 何賴傑 [Lai-jier Her], '論刑事訴訟法之傳承與變革–從我國與德國晚近刑事訴訟法修法談起' [On the Tradition and Reforms of the Criminal Procedural Law: An Analysis Starting from the Latest Revisions of Taiwanese and German Criminal Procedural Laws], 月旦法學教室 [Taiwan Jurist] 100 (February, 2011): 173. The adversarial system was commonly translated as "*dangshirenjinxingzhuyi*" (當事人進行主義) or "*dangshirenzhuyi*" (當事人主義), connoting that the trial is "controlled" or "run" by the parties of the case. The inquisitorial system was commonly translated as "*zhiquanjinxingzhuyi*" (職權進行主義) or "*zhiquanzhuyi*" (職權主義), connoting that the trial is "controlled" or "run" by the judge. See, for example, 嚴泓 [Hon Yen], 刑事訴訟實用 [Practical Criminal Procedure] (Taipei: 自刊 [self-publication], 1957): 6–7; 梁恆昌 [Heng-tsang Liang], 刑事訴訟法新論 [A New Thesis on Criminal Procedural Law] (Taipei: 自刊 [self-publication], 1960): 3; 俞士英 [Si-ing Yu], 刑事訴訟法釋論 [The Interpretation of Criminal Procedural Law] (Taipei: 自刊 [self-publication], 1965): 7. While these translations reflect important dimensions of these two systems, they have also led to misunderstandings.

83 In fact, the majority of law professors have graduated from German doctoral programs. Scholars who obtained their degrees from the US or Japan tended to favor the adversarial system. But they

one prominent criminal law professor in National Taiwan University. They rejected the notion that the problems that existed in Taiwan's criminal procedure stemmed from the inquisitorial system and defended the inquisitorial system by using modern German criminal procedure as an example.[84] They also suggested alternative plans of judicial reform.[85] Three weeks before the NJRC, dissenting scholars worked with other opponents to establish an alliance, the "Judicial Reform Oversight Front" (司法改革監督陣線), against the JY's version of judicial reform. They pointed out the dangers and blind spots of the JY's plan, including the "bourgeois-ification of the criminal justice system" – the view that only the rich would be able to afford lawyers and get justice in the adversarial system, sacrificing justice in most cases because the majority of cases would be handled unfairly through plea bargaining.[86] These scholars' actions strengthened the MOJ's position.

Facing mixed reactions to their plan and increasingly stronger opposition, the JY worked hard to resolve disputes and differences before the NJRC. It called pre-conference meetings with the MOJ, bar associations, and the JRF. Most representatives from the different organizations agreed to adopt quite a few measures to make trials fairer and to reduce the workload for judges and prosecutors. However, on two core issues – the judge's role at trial and adopting the "principle of the simple bill of indictment" – representatives from the MOJ refused to make any concessions.[87] The MOJ's tough attitude was not only backed up by law scholars, but it also received help from the press. On the day the NJRC convened, the *United Daily News*, a major newspaper, published an editorial

did not unquestionably support the JY's plan. For example, Professor Wang Jaw-perng (王兆鵬), who graduated from a US law school, claimed that the JY neglected the rights of the defendant in the National Judicial Reform Conference. 王兆鵬 [Jaw-perng Wang], 審判中被告之地位 – 當事人進行主義與職權主義之不同 [The Position of the Defendant at Trial: The Differences between the Adversarial System and the Inquisitorial System] (Taipei: 月旦 [Taipei Law Review], 1999: 115–25. Professor Chen Yun-tsai (陳運財), who received his doctoral degree in Japan, disagreed with how the JY and the JRF defined the inquisitorial system. 陳運財 [Yun-tsai Chen], 釋字第392號解釋與刑事訴訟制度的變革, 刑事訴訟與正當之法律程序 [JY Interpretation No. 392 and the Changes in the Criminal Justice System: Criminal Procedure and Due Process] (Taipei: 月旦 [Taipei Law Review], 1998): 93–5.

84 See, for example, 林山田 [Shan-tien Lin], '別迷失在主義的叢林中－為職權原則與調查原則喊冤' [Do Not Get Lost in the Jungles of Systems: A Defense for the Principle of Duty and the Principle of Investigation].

85 林山田編 [Shan-tien Lin, ed.], 刑事訴訟法改革對案 [Alternative Proposals for the Reform of Criminal Procedure] (Taipei: 元照出版公司 [Yuanzhao Publishers], 2000).

86 黃錦嵐 [Jin-lan Huang], 「監督陣線」成軍 提司改危險與盲點 [A Supervision Alliance Was Established to Provide Warnings about Dangers and Blind Sides of Judicial Reform], *China Times* (June 15, 1999): 8.

87 黃錦嵐 [Jin-lan Huang], 司改會前會 院部共識高 [The JY and the MOJ Have a High Level of Consensus in the Preliminary Meeting of the National Judicial Reform Conference], *China Times* (July 3. 1999): 8.

questioning the necessity of adopting the adversarial system.[88] The JY faced a difficult road to getting this part of its plan accepted at the NJRC.

The National Judicial Reform Conference: a failure on the verge of success

In the history of Taiwan, the NJRC in 1999 was an exceptional event with no predecessors or successors. Previously, the JY at most invited limited numbers of privileged elites to its special committees to provide suggestions.[89] In 1999, the JY invited a greater number of elites to participate in deliberations about major reforms to law. Most attendees were representatives from groups, such as lawyers, scholars, judges and prosecutors. Some were not in the legal profession. The decisions reached at the NJRC were expected to become the blueprint for subsequent legislation. Being aware of the importance of this conference, different groups, including the JY, craftily issued opening statements, hoping to influence public opinion and thus the outcome of the NJRC. They also disputed over who should participate in the conference.

Even though the JY enthusiastically used the NJRC as an important battlefield to fight for the acceptance of the adversarial system, this conference was actually not initiated by the JY. The idea of having a national conference to solve policy disputes appears to have originally come from the JRF. Disappointed with the scale and speed of judicial reform led by the JY, and unsatisfied with providing alternative opinions merely through articles and conferences, the JRF pressured President Lee Teng-hui (李登輝) in May 1997 to organize a legal reform gathering modeled on the Conference on National Development in 1996.[90] The JY was later forced to organize this conference.[91] But at first, the JY tried to limit the issues and participants in the NJRC.[92] The JRF boycotted the JY's plan and initiated a demonstration in October 1997, in which many lawyers, scholars,

88 「當事人進行主義」不是司法改革萬靈丹 [The Adversarial System is Not a Magic Cure for Judicial Reform], *United Daily News* (July 6, 1999): 2.

89 When Chi-yang Shih (施啟揚) became the JY's president in 1994, he asked his staff to organize an official committee for judicial reform. A limited numbers of people, including legislators, scholars, lawyers, senior judges and prosecutors, and respected social elites, were invited to the committee. In fact, it was not the first time the president of the JY swore to reform the judicial system and to improve people's confidence in the judicial system. But the general impression of the JY's efforts was that it was merely empty promises. 寄望這次司法改革真是「玩真的」 [It is Hoped that Judicial Reform is 'For Real' This Time], *China Times* (October 21, 1994): 3.

90 Like the Conference on National Affairs in 1990 or the Conference on National Development in 1996, the NJRC was pushed by reformers as a strategy to include liberal voices from civil society to challenge the government's domination over judicial policies. If properly administered, the national conference could have been used by the President to overcome resistance in the judicial bureaucracy and to speed up reform.

91 李總統：贊成司法預算獨立 [President Lee: I Approve the Independence of Judicial Budget], *United Daily News* (May 9, 1997): 17.

92 鍾沛東 [Pei-tong Chong], 全國司改會議 決15日開籌備會 [The JY Decided to Hold a

judges and prosecutors participated, to put pressure on the government. The impasse between the JY and reform groups did not change until President Lee replaced Shih Chi-yang (施啟揚) with Weng Yueh-sheng (翁岳生) as the president of the JY in February 1999.[93] The NJRC was quickly re-examined.[94] Over the next few months, the JY worked closely with scholars and reform groups to prepare for the NJRC. Interestingly enough, the JRF had become the JY's allies at the NJRC, at least on the issue of adopting the adversarial system.[95]

The NJRC was held from July 6 to July 8, 1999. The first two days were panel discussions. One hundred and twenty-five representatives were divided into three panels and tasked with discussing over 12 topics and reaching preliminary resolutions. The preliminary resolutions made in each panel would be voted on in a grand assembly on the last day.[96] The topic of the reform of criminal procedure was assigned to Panel Two. On this topic, the core issue was whether criminal procedure should be transformed to the adversarial system. Based on proposals submitted to the NJRC in advance, representatives in Panel Two were asked to discuss several issues relating to the future contours of criminal procedure.

Among the issues Panel Two discussed, three were linked to the adoption of the adversarial system, or more specifically, the Japanese-style adversarial system: (1) whether to adopt "the principle of the simple bill of indictment," (2) "the cause of action system" (訴因制度), and (3) whether judges should have the obligation to investigate evidence unfavorable to the defendant.[97] The third issue involved overturning a core feature of the inquisitorial system. "The principle of the simple bill of indictment" was intended to help make adversarial trials fair. It aimed at changing a common practice in Taiwan's inquisitorial system, under which the prosecutor would transfer all evidence to the judge prior to trial. Under "the principle of the simple bill of indictment," the judge would only be given the charges against the defendant and a list of evidence prior to trial, with the content of the evidence only emerging later at trial. "The cause of action system" circumscribes the scope of the charge(s) against the defendant at trial. Under this system, the judge cannot expand the scope of the charges at

---

Preliminary Meeting for the National Judicial Reform Conference], *United Daily News* (October 2, 1997): 6.

93 鍾沛東 [Pei-tong Chong], 施啟揚為什麼下台？[Why did Shih Chi-yang Step Down?], *United Daily News* (January 12, 1999): 8.

94 鍾沛東 [Pei-tong Chong], 全國司改會議 七、八月間召開 [The National Judicial Reform Conference will be Held in July or August], *United Daily News* (March 2, 1999): 8.

95 民間司法改革基金會 [JRF], '民間司法改革基金會簡介' [The Overview of the Judicial Reform Foundation], in 澄社、民間司法改革基金會編, 司法的重塑－民間司法改革研討會論文集（一） [The Reconstruction of the Judicial System: Essays on the Civilian Conference of the Judicial Reform I], eds. 澄社、民間司法改革基金會 [Taipei Society and JRF].

96 司法院 [Judicial Yuan], 全國司法改革會議實錄 [National Judicial Conference Minutes], 1581–3.

97 Ibid., 1025–6.

trial. Only charges specifically stated in the bill of indictment could be tried. This system was intended to change a common practice in Taiwan's inquisitorial system. It was not only meant to make the trial more predictable for the defendant, but also to limit the discretion of the judge. The judge would become a more passive but neutral "referee" in a battle between the prosecutor and the defendant.

Unsurprisingly, representatives could not agree on adopting these three issues, even though both the JY and the MOJ claimed that they were willing to make concessions. The JY was willing to give the judge the discretion to investigate the truth of the crime at trial when necessary, while the MOJ was willing to ask the prosecutor to bear a substantial burden of proof. Representatives of the MOJ insisted that judges should share the burden of proof with the prosecutor. They also rejected the adoption of "the principle of the simple bill of indictment" and "the cause of action system." Many representatives were convinced that the adoption of "the principle of the simple bill of indictment" would prevent the judge from being biased against the defendant prior to the trial and that removing judges' obligation to investigate the facts of crimes would make the trial fairer. Most of the time, representatives of the MOJ stood alone to fight against almost all other representatives, including those of the JY, judges, lawyers and scholars.[98] Even though the majority of representatives in Panel Two favored the adversarial system, consensus on these core issues could not be reached. Only temporary resolutions could be submitted to the grand assembly for further consideration.[99]

According to the rules of the NJRC, final resolutions could be decided on in only two situations: (1) Representatives in the panel had consensus over one issue and submitted a preliminary resolution to the grand assembly. Later, the majority of representatives in the grand assembly approved that preliminary resolution; (2) If representatives in the panel did not have consensus over one issue, and the panel submitted two to three temporary resolutions to the grand assembly, a final resolution on one issue could still be made if all four vice presidents of the NJRC reached a consensus over that issue, recommended one temporary resolution to the grand assembly, and the majority of the representatives

98 There were three criminal law scholars in Panel Two. One was Tuan Chung-min (段重民), who graduated from University of California, Hastings College of the Law. The other two were Chen Yun-tsai (陳運財) and Huang Chaur-yi (黃朝義). They received their doctoral degrees in Japan. Three of them were important consultants for the JY in planning to adopt the adversarial system. Scholars who obtained their doctoral degrees from Germany and strongly opposed the JY's plan did not attend the NJRC. Records show that one leading dissenting professor, Shan-tien Lin (林山田), was invited. 司法院 [Judicial Yuan], 全國司法改革會議實錄 [National Judicial Conference Minutes], 662. It was not clear why he did not attend. It is very likely that Professor Lin did not want to endorse the resolution of the NJRC, because opponents to JY's plan were clearly outnumbered by proponents.

99 司法院 [Judicial Yuan], 全國司法改革會議實錄 [National Judicial Conference Minutes], 1372–91.

in the grand assembly approved that resolution. In the second situation, the opinions of vice presidents of the NJRC would be crucial. If any of the vice presidents of the NJRC had a dissenting opinion, no resolution on the issue could be recommended to the grand assembly, and no relevant resolution could be made. It did not matter even if the majority of the representatives in the panel or in the grand assembly favored one temporary resolution. The rationale of this rule was to prevent the "tyranny of the majority." The rule-makers believed that a reform would not work well if it could not gain consensus from representatives.[100]

The resolution rules had a clear impact on the outcome of the NJRC regarding the issues relating to the adoption of the adversarial system. Representatives in Panel Two could not agree on the three controversial issues. Therefore, only temporary resolutions were submitted to the grand assembly for consideration. In the grand assembly, the Minister of Justice Yeh Jin-Feng (葉金鳳), who had been a judge and later became the Minister of the Interior and the Chair of the Central Election Commission, disagreed with the other three vice presidents. She did not consent to the adoption of "the principle of the simple bill of indictment" and "the cause of action system." She wanted the judge to share the burden of proof with the prosecutor at trial. Even though the majority of representatives favored the adoption of the adversarial system, the conference rules dictated that no resolutions on these issues could be made. The Minister of Justice literally vetoed the decision of the majority of the representatives, and vetoed the JY's plan. Although it was on the verge of success, the JY's plan to make criminal procedure more adversarial failed.

The global trend toward the adversarial system

The goal for reformers in pursuing the NJRC process was to challenge the government's domination of judicial policies and to create a democratic space for people to decide judicial policies as equal partners. The legitimacy of the resolutions of the NJRC as the blueprint for subsequent legislation was derived from the democratic nature of the conference. But whether the participants of the NJRC could really represent society (or at least the legal community), to what extent participants were well-informed, and whether the discussions were rational are all open questions.

The day after the NJRC, 17 criminal law scholars issued a joint statement questioning the representativeness of the NJRC. The statement pointed out that only three criminal law professors participated in the NJRC. The NJRC thus lacked sufficient legal expertise to formulate policies to reform Taiwan's criminal procedure.[101] Three months after the NJRC, several criminal law scholars

100 Ibid., 1608–13.

101 宋伯東 [Pao-tong Song], 刑法學者批司改會不專業 [Criminal Law Scholars Attacked the National Judicial Reform Conference as Unprofessional], *United Daily News* (July 10, 1999): 8. Criticisms of the legitimacy of the NJRC were also raised before the NJRC. 宋伯東

organized a symposium to debate the appropriate ways for reforming Taiwan's criminal procedure. In that symposium, one senior criminal law professor, Gan Tien-guei (甘添貴), complained that he was neither invited to the NJRC nor consulted before it. He criticized the NJRC process as being so hasty that it could produce catastrophic results for Taiwan's criminal justice system.[102] The backlash against the JY and the NJRC from law scholars looked huge, which helped the MOJ. But the JY had the legal experts it needed to endorse its plan. In Taiwan, law scholars are influential in policy-making, mainly through the government or legislators inviting them to help in law-drafting or revising existing law. However, whether Taiwan would shift to the adversarial system still hinged on the result of the battle between the JY and MOJ.

Even though the criticisms against the NJRC had exposed weaknesses in its organization and challenged its legitimacy, the MOJ was under greater pressure. On its face, the MOJ won the battle with the JY over whether Taiwan should adopt the adversarial system. But it immediately faced criticisms. It was attacked as a "factionalist" (本位主義) mainly concerned with defending its bureaucratic turf and was labeled anti-reform.[103] Even one friendly journalist pointed out that the MOJ inevitably had to take the full responsibility for any problem in the criminal justice system from now on, even though no one knew for sure whether the adoption of the adversarial system would have been a panacea.[104] The MOJ denied the accusations and emphasized that it supported judicial reform and was willing to find common ground with the JY. The JY also expressed its intention to keep negotiating with the MOJ.[105] A second round in the battle between the JY and the MOJ began.

Following the NJRC, more and more judges asked prosecutors to bear the substantial burden of proof. Those who failed to prove the guilt of defendants at

[Pao-tong Song], 檢改會陳瑞仁 籲停止官式大拜拜 [Eric Chen from the Prosecutors' Reform Association Calls for the Cancellation of the Meaningless Ritual-like JRC], *United Daily News* (July 4, 1999): 8. Such critiques can still be seen today. See, for example, 何賴傑 [Lai-jier Her], '論刑事訴訟法之傳承與變革–從我國與德國晚近刑事訴訟法修法談起' [On the Tradition and Reforms of the Criminal Procedural Law: An Analysis Starting from the Latest Revisions of Taiwanese and German Criminal Procedural Laws], 月旦法學教室 [Taiwan Jurist] 100 (February, 2011): 172.

102 甘添貴 [Tien-guei Gan], '本書緣起' [Prologue], in如何建立一套適合我國國情的刑事訴訟制度 [How to Build a Criminal Justice System that is Suitable for Our Country], eds. 林山田 [Sheng-tien Lin] and甘添貴 [Tien-guei Gan] (Taipei: 新學林 [New Sharing Publishing Co.], 2000).

103 楊肅民 [Su-ming Yang], 法務部硬爭 叫改革太沈重 [The Struggle by the MOJ Made Reform Unbearable], *China Times* (July 9, 1999): 2.

104 鍾沛東 [Pei-tong Chong], 用否決權後 法部有無限責任 [After Using the Power of Veto, the MOJ Has to Shoulder Unlimited Responsibilities], *United Daily News* (July 10, 1999): 8.

105 張瓈文 [Li-wen Chang], 翁岳生：繼續溝通 尋求院部共識 [Weng Yueh-sheng: The JY Will Continuingly Seek Communication and Consensus with the MOJ], *China Times* (July 10, 1999): 8.

trial increasingly received not-guilty verdicts.[106] Facing pressure from the courts and society, the MOJ became even more aggressive than the JY in pushing the adversarial system – or at least the MOJ's version of it. The MOJ planned to adopt "the principle of the simple bill of indictment." It also asked prosecutors in two prosecution offices to more actively participate in trials.[107] But despite these moves, the MOJ still insisted that judges should share the responsibility of investigating evidence at trial. This became the main disagreement between the JY and the MOJ. The MOJ's intent was not only to show Taiwanese society that it was not anti-reform, but to force the JY to admit that the JY's version of adversarial system was not suitable for Taiwan. But more importantly, the MOJ strongly believed that by doing so, prosecutors could also maintain their equal status as judges.[108] Some prosecutors became more aggressive at trial, so much so that they sometimes made district court judges look unprepared, ironically.[109] This could have forced the JY to reconsider its reform plans. Even though the MOJ admitted that the adoption of the adversarial system was a global trend, it did not want to give in to the JY's plan.[110]

While the battle between the JY and the MOJ still looked tight, the JY sent its legislative bill to revise the criminal procedural code to the Legislative Yuan. Due to the JY's aggressive lobbying, the bill was approved by the judiciary committee of the legislature on October 29, 2001. The JY's bill not only gave the judge the discretion to initiate the investigation of the truth of a crime at trial when necessary (Art. 163 of the Criminal Procedural Code), it also gave the judge the option to return the indictment to the prosecutor if evidence was clearly insufficient to support the charges (Art. 161 of the Criminal Procedural Code). But it did not adopt "the principle of the simple bill of indictment" and "the cause of action system." The adoption of the adversarial system was thus incomplete.

The JY's legislative bill once again aroused debate.[111] The MOJ was still the number one opponent of the change.[112] But the situation changed when the new

106 林河名 [Her-ming Lin], 上訴駁回 高院數落檢方未到庭 [High Court Denies Prosecutor's Appeal on the Grounds that He Failed to Show up to Trial], *United Daily News* (August 8, 1999): 8.

107 楊肅民 [Su-ming Yang], 簡化起訴書 開庭再攻防 [The Bill of Indictment will be Simplified. The Prosecutor will Argue the Case at Trial], *China Times* (January 2, 2000): 8.

108 楊肅民 [Su-ming Yang], 三角習題 牽絆司改步伐 [Triangle of Issues Hold Judicial Reform Back], *China Times* (July 10, 1999): 8.

109 宋伯東 [Pao-tong Song], 當事人進行主義 未必適合我民情 [The Adversarial System is Not Necessarily Appropriate for Our Society], *United Daily News* (April 24, 2000): 8.

110 王鵬捷 [Perng-jei Wang], 當事人進行主義六月實施 葉金鳳表示 檢察官專責蒞庭制度將配合國情改良 迎合世界潮流 [The Adversarial System will be Adopted in June. Yeh Jin-feng Claimed that the Participation of the Prosecutor at Trial will be Adjusted to the Culture of Our Country and Follow the Global Trend], *CDNews* (May 3, 2000): 9.

111 See, for example, 理性思辯刑訴法第161、163條修正案 [A Rational Debate over the Revisions of Art. 161 and Art. 163 of the Criminal Procedural Code], *China Times* (December 20, 2001): 6.

112 王文玲 [Wen-ling Wang], 刑訴法變革 院部針鋒相對 [The JY and the MOJ Disagree on the Issue of Judicial Reform], *United Daily News* (October 30, 2001): 9.

ruling party – then the Democratic Progressive Party (DPP) – turned to support the JY's bill. The MOJ had no choice, and was left merely insisting on a sunrise clause to delay the start to the new law. This gave the JY as well as the MOJ a period of time to adjust to the new system.[113] In fact, the MOJ did not completely lose the battle. To reduce opposition from the MOJ, the JY agreed to make concessions on deferred prosecution. Originally, prosecutor's discretion to defer prosecution would be reviewed by judges and citizens, but the JY dropped its insistence on this.[114] On January 18, 2002, the legislature passed the JY's bill. But the LY unexpectedly failed to pass the sunrise clause at the same time, and Taiwan's criminal procedure was instantly shifted toward the adversarial system.[115]

In 2002, the LY took the first and the decisive step to pull Taiwan's criminal procedure away from a pure inquisitorial system and to push toward an "improved" adversarial system under which the judge is no longer legally obligated to actively investigate evidence. One year later, the LY also passed procedural rules that are key to the adversarial system, such as rules on cross-examination (Art. 166~167–7). Hearsay rules (Art. 159~159–5), which are designed to prevent the judge from using the evidence that has not been cross-examined at trial, were also adopted.[116] In April 2004, the LY added an important supplementary measure to its adversarial system – a sentence bargaining system (Art. 455–2~455–11). This was added quite possibly to reduce the workload of judges and prosecutors that had increased with the adoption of the adversarial trial.[117] Within three years, the LY transformed Taiwan's criminal procedure from a pure inquisitorial system to the so-called "improved adversarial system." It is believed to be an improved version because the judge can still investigate the truth of the case if the prosecutor or defense lawyer does not do their job well. The JY got the reforms it wanted with some concessions. The MOJ lost the battle, but did not walk away without gaining anything. The newly adopted deferred prosecution policy has given prosecutors more discretion in deciding whether to prosecute. Instead of prosecuting suspects, prosecutors can bargain with the defendant to drop charges in exchange for community service or a donation to government or non-profit organizations (Art. 253–1~253–3).

113 鍾年晃 [Nian-huang Chong], 當事人進行主義 民進黨決支持 [The DPP Decided to Support the Adoption of the Adversarial System], *United Daily News* (December 20, 2001): 4.

114 王文玲 [Wen-ling Wang], 當事人進行主義 日出條款初定 [The Sunrise Clause was Added to Halt the Adoption of the Adversarial System], *United Daily News* (December 26, 2001): 1.

115 劉添財 [Tien-tsai Liu], 刑訴改採當事人進行主義 [The Criminal Procedure has Adopted the Adversarial System], *China Times* (January 18, 2002): 4.

116 Compared to the US Federal Rules of Evidence, the hearsay rules in Taiwan's Criminal Procedure Code are much simpler. Fewer hearsay exceptions are recognized in the code.

117 Compared to the US plea bargaining system, Taiwan's bargaining system does not allow the prosecutor to negotiate with the defendant about the content or number of charges. The only thing that can be negotiated is the sentence. See Art. 455–2~Art. 455–11 of Taiwan's Criminal Procedural Code.

An overtime debate

In retrospect, it is debatable whether Taiwan's new criminal procedure is an improved and thus better version of the adversarial system. In fact, it is even not very clear whether Taiwan's new procedure improves upon the adversarial or inquisitorial system. The answer is not so straightforward, because all modern criminal legal systems are to some extent hybrids.[118]

Taiwan's new criminal procedure does have the core characteristics of the adversarial system – the judge in principle has no absolute legal obligation to actively investigate the truth of a crime at trial. But it should be noted that legislators also gave the judge an obligation to investigate the evidence when he or she believes that such an investigation is crucial to maintain justice or to protect the interests of the accused (Section 2 of Article 163). As many researchers have already pointed out, since every piece of relevant evidence inevitably involves justice or the interests of the defendant, the judge essentially has an obligation to investigate all evidence.[119] Various Supreme Court decisions have confirmed researchers' views. At least by 2010, most Supreme Court criminal decisions asked the lower courts to investigate any evidence that is insufficiently clear. If a lower court fails to do this, their judgments may be vacated and remanded for retrial.[120]

The main difference between the old and new systems is that the new system allows the prosecutor and the defendant to participate in the trial more actively. If the judge chooses to, and the defense lawyer does not complain, the judge can still dominate the investigation of evidence at trial. In these situations, the prosecutor bears a minimal burden of proof, just as before. This is what generally happens now at the High Court level. In addition to the investigation of evidence, many provisions in Taiwan's criminal procedure remained unchanged and thus still follow the logic of the inquisitorial system.[121] As a result, Taiwan's criminal procedure after 2004 seems more like an *improved inquisitorial system*. It is ironically what the MOJ advocated in the early twenty-first century. The MOJ was willing to have prosecutors more actively participate in the trial, but insisted that prosecutors should not bear the complete responsibility of evidence investigation. It has insisted all along that the court still needs to share the burden of investigating evidence.

118 Brian Kennedy, LA Law in Taiwan? (May 1, 2002) Retrieved on April 10, 2014 from http://taiwantoday.tw/fp.asp?xItem=722&CtNode=124.

119 林鈺雄 [Yu-hsiung Lin], 刑事訴訟法（上）-總論篇 [Criminal Procedural Law I: General Principles] (Taipei: 元照出版公司 [Yuanzhao Publishers], 2013): 70.

120 See, for example, 91台上6474; 93, 台上, 665; 95, 台上, 1055; 96, 台上, 3125; 97, 台上, 1910; 99台上， 5292.

121 For example, prosecutors still enjoy discretion on evidence inspection (Art. 212), similar to judges. Prosecutors can authorize forensic analysis, like judges. Lab reports by prosecutors' expert witnesses are exempted from hearsay rules. In comparison, lab reports by a defendant's expert witnesses are hearsay evidence and cannot be admitted at trial.

Nevertheless, things began to change in 2011. Some Supreme Court judges changed their position on the issue of judges' responsibility to investigate evidence at trial. In three criminal court judgments,[122] these judges held that if the prosecutor fails to present solid evidence of a defendant's guilt, the judge can acquit the defendant of the unproven charges. They argued that if the trial judge initiates the investigation of evidence unfavorable to the defendant, the trial judge is essentially doing the prosecutor's job, and the trial will be unfair to the defendant. They believed that the application of the judge's obligation of evidence investigation prescribed in Section 2 of Article 163 of the Criminal Procedural Code should be strictly interpreted, or else it would violate the principle of the presumption of innocence, a principle that has been formally recognized in law since 2003. Facing conflicting points of views, the Supreme Court called a meeting among criminal court judges and issued a resolution (最高法院101年第2次刑庭決議). This resolution followed three judgments in 2011. It immediately aroused a backlash from prosecutors and some law scholars. But the move received support from lawyers. The similarity of the arguments and lineup of opposing sides strongly suggested the debate in 2012 was an extension of the 1999 debate that had gone into overtime.

Conclusion

In tracing how Taiwan has transformed its criminal procedure from the inquisitorial system to the "improved adversarial system" at the turn of the twenty-first century, and explaining how this transformation was made possible, this chapter offers a complex picture of judicial reform.

This transformation was encouraged by the transition to democracy since the 1980s. Adversarial reforms in criminal procedure were part of US-style democratic reforms. But ironically, it is questionable whether the way this new system was adopted was democratic. The controversies it aroused were far larger than the question of which system was better. They involved conflicting institutional interests (the JY, the MOJ, and the bar). The needs of convenience (judges' burdensome caseloads) have substantially affected the contours and content of the reform. Relevant debates can also be seen as a cultural war – between the traditional image of justice, as seen in stories of Judge Bao, and the new image of justice, provided by US court dramas (*L.A. Law*). From another angle, debates looked like a turf war between scholars who earned law degrees from Germany versus those who studied in the US or Japan.

But the debates did not fully represent a tradition versus modernity argument, because even opponents to the adversarial system were not satisfied with Taiwan's inquisitorial system. Taiwan's inquisitorial system followed Japan's pre-war criminal procedural code, and thus was based on an old-fashioned, pre-war

122 100, 台上, 6259、100, 台上, 6287、100, 台上, 7167.

German criminal procedure. But at the turn of twenty-first century, opponents to the adversarial system advocated a modern German system. Those who obtained their doctoral degrees in Germany provided an alternative reform plan to JY's version based on the modern German system. They organized symposiums, published books and even established an academic group, the Taiwan Criminal Law Society (台灣刑事法學會), to promote their plans. Nevertheless, even though these scholars were far more powerful in academia than those who got their degrees from the US and Japan at that time, they could not stop the JY's ambitions. The transformation (or to be more specific, the incomplete transformation) of Taiwan's criminal procedure was thus a dialectical result of various factors on different levels. As legal history never flows inevitably in one direction, the question of whether Taiwan's criminal procedure will incline further toward the adversarial system will depend on future factors and problems that arise in the development of the criminal justice system.

10 The evolution of the right to counsel in Taiwan

Rong-Geng Li

Introduction

The primary statute governing criminal procedure in the Republic of China (ROC; unofficially, "Taiwan") is the Code of Criminal Procedure (CCP), whose roots can be traced back to 1906.[1] Taiwan's criminal procedure did not, until recently, strongly emphasize the right to counsel – a defendant's right to be represented by a lawyer in a criminal investigation and trial. Generally, it was believed that an innocent person did not need counsel because he was innocent and so law enforcement and the courts would reach that conclusion and release or acquit him. A guilty person did not need a lawyer either, it was thought, because as a perpetrator he did not need to be represented by a counsel to be acquitted. Thus it was long believed that the innocent did not need and the guilty did not deserve to have access to counsel in criminal proceedings. The historical influence of Chinese culture also de-emphasized the importance of lawyers. In the past, judges heard cases as if they were parents, not arbitrators resolving disputes between parties. Harmony was highly valued and litigation was not encouraged. Consequently, defense lawyers, who raised issues and argued for people against the state were usually ignored and people's rights to counsel were disregarded.

Another reason that explains the ignorance surrounding the right to counsel is related with the democratization. During the period of martial law (1949–92), Taiwan was an authoritarian country. People's rights were under strict restraints. The government did not want too many lawyers in society because their job was to challenge prosecutors, judges, and even the government, argue for criminal defendants, and protect people from abuses of governmental power. Doing those

1 The current CCP is the successor to the "Code of Criminal and Civil Procedure" (1906) and the "Code of Criminal Procedure" (1911). After the end of Qing Dynasty in 1911, the Republic of China (ROC) was established. Twenty-four years later, the ROC Code of Criminal Procedure (CCP) was enacted (1935), and it has formed the basic structure of the current CCP and is its precursor. 黃源盛 [Huang Yuan-Sheng], "民國初年近代刑事訴訟的生成與開展" [A Study of the Chinese Supreme Court's Criminal Procedure Decisions During the Period of 1912–1914], 政大學法學評論 [NCCU Law Review] 61 (1999): 47–8.

jobs well usually means embarrassing the government and compromising its authority. Thus, the passage rate of the bar exam was kept extremely low. From 1940 to 1988, about 22 people passed the bar exam per year. In several years, even less than ten people passed the bar exam. For example, in 1982, six people did, and in 1977, seven people did. The number of lawyers was closely identified with democratization. With the ending of martial law, the bar pass rate started increasing in 1989. In that year, 288 people passed the bar exam. By 2014, more than 900 people passed the bar exam. It is fair to say that people place importance on the right to counsel nowadays because it is much easier for people to obtain lawyers when necessary. There is a very close connection between the accessibility of lawyers, the emphasis of the right to counsel, and the democratization of a country.

After 1995, more and more law professors who had obtained doctoral degrees in the US, Japan, or Germany came back to Taiwan, taking faculty positions in law schools. They introduced ideas from the legal systems where they had studied, conducted comparative studies, and offered opinions with respect to criminal procedure. In addition, those law professors pushed for the revision of the CCP. Under the influence of foreign legal systems and democratization, the legislature revised the CCP several times. Statutes were also enacted to improve people's rights in criminal proceedings. International human rights covenants greatly influenced legislative changes and judicial judgments. In addition, the Constitutional Court also made several important decisions with respect to criminal procedure. These revisions, enactments, judgments, and judicial decisions significantly strengthened the defendant's position in criminal procedure, including his right to counsel. In other words, more and more, people have been provided an effective right to counsel.

This chapter will examine how the right to counsel has developed in Taiwan. First, it will explain the recent adoption of international human rights standards that provide for the right to counsel. Next, the chapter will discuss the statutory reforms that granted unindicted suspects the right to retain counsel and also gave arrested suspects the right to immediately meet with counsel. Following that, this chapter will analyze detainees' right to consult with their defense lawyers and freely and fully hold discussions with them. It will then explain the reconceptualization of the right to counsel as a constitutional right in a landmark Constitutional Court decision. Finally, the new system of legal aid will be explained, and our conclusion will be presented.

The impact of international human rights standards

The international status of the ROC is unique. The ROC cannot participate in most international organizations, and it cannot sign most international human rights covenants. Taiwan, however, still makes great efforts to improve its human rights protections and keep them in compliance with international standards, despite its difficult situation.

In 1971, the ROC lost its seat in the United Nations (UN). In addition, since then Taiwan has not been recognized as an independent nation by most countries. Nevertheless, Taiwan has still maintained membership in several international economic organizations, such as the Asia-Pacific Economic Cooperation and the World Trade Organization. At the same time, the ROC has been careful to align its rights protection standards with international human rights standards. Taiwan signed both the International Covenant on Civil and Political Rights (ICCPR) and International Covenant on Economic, Social, and Cultural Rights (ICESCR) in 1967. However, Taiwan could not deposit instruments of ratification with the UN.

But the situation changed in 2008, when Ma Ying-Jeou was elected as president of the ROC. President Ma declared that these two covenants should be ratified by the legislature as quickly as possible and incorporated into Taiwanese law so that they would be directly applicable in the courts. He emphasized that the government should strengthen human rights safeguards and bring them into close accord with international standards.

On March 31, 2009, Taiwan's national legislative body, the Legislative Yuan, ratified the two covenants. To give the two covenants the force of domestic law, the Legislative Yuan also passed the "Act to Implement the International Covenant on Civil and Political Rights and the International Covenant on Economic, Social, and Cultural Rights." The law was proposed on May 14, 2009 and became effective on December 10 of the same year. It stated that "human rights protection provisions in the two Covenants have domestic legal status" (Art. 2). After the ratification of the two covenants and the enactment of the implementation law, the international human rights covenants have directly applied to national courts in the ROC.

To consolidate the concepts and values of human rights within the government, President Ma established the Presidential Human Rights Consultative Committee on December 10, 2010. The following year, the committee resolved that Taiwan would submit an initial human rights report under the ICCPR and ICESCR, although the report was published rather than given to the UN.[2] Accordingly, in April 2012, the common core document[3] and treaty-specific documents for the ICCPR[4] and ICESCR[5] were submitted. The reports fully examined Taiwan's human rights record according to the requirements of the

2 According to the two covenants, a signatory state must submit a human rights report annually to the UN. The ROC, however, is not a member of the UN so she cannot submit those reports to the UN. Even if it did, the UN would not accept them. Therefore, the submission of those human rights reports by the ROC is more like publication or announcement of them to the public.

3 Republic of China (Taiwan), Core Document Forming Part of the Reports 2012 (www.humanrights.moj.gov.tw/public/Attachment/2104105692.pdf) (last visited: June 13, 2014).

4 Republic of China (Taiwan), Implementation of the International Covenant on Civil and Political Rights 2012 (www.humanrights.moj.gov.tw/public/Attachment/21041062855.pdf) (last visited: June 13, 2014) (hereinafter "the 2012 report of ICCPR").

5 Republic of China (Taiwan), Implementation of the International Covenant on Economic, Social and Cultural Rights 2012 (www.humanrights.moj.gov.tw/public/Attachment/21041071263.pdf) (last visited: June 13, 2014).

two covenants. The domestic adoption of the ICCPR and ICESCR have enabled citizens to enjoy the rights they declare, which include the right to counsel.[6] This right may now be invoked by criminal suspects and defendants.

Suspects' rights to counsel during an investigation

Suspected criminals formerly had no right to counsel. After several revisions of the CCP, suspects' rights to counsel gradually came to be protected. Before 1982, the CCP stated that a defendant could not hire a defense lawyer until he had been indicted.[7] According to the relevant provision, only defendants who had been indicted were permitted to retain defense lawyers who could be present and advocate for defendants during pre-trial interrogation. In other words, unindicted suspects did not have the right to be represented by a counsel. A defense lawyer could be consulted, but could not provide assistance during interrogation even if hired by a suspect. Thus, a defense lawyer could meet and correspond with an indicted, detained defendant, who did have the right to counsel. Detained suspects who had not been indicted, however, had no such right.[8]

Because of this, prior to 1982 unindicted suspects were interrogated alone by law enforcement without a hired or state-provided defense lawyer present. During that time, torture often took place, and the police usually employed various illegal methods to obtain confessions because no third party was present to protect the suspect under interrogation. A suspect whose rights were violated during interrogation could hardly challenge the admissibility of the confession because of the absence of evidence or witnesses to prove police misconduct. The absence of suspects' rights to counsel resulted not only in human rights violations, but also in countless false confessions and wrongful convictions.

The circumstances were obviously unreasonable and unjust to suspects. In 1982, the very sad case of Wang Ying-Xian (王迎先) occurred and resulted in reform to the right to counsel. In that year, Wang was suspected of armed robbery of a bank, was arrested, and confessed after a police interrogation. He asked to urinate while being escorted. The police agreed, but Wang took the

6 Sec. 3 of Art. 14 of ICCPR provides that

> [i]n the determination of any criminal charge against him, everyone shall be entitled to the following minimum guarantees, in full equality: … (d) … to defend himself … through legal assistance of his own choosing; … and to have legal assistance assigned to him, in any case where the interests of justice so required, and without payment by him in any such case if he does not have sufficient means to pay for it; ...

7 The CCP of 1935, Art. 27 provided: "An accused may at any time retain defense attorneys."

8 The CCP of 1935, Art. 34 provided:

> A defense attorney may meet and correspond with an accused under detention, but if facts exist sufficient to justify a suspicion that such a defense attorney may destroy, fabricate, or alter evidence or form a conspiracy with a co-offender or witness, such interviews or correspondence may be limited.

chance to jump into a river, committing suicide. The police claimed that Wang committed suicide to escape punishment. However, a few days later, a man informed the police that one of his friends, Li Shi-Ke (李師科), had left some objects that looked like bills in his house. The police found after an investigation that those objects were the stolen money and that Li was responsible for the robbery. Subsequently, the police admitted that Wang was tortured, the confession was false, and that he was innocent.

The Wang case caused a great shock to Taiwanese society and caught the attention of the legislature. They realized that an innocent person could be mistreated during investigation and that his rights should be protected by a defense lawyer, rather than law enforcement. After *Wang*, the legislature revised several provisions of the CCP and offered suspects more procedural rights to legal assistance from defense lawyers.[9]

First, according to the revised CCP, not only defendants but also unindicted suspects had the right to retain a counsel at any time.[10] A suspect's lawyer, therefore, was entitled to be present to provide legal assistance when a suspect was interrogated by the police.[11] In addition, a lawyer could meet and correspond with a suspect held in detention.[12] A detained suspect isolated from his family

9 See 王兆鵬 [Wang Jaw-Perng], 辯護權與詰問權 [The Right to Counsel and Confront] (Taipei: 元照[Yuanchao], 2008): 80 n. 4.

10 Sec. 1 of Art. 27 of CCP provides: "An accused may at any time retain defense attorneys. The same rule shall apply to a suspect being interrogated by judicial police officers or judicial policemen."

11 Secs. 2, 3, and 4 of Art. 245 of CCP provide:

> The defense attorney of an accused or suspect may be present and state his opinion when a public prosecutor, public prosecuting affairs official, judicial police officer, or judicial policeman examines the accused or suspect, but if facts exist sufficient to justify an apprehension that such presence may jeopardize national security or destroy, fabricate, alter evidence or form a conspiracy with a co-offender or witness, or may be detrimental to the reputation of others, or that the behavior of the defense attorney is so inappropriate that it would interfere with the order of the investigation, such presence may be limited or prohibited (Sec. 2). The public prosecutor, public prosecuting affairs official, judicial police officer, judicial policeman, defense attorney, agent of the complainant, or any other person performing his duty under law during the investigation shall not disclose whatsoever information acquired through the performance of the duty during the investigation, unless otherwise permitted by law, or it is necessary for the protection of public interest or legitimate interest (Sec. 3). The time, date, and place of the examination of an accused or suspect during the investigation shall be notified to the defense attorney unless urgent circumstances exist (Sec. 4).

12 Art. 34 of CCP provides:

> A defense attorney may interview and correspond with a suspect or an accused under detention, provided that if facts exist sufficient to justify an apprehension that such a defense attorney may destroy, fabricate, or alter evidence or form a conspiracy with a co-offender or witness, such interviews or correspondence may be limited.

and society thus had the opportunity to consult with a defense lawyer, and learn more about the rights he had and situations he was dealing with.

These revisions to the CCP in 1982 represented a turning point. They officially extended the right to hire counsel from trial to the investigative process. The CCP, therefore, provided suspects with more comprehensive protection. Because of these revisions, suspects could gain better understandings of their situations and obtain legal advice from a defense lawyer while being interrogated by the law enforcement. A defense lawyer could protect a suspect from possible violations of human rights during the investigation and challenge police misconduct. These revisions allowing a suspect to retain a defense lawyer were a significant strengthening of the right to counsel in criminal procedure.

The right to appointed counsel

The right to counsel consists of two rights: the right to privately hire counsel and the right to a court-appointed lawyer paid for by the state. Before 1997, only felony defendants at trial had the right to be appointed counsel by presiding judges. However, presiding judges were not required to appoint defense lawyers for defendants with low incomes or those unable to make complete statements due to intellectual disabilities if they were not indicted of felonies. Suspects, moreover, did not have the right to appointed counsel even if they were under interrogation for felonies. Defendants ineligible for court-appointed lawyers therefore potentially had to confront complicated trial proceedings and hostile prosecutors without any assistance from defense lawyers. In addition, suspects who were intellectually disabled were often interrogated by prosecutors without access to legal advice from defense lawyers. Without advice from defense lawyers, defendants and suspects, especially those from disadvantaged backgrounds, often made unwise decisions or statements unfavorable to themselves.

In 1997, the legislature revised the CCP, extending the right to appointed counsel to any defendant who could not make complete statements due to an unsound mind and who did not retain defense lawyers.[13] In 2003, the legislature again revised the CCP, guaranteeing low-income defendants the right to appointed counsel at trial.[14] The legislature, in 2013, extended the protection of

13 Sec. 1 of Art. 31 of the CCP of 1997 provided that in cases where the minimum punishment is no less than three years imprisonment, where a high court has jurisdiction over the first instance, or where the accused is unable to make a complete statement due to unsound mind, the presiding judge shall appoint a public defender for him if no defense lawyer has been retained. If it is considered necessary, the same rule shall apply.

14 In 2003, the legislature added the following sentence to the end of Sec. 1 of Art. 31 of the CCP of 1997: "[;] in other cases, if no defense attorney has been retained by an accused with low income and a request for appointing one has been submitted ... the same rule shall apply."

the right to counsel to indigenous and middle-income suspects.[15] Revisions, especially in 2003 and 2013, were made to respond the resolution of the National Judicial Reform Conference held in 1999. The Conference resolved that the ROC's criminal procedure should adopt the concept of the adversarial system. And therefore, a defendant needed to be provided effective procedural rights to defend himself in criminal proceedings with a government-paid lawyer.

The right to appointed counsel also applies to the bargaining process, which has some similarities to American plea bargaining.[16] The original provisions of this process were drafted by the Judicial Yuan. When enacting these provisions, many scholars and NGOs were deeply involved, including Professor Wang Jaw-Perng (王兆鵬), the Judicial Reform Foundation, the Taipei Bar Association, Taiwan Bar Association, and the Center for Criminal Law Research of National Taiwan University's College of Law. They suggested another version of the plea bargaining process, arguing that a defendant usually had no ability to negotiate with a prosecutor. Without proper assistance, a defendant could not make a fair agreement with the prosecutor. To narrow the gap between defendants and prosecutors, it was necessary to provide defendants with sufficient assistance from defense lawyers. The legislature required the Judicial Yuan to reach a consensus with scholars and NGOs.[17] Therefore, when adopting the bargaining process in 2004, at the insistence of scholars and NGOs, the legislature required judges to appoint defense lawyers for defendants who had not retained counsel if they were facing over six months of imprisonment not subject to suspension (Art. 455–5 of CCP). These reforms moved the CCP in the direction of providing a stronger and broader right to counsel. According to the CCP, the state was obliged to appoint defense lawyers in an increasing number of cases and conditions for defendants who were intellectually, economically, or socially disadvantaged, or who had inadequate knowledge of the procedures. This reform was a huge victory for professors like Professor Wang and NGOs such as Judicial Reform Foundation, who fought to strengthen the right to counsel.

15 Sec. 1 of Art. 31 of CCP states:

> In one of the following circumstances, the presiding judge shall appoint a defense lawyer for the defendant: 1. the case is punishable by no less than three years imprisonment; 2. a high court has jurisdiction over the first instance; 3. the defendant cannot make a complete statement due to unsound mind; 4. the defendant is indigent and has been indicted or tried through the regular proceeding; 5. the defendant is low-income or middle-income and makes a request to appoint one; and 6. in other cases which the presiding judge considers necessary.

16 The bargaining process is similar with plea bargaining in the US. However, the bargaining process only applies to offenses that are punishable with imprisonment for less than three years, and the negotiable items in bargaining are limited (Arts. 455–2 of the CCP).

17 王兆鵬 [Jaw-Perng Wang], '論刑事訴訟新增訂之協商程序（上）' [The New Bargaining Process in the Criminal Procedure (Part. 1)], 2; 司法週刊 [Judicial Weekly] 2 (April 22, 2004).

The legislature also extended that right to counsel to the investigation process. It was previously believed that a suspect did not need to be appointed a defense lawyer during an investigation because he was not necessarily going to be indicted and face the risk of punishment. Additionally, public prosecutors are required to "give equal attention to circumstances both favorable and unfavorable to the accused."[18] Therefore, it was not thought necessary for the government to provide suspects with defense lawyers during an investigation. However, in 2006, the government was required to appoint defense lawyers for suspects unable to make complete statements due to unsound mind at the investigation stage.[19] In 2013, indigent suspects were included in the protection of the right to appointed counsel during investigations.[20] These revisions were extremely significant for the reform of the right to counsel. In the past, it was believed that state was only obligated to appoint counsel for defendants at trial. During the investigation, before a defendant was indicted, the state had no obligation to appoint counsel for suspects. The right to appointed counsel was limited to the trial period and preparations. The revisions in 2006 and 2013 broke through the old way of thinking, declaring that the state was obliged to appoint defense lawyers for disadvantaged suspects even before they were indicted.

It should be noted that public prosecutors are obligated to appoint counsel for suspects during investigation and judges for defendant at trial. In other words, different officials appoint counsels at different procedural stages. The reason is that, according to the CCP, public prosecutors take charge of investigations and judges preside over trial. These rules reflect the traditional Taiwanese legal view of prosecutors as "judicial officers," essentially equivalent to judges in status.

The CCP currently provides greater protection than ever before with respect to the right to counsel. However, the initial government report on the ICCPR written by the government indicated that at the investigation stage, a suspect with an intellectual disability had the right to court-appointed counsel. But the relevant provision still does not give the same right to those with autism, mental disorders, learning disorders, or other similar conditions. To apply the requirements of the ICCPR consistently, the CCP should be revised to provide necessary assistance in these situations according to the essential provisions of the ICCPR.[21]

18 Sec. 1. of Art. 2 of the CCP.

19 Sec. 4 of Art. 31 of the CCP of 2006 provides that in cases where the suspect is unable to make a complete statement due to unsound mind, the prosecutor shall appoint a defense lawyer for him at investigation if no one has been retained.

20 Sec. 4. of Art. 31 of the CCP provides that in cases where the suspect is unable to make a complete statement due to unsound mind or is indigent, the prosecutor shall ask a legal aid organization to appoint a defense lawyer for him at investigation if one has not been retained at investigation. A prosecutor or the police representative shall interrogate the suspect immediately if he requests this or if the defense lawyer does not present after four hours.

21 Republic of China (Taiwan), 90/¶212 Implementation of the International Covenant on Civil and Political Rights 2012 (www.humanrights.moj.gov.tw/public/Attachment/21041062855.pdf).

Arrested suspects' rights to interview with counsel

In Taiwan, as in other countries, arrests are usually made by police. Arrested suspects are sent to police stations, or to a public prosecutor's office directly and then to police stations.[22] There, arrested suspects are initially interrogated by the police. However, police stations can be hostile, unfamiliar environments to arrested suspects. Suspects typically feel nervous, terrified, helpless, and upset in police stations.[23] The police take advantage of the psychological condition of those arrested and typically increase pressure on them in order to obtain confessions. Nevertheless, confessions obtained under such circumstances are very likely to be coerced, resulting in intrusions onto suspects' rights and wrongful convictions. For this reason, ensuring an arrested suspect's right to meet with his defense lawyer has become a critical issue.

After 1982, defense lawyers were allowed to advise arrested suspects when they are interrogated by the police. However, law enforcement would formerly delay or even cancel defense lawyer interviews, claiming that these interviews might compromise the ongoing investigation or that the interrogation was not yet completed. Thus, arrested suspects were usually allowed to consult with their counsel only after being interrogated by the police. The actual reason for the police to delay or cancellation of defense attorney interviews was very simple: the police wanted to use the coercive circumstances of the interrogation to obtain confessions from suspects. The police might not able to do so after suspects had spoken with their defense lawyers. However, by the time a defense lawyer arrives, a suspect in custody might already have made unwise decisions or unfavorable statements.

In 2010, the CCP was revised because of Judicial Interpretation No. 654 (2009) by the Constitutional Court, which held that suspects have a constitutional right to counsel. One of the revisions was that a defense lawyer could meet and correspond with an arrested suspect and such meetings and correspondence could not be limited. An arrested suspect had the right to meet his attorney at least once for no less than one hour (Sec. 2 of Art. 34 of CCP). An arrested suspect's right to meet or correspond with his defense lawyer could not be limited or prohibited, only deferred. A public prosecutor could postpone such meetings for another time and place if proper reasons existed. Additionally, the assignment of a time and place for the defense lawyer to interview the arrested suspect must not interfere with the suspect's right to defense and the lawyer's legitimate rights to fairly advise his client (Sec. 3 of Art. 34 of CCP). The suspect or his defense lawyer could file a motion to withdraw or change a meeting time and place to the competent court if he disagreed with the public

22 Art. 91 of the CCP states, "If an accused is arrested with a warrant or because of a circular order to arrest without a warrant, he shall be brought immediately to the place designated…." In practice, "the place designated" is usually a public prosecutor's office. However, a public prosecutor usually sends the arrested suspect to the police, asking them to interrogate the suspect first.

23 *Miranda* v. *Arizona*, 384 U.S. 436, 455–7, and 460 (1966).

prosecutor's decisions regarding it (Sec. 1 of Art. 416 of CCP). Any confession resulting from the violation of an arrested suspect's right to consult with his defense lawyer may be excluded from evidence (Art. 158–4 of CCP).

The revision creating a suspect's right to consult with his defense lawyer was critical. First, the new CCP clearly provided suspects with the right to consult their defense lawyers' right after arrest. The right to counsel was thus more comprehensively protected. With immediate access to a lawyer, a suspect is more able to fully understand his situation, learn of his options and rights, determine his best options, and, most importantly, receive necessary legal advice. With this knowledge, the suspect could make statements more voluntarily as well as make wiser decisions. Interrogations conducted by the police, moreover, become fairer and more reasonable when defendants received legal advice beforehand.

Second, a suspect and his defense lawyer were given the right to challenge the ruling of a public prosecutor who deferred their meeting together. They could file a motion to withdraw or change the time or place the prosecutor assigned. This has ensured that suspects are able to immediately challenge prosecutors' assignments and consult with their defense lawyers as soon as possible before police interrogation. Third, the exclusionary rule of evidence now applies to a suspect's statements if his right to meet with counsel right after being arrested was infringed – prosecutors might not use the suspect's confession at trial. The application of this rule provided suspects with sufficient and effective remedies if their rights to private consultation were violated. With these new provisions, suspects' rights to counsel from defense lawyers before being interrogated have become more completely protected.

Detainees' rights to consult with counsel

According to the CCP of 1982, a defense lawyer may correspond with a client held in custody. The communications might be limited if sufficient facts existed to justify a suspicion that the defense attorney could destroy, fabricate or alter evidence, or collude with a co-offender or witness (Sec. 1 of Art. 34 of the CCP). That provision had at least two defects. First, a defense lawyer's meeting with his client in detention could be limited on the grounds of mere "suspicion." The standard was extremely vague and was too easily used to limit meetings between detainees and their defense lawyers. Second, the CCP determined neither who had the authority to make such rulings, nor how to make them. Therefore, there was no provision about how to file a motion to challenge limits on meetings between detainees and their defense lawyers.

The legislature, in 2010, revised several provisions of the CCP to improve detainees' rights to meet with their defense lawyers. This was done because of the Constitutional Court decision in 2009 that held that defendants had the right to freely and fully communicate with their defense lawyers.[24] The revision

24 Judicial Interpretation No. 654 (2009).

altered the conditions for limiting meetings between detainees and defense lawyers. Limitations required sufficient facts proving that the defense attorney would destroy, fabricate or alter evidence, or collude with co-offenders or witnesses (Sec. 1. of Art. 34). Suspects or defendants in detention were no longer arbitrarily prohibited from consulting with their counsels on grounds of "suspicion."

Second, public prosecutors could not limit meetings or correspondence on their own. Only through a court order ("limitation warrant") issued by a judge could meetings or correspondence be limited (Sec. 1 to 4 of Art. 34–1). A public prosecutor could make a necessary ruling to limit detainees' contact with their defense lawyers if exigencies existed. However, the public prosecutor had to apply for a court order within 24 hours, and the court would have to decide whether or not to issue the order. A limitation ruling by a public prosecutor would cease to be effective if the court rejected the application or the public prosecutor failed to apply to the court (Art. 34–1, Sec. 5).

This new provision was more reasonable; it protected detainees' rights to counsel more effectively. The revised CCP provided for proceedings to regulate the restrictions on meetings and correspondence between detainees and their counsels. More importantly, public prosecutors were not allowed to limit such meetings or correspondence. The new CCP provided that only judges had the authority make such rulings, rather than public prosecutors, who were usually overzealous regarding the investigation and could arbitrarily violate suspects' rights.

Third, those revised provisions provided detainees and defense lawyers the right to file a motion against restrictions on contact between detainees and counsels (Sec. 1 of Art. 404). With these new provisions, detainees' rights to counsel were more properly and fully protected.

Detainees' rights to freely and fully interview with counsel

The CCP addresses both trial and pre-trial detention.[25] According to the Detention Act, defendants or suspects were to be held in detention centers if necessary (Sec. 1 of Art. 1 of the Detention Act). Before 2009, detention centers were permitted (and required) to monitor all meetings between detainees and interviewers (Sec. 2 of Art. 23 of the Detention Act of 2006). Detention centers were to provide prosecutors or courts with any detainees' conversations, actions, and mail that could be used for investigation or trial (Art. 28 of the Detention Act of 2006). This provision not only applied to conversations between detainees and their families or friends, but also to those between detainees and their defense lawyers (Sec. 3 of Art. 23 of the Detention Act of 2006).

25 Art. 93, 101, 101–1, and 108 of the CCP.

Therefore, detention centers used to monitor and record all conversations and interviews between detainees and their defense lawyers, providing the records to public prosecutors and courts. Under these provisions, detainees were unwilling to talk openly to their defense lawyers about their needs, and could not fully consult with their defense lawyers because all conversations with respect to defense strategy and facts were under law enforcement surveillance. Defense lawyers, therefore, often could not give detainees helpful advice. Thus, suspects and defendants had no effective rights to counsel once they were detained. These provisions were obviously unreasonable.

In 2009, the Constitutional Court held that provisions allowing detention centers to monitor conversations between detainees and their defense lawyers were unconstitutional.[26] The Court first indicated that Art. 16 of the Constitution guaranteed people the right to litigate. That constitutional right included the defendant's right to make a full defense under due process of law. Defendants, therefore, also enjoyed the right to retain an entrusted counsel. To fulfill the function of the right to defense, the right to counsel was therefore effectively protected. Thus, full and free communications between defendants and defense lawyers, critically important for defense lawyers to effectively assist their clients, was held to be protected by the Constitution.

The Court explained that only when a defense lawyer is able to meet with the detainee in detention without monitoring or surveillance could the detainee obtain substantial and effective legal assistance. The relevant provision of the Detention Act asked detention centers to monitor or record all conversations between defense lawyers and detainees regardless of necessity. It was problematic in two ways. First, it resulted in unnecessary intrusions into detainees' rights, violating the proportionality requirement provided by Article 23 of the Constitution. Second, the provision was inconsistent with Article 16 of the Constitution, which provided the right to litigate. This was because a detainees could not obtain effective legal advice.

The revised Act provided that, unless the law specified otherwise, detention centers could only visually monitor interviews between detainees and their defense lawyers.[27] Correspondence between detainees and their defense lawyers could only be inspected for maintaining order and safety.[28] The legislature also deleted the provision that admitted recorded or noted communications as evidence. Consequently, detainees were then able to freely and fully consult their

26 Judicial Interpretation No. 654 (2009).

27 Sec. 1 of Art. 23–1 of the Detention Act states that "during the visitation between a criminal lawyer and a defendant, officers only can watch over, but cannot listen, except for other specific regulations."

28 Sec. 2 of Art. 23–1 of the revised Detention Act states, "For maintaining the order and safety, all correspondence and documents between a criminal lawyer and a defendant will be examined except for other specific regulations." Specific regulations include, but are not limited to, the limitation warrant issued by courts according to Art. 34–1 of the CCP.

counsels, obtain necessary legal advice, and provide effective defenses in criminal proceedings.

The Constitutional Court's Interpretation and the subsequent revision of the Detention Act were significant landmarks for a detainee's right to counsel. After 2009, it was fair to say that detainees' rights to counsel were much better protected.

These two Constitutional Court decisions did not specifically recognize that criminal defendants had the right to appointed counsel. They just abstractly held that a defendant had the constitutional right to retain an entrusted counsel. The state was not obligated to give defendants defense lawyers because of these two decisions. And the CCP provided that defendants or suspects had the right to retain counsel and the right to appointed counsel in certain circumstances. However, these two decisions are still significantly important because they declared that the right to counsel is a constitutionally protected right, not merely a statutory one. Therefore, the legislature cannot limit a defendant's right to counsel at will. For example, the statute cannot authorize prison officials to monitor all conversations between detained defendants or suspects and their counsels. Therefore, the two decisions of the Constitutional Court have been crucial for the development of the right to counsel.

Legal aid

Legal aid in Taiwan was mainly provided in the form of public defenders appointed by courts. The CCP has adopted an adversarial model since the National Judicial Reform Conference in 1999, and since then defense lawyers have played an increasing role in criminal procedure. Because of this, a new statute was enacted and a new system established to provide defendants with more procedural rights regarding the right to counsel.

From an inquisitorial to adversarial model

The basic structure of the CCP has followed German Criminal Procedure. Therefore, the CCP was typically inquisitorial. Public prosecutors had wide power during investigations, and judges were obligated to gather evidence, even against defendants, at trial. However, society became dissatisfied with the judicial system, complaining that defendants have usually been under attack from both prosecutors and judges. Moreover, defendants, who had the right to appointed counsel, might only obtain legal assistance from one of the very few public defenders. They had to handle a considerable numbers of cases and therefore few defendants could obtain effective legal assistance. In addition, they were not strongly motivated to fight for defendants because of their public official position. Therefore, many people were dissatisfied with the legal assistance provided by the state. Many NGOs, attorneys, and professors argued that the public defender system seriously undermined people's rights to counsel and should be reformed.

In 1998, reform efforts were initiated by attorneys Lin Yong-Song (林永頌) and Cheng Wen-Long (鄭文龍), the Judicial Reform Foundation, Taipei Bar Association, and the Taiwan Association for Human Rights. They allied to promote and enforce people's rights to equal access legal aid. This group – which included attorneys and professors, such as Wu Zhi-Kuang (吳志光) – met monthly to discuss comparative research into legal aid systems.

In 1999, Dr. Weng Yueh-Sheng (翁岳生) became President of the Judicial Yuan and held the National Judicial Reform Conference to respond the outcry for a modern judicial system. There is no doubt that the democratization of the society played a crucial role that facilitated the conference. Judges, public prosecutors, public officials, members of civil society, and lawyers, and scholars participated in the conference. Several scholars had studied in countries adopting the adversarial system, such as Fa Zhi-Bin (法治斌, US), Duan Chong-Min (段重民, US), Chen Yun-Cai (陳運財, Japan), and Huang Chao-Yi (黃朝義, Japan). The study-abroad backgrounds of these scholars significantly shaped the resolutions of conference. The conference resolved that the criminal trial system should shift from an inquisitorial model to an adversarial one.[29] Judges, accordingly, would no longer have a primary duty to investigate facts or the duty to decide the truth. Instead, judges would play a more neutral role at trial, and parties bore the burden of proof and had to play a much more active role in court proceedings. The defendants' rights to counsel, therefore, became more important than before. Because defendants could no longer rely on judges to actively protect their interests in court, defendants required defense lawyers who would be able to make favorable arguments and wise decisions on behalf of their clients. Therefore, the criminal justice system needed to provide more opportunities for defendants to obtain legal assistance. The conference also resolved that the Judicial Yuan should establish an organization providing legal aid.

In 2000, the Judicial Yuan organized "The Research Team for the Draft of the Legal Aid Act." The draft was finalized in 2001 and sent to the Legislative Yuan. In order to press for the passage of the act, the Judicial Reform Foundation, Taipei Bar Association, and Taipei Society formed an alliance, which was staffed by Professor Qu Hai-Yuan (瞿海源), Judge Su Su-er (蘇素娥), Judge Tsai Jiong-Dun (蔡炯墩), attorney Lin Yong-Song (林永頌), attorney Chen Chuan-Yue (陳傳岳), attorney Wellington Koo (顧立雄), prosecutor Chen Rui-Ren (陳瑞仁), and prosecutor Wu Wen-Zhong (吳文忠), among others. The alliance lobbied in the Legislative Yuan, visiting the President of the Legislative Yuan, Mr. Wang Jin-Pyng (王金平), parties, and legislators. The alliance received much support for the new system. In addition, the alliance also visited the President of the Executive Yuan, Mr. Yu Xi-Kun and the President Chen Shui-Bian to discuss the legal aid budget. They both expressed strong support

29 Jaw-Perng Wang, *The Evolution and Revolution of Taiwan's Criminal Justice*, 3 Taiwan in Comparative Perspective 8, 8–9 (2011).

for the legal aid system, promising that the Executive Yuan would contribute to the legal aid budget. That eventually resolved the funding issue. The Legislative Yuan enacted the Legal Aid Act (LAA) in 2003, and it became effective in 2004. Through the Legal Aid Act, the Legal Aid Foundation (LAF) was established in 2004, and it currently has 21 branches nationwide to serve those needing legal counsel. The reason that the LAA adopted an NGO-type organization to provide aid rather than a government agency, was to avoid creating an inactive, inefficient, overly-bureaucratic delivery system for legal aid.

Legal assistance provided by the Legal Aid Foundation

The LAA was enacted to ensure legal assistance for those who are indigent or otherwise unable to receive legal protection, and to fulfill their rights to litigate (Art. 1 of LAA). The legal aid provided by the LAF involves provision of legal consultation, mediation, settlement, drafting of legal documents, acting as a representative or defender in litigation or arbitration, and necessary assistance for other legal matters (Art. 2). Criminal, civil, and administrative trials are all included in the LAF's activities. The funding for the LAF (ten billion NT dollars, about 334 million US dollars) mainly comes from its governing authority, the Judicial Yuan, which compiles its annual budget (Art. 6). The ten billion NT dollar fund was not donated to LAF all at once. The provision states that the Judicial Yuan should donate annually to the LAF. From 2004 to 2015, the Judicial Yuan donated 47 to 75 million NT per year. Based on the population of those needing help and the number of branches the LAF has (21), the budget is very insufficient. This low budget results in a situation in which lawyers get limited compensation from legal aid cases, and therefore few lawyers are willing to join the LAF.

All who are indigent are qualified to apply for legal aid (Art. 13). An "indigent" person indicates a certified "low-income resident" under the Social Relief Act, or one whose monthly income and disposable assets are under a specific standard set by the LAF (Art. 3). The following non-indigent people may also apply for legal assistance: (1) a defendant who is on trial for a crime punishable by than three-years of imprisonment or is in a trial adjudicated by the high court for the first instance and does not retain a defense lawyer; (2) a defendant unable to make complete statements due to mental disability, who does not retain a defense lawyer, and for whom a presiding judge deems it is necessary to appoint one (Art. 14).

Procedures for obtaining legal aid

Application for legal aid is made to a branch of the LAF (Art. 18 of LAA). The branch decides whether to approve the application, and if so, the form and extent of legal aid that will be granted, the amount and deadline for the payment by the recipient if partial legal aid is granted, and the lawyer who will provide the legal aid. The above items must be specified in written form (Art. 19). In exceptional circumstances, the regular processing of an application for legal aid may not be able to provide necessary help in time, and so a branch may make a preliminary decision to grant legal aid in emergencies, even though the applicant fails to meet application requirements (Art. 21). An application shall be declined if one of the following conditions exists: (1) the statements and information provided by the legal aid applicant apparently show no legitimate justification for legal aid; (2) the value of the award the applicant may recover from prevailing in litigation is less than the litigation costs and the lawyer fees, except in cases where the controversies at issue are significant to the law or to society; (3) the applicant has already received legal aid according to the LAA or other statutes for the same matter, and is no longer eligible to receive further legal aid; (4) the application for legal aid is made to sue the LAF; (5) extraterritorial litigation; and (6) the issue for which the applicant applies for legal aid does not correspond to the purposes of providing legal aid (Art. 16).

The LAA also has provisions for applicants and recipients to challenge the decisions of branches. It provides that an applicant or recipient who disagrees with a decision made by the review committee of a branch may file a petition to the Appeal Committee of the LAF within 30 days after receiving a written decision (Sec. 1 of Art. 36). The appeal process guarantees applicants and recipients' procedural rights. To settle such issues as quickly as possible, the decisions of the Appeal Committee of the LAF are considered final, and applicants or recipients are not allowed to appeal such decisions (Sec. 3 of Art. 36).

Lawyers' duty

Except for legitimate reasons for exemption, every lawyer has a duty to provide legal aid (Sec. 1 of Art. 25). While this provision looks as if it adopts the pro-bono system of the US, it does not. In reality, lawyers in Taiwan are not mandated to provide pro bono services. In practice, a lawyer who is willing to provide legal aid needs to join a branch of the LAF first. The branch of LAF then may assign approved cases to the lawyer. Until now, an LAF branch has never assigned a case to a lawyer who has not joined an LAF branch. The concept of the lawyer's duty to the legal aid system did not follow any particular foreign model, even though Taiwan has adopted many criminal justice ideas from abroad. This LLA provision was designed with practical concerns in mind. Lawyers would oppose the LLA's enactment if it would have subjected them the duty to provide legal aid.

A lawyer who joins a branch of the LAF and accepts an assigned case but disregards his duty may be sanctioned by the Attorney Disciplinary Committee, which consists of three judges assigned by the High Court, one public prosecutor nominated by the High Prosecutors Office, and five attorneys designated by Taiwan Bar Association, according to the Attorney Regulation Act (Art. 27 of LAA). To help a legal aid recipient to choose a lawyer, branches of the LAF shall provide recipients with a list of lawyers providing legal aid (Sec. 1 of Art. 26). Aid is always paid by the relevant branch according to the LAF's remuneration standards (Art. 28). Except for lawyers joining a branch and providing legal aid on an individual-case base, the LAF may retain full-time lawyers (Sec. 3. of Art. 24).

Litigation aid provided by other statutes

The Code of Civil Procedure has provisions regarding litigation aid that were made before the enactment of the LAA. This code provides that except in cases where there is manifestly no prospect for a party to prevail in the action, when a party lacks the financial means to pay the litigation expenses, the court shall, after ruling on a motion, grant litigation aid (Sec. 1 of Art. 107). The Administrative Litigation Act, moreover, has the same provisions regulating litigation aid in administrative trials (Art. 101).

For civil or administrative trials, parties who lack financial means may be granted litigation aid by the court. The "lacking financial means" requirement aligns with the "indigence" standard in the LAA. Therefore, when people who are granted legal aid by a branch of the LAF according to the LAA and apply for litigation aid to the court, the court shall grant it (Art. 62 of the LAA). In that situation, the court's budget covers the expense of legal aid (litigation aid). That provision may avoid courts' investigation of parties' finances and consolidate the courts' litigation aid responsibilities, as well as save the LAF's budget.

Conclusion

It is fair to say that rights to counsel are increasingly protected even though the whole system is imperfect. There were several factors that caused revisions to the CCP and the enactment of the LAA. Suspects have the right to retain counsels, they may present to provide legal advice, and meet with their client in detention because of the *Wang* case. Democratization played an irreplaceable role in the reform of the right to counsel. The number of lawyers significantly increased with the end of the period of martial law and lawyers were more accessible to the people. Therefore, the right to counsel became meaningful and realistic for citizens.

Interpretations of the Constitutional Court have held that the right to counsel is protected by the Constitution. The right to counsel is not merely statutory. In particular, Judicial Interpretation No. 654 stated that people have the rights to retain entrusted counsels and freely communicate with their defense lawyers. Due to that decision, the CCP was revised and defense lawyers were allowed to meet with suspects soon after they were arrested. Moreover, the government has lost the power to monitor communications between suspects/defendants and defense lawyers.

In order to respond to the democratization of society, the National Judicial Reform Conference was held in 1999. According to the resolutions of the conference, the LAA was enacted. The LAA provides indigent people with the opportunity to obtain legal assistance and strengthens the right to counsel. In the reform process, professors and NGOs were extremely important. Professors with study-abroad backgrounds, especially those who studied in the US and Japan, introduced ideas from foreign legal systems, conducted comparative studies, and promoted criminal justice reform. NGOs, such as Judicial Reform Foundation and Taipei Bar Association, actively pressed for judicial reform. It is fair to say that without their participation, the right to counsel "system" that was achieved would have not been what it is now.

Taiwan has made great progress in reforming the legal framework of the right to counsel. There are still many changes to be made. However, we are confident that within a decade, people in Taiwan will be able enjoy more proper and complete rights to counsel.

11 A leap forward not yet achieved

Civil procedure reform in Taiwan

Jing-Huey Shao

Introduction

Inheriting the legal legacy of Continental systems, Taiwanese civil procedure law is essentially closer in design to the inquisitorial mode than the adversarial mode, as represented by the US law system. This means that the litigation process is theoretically mostly controlled by judges rather than led by the parties.[1] However, in the practice, litigants still exert a quite substantial influence on the pace of litigation in Taiwan.[2] Taiwan's Code of Civil Procedure ("TCCP") gives the court limited control with regard to when to conclude a case, and it must wait until the parties agree that all the evidence and issues have been investigated and addressed.[3] Therefore, the court generally hears several cases at the same time.[4] This creates hurdles for efficiency in litigation. If the parties abuse their liberty to control the pace of proceedings, they delay the progress of litigation, wasting resources and time. Some litigants even keep some evidence from being unveiled at the first instance in order to ambush the opposing party with new facts at the second instance.[5] These problems may cause the first trial to lose its theoretical function of being the first true airing of all the facts that serves as the best opportunity to resolve disputes.

As Ernest Friesen has said, "Justice is lost with the passage of time.... No matter how you look at it, whether it's a civil or a criminal matter, time destroys the purposes of courts."[6] There have been numerous cases in Taiwan that

1 黃國昌 [Kuo-Chang Huang], 民事訴訟法教室I [Classes of Civil Procedure I], 53–4.

2 許士宦 [Shu-Huan Shyuu], 集中審理與審理原則 [The Principles of Trial and The System of Concentrated Trial], 137–8.

3 陳榮宗、林慶苗 [Rong-Zong Chen, Lin Qing-Miao], 民事訴訟法(上) [Code of Civil Procedure Vol. 1], 55–6.

4 許士宦 [Shu-Huan Shyuu], 集中審理與審理原則 [The Principles of Trial and The System of Concentrated Trial], 138.

5 Ibid.

6 David C. Steelman with John A. Goerdt and James E. McMillan, (2004), "Caseflow Management: The Heart of Court Management in the New Millennium," xvi, citing Ernest C. Friesen, "The Delay Problem and the Purposes of Courts," in National Center for State Courts, Institute

illustrate the seriousness of delayed justice. The "921 earthquake" that occurred on September 21, 1999, also known as the Jiji earthquake, killed 2,415 people, injured 11,305, and caused damages amounting to NT$300 billion (about US$9 billion).[7] Claims mounted over shoddy construction practices, and several defendants were sued in 1999 and 2000.[8] After about 15 years of litigation, many cases received their final court decisions in 2014.[9] In another case, ex-employees of the Radio Corporation of America (RCA) sued RCA and Thomson over the company's handling of industrial waste and organic solvents that were cancer-inducing toxins.[10] Over 30,000 of RCA's ex-employees suffered from toxic chemical poisoning.[11] They formed the Self-Help Association for RCA Employees Suffering from Cancer (SHA), and they encountered various difficulties and delay tactics from the defendants in their lawsuit. For example, the defendants claimed that the SHA was not a legal person and hence did not qualify as a plaintiff according to the old TCCP.[12] Although litigation began in 2004, it was not until 2015 that the Taipei District Court finally ruled that RCA should pay damages to its ex-employees.[13] The case is currently on appeal. In the meantime, 216 people involved in the case have already died from cancer, and 102 others have various kinds of tumors.[14] For those who suffered and could not see the outcome of the case, what does justice mean for them? Is justice delayed still justice? Such delays in trials have worsened the burden on the courts, which are already facing large increases in their caseloads, while the growth in the

for Court Management, *Caseflow Management Principles and Practices: How to Succeed in Justice* (Videotape, 1991).

7 Chi-Chi, EERI, www.eeri.org/1999/09/chi-chi.

8 Ibid.

9 纏訟14年，921東星受災戶僅獲賠1.9億定讞 [Litigating for Fourteen Years, the Victims of Tonghsin Building Collapse in the 921 Earthquake Only Awarded NT$190 Million], www.apple-daily.com.tw/realtimenews/article/new/20141003/481047.

10 *RCA – The Unacceptable Face of Capitalism in Taiwan*, September 11, 2007, www.amrc.org.hk/alu_article/occupational_health_and_safety/rca_the_unacceptable_face_of_capitalism_in_taiwan.

11 Ibid.

12 The Taipei District Court held that the SHA organized by the victims was not qualified to be a representative party under Article 44–1 of the TCCP on the grounds that the association had not been registered as a juridical person and thus was not a qualified incorporated charitable association. The court also reasoned that although the association met the condition set in Article 40(3) of the TCCP as an unincorporated association and thus had capacity to be a party, since the victims in that case were the members of the association, not the association itself, the association was neither qualified to sue on its own nor qualified as a representative party under Article 41 of the Taiwan Code of Civil Procedure. *The First Hearing of the RCA Case, The Ex-employee Who Suffered Cancer Testifies*, November 10, 2009, www.coolloud.org.tw/node/48273.

13 臺北地方法院95年度重訴更一字第4號 [Taiwan Taipei District Court 2006 Major Case Remanded No. 4], 司法院法學檢索系統 [Law and Regulations Retrieving System, The Judicial Yuan of The Republic of China], http://jirs.judicial.gov.tw/Index.htm.

14 LAF's Annual Report of Year 2009, www.laf.org.tw.

number of judicial personnel has not kept pace.[15] Therefore, many voices have urged for the reform of civil procedure. Also, according to a survey conducted by the Judicial Reform Foundation (JRF) on social trust in judicial system, 82 percent of those surveyed wish to obtain a final decision to a legal dispute within one year.[16] People's desire to obtain timely justice has become a pressing issue, underscoring the need for efficient court systems and procedure.

Many countries have been perplexed by similar delay problems and have adjusted or refined their trial systems to enhance efficiency. The TCCP, enacted over 80 years ago in 1930, did not undergo substantial review and amendments until the 1990s. Because of the long martial law era, many laws were frozen to preserve the stability of government control over society. After the lifting of martial law in 1987, Taiwan began her transition to democracy, and various reforms aiming for adjustments of the law to meet social needs were launched. Several important judicial reforms, including many related to civil procedure, were undertaken starting in the 1990s.

There are several reasons why reform was needed. First, most fundamental statutes in Taiwan were enacted more than half a century ago. Given social, political, and economic changes in society, Taiwan today is very different from the Republic of China in which the fundamental legislation was written, both in social needs and people's awareness of rights.[17] Second, due to the urgent need to create a systematic and complete legal framework in the early Republic of China, transplantation was deemed the most efficient way to create civil procedure. Hence, the law was mostly modeled, without much accommodation, on Japanese civil procedure, which was in turn adopted from German law. Public disappointment with the judicial system arises because either the law does not fit society or because it once did but now is outdated. Former President of the Judicial Yuan (JY), Weng Yueh-Sheng (翁岳生), spoke of this phenomenon:

> We have endeavored to advance the judicial system, but cannot meet the current needs of people, which has resulted in low credibility of the judicial system in people's minds. Probing into such problems, we found there are three reasons behind this: (1) most judicial reforms are not made standing in people's shoes and do not accommodate people's needs, so people are not aware of any advancement of the judicial system. (2) Judicial proceedings

15 鍾秀瑋 [Hsiu-Wei Chung], 民事訴訟進行遲延之防止 [The Prevention of Delay in Civil Procedure], 26–7.

16 黃旭田 [Xu-Tiang Huang], 1999、2002年年司法信賴度網路民調 [Online Poll on the Reliability of the Judicial System in 1999 and 2002], www.jrf.org.tw/newjrf/index_new2014.asp?id=1008.

17 邱聯恭 [Lian-Gong Chiou], 民事訴訟審理原則之新容貌及機能演變(一) – 著重於評析其如何受最近立法走向所影響及相關理論背景 [The New Look and Functional Transition of Civil Procedure Law – An Analysis of New Amendments and Related Theoretical Background], 月旦法學雜誌 [Yuedan Law Magazine], Vol. 53, 143 (October 1999).

are lengthy, complicated and inefficient and hence the people's rights cannot be realized in a timely fashion. (3) Judicial personnel lack professional dedication, and this results in the low quality of judicial work that is criticized by the people.[18]

Weng Yueh-Sheng convened the National Judicial Reform Conference (NJRC) in 1999, where monumental reform issues were discussed by distinguished scholars and practitioners from around the nation. As one of the NJRC topics, the reform of civil procedural law was less controversial than other issues as its objectives were relatively clear, and a preliminary consensus about promoting the efficiency of the judicial system was not disputed. Most of the issues were discussed prior to the NJRC through regular meetings or conferences among civil procedure scholars and practitioners. The NJRC essentially confirmed general agreements reached beforehand. The meeting's official nature ensured that the authorities would proceed with reform.

Unlike other reforms that were more sensitive due to their political nature, civil procedure law governs private law as it applies to the general public. Reform in this field does not significantly affect the power of state authorities. Since civil procedure reform did not entail a restructuring of judicial authorities, civil procedural reform was relatively smooth and was spared undue political wrestling. The reforms, discussed below, eventually made huge progress toward addressing the obligations of the courts, legal professionals, and lay people who participate in litigation.

But, more than a decade after the implementation of the reforms, the results are disappointingly not as significant as expected. Statistics and surveys of judges show that there are still gaps between ideology and reality. Without adequate support for surrounding mechanisms and mandatory personnel training, any new law may only have a limited effect. Although the reform has not met its set goals, it is still a positive development that academics and practitioners recognized the necessity of reform and made an effort to improve the system and accommodate people's needs. Continuous review and adjustments to the reforms are still needed, and future developments in civil procedure can be anticipated.

This chapter is organized as follows. The next section identifies the pre-reform problems. Section three explains the origins of civil procedure reform, including in the NJRC. Section four examines the objectives of the reform and the content of the amendments. Section five explains how reforms were concluded and implemented. Section six evaluates the results of reform. The prospects for future reform are discussed in the final section.

18 翁岳生 [Yueh-Sheng Weng], 迎接新世紀的挑戰, 加速改革司法 [Meet The Challenges of the Next Century, Speed up Reforming the Judiciary], www.judicial.gov.tw/aboutus/aboutus05/aboutus05-01.asp.

The pre-reform problems

Due to the transplantation of the old German code, the courts in Taiwan used to hear several cases over a long period of time, and the time allocated to each case was scattered and limited.[19] A court would hear several cases, usually in a morning or afternoon session, where the parties would state their claims or exchange pleadings in a matter of a few minutes.[20] The absence of "concentrated proceedings" is due to Taiwan's lack of a US style jury system, and hence there was no need to concentrate hearings to accommodate the schedule of the jury. The result is that professional judges who hear several cases at the same time often depend on written documents to refresh their memories of the cases.[21] The overly lengthy trial and document-based proceedings are inefficient, not only because they lengthen the time for people to realize their rights, but also because they tax judges' memories and waste judicial resources.[22] Also, with the rising legal consciousness among Taiwanese people, there has been a steady increase in the number of cases that have gone to trial,[23] especially since Taiwan does not require legal representation in civil litigation, which makes it relatively cheap. Actually, nearly 90 percent of civil cases at the first instance involve a party acting without lawyers.[24] Cases initiated by lay people without attorney representation have flooded into the courts without professional evaluation of the merits, causing difficulties in expediting court proceedings involving legally untrained litigants. Also, over the past two decades, the growth in the number of judges has not kept pace with rising demand in the courts.[25] Judges' inundation with work has worsened delays in trials. Long cases and judges working overtime may cause low-quality decisions, which eventually undermines people's confidence and trust in the judicial system.

In addition to the problem of trial delays, an unreasonably high percentage of appeals are heard at the second instance, exacerbating the delay problem. Taiwan's civil court system has three instances, including two instances of trial courts (district and high) and the court of last resort – the Supreme Court, which only deals with questions of law. The first instance district courts should be the focus of the trial courts in resolving the majority of the cases as they are in the best position to investigate cases and resolve disputes promptly. The second

19 陳榮宗、林慶苗 [Rong-Zong Chen, Lin Qing-Miao], 民事訴訟法(上) [Code of Civil Procedure Vol. 1], 55–6.

20 Ibid.

21 陳榮宗、林慶苗 [Rong-Zong Chen, Lin Qing-Miao], 民事訴訟法(上) [Code of Civil Procedure Vol. 1], 51.

22 Ibid.

23 鍾秀瑋 [Hsiu-Wei Chung], 民事訴訟進行遲延之防止 [The Prevention of Delay in Civil Procedure], 19–25.

24 鍾秀瑋 [Hsiu-Wei Chung], 民事訴訟進行遲延之防止 [The Prevention of Delay in Civil Procedure], 30–2.

25 Ibid.

instance courts, the high court level, should ideally only hear cases with larger stakes or disputes that cannot be resolved at the first instance. This is for the aforementioned reason of prompt and correct investigation and also for the objective of delivering timely justice in light of limited judicial resources. However, there is no substantial limitation on appeals to the high courts, and new evidence can still be adduced in the second instance.[26] Without proper evaluation of the merits of the cases at the district level, litigants are inclined to appeal to high courts. Another reason for appeals seems to be that citizens have less confidence in the young judges that serve in district courts.[27] Because the judges in Taiwan have traditionally been selected through the judicial examination, law graduates who pass the exam and take their training immediately might be able to serve at district courts at the age of 24 or so.[28] Also, in district courts, cases are usually heard by a single judge, except for complicated ones. Many litigants are not confident in the abilities of young judges and are inclined to appeal to high courts where cases are heard by panels and the judges are usually more senior. Therefore, many litigants devalue the function of district courts and withhold evidence at the first instance, planning to disclose it at the second instance instead.[29] This turns the district court into a figurehead, and the caseload at the second instance becomes unreasonably high as most cases are appealed.

Overly lengthy proceedings and the flood of litigation cause serious delays in trials, which in turn obstructs people's access to the vindication of their rights and resolution of disputes in a timely fashion. The old TCCP has reached its limits in resolving civil disputes efficiently. Thus many voices have called for change, urging reform of civil procedure. With the efforts of both academics and practitioners, review and discussion started in the 1980s and later became the basis for reform in the 1999 NJRC.

The origins of the reform of civil procedure and an overview of the NJRC

It is generally accepted that the ideal court system is pyramid-shaped, where most cases are resolved in the first instance and only cases that clearly err in fact or procedure can be appealed to higher courts.[30] However, Taiwanese litigants

26 許士宦 [Shu-Huan Shyuu], 集中審理與審理原則 [The Principles of Trial and The System of Concentrated Trial], 138.

27 司法院 [Judicial Yuan], 全國司法改革會議實錄 [National Judicial Conference Minutes] (Taipei: 司法院 [Judicial Yuan], 1999), 分組會議及紀錄 967 [Record No. 967], 陳清秀發言 [Speech of Ching-hsiou Chen].

28 In recent years, there are also some senior judges who are willing to serve at district courts.

29 許士宦 [Shu-Huan Shyuu], 集中審理與審理原則 [The Principles of Trial and the System of Concentrated Trial], 138.

30 陳榮宗、林慶苗 [Rong-Zong Chen, Lin Qing-Miao], 民事訴訟法(下) [Code of Civil Procedure Vol. 3], 673–4.

tend to appeal to the second instance, worsening the situation of unreasonably high caseloads at the district and high court levels.

To resolve the existing problems, including the lengthy litigation process and enormous caseloads in courts, after years of accumulating of experience and knowledge, most scholars and practitioners acknowledged and identified the shortcomings of civil procedural law and practice. The law was originally modelled on the German Civil Procedure Law of 1877, which was transplanted to Japan and was later adopted by the Republic of China.[31] Hence, later theories and interpretations of civil procedure mostly referred to Germany and Japan up to the 1980s. With the ambition of refining the civil procedure law to conform to Taiwan's needs, starting in 1980 Professor Chiou Lian-Gong (邱聯恭), who later become a vice president of the NJRC, held regular meetings where academics and practitioners discussed important issues of civil procedure law. The meetings later turned into the Civil Procedure Law Research Association (民事訴訟法研究會, CPLRA), a non-profit organization that regularly held such meetings and published articles that were the basis for its discussions. Hence, to some extent, civil procedure law reform unofficially started 20 years before the government-led conference in 1999. Through the nearly two decades of exchanging of ideas and experiences in the meetings, disagreements at the NJRC were minimized. Driven by Professor Chiou, even the bill of the amendments to the TCCP was sent to the Legislative Yuan (LY) before the actual commencement of the NJRC.

The NJRC of July 1999 invited many distinguished academics, practitioners, and social elites to discuss critical reforms, which showed the government's efforts to reorganize and advance the judicial system. There were three panels at the NJRC.[32] Panel 1 included the "position of Judicial Yuan" (司法院定位), "protection of the people's right to litigation" (人民訴訟權之保障), civil participation in trials (人民參與司法審判), reform of civil procedure (民事訴訟制度之改革), and the implementation of judicial panels (合議制度之落實). Panel 2 was concerned with criminal procedure law reform. Panel 3 examined appointment and review mechanisms for judges and prosecutors (法官與檢察官之人事改革).[33]

As a major topic for Panel 1, specific civil procedure reforms were itemized under relevant proposals. The first proposal involved introducing concentrated proceedings in civil cases (民事事件審理集中化) and strengthening of the functioning of the first instance of trial courts (強化第一審之事實審功能). The second proposal concerned "strict limitations on appeals" to second

31 許士宦 [Shu-Huan Shyuu], 戰後臺灣民事訴訟法學發展史 [History of the Development of Postwar Taiwan's Civil Procedure Studies], 月旦民商法雜誌 [Cross-Strait Law Review], Issue 35, 6–7 (March 2012).

32 全國司法改革會議結論具體措施時間表 [Timetable of Specific Measures from the Conclusion of National Judicial Reform Conference] (July 26, 1999), www.judicial.gov.tw/aboutus/aboutus05/aboutus05-05.asp.

33 Ibid.

instance courts (事後審或嚴格限制的續審制) and strict limitations on appealing and permission to appeal to the Supreme Court on questions of law (嚴格法律審並採上訴許可制). The third proposal was that the first instance of trial courts should hear cases by panels of judges, except for summary proceedings and small-claim proceedings (除小額及簡易訴訟外，應採合議制).[34] All three proposals implied an underlying objective of "pyramidizing" Taiwan's court system – that is, reducing the number of cases rising to higher levels of adjudication. After the discussions in the NJRC, the JY requested that the LY expedite its review of proposed legislative amendments that had been approved at the NJRC. Thus, starting from 1999, the TCCP went through several crucial amendments, the most important of which were those of 1999, 2000, and 2003.

Reform objectives and content of the amendments

Overall, the amendments and revisions of the TCCP during these years went smoothly and in accordance with the consensus developed within the CPLRA. Drawing on novel theories developed by Taiwanese scholars with reference to ideas from Germany and Japan, the content of the amendments as well as the big picture of civil procedure reform was mostly guided by the founder of the CPLRA, Professor Chiou.

Among the three proposals for reform in the NJRC, the "concentrated trials" proposal was undoubtedly at the heart of civil procedure reform as it could reduce judges' workloads and promote efficient trials, thus rebuilding parties' trust in the judicial system. In order to achieve the objectives of concentrated trials, the main themes of the three amendments all related to the efficiency of court proceedings as well as the enhancement of the first instance in order to make it central to civil adjudication. By specifying the obligations of parties and judges, the new law aimed to facilitate the litigation process by providing mechanisms to organize disputed facts, refine evidence rules, expand courts' elucidation powers (闡明權),[35] and limit appeals. For example, the new law requires parties to prepare evidence beforehand and produce pleadings and documents with required information within specified times,[36] and it also narrows down the relevant facts and issues between opposing parties at an

34 Ibid.

35 Elucidation power refers to judges' authority to clarify their opinion of law or fact to the parties, as well as to command the parties to refine their unclear statements.

36 Article 267 of TCCP:

> (section 1) The defendant shall, if he/she considers it necessary to do so, submit his/her answer to the court, with a written copy or photocopy thereof sent directly to the plaintiff within ten days after receiving the complaint, and no later than five days prior to the oral-argument session if one has been designated.

earlier stage.[37] Essentially, the court must direct the case using its expanded authority of elucidation, to help parties clarify and organize their disputed issues. The rules regarding activities in courts include the timely provision of evidence and presenting attacks or defenses in due course. If a party acts in a dilatory manner, sanctions such as the exclusion of evidence or claims, may be imposed.[38]

With regards to the second NJRC proposal, namely, to limit the number of appeals to the second instance, the new law specifies that if a case is appealed to the high court, the parties cannot present new evidence except under specified conditions.[39] Participants are thus encouraged to litigate their cases efficiently at

37 Article 268–1 of TCCP:

> The defendant shall, if he/she considers it necessary to do so, submit his/her answer to the court, with a written copy or photocopy thereof sent directly to the plaintiff within ten days after receiving the complaint, and no later than five days prior to the oral-argument session if one has been designated. Where any matter which should be notified to the opposing party in preparation of the case is not indicated in the complaint or answer, the parties shall submit to the court a preparatory pleading indicating such matter with a written copy or photocopy thereof sent directly to the opposing party within the period which the opposing party needs to prepare for such matter, and no later than five days prior to the oral-argument session if one has been designated. The parties shall submit to the court the preparatory pleading, if any, to dispute or respond to the matters indicated in the pleadings provided in the two preceding paragraphs with a written copy or photocopy thereof sent directly to the opposing party within five days after receiving such pleadings as provided in the two preceding paragraphs, and no later than three days prior to the oral-argument session if one has been designated.

Ibid.

38 Article 196:

> Except as otherwise provided, the means of attack or defense shall be presented in due course according to the phase of litigation before the conclusion of the oral-argument sessions. Where a party, attempting to delay litigation or through gross negligence, presents an attack or defense in a dilatory manner at the possible cost of a timely conclusion of the litigation, the court may deny the means of attack or defense so presented. The same rule shall apply when the purpose of the means of attack or defense presented is unclear and the presenting party fails to provide a necessary explanation after being ordered to do so.

39 Article 447:

> No additional means of attack or defense shall be presented, except in case of any of the following: 1. Where such additional means of attack or defense were prevented from being presented as a result of the court of first instance acting in contravention of the laws and regulations; 2. Where the occurrences giving rise to such additional means of attack or defense took place after the conclusion of oral arguments in the court of first instance; 3. Where additional means of attack or defense are presented for purposes of supplementing those already presented in the first instance; 4. Where the occurrences giving rise to such additional means of attack or defense are generally known or known to the court in the course of performing its functions, or the court should take evidence on its own initiative with regard to such occurrences; 5. Where the party was unable to present such additional means of attack or defense due to reasons not imputable to him/her; 6. Where it would be

the first instance trial courts rather than re-argue the same issues again at the second instance. The goal is to conserve judicial and litigant resources.[40]

To elaborate, the first amendment in 1999 mainly aimed at reducing the caseloads inundating the first instance trial courts by utilizing Alternative Dispute Resolution (ADR) mechanisms such as mediation to reduce the amount of litigation.[41] In order to increase the application of mediation, the types of mandatory mediation were expanded, and the authority of mediation committees was strengthened. Also, besides mediation, "small-claim proceedings" were introduced for the first time to let people litigate disputes under NT$100,000 (about US$3,000). The new small-claims proceedings have several efficient and convenient features: simplified pleadings; night courts and holiday courts; settlement incentives such as refunds of filing fees; enlargement of judges' discretion and authority; and simplified evidence rules.[42] These changes mean that courts can resolve small claims cases efficiently, economically, and without utilizing disproportionate resources.

The second amendment in 2000 was the core of the three amendments. The 2000 amendments followed five guidelines: to provide convenient access to civil procedure for the parties; to prevent disputes from arising or expanding, to strengthen the conflict resolution function of civil procedure, to proceed with litigation efficiently, and to reduce court caseloads.[43] These five guidelines[44] not only clearly restate the spirit of the concentrated trial, but highlighted another important objective – "one-time dispute resolution" (紛爭解決一次性), which means resolving relevant issues at one time rather than repeatedly utilizing the same procedures. First, the amendment in 2000 provided more access to courts through the relaxation of procedural hurdles to the modification and adding to of claims and counterclaims if the case had additional issues arising from the same

manifestly unfair to prevent the party from presenting such additional means of attack or defense. The party shall make a preliminary showing of the existence of one or more of the circumstance provided in the provisos of the preceding paragraph. The court of second instance shall reject any additional means of attack or defense presented in violation of the provision of the two preceding paragraphs.

40 黃國昌 [Kuo-Chang Huang], 限縮爭點之拘束與新攻擊防禦方法之駁回──以「促進訴訟之效率性價值是否為當事人所能處分？」為中心 [A Study on Binding Force of Issue-Narrowing and Dismissal of Allegations/Defenses: Centering on "Can the Efficiency Value of Procedural Promotion be Decided by the Parties?"], 台灣法學雜誌 [Taiwan Law Journal], Issue 119, 210 (January 1, 2009).

41 See the preamble of the Amendment to the TCCP in 2000.

42 王甲乙 [Jia-Yi Wang], 五十年來我民事訴訟法之修正 [Amendments of Code of Civil Procedure in Taiwan over 50 years], 法令月刊 [The Law Monthly], Vol. 51, Issue 10, 462–5 (October 2000).

43 See the Amendment of TCCP in 2000.

44 張劍男 [Jian-Nan Zhang], 民國八九年、九二年修正民事訴訟法若干問題 [Issues from The Amendments of the Code of Civil Procedure in 2000 and 2003], 法官協會雜誌 [Journal of the Judges Association], Vol. 6, Issue 1, 10 (June 2004).

material facts. This helps to avoid the initiation of new lawsuits.[45] It also relieves the burden on the judicial system of arranging additional trials as well as saves the resources of the parties. The amendment also enlarges the possibility of filing claims to demand future performance and obtain preliminary "declaratory judgements" to resolve or prevent disputes from occurring by ascertaining rights and obligations.[46]

Substantial fairness to parties' litigation status is also addressed in the 2000 amendments, with an emphasis on equal opportunities being conferred on parties to proceedings. Civil procedure in Taiwan does not require parties have attorney representation, except at the Supreme Court.[47] With a large percentage of cases litigated by lay people, judges have had to play important roles in directing proceedings and clarifying legal issues. Inquisitorial intervention by judges is fairly common in practice and is encouraged as a means to protect litigants' rights.[48] Expanding the scope of judicial elucidation authority[49] is one way to ensure substantial fairness. If a party's statements and factual presentations are ambiguous or incomplete, the court may direct them to clarify or supplement their positions,[50] which not only promotes substantial fairness to the parties in exerting their rights, but resolves disputes efficiently. Substantial fairness is also addressed in evidence rules. The default rule of the burden of proof is that a party bears the burden of proof for facts if the party alleges a fact in his or her favor.[51] However, to put parties on equal footing, a proviso to the burden of

45 王甲乙 [Jia-Yi Wang], 五十年來我民事訴訟法之修正 [Amendments of Code of Civil Procedure in Taiwan over 50 years], 法令月刊 [The Law Monthly], Vol. 51, Issue 10, 473 (October 2000).

46 Article 246 of TCCP: An action demanding future performance may not be initiated unless it is necessary to make such a demand in advance.

47 Article 466–1 of TCCP: (section 1) Unless the appellant or his/her statutory agent himself/herself is qualified to act as an attorney, an appellant shall appoint an attorney as his/her advocate in the appeal from the judgment of a court of second instance.

48 魏大喨 [Da-Liang Wei], 訴訟基本權在民事訴訟法之實現 [The Realization of Fundamental Rights in the Code of Civil Procedure], 月旦法學雜誌 [The Taiwan Law Review], Issue 105, 131 (February 2004).

49 Article 199–1 of TCCP:

> Where the plaintiff's statements and factual representations may lead to an assertion of several legal relations and his/her assertion is ambiguous or incomplete, the presiding judge shall direct him/her to clarify or supplement. Where the defendant asserts a reason to extinguish or prevent the plaintiff's claim and there exists ambiguity as to whether such a reason is raised as a means of defense or counterclaim, the presiding judge shall elucidate.

50 Ibid.

51 TCCP Article 277:

> A party bears the burden of proof with regard to the facts which he/she alleges in his/her favor, except either where the law provides otherwise or where the circumstances render it manifestly unfair. For cases regarding pollution or consumer disputes, as the defendant companies are usually economically superior, the party that does not have access to evidence may petition to the court to order the defendants to produce necessary documents. If

proof was added: the burden of proof can be reversed when the law provides otherwise or where the circumstances render it manifestly unfair, as determined at the court's discretion.[52] This may occur where the party has the burden of proof but has extreme difficulties in producing evidence. The court may reverse the burden of proof on a hospital, for example. Furthermore, the amendment also expanded the application and function of the perpetuation of evidence (i.e., seizing evidence), which includes agreements reached by the parties with regard to claims, facts, evidence, or other matters that are binding on later trials.[53] Also, for efficient fact-finding, the amendment introduced judicial examination of parties (i.e., making them witnesses) as a way of producing evidence when necessary.[54] Sanctions may be imposed if a party refuses to take an oath without justification or makes false statements.[55]

> the defendant company refuses to do so without justifiable reasons, the court may take such evidence or the disputed facts as true to prevent the evidence holders from obstructing truth finding. This is an example of the reforms aiming at achieving the substantial procedural fairness.

52 TCCP Article 277:

> A party bears the burden of proof with regard to the facts which he/she alleges in his/her favor, except either where the law provides otherwise or where the circumstances render it manifestly unfair. For example, a patient claims damage resulting from medical negligence against a hospital but does not have the medical record kept by the hospital.

53 Article 376–1:

> Before an action is initiated, when both parties appear on the date designated for the perpetuation of evidence and reach an agreement with regard to the claim, the facts, the evidence or other matters, then the court shall make a note of such agreement in the transcript. Where the agreement provided in the preceding paragraph is reached with regard to the claim, the court shall also make a note in the transcript of the agreed legal responsibility and the circumstances under which the dispute arose. Where a party shall tender specific performance according to the agreement, the transcript may serve as a writ of execution. Where an agreement has been reached, the authenticated copy of the transcript shall be served upon the parties within ten days. The provisions of Articles 212 to 219 inclusive shall apply mutatis mutandis to the transcript provided in the preceding paragraph.

54 許士宦 [Shu-Huan Shyuu], 戰後臺灣民事訴訟法學發展史 [History of the Development of Postwar Taiwan's Civil Procedure Studies], 月旦民商法雜誌35期 [Cross-Strait Law Review, Issue 35], 12 (March 2012). Article 367–1 II:

> In the case provided in the preceding paragraph, the presiding judge may, either before or after the examination, order the examined party to sign a written oath, and in such case the provisions of the second paragraph of Article 312, Article 313, and the first paragraph of Article 314 shall apply mutatis mutandis.

55 Article 367–1 III:

> Where a party refuses to state or sign a written oath without giving a justifiable reason, the court may take such refusal into consideration in finding the truth of the disputed fact.

As most of the reforms were stipulated in the year 2000 amendment, the 2003 amendment contained the rest of the reforms, and more mechanisms for the "one-time dispute resolution" goal were provided. The amendment offered new standing provisions for suing in multiple-litigant cases (i.e., class actions) and allowed government-sanctioned organizations (GSOs) or nonprofit organizations (NPOs) as representatives for filing class actions. In addition to monetary claims, GSOs or NPOs can seek injunctive relief in the public interest,[56] so that harms and damages can be prevented and the general public can benefit.[57]

While the three amendments mainly focused on concentrated proceedings and "one-time dispute resolution," there has been an important guiding spirit throughout the whole reform of the TCCP – that is, the "guarantee of procedural rights" (程序權保障). This is the concept that everyone has the "right of instituting legal proceedings" under the Constitution, which is analogous to the notion of "access to court."[58] This also could equate to the concept of "due process of law," for they both emphasize the legitimate basis for people to participate in a process that will influence their rights and to participate in litigation where a binding decision will be entered and res judicata takes effect.[59] As Constitutional Court Interpretation No. 482 states on the meaning of procedural rights:

> People shall have the right to petition and to bring administrative appeals, and the right of instituting legal proceedings under Article 16 of the Constitution.

> Where a party has been ordered by the court to appear in person and he/she fails to appear without giving a justifiable reason, he/she shall be deemed to have refused to testify, except in cases where the summons is served by deposit or constructive notice. Article 367–2: Where a party, after signing a written oath in accordance with the provision of the preceding article, intentionally makes false statements which will affect the outcome of the decision, the court by a ruling may impose a fine not exceeding NT$30,000 [about US$1,000]. An interlocutory appeal may be taken from the ruling provided in the preceding paragraph; the execution of such a ruling shall be stayed pending appeal. Where the party or statutory agent provided in the first paragraph confesses that his/her statements are false before the conclusion of the oral argument in the second instance, the court in which the action is pending may, in its discretion, revoke the original ruling.

56 Consumer Protection Law Article 53: Consumer ombudsmen or consumer protection groups may petition the court for an injunction to discontinue or prohibit a business operator's conduct which has constituted a material violation of the provisions of this law relating to consumer protection.

57 However, due to lack of incentives, such as the contingency fee arrangement and the opt-out system in the US, class action mechanisms have seldom been utilized. There have been less than 20 such cases over the past ten years.

58 Constitution of the Republic of China (Taiwan), article 16: The people shall have the right of presenting petitions, lodging complaints, or instituting legal proceedings. 黃國昌 [Kuo-Chang Huang], 既判力：第一講 – 既判力總論 [Res Judicata: Session One – Introduction of Res Judicata], 月旦法學教室30期 [The Taiwan Law Review, Issue 30], 90–1 (April 2005).

59 許士宦 [Shu-Huan Shyuu], 戰後臺灣民事訴訟法學發展史 [History of the Development of Postwar Taiwan's Civil Procedure Studies], 月旦民商法雜誌35期 [Cross-Strait Law Review, Issue 35], 12 (March 2012).

> The so-called "right of instituting legal proceedings" denotes the people's right to enjoy judicial benefits, namely, the right to entreat the court to hold a timely trial in case one's right is encroached upon, and this right of instituting legal proceedings includes the right to apply for a hearing, due process, an open trial, and equality in procedures. The retrial proceedings provided in the Code of Civil Procedure are a special remedial system, making it possible for a case determined by an irrevocable final judgment to be put under trial once again … and such restrictions do not contradict the intent of the Constitution in protecting the people's right of instituting legal proceedings.[60]

The notion of "procedural rights" served as one of the underlying guidelines of the amendments and was the spirit incorporated in the reforms. Taiwanese scholars have further elaborated on "procedural rights" and the concept of "justice" in civil procedure, saying they include not only the substance of disputes, but also the process for pursing such rights.[61] That is, the parties and courts should pay attention to the resources the parties and the judicial system spend on discovering truth when seeking justice.

Even though the tone of the reform had been set and the amendments were under review in the LY committee, during the NJRC panel discussion on civil procedure reform, there were dissenting voices. While the necessity of the first proposal was rarely challenged, with respect to the second proposal on strict limitations on appeals, commentators questioned whether the limitations on appeals should be adopted before supporting mechanisms were ready. First, because legal representation is not required in trial courts, lay litigants might not understand their obligations at the first instance and their rights may be adversely affected in the second instance. This is contrary to the objective of promoting substantial justice. Second, if the reform aimed to enhance the first instance so that it would become "the center of the trial," the premise is that there would be experienced judges serving in district courts. However, many judges in the district courts are still young and may lack adequate social experience in the parties' eyes, which undermines litigants' trust in court decisions, especially when they preside over cases as single judges (獨任法官). Third, without enhancing lawyers' powers in investigation, as in American-style discovery and the obligation of judges to disclose judges' deliberations of fact or law for efficient fact-finding, it would be inappropriate to limit appeals. With respect to the third

60 Constitutional Court, Interpretation No. 482: "In order to ensure that the lawsuit will proceed in an equal and fair procedure for both parties and to maintain the stability of an irrevocable final judgment, the Code of Civil Procedure imposes relatively strict restrictions on the institution of retrial proceedings…."

61 許士宦 [Shu-Huan Shyuu], 民事訴訟之程序權保障：以通常訴訟程序當事人之程序權為中心 [The Guarantee of Procedural Rights in Civil Procedure: Focusing on the Parties' Procedural Rights in General in Ordinary Proceedings], 國立臺灣大學法學論叢 [National Taiwan University Law Journal], Vol. 38, Issue 4, 229–71 (December 2009).

proposal that cases should be heard by a panel of judges, most commentators agree with this direction for reform.[62]

The chair of the panel, Professor Chiou, responded to the misgivings over the second proposal by arguing that the relevant amendments did not actually strictly prohibit appeals to the second instance. With respect to the question of whether to adopt a discovery rule, as in the US, research into this was undertaken, but Professor Chiou did not personally participate.[63] The issue of mandatory representation at the first instance did not receive a clear response in the panel discussion. Other comments relating to judicial personnel and panel trials were noted and incorporated into the conclusions of NJRC and the to-do list of the JY for civil procedure law reform.

The final civil procedure reforms and supporting mechanisms

As a newly-introduced reform measure, concentrated proceedings might have been novel to jurists and lay people. Black-letter law reforms must be backed up by supporting mechanisms such as education and incentives. At the end of the NJRC, the following conclusions regarding the first proposal were reached: (1) The LY should expedite its review process and pass the amendments to the TCCP as soon as possible. (2) The JY should oversee the implementation of the newly enacted small-claim proceedings. (3) The professional education of judges and lawyers should be enhanced, and the bar association should devise substantive rules to implement this. (4) Judges' job transfers should not hinder progress in cases and cause delays in litigation. (5) Law schools in Taiwan should provide courses that emphasize the skill of fact determination. (6) The JY should devise rules for probationary judges to join panels to gain training and become experienced. With respect to the second proposal, the conclusion was that a strict limitation on appeals to the second instance should wait until after the quality of judges and court decisions were raised.[64] Lastly, to carry out the third proposal of panel trials in district courts, probationary judges should not preside over cases alone until they gained one or three years of experience, depending on their completion year. Also, it was decided that the JY should propose rules to encourage senior judges to serve in district courts.

62 司法院 [Judicial Yuan], 全國司法改革會議實錄 [National Judicial Conference Minutes] (Taipei: 司法院 [Judicial Yuan], 1999), 分組會議及紀錄, 967, 陳清秀發言 [Speech of Ching-hsiou Chen].

63 司法院 [Judicial Yuan], 全國司法改革會議實錄 [National Judicial Conference Minutes] (Taipei: 司法院 [Judicial Yuan], 1999), 分組會議及紀錄, 968, 主席邱聯恭發言 [Speech of Chair Lian-Gong Chiou]. In fact, most civil procedure law scholars at that time were educated in Continental law countries. Eventually, the US discovery system was not adopted in the new law advocated by Chiou.

64 司法院 [Judicial Yuan], 全國司法改革會議實錄 [National Judicial Conference Minutes] (Taipei: 司法院 [Judicial Yuan], 1999), 1529–31.

To support the conclusions reached in NJRC, the JY created a substantial to-do list, which included enhancement of the education of judges and lawyers, emphasizing law school education on fact-finding, and combining theory and practice.[65] Also, in order to help judges and other judicial personnel understand and be able to utilize the new law, the JY invited academics to hold conferences and educational seminars for practitioners. The new law has been accepted relatively smoothly by law school students because they have strong incentives to learn and pass the judicial or lawyer exams. In order to encourage more experienced judges to serve at trial courts to promote efficient trials, the JY announced rules encouraging such job transfers. Experienced trial court judges can be promoted to the highest grade of seniority and pay rate. And in order to avoid delays in trials, the JY also devised a rule limiting judges' transfers if they have not been in their current office for more than two years.

Evaluations and results of the reform

In the years since the enactment of the amendments, there have been several evaluations of the reforms. The JY even formed the Civil Litigation Reform Effectiveness Assessment Committee to evaluate the reforms (民事訴訟改革成效評估委員會).[66] Academia Sinica also held the Conference on the Review and Prospects for Judicial Reform to mark the tenth anniversary of the 1999 NJRC.[67] Also, there have been some reports from the government[68] and academics that have used quantitative methods to analyze the reforms.

Statistical overview of the amendments

Disappointingly, many judges have not adopted the mechanisms of concentrated trials. According to the Department of Statistics of the Banqiao District Court, only 25 percent of cases involved concentrated trials in all district courts and 29 percent at all high courts. In cases involving attorney representation, the percentage rose to 54 percent in district courts and 46 percent in high courts. Even though the overall rates of the implementation of concentrated trials are below expectations, the representation of attorneys still significantly enhances the implementation of the ideal.[69]

65 Ibid.

66 司法院 [Judicial Yuan], 民事訴訟改革 [The Reform of Civil Procedure], www.judicial.gov.tw/revolution/judReform04.asp

67 See generally, 湯德宗, 黃國昌主編 [Te-Chung Tang, Kuo-Chang Huang], 司法改革十週年的回顧與展望 [Looking Back and Ahead at the 10-Year Anniversary of Judicial Reform].

68 民事訴訟制度改革成效初步評估報告 [A Preliminary Assessment of Civil Procedure Reform], www.judicial.gov.tw/revolution/司法院民事訴訟制度改革初步評估報告(集中審理部分).doc.

69 Ibid., 13–14.

To evaluate whether the heart of the reforms – concentrated proceedings and the enhancement of the first instance – has succeeded, it is reasonable to check whether the new law has shortened the trial period, whether ADR has reduced the number of cases entering the courts, and the rate of appeals to higher courts. Even though the JY has a statistics department that publicizes basic statistics of trial-related information, it does not make the raw data available for researchers or the general public for further analysis. Without information on the number of hearings per case and days between the hearings, researchers can only rely on less direct indicators offered by the JY to evaluate the first proposal of civil procedure reform, which includes settlement and mediation rates, the number of days needed to conclude a case, and appeal rates. These "before and after" numbers can somewhat reflect how far we are from the ideal of a pyramidized judicial system that reduces caseloads. After adjusting for the overall trend of case growth, according to the research of Professor Kuo-Chang Huang, the days it takes to conclude a case has slightly decreased in the first instance and the settlement rate has increased.[70] With regard to the appeal rate, although it is decreasing, conclusions cannot clearly be drawn as this trend existed before the reform. Among these three indexes, the settlements rate is the most quantitatively significant for showing a positive result of the reform.

Another way the reforms can be evaluated is through a general survey of judges at all levels released in a report by the Civil Affairs Department of the JY. The opinion survey of judges handling civil cases, conducted by Kuo-Chang Huang, asked about civil procedure reforms and especially the concentration of trials. According to the report, nearly half of judges (48 percent) think that the time spent on cases before and after the concentrated trial reform is about the same, with another 36 percent of judges believing that it takes more time to hear a case under the new rule.[71] Also, more than half (63 percent) of the judges think the new rules do not favor case deliberation, and only 32 percent agree that the new rules help. As for the time spent on producing court decisions, more than half (62 percent) of judges think there is no difference between the new and old systems.[72] The survey thus indicates that judges believe that the new law regarding concentrated trials has had a limited impact: it improves settlement rates, but does not shorten the length of trials or reduce appeal rates.[73]

The results of both the statistics and the survey are not impressive. The before and after numbers do not show significant advancements in the problems that were to be addressed. Improvements to the appeals rate and the days to conclude

70 黃國昌 [Huang Kuo-Chang], 程序法學的實證研究 [Empirical Studies of Procedural Law], 元照出版 [Angle Publishing Company], 2012, 19–64.

71 民事訴訟制度改革成效初步評估報告 (集中審理部分) [A Preliminary Assessment of Civil Procedure Reform (Session on Concentrated Trials)], 7–8.

72 Ibid.

73 黃國昌 [Huang Kuo-Chang], 程序法學的實證研究 [Empirical Studies of Procedural Law], 19–64.

a case have not been significant, implying that concentrated trials have not really served their function. Also, the survey of judicial opinions indicates that the function of the new law is of limited help to trial practice.

In the 2008 conference at Academia Sinica, scholars and practitioners suggested several possible obstacles for the reform. First, Taiwan did not adopt mandatory representation in civil actions, which made it difficult for lay litigants to understand court instructions or even to follow judicial directions. Much of the work fell to judges, adding to the burden on judicial workloads, to the detriment of concentrated proceedings. Relatedly, since the general public has lacked knowledge of the legal effects of litigation procedures in court, judges may be hesitant to exert their authority to exclude litigants' rights in certain circumstances. Second, although the JY held numerous training sessions, meetings, and conferences for judges to exchange ideas and learn the new mechanisms created by the amendments for concentrated trials, some judges were reluctant to attend, since judges are tenured and there are no sanctions for judges not engaging in mandatory continuing education.[74] Third, even though the JY had requested that bar associations devise rules for lawyers to fulfill their continuing education requirements, so far this is still not mandatory, and so lawyers have not felt pressured to learn the new law, hindering the understanding and acceptance of the reform. According to some judges at a meeting of the CPLRA discussing the effect of concentrated trials, between less than half or one-third of judges attended the seminars on concentrated proceedings.[75] Finally, judges have had the discretion to decide whether to adopt the new mechanisms for concentrated trials or not. Furthermore, to determine whether the case has utilized concentrated proceedings, the JY adopted a form for judges to fill out on whether they used certain procedures, making the determination superficial rather than substantial.[76]

Some commentators believe that without clear definitions of important terms, it would be difficult for the reforms to proceed. For example, there is no definition of "concentrated trial" stipulated in the new law, so practitioners or the general public may have different attitudes toward the interpretation and implementation of this.[77] Furthermore, because concentrated trials in the first instance have not yet been fully institutionalized, judges at the second instance are hesitant to exclude litigants' rights if they raise the objection that it would be "manifestly unfair" to do so. This term is itself vague in its legal meaning.[78]

74 Judges Act, section 81: A judge shall engage in on-the-job studies every year. The Judicial Yuan shall provide a budget every year to dispatch judges at all levels of courts for judicial studies or continued education domestically or overseas.

75 爭點集中審理制度在各法院之施行狀況及其檢討 – 民事訴訟法研究會第94 次研討會 [The Examination of Concentrated Trial: CPLRA no. 94], 黃柄縉發言記錄 [Speech of Huang Bing-Jing], 法學叢刊 [China Law Journal], Vol. 205, 334 (January 2007).

76 Ibid.

77 湯德宗, 黃國昌主編 [Te-Chung Tang, Kuo-Chang Huang], 司法改革十週年的回顧與展望 [Looking Back and Ahead at the 10-Year Anniversary of Judicial Reform], 421.

78 湯德宗, 黃國昌主編 [Te-Chung Tang, Kuo-Chang Huang], 司法改革十週年的回顧與展望 [Looking Back and Ahead at the 10-Year Anniversary of Judicial Reform], 442–5.

The second reform proposal, on limitations on appeals, has also had mixed results. According to a report by the JY's Civil Affairs Department in 2011, the days needed to conclude a case at the second instance show a slight decrease from 257 days in 2003 to 211 in 2010.[79] The rate of appeals to the third instance (the Supreme Court) also show a slight decrease.[80] However, as specified in the report, it is unclear that the second proposal has achieved its goals, since the change is fairly minor over a ten year span and other factors might be at work. Regarding the second part of the second proposal, concerning limiting appeals to the Supreme Court to only cases with errors of law or procedure, there has been relatively encouraging progress.[81] Nearly half of cases appealed to the highest court have been rejected, showing a positive outcome in this part of the reforms.

In terms of the third proposal – that the first instance trial courts should hear cases with a panel of judges, except for small claims – the JY has announced that probationary judges will participate in such panels in order to learn from senior judges. This has also had the beneficial effect of encouraging experienced judges to stay in trial courts at the first instance. However, because the increase in the number of cases is many times more than the increase in judge numbers, there is still a problem of an inadequate judicial personnel in the first instance.[82]

79 民事訴訟制度改革成效初步評估報告 [A Preliminary Assessment of Civil Procedure Reform], 5–6. (2010).

80 Ibid.

81 Section 468:

> A judgment is in contravention of the laws and regulations if the applicable laws are not applied or are erroneously applied. Section 469: A judgment shall be automatically held in contravention of the laws and regulations in the following situations: 1. Where the court is not organized in conformity with the laws; 2. Where a judge who should have disqualified himself/herself by operation of law or by decision has participated in making the decision; 3. Where the court lacks the subject matter jurisdiction or acts in violation of exclusive jurisdiction; 4. Where the parties are not legally represented in the action; 5. Where the court violates the provision that the oral argument should be open to the public; 6. Where the judgment does not provide reasons or provides contradictory reasons. Section 469–1: A court of third instance must permit an appeal taken to a court of third instance on grounds other than those provided in the preceding article. The permission provided in the preceding paragraph shall be granted only when such an appeal is necessary for the continued development of the laws, or to ensure coherence of decisions, or when other legal opinions involved are significant in principle.

82 90年度中央政府總預算案審查專輯 [Annual Record of Deliberation of Budgetary Bills in the Central Government of 2001], 立法院預決算資料影像調閱系統 [Image Accessing System, Legislative Yuan], 201–02. http://lis.ly.gov.tw/lgcgi/ttstoc?/disk1/TTSWORK/_T94.TOC:N033159:93:0008@@1192707556.

Conclusion

While it is not easy to strike a balance among different objectives and ensure the justifiability of res judicata,[83] the civil procedure reform has shown great ambition. The objectives of the reform overall have not been fully accomplished, especially those at the heart of the reform – concentrated trials. The reason for such unsatisfactory results is not mainly the law, but the supporting mechanisms and the people involved. The amendments were written and passed in a fairly efficient way, however the habits and the mindsets of practitioners and the general public are not easy to change. The reform's voluntariness also made it difficult to push and may diminish its effect if the people impacted by it become confused and gradually lose faith in the new law. The whole system, without mandatory supporting mechanisms or a change in mentality, is stalling in further transforming civil procedure in practice.

Although we cannot triumphantly declare that we have achieved the ideal of a pyramid-shaped trial system, the amendments have still provided a framework for future refinement. Also, the JY has proceeded with case management reforms, based on US and Singaporean procedures, which have been trialed in the Kaohsiung District Court since 2007.[84] Case management so far has reduced judges' caseloads by dividing case work into trial-related and non-trial-related categories and arranging trials into pre-trial and trial periods. Junior judges are assigned to organizing cases in the pre-trial phase, providing senior judges with more time to focus on the trial without distraction.[85] This might be another option for the concentrated trial reform. As for the possibility of mandatory representation in proceedings, it might have to wait until the overall quality of the legal profession has been raised and mechanisms for attorney fees and legal aid have been properly designed.

As academics have said, the 1999 reform has only been implemented for about ten years, and it was done without prior surveys or experimentation. It is advisable to revisit the reforms after accumulating experience from judicial practice over these years. Taiwan has continued to reform its law in other respects, such as the recent enactment of the Family Act, which centralizes relevant resources to family courts for special needs. As with the more than 50 years of postwar reforms in Japan,[86] further adjustments to Taiwan's legal reforms can be expected.

83 黃國昌 [Kuo-Chang Huang], 既判力： 第一講 – 既判力總論 [Res Judicata: Session One – Introduction of Res Judicata], 月旦法學教室30期 [The Taiwan Law Review, Issue 30], 91 (April 2005).

84 高雄地院率先試辦「民事案件流程管理制度」首創民事審查庭規劃案件流程管理落實案件密集審理加速實現當事人權利, [Kaohsiung District Court Pioneered in Attempts of "Civil Cases Process Management System": First Installation of Civil Tribunals, Planning Case Process Management, Implementing Concentrated Trial, Accelerating the Realization of Rights for the Parties], 司法周刊 [Judicial Weekly], Issue 1338 (May 7, 2007).

85 Ibid.

86 湯德宗, 黃國昌主編 [Te-Chung Tang, Kuo-chang Huang], 司法改革十週年的回顧與展望 [Looking Back and Ahead at the 10-Year Anniversary of Judicial Reform], 428.

12 Administrative law reform in Taiwan

Ching-Hui Chen

Introduction

Since the end of World War II, Taiwan's politics, society, economy, and circumstances of constitutional development have undergone gigantic changes. The repeal of martial law in 1987 was not only a turning point for Taiwan's democracy, but also for its society and economy. Administrative law reform before and after democratization reflects these momentous changes and provides a helpful perspective on them. This article explains the experience and development of administrative law in Taiwan before and after the repeal of martial law and highlights its relation to democratic consolidation and the diffusion of law. It also discusses whether administrative law adequately deals with contemporary problems as well as new challenges in the future.

Administrative law before the lifting of martial law

Administrative law existed in Taiwan's legal system before the repeal of martial law. However, the main goal of administrative regulation in this period was to regulate people. Purposes and rules of administrative law were determined by unelected policy makers. Citizens did not have the right to participate in public affairs. Those whose rights were violated did not have access to effective remedies. During this period, the main tools of governance were not laws passed by legislators, but executive orders published by administrative agencies.[1] With this background, the development of administrative law in Taiwan at its early stage focused on controlling the legality of administrative action and broadening the availability of legal remedies for those whose rights or interests were infringed by illegal dispositions of administrative agencies. Theories and practices in other countries, particularly in Germany and Japan, strongly affected the development

1 翁岳生 [Weng Yueh-Sheng], 臺灣民主憲政的發展與法律概念及立法功能的演變 [*The Development of Taiwan's Constitutional Democracy and the Advance of Legislative Function*], 月旦法學雜誌 [Yuedan Law Magazine], 200 (January 2012): 47.

of administrative law within this period because a majority of those who acted to make this progress did advanced studies in Germany and Japan.

Major developments have included: (1) Adopting "the principle of legal reservation" and principle of "clarity and definiteness of law" to deal with orders which directly infringe on peoples' rights, but were not agreed on by legislators; and (2) expanding the extent of the concept of "administrative act" to enlarge chances of remedies.[2] Landmark legislation of the reform process included the Administrative Procedure Act as well as reform of the Administrative Appeal Act and Administrative Litigation Act. Theories and practices in other countries have been the most important foundation for improving administrative law. Crucial achievements up to the end of the 1990s have been codified in the Administrative Procedure Act, which marked a milestone for administrative law reform in Taiwan.[3]

Administrative law after the termination of martial law

Sets of administrative laws were passed in the late 1990s to react to rapid economic growth. By then, the middle class had formed and national wealth has increased. Public concern to uphold civil and political rights was strengthened, and civil society had become increasingly vibrant since the 1980s. During this period, Taiwan's authoritarian social atmosphere opened step by step, and platforms were created for interest group to participate in and influence policy makers. In this transformation, administrative law recognized the value of gathering multiple opinions and offering fair, public, and equitable procedures.[4] Above all, the legislation of Administrative Procedure Act and reform of procedures for administrative remedies were the most important steps to fulfill this duty and protect human rights. Furthermore, the organizational structure of administrative agencies influences whether or not the agencies work well. This section will thus also look at the reengineering of government.

The legislating of Taiwan's Administrative Procedure Act: strong influences from foreign legal systems

After World War II, the enactment of administrative procedure acts was a worldwide trend. Some administrative law scholars in Taiwan gave advice on the

2 葉俊榮 [Yeh Jiunn-Rong], 臺灣行政法學的發展與挑戰 – 一個批判的觀點 [*Administrative Law's Development and Challenges for Taiwan. – in Critical View*], 月旦法學教室 [Yuedan Law Magazine], 100 (February 2011): 71.

3 翁岳生 [Weng Yueh-Sheng], 臺灣近年來行政法之發展 [*The Development of Taiwan's Administrative Law in Recent Years*], 法令月刊 [The Law Monthly], 50(3) (March 2001): 3.

4 葉俊榮 [Yeh Jiunn-Rong], 「行政程序法草案」立法取向之評估 [*Legislative Orientation of the Administrative Procedure Bill*], 立法院院聞 [Legislative Yuan Gazette], 283 (August 1996): 86.

drafting of an administrative procedure act in the 1950s. The Research, Development, and Evaluation Commission of the Executive Yuan commissioned some scholars to write a research report on this in 1974. Taiwan's Administrative Procedure Act was thus first drafted in the 1970s.[5] However, the political environment was sensitive and conservative then. The draft bill languished until the late 1980, when the country's political economic structure changed, and a revised version of the draft bill was released. Both private and public agencies participated in the legislative process. Taiwan's Administrative Procedure Act (TAPA) was finally announced on February 3, 1999 and came into force on January 1, 2001.

Scholars who had studied abroad were actively engaged in the drafting process. In this sense, the drafting tended to bring features that characterize other legal regimes together.[6] These legal regimes may be divided into two main systems: the American and the German/Austrian system. The legislative outlines came mainly from two sources: one was to introduce the concept of "due process of law" and "information disclosure" from the US legal system. The other motivation was "codification" of both substantive law and procedural law, which emulates the German and Austrian model. Thus, the law's chapters concerning the "disclosure of information," "process for hearing proceedings," "legal orders," and "administrative rules" were inspired by American law. Chapters concerning "administrative guidance" and "petitions" were based on Japanese law. The rest of the chapters, such as "administrative acts," "administrative contracts," and "administrative plans," were introduced from German law. Although there may be some advantages from collecting strong points from different legal systems, the system created by TAPA is to some extent in disarray and complicated.

Most general principles of administrative law are codified in Taiwan's Administrative Procedure Act (Articles 4–10 TAPA). This feature is unique, since it is rarely seen in the legal system of other countries. Even the corresponding statute in Germany lays down only a few of these principles. In addition, Taiwan's Administrative Procedure Act, like the German Administrative Procedure Act, prescribes important types of administrative actions, which it defines, provides criteria for, and makes provisions that administrative authorities must follow in performing administrative actions. Taiwan's Administrative Procedure Act thus combines both substantive and procedural regulation.

5 翁岳生 [Weng Yueh-Sheng], 我國行政法四十年來之發展 [*The Development of Taiwan's Administrative Law for Forty Years*], 收於：氏著, 法治國家之行政法與司法 [*The Development of Taiwan's Administrative Law for Forty Years*], 2nd edn, 2009: 275–6.

6 陳愛娥 [Chen Ai-Er], 我國行政程序法立法過程的幾個特點 [*Features of Taiwan Administrative Procedure Act's Legislation*], 月旦法學雜誌 [Yuedan Law Magazine], 50 (July 1999): 35–6.

The main purposes and functions of Taiwan's Administrative Procedure Act

The main purposes and functions of the law are enshrined in Article 1 of TAPA, which states that its main purposes are to enhance democracy, to carry out the principle of administration by law, to protect the interests of citizens, and to raise administrative efficiency. These can be described as follows.

Enhancing democracy

There are two sets of provisions that focus on public participation and the enhancement of democracy. The first relates to setting procedures to establish administrative orders: "legal orders" and "administrative rules." The second focuses on the disclosure of information. Both of these sets of provisions are heavily influenced by the United States' Federal Administrative Procedure Act. There are no such similar rules in the German or Japanese general administrative procedure acts. In Taiwan, whether or not to enact these provisions in TAPA was heavily debated. Scholars who had studied in Germany argued that the establishment of legal orders and administrative directives falls essentially under "legislative procedure" and that TAPA should govern how the executive branch enforces the laws written by the legislature.[7] Conversely, scholars who had studied in America took the view that because administrative ordinances have a great impact on petitions and interest groups,[8] administrative legislation should be made transparent to improve democracy. The latter approach won out. It stipulates, for example, that legal orders require notice and public comments before being released. Therefore, legal orders made by public agencies should be published in the media, and citizens should have the opportunity to present their opinions. These procedures illustrate a concern for participatory democracy.

In the Administrative Procedure Act, the administrative orders are divided into two categories: "legal orders" and "administrative rules." This distinction arouses controversy over whether or not an ordinance issued by a government agency by its officer is valid when the government agency is not delegated by statues to do this. Such an ordinance is called a non-delegated administrative order. The first three amendments to TAPA after its enactment aim to solve this problem. Article 174–1 TAPA states that:

> All legal orders established by administrative authorities before this Act comes into force in accordance with article 7 of the Standard Act for

7 陳愛娥 [Chen Ai-Er], 於「為行政程序法催生」座談會之發言 [*Oral Script of the Forum – Birth of Taiwan's Administrative Law*], 月旦法學雜誌 [Yuedan Law Magazine], 32 (January 1998): 54; 翁岳生 [Weng Yueh-Sheng], *supra* note 1 at 62.

8 湯德宗 [Tang Dennis Te Chung], 論行政程序法的立法目的 [*The Purpose of Legislating Administrative Procedure*], 月旦法學雜誌 [Yuedan Law Magazine], 56 (January 2000): 147; 葉俊榮 [Yeh Jiunn-Rong], *supra* note 4 at 90.

> Making of Laws and Regulations by the Central Government, of which the basis of authorization is required to be provided for or specified by law, shall be amended or established after their respective basis of authorization is so provided for or specified by law, within two years after this Act comes into force, and shall become inoperative thereafter.

One possible solution is that, according to this provision, non-delegated administrative orders are no longer allowed. Against to this viewpoint, some back the legality of non-delegated administrative orders. These opinions indicate that the source of the legality of administrative orders may be found in the transition to direct election of the president and the six modern amendments to the Constitution supporting democratization.

It is worth noting that the concept of "democracy" in Taiwan's democratic constitutional system has gradually come to be seen as "dual democracy." Owing to the impact of German constitutional theory, the concept of democracy in Taiwan's Constitution was traditionally understood as "monolithic democracy," that is, it only emphasizes democratic legitimacy achieved by elections. But after the direct election of the president and six constitutional amendments, the executive branch has come to obtain democratic legitimacy direct from the Constitution – a second source. Furthermore, by enacting the Administrative Procedure Act, the executive branch can get democratic legitimacy by operating transparently, openly, offering public participation, and building partnerships with the private sector.[9] This transparency is seen as an alternative second pillar of democratic legitimacy, or even a third pillar. Thus, according to the view of non-delegated administrative orders as permissible, since the executive branch receives democratic legitimacy directly from the Constitution, the autonomy of the executive branch cannot be totally denied.[10] This dispute over non-delegated administrative orders is still an ongoing issue.

Another way in which TAPA enhances democracy is its rule of disclosure of information. There are two legal models available to reach this end: the American and the German/Japanese model. The former not only contains publishes government information and facilitates its dissemination, but also involves the right to privacy. The latter model gives interested parties the right to view relevant records and documents, while other rules concerning disclosure of information are left to be legislated in other statutes. The differences between

9 葉俊榮 [Yeh Jiunn-Rong], 二元民主與行政程序 [*Dual Democracy and Administrative Procedure*], in 台灣行政法學會 [Taiwan Administrative Law Society], 行政程序法之檢討、傳播行政之爭訟 [Reviewing Administrative Procedure Law, Disseminating Disputes of Administration], July 2003: 32–3.

10 黃舒芃 [Haung Shu-Perng], 再論「二分」與「三分」之爭：從憲法觀點檢討職權命令的存廢問題 [*Dichotomy instead of Trichotomy? On the Constitutional Basis for Non-Delegated Administrative Legislation in Taiwan*], 東吳法律學報 [Soochow Law Review], 23(2) (October 2011): 22–3.

the two models boil down to the level and extent of disclosure of information.[11] The German and Japanese model enables persons involved to apply to an administrative authority to examine, transcribe, copy, or take photographs of relevant materials that are necessary for the protection of their legal interest. In contrast, the United States model focuses on the public supervision of government agencies by expanding the extent of disclosure of information. Although TAPA follows the United States' model (Articles 44–47 TAPA), its rules are not as complete.

Article 44 TAPA, which was deleted in 2005, provided that government information must be made available to the public actively on principle, with restriction being exceptional. The scope of government information required to be disclosed was prescribed by other laws. For this reason, "The Freedom of Government Information Law" was enacted in 2005 to replace Articles 44–45 TAPA. According to this law, the right to claim disclosure of government information is not only applicable when administrative authorities carry out a relevant administrative act, but it can also be requested independently of any act. This law institutionalized the publication of government information, which is relevant to protect people's right to know about government, furthering citizens' oversight of public affairs, and encouraging public participation in democracy.

Ensuring the principle of administration according to law

There is a considerable difference as to the concept of "law" among the various legal systems that espouse "administration according to law." On the whole, civil law countries emphasize that all acts carried out by public agencies should be made according to law to prevent the abuse of administrative power. Therefore, the concept of law under the term "administration according to law" equals substantive administrative law. In contrast with this viewpoint, common law countries put more stress on procedure, emphasizing that there is no legal protection without procedural safeguards. In the past, the development of Taiwanese administration law was influenced by German law. As a result, it puts more emphasis on compliance with substantive law. But with the establishment of TAPA, Taiwanese administrative law now puts more stress on the rules of due process, which deeply alters the connotation of the phrase "administration according to law."

Protecting the rights and interests of the people

Before the Administrative Procedure Act came into effect, people could not file an administrative appeal or lawsuit until their right or interest had been unlawfully or improperly injured by a government agency's administrative action. And

11 湯德宗 [Tang Dennis Te Chung], *supra* note 8 at 147.

once a public agency did so, the enforcement of that act would not be halted by the commencement of an administrative appeal or lawsuit, provided that other laws allow it to continue. Meanwhile, *ex post* remedies are often too late or insufficient to repair any damage.

In the order to protect the rights of citizens, TAPA provides petitioners and interested parties with access to participation in the administrative process in which the relevant action was made. Such participation involves rules related to public hearings (Article 107 TAPA), the opportunity to state opinions before rendering a non-beneficial administrative disposition (Article 102 TAPA), and public agencies' obligation to give reasons and show the legal basis of an administrative act (Article 96 TAPA). When providing a person with administrative guidance, the administrative authority must expressly give the person details relating to the purpose and substance of the guidance and the officer in charge of providing guidance (Article 167 TAPA). These provisions create a platform for citizen involvement that enhances the legitimacy and efficiency of administrative actions.[12]

Enhancing administrative effectiveness

During the drafting process, administrative agencies questioned whether the Act might reduce administrative effectiveness. In this sense, one of the tasks for legislator was thus to coordinate the conflict between administrative effectiveness and the protection of rights. Three major devices were developed in the harmonizing process. The first device was the "exceptional clause." For example, the right to review files pertinent to an administrative act may not be given to an affected party under special circumstances (Article 46 TAPA).

Second, the Act allows for the legal effect of an unlawful action. Although the concept of due process is mentioned in many articles, an administrative action rendered contrary to required procedure or form does not automatically become invalid. This differs from the Administrative Procedure Act in the United States. In some cases, an administrative disposition rendered contrary to the required procedure or form is amendable before the administrative appeal procedure is concluded (Article 114 TAPA). If an affected party is dissatisfied with an action taken by an administrative authority on a procedural basis, he may file a statement to this effect only if he is also dissatisfied with the substantive decision and files a statement on this basis (Article 174 TAPA). These rules are modeled after the Administrative Procedure Act in Germany and demonstrate that Taiwan's Act does not emphasize due process as strongly as the United States.

12 李建良 [Lee Chien-Liang], 行政程序法與人民權利之保障 [*Protection of Administrative Procedure Law and People's Rights*], 月旦法學雜誌 [Yuedan Law Magazine], 50 (July 1999): 46.

The third device to harmonize administrative effectiveness and rights' protection involves that granting to administrative authorities of a certain degree of discretion. For example, public agencies have discretion in whether or not to investigate evidence, how and to what extent to conduct inquiries (Article 37 TAPA), and whether or not to hold a hearing (for those which are not required by law). Critics have claimed that the aforesaid rules show that Taiwan's Administrative Procedure Act tends to favor administrative effectiveness in a conflict between individual rights and administrative efficiency.[13]

The evolution process of the system of administrative remedies

Procedures for administrative remedies in the past followed a three-level system: administrative appeal to the public agency, administrative re-appeal, and administrative litigation to a court. As for the litigation stage, there was only a revocation remedy available for petitioners to protect their interests. This could not deliver adequate relief for people to secure their rights and interests though. The problem was not solved until the Administrative Appeal Act and Administrative Litigation Act were amended in October 1998. The new acts came into force on July 1, 2000. The revised legislation provided a more integrated framework of administrative remedies, enabling the judicial system to check and balance executive power effectively. The development of the revisions is discussed below.

Revision of the Administrative Appeal Act

When the amendments were proposed, abolishing the second-stage re-appeal rule was debated. The point of dispute was whether administrative appeals (in the Executive Yuan's opinion) or administrative litigation review (in the Judicial Yuan's opinion) should be placed at the center of the system of administrative remedies.[14] The Executive Yuan presented Administrative Appeal Act revision bills to the Legislative Yuan. Though the Executive Yuan endorsed the reform of the administrative appeals system, it expected the system to maintain the administrative re-appeal stage, in order to shield administrative acts from judicial review by the administrative court as far as possible.

Another draft amendment to the Administrative Appeal Act proposed by the Judicial Yuan was also submitted to the Legislative Yuan. According to it, the administrative re-appeal stage would be abolished and replaced with a two-level two-instance administrative litigation review system. This would follow the first instance administrative appeal to the relevant agency. After several rounds of consultation, supporters of the Judicial Yuan's view became the majority. The

13 Ibid., p. 47.
14 *Supra note* 1, p. 58.

draft submitted by Judicial Yuan was adopted by the Legislative Yuan, and the administrative re-appeal was finally abolished.

Some scholars view administrative appeals as part of administrative procedure. Thus, rules of administrative appeals may be enumerated in an administrative procedure law, which is the case with the legislation of German, Austria, and Switzerland.[15] The Legislative Yuan did not approve this approach though. In fact, at least 60 percent of the provisions set forth in the Administrative Appeal Act are highly similar to those in the Administrative Procedure Act. About 20 percent overlap with those in the Administrative Litigation Act. These three statutes sometimes regulate the same object, although they often use different terms. The reason is that they were drafted separately by different government agencies at different times, without coordinating with each other. The Administrative Appeal Act was written by the Committee of Administrative Appeals (under the Executive Yuan); the Administrative Procedure Act by the Ministry of Justice and the Research, Development, and Evaluation Commission together; and the Administrative Litigation Act was drafted by the Judicial Yuan. If the current legislative pattern of separating the Administrative Procedure Act and Administrative Appeal Act were to continue, there are good reasons to believe that provisions of the Administrative Procedure Act would apply *mutatis mutandis* to the corresponding objects prescribed in Administrative Appeal Act.[16]

The Administrative Appeal Amendment Act of 1998 expanded the statute's number of paragraphs from 28 to 101. It comprehensively regulates the types, subjects, and procedures of administrative appeals in order to achieve the goal of improving the legitimacy of this institution. It also aims at resolving administrative disputes inside the administrative system as much as possible. The following key revisions relate to deepening democracy and protecting the rights of the people.

First, the agency with jurisdiction for administrative appeals is in principle the superior agency of the agency that made the contested administrative action. According to the new legislation, an administrative appeal must be filed to the agency that performed the administrative act in question. This subordinate agency must first review the legality and propriety of the administrative action. While the administrative appeal is underway, the agency may revoke or modify the administrative action and report to the superior agency with jurisdiction for administrative appeals. If the inferior agency refuses to revoke or modify the administrative action, that agency must prepare a written answer promptly and transfer all related documents to the superior agency with appellate jurisdiction (Article 58 Administrative Appeal Act). The purposes for amending Article 58

15 吳庚 [Wu Geng], 於「為行政程序法催生」座談會之發言 [*Oral Script of the Forum – Birth of Taiwan's Administrative Law*], 月旦法學雜誌 [Yuedan Law Magazine], 32 (January 1998): 51.

16 行政院訴願審議委員會 [*Committee of the Administrative Appeal of Executive Yuan*], 訴願制度回顧與展望 [*Administrative Appeal Review and its Prospects*], 2011: 223.

are to prompt administrative agencies to reconsider their decisions, to enable appellants to acquire remedies as soon as possible, and to avoid jurisdiction mistakes.

Second, Article 63 II and III of the Administrative Appeal Act give administrative appellants or intervenor appellants the right to put forward their opinions when they file an application for stating them, so long as they have reasonable grounds. This enables an administrative appellant or intervenor appellant to actually participate in the administrative appeal process.

Third, the composition of an administrative appeal review committee was adjusted. Before the amendment in 1998, members of this body were commonly chosen from the staff of agencies with jurisdiction for administrative appeals. After the amendment, no more than half of the members of an administrative appeal review committee must come from the administrative agency with jurisdiction, to ensure the impartiality in decision-making.

Overall, the main points of the 1998 amendments were mostly implemented in administrative practices.[17] The current problem is rather that in many administrative fields there is a mandatory procedure preceding the administrative appeal, i.e., a pre-procedure must be conducted before the administrative appeal may proceed. Even though it has been decided that administrative litigation review should be placed at the center of the system of administrative remedies, mandatory procedures preceding the administrative appeal have not diminished but rather increased. In fact, almost all determinations of pre-appeals refuse citizens' complaints on the grounds that they would lead to disadvantages to industrial and commercial development. All companies desire to solve legal disputes rapidly, and the current system serves them well. But it is necessary to integrate administrative appeals and pre-appeals into one procedure to avoid functional redundancy and delays in the granting of remedies.[18]

Revision of the Administrative Litigation Act

The Administrative Litigation Act has been drastically revised, with the number of articles rising from 34 to 308. The Administrative Court, established on September 1, 1933, had historically followed a one-level one-instance system, and it made final judgments for which there were no appeals. On July 1, 2000, the administrative litigation system was transformed into a two-level two-instance system. It was further revised into a three-level two-instance system after September 6, 2012. Furthermore, previously, administrative litigation could only be initiated for disputes arising over illegal administrative acts believed to damage

17 郭介恒 [Kuo Chih-Heng], 行政三法實施十週年之回顧與檢討 – 訴願法 [*The Tenth Anniversary of Enforcement of Three Administrative Laws: Review and Outlook with a Focus on Administrative Appeal Act*], 月旦法學雜誌 [Yuedan Law Magazine], 182 (July 2010): 84.

18 行政院訴願審議委員會 [*Committee of the Administrative Appeal of Executive Yuan*], *supra* note 16 at 221–2.

rights or legal interests. Now, for all disputes arising under public law, unless expressly provided otherwise by other statutes, administrative litigation may be initiated. In other words, previously there was only one type of appeal-revoking litigation. But under the new system, in addition to revoking litigation, there are also requests for obligatory litigation, confirmation litigation, regular settlement litigations, and special litigations for protecting the public interest (so-called "public interest litigation").

It is worth mentioning that public interest litigation can be raised by members of public-interest groups on matters not relevant to their own rights and legal interests. This design allows, for example, environmentalists to pressure to administrative authorities to in situations that do not directly affect them. Public interest litigation may also be initiated if it is expressly allowed by other statutes. It is doubtful that this legislative model is beneficial. Currently, the statutes that expressly provide for public interest lawsuits only involve environmental issues: the Air Pollution Control Act (Article 81), Waste Disposal Act (Article 72), and Soil and Groundwater Pollution Remediation Act (Article 54) allow public interest litigation. However, public interest lawsuits are needed in other fields, especially those involving communicable diseases and public health, food safety, labor safety, and health protection. Public interest litigation is needed in these fields when the authorities do not execute their duties after victims or charity associations requested for them to do so.[19]

Over the more than ten years' of public interest litigation in Taiwan, over 60 percent of cases were filed under the Environmental Impact Assessment Act. Administrative agencies have won most of them. Yet citizens have won some cases recently because the competent authority did not precisely follow the environmental assessment procedure before making the environmental impact statement. These decisions emphasize that it is necessary to let people fully participate in the environmental assessment process before making an administrative decision because this can reduce later resistance to it and improve the efficiency of government agencies.[20] This demonstrates that the administrative courts have become more interested in the proper functioning of administrative procedure.

As for litigation procedure, the most important change was a shift from written to oral proceedings. Under new rules, administrative litigation judgments could only be rendered after oral arguments between the litigating parties, except at an instance of legal review. This marked a major change when compared to the old rules, whereby adjudication was mainly based upon written submissions to the court. Owing to this change, officials in charge needed to improve their

19 廖義男 [Liao Yi-Nan], 行政法之回顧與展望 [*Administrative Law Review and Its Prospects*], 月旦法學雜誌 [Yuedan Law Magazine], 200 (January 2012): 84.

20 葉俊榮 [Yeh Jiunn-Rong], 捍衛環評制度尊嚴的行政法院中科裁判 [*The Judgment of the Central Scientific Area by the Administrative Court that defended the Dignity of Environmental Impact Assessment*], 月旦法學雜誌 [Yuedan Law Magazine], 185 (October 2010): 73–4.

preparedness for lawsuits in order to clearly indicate the facts and reasons in pending cases.

On January 13, 2011, amendments to the Administrative Litigation Act were announced, and 66 paragraphs were amended. This was an enormous modification of the new administrative litigation system. The focus of these amendments was to enhance peoples' convenience in commencing administrative lawsuits. For example, parties may submit pleadings to the court by fax or electronically.

Revision of the Administrative Court Organization Act

In response to the revised Administrative Litigation Act, the Legislative Yuan passed an amendment to the Administrative Court Organization Act on February 3, 1999. It came into force on July 1, 2000. The most controversial part of the reform was the issue of capacity to be a judge, i.e., whether professionally qualified judges alone could serve on the Administrative Court. Under the old rules of the Administrative Court Organization Act, each panel consisted of one or two professional judges. This resembled the "Conseil d'Etat" in France, in which administrative court judges come mainly from outside the judicial system (primarily from the administrative system), while professional judges are subsidiary.[21] However, the legal profession argued that judges from the administrative system were not as qualified as professional judges. The Judicial Yuan's drafting team accordingly recommended a lower number of judges from administrative system, but this suggestion was not adopted by the Legislative Yuan. The Legislative Yuan abolished the old rules, but introduced new rules to strengthen the qualifications of administrative court nominees. According to these new rules, in addition to professional judges, candidates who have been lawyers, law-related teachers, researchers, or civil servants for at least eight years could be appointed as judges of the Administrative Court.

Governmental reform

An amendment of the Executive Yuan Organization Act, passed by the Legislative Yuan in January 2010 and promulgated on February 3 of the same year, aimed at re-engineering government. It belonged to a legislative package of laws that included revisions to the Basic Code Governing Central Administrative Agencies Organizations and the Act Governing the Total Personnel Headcount of Central Government Agencies. The Basic Code Governing Central Administrative Agencies Organizations determinates the basic organizational structure of the central administrative agencies, and the amendment to it created a new basis for discussion of administrative organization law. What was especially remarkable in this legislative package was the legal admissibility of establishing

21 吳庚 [Wu Geng], 行政爭訟法論 [*Administrative Litigation*], 6th edn, 2012: 13.

so-called "independent agencies" having some independence in exercising legal authority without full supervision by a superior government agency. These independent agencies represent an exception to the hierarchical structure of administrative agencies.

The adjustment to the organizational structure of central administrative agencies was just one part of the government re-engineering program. Another key area of reform involved introducing the resources of private entities (including private enterprises, NGOs, specialists, etc.) to governance epitomized the other important goal of reinventing government. These changes allowed for partnerships between government and private sectors. Also, the category of "non-departmental public body" was created in 2011 to allow for hybrid organizations, neither fully public nor private, to improve government efficiency and to bring non-officials into decision-making bodies.

However, a democratic deficit exists where outsourcing public functions to the private sector and hybrid organizations occurs. Although the "Administrative Procedure Act" provides a legal framework for the cooperation between public and private sectors, these provisions can only be applied to government agencies (Articles 93–94 TAPA, dealing with incidental provisions of administrative dispositions; Articles 135–139 TAPA, on administrative Contracts; and Articles 165–167 TAPA on administrative guidance). As for "contracting-out" a governmental function, it comes out from under the control of the legislature, and the public interest may also be easily ignored in these situations. In these cases the public may not know the content of the contract or participate in the decision-making. The Electronic Toll Collection (ETC) system is a case in point. The dichotomy of public law and private law in such situations comes with an obvious disadvantage. Therefore it is necessary to increase public participation and transparency in the policy-making processes when a public function moves from government to the private sector.[22]

The relationship between central and local government involves another goal of government re-engineering. The leading concern here is assigning the competences of the central government to local authorities, as long as the local government is able to carry it out. Promoting local autonomy to deepen democracy corresponds to an international trend as well. The division of powers between the central and local governments is regulated by the Constitution of 1947, which was designed mainly for governing mainland China but its effective jurisdiction has been limited to Taiwan. The government of the "province" level has thus been suspended following the 1997 amendments to the Constitution. The Local Government Act was formulated in accordance with Article 9 paragraph 1 of a 1999 amendment to the Constitution. This Act intended to establish a local

22 廖元豪 [Liao Yuan-Hao], 政府業務外包後的公共責任問題研究 [*On the Problems of Public Responsibilities after Out-Sourcing the Government's Tasks*], 月旦法學雜誌 [Yuedan Law Magazine], 178 (March 2010): 161.

government system appropriate for Taiwan. Since then, "horizontal cooperation" across regions has improved alongside vertical decentralization. This is of particular importance to counties that are small in area but densely populated. To handle self-government matters that involve other areas, to facilitate the use of resources within the region, or to improve the well-being of the residents in the region, a local self-governing body may, together with other local self-governing bodies, establish organizations for regional collaboration, enter into agreements, or use other methods of collaboration.

Since the Local Government Act came into force in 1999, local governments have pressed for local autonomy. Some supervisory conflicts, involving legislative autonomy, financial autonomy, and personnel rights, have occurred between central and local governments. Although several Constitutional Court Interpretations (No. 498, 527, 550, and 553) have favored the autonomy of local government, there are still unresolved problems. Clarifying criteria for the central/local division of power and local autonomy supervision continue to be major issues with Taiwan's local self-government.[23]

IV Conclusion and prospects

During the period of martial law, many administrative regulations were created unilaterally by public agencies. Even though there were some administrative regulations passed by the Legislative Yuan, they still suffered from a democratic deficit, because legislators were not re-elected for a long time. Democracy was not actually implemented. After the reform of administrative law in the late 1990s, people gained the right to participate in rule-making processes and the establishment of legal orders. A person now has the right to express his opinion before an administrative disposition unfavorable to him has been made. Meanwhile, government agencies have had to give reasons and explain the legal basis of their dispositions, and affected parties have gained the right to inspect relevant materials or records. The early modernization of Taiwan's administrative law was primarily based on the Continental European legal system, especially the administrative law of Germany. But in recent years, the influence of the United States' legal system, especially in the field of health and the environment, has increased. New elements such as the concept of due process of law and mechanisms for consultation and dialogue were adopted. The system of administrative law has been fundamentally re-established in Taiwan.

There are still challenges to overcome after the transition from the martial law regime to democracy. First, more attention should be paid to the internalization of transplanted foreign administrative laws. In other words, it is necessary after transplantation to apply, interpret, and revise laws to fit local culture. In addition,

23 Lo Cheng-Chung, Taiwan's Local Government Reform – Unresolved Issues, Taiwan Brain Trust Newsletter No. 10, December 2010, 15–17.

there have been considerable changes in Taiwan's administrative environment since TAPA has come into effect. The Ministry of Justice is thus drafting an amendment to the Administrative Procedure Act. It is suggested that the Ministry of Justice should consider practical experience as the basis for the draft amendment. For example, litigation cases related to administrative acts form the majority of cases, while the number of cases related to other types of administrative actions stipulated by the Administrative Procedure Act are far less than the former. In this sense, it is worth pondering to what extent the provisions of the Administrative Procedure Act meet the needs of the social reality.[24]

Second, elements of American law have gradually become integrated into the previously established Continental European framework, and they have had a strong influence on existing rules and structures of Taiwan's administrative law. There are more and more mid-level and high-level officials and scholars who have studied in the United States. It is predicable that in the near future, theories and institutions of common law will play an important role in Taiwan's legal system. How we should reconcile the two legal systems will hence become an essential issue in developing a functioning legal system.

Since the enactment of the new Administrative Litigation Act over ten years ago, the administrative court system has become more efficient than ever.[25] However, administrative authorities have not always complied with judgments of the administrative courts. There have recently been disputes involving environmental impact assessments in which affected persons won administrative lawsuits but the administrative agency at issue did not follow the court's decision. This shows that the principle of administration according to law has not yet been deeply rooted in the whole system of government. Though the values of public participation, transparency in administration, and administrative efficiency are codified in law, there is room for improvement regarding the government's implementation of those rules and regulations.

24 陳愛娥 [Chen Ai-Er], 行政程序法施行十週年的回顧與前瞻 [*The Tenth Anniversary Review and Outlook – The Implementation of Administrative Procedure Law*], 月旦法學雜誌 [Yuedan Law Magazine], 182 (July 2010): 79.

25 李建良 [Lee Chien-Liang], 行政訴訟實務十年掠影 [*Glimpse for Practicing Administrative Litigation for Ten Years*], 月旦法學雜誌 [Yuedan Law Magazine], 182 (July 2010): 62.

Afterword

President Tsai's 2017 National Conference on Judicial Reform

Neil Chisholm

The 2016 election of Tsai Ing-wen to the presidency marked the end of the judicial reform agenda under KMT President Ma Ying-jeou, which was masterminded by Judicial Yuan Vice President Su Yeong-chin (蘇永欽). Her party's simultaneous victory in legislative elections meant that, for the first time in the history of the Republic of China, the Democratic Progressive Party (DPP) controlled the Legislative Yuan. In addition, a strong supporter of judicial reforms, Huang Kuo-Chang (黃國昌), was elected to the Legislative Yuan as leader of the newly-created New Power Party (時代力量). Formerly a professor at Academia Sinica, Huang's research focused on judicial reform. Through media appearances, he became famous as a charismatic advocate for reform and fierce political debater. He eventually decided to enter politics to effect change directly. These developments meant that President Tsai's term appeared to be an auspicious time for judicial reform.

In her inaugural speech, President Tsai listed her major priorities: (1) changing Taiwan's economic model by expanding ties with India and ASEAN counties (the "New Southbound Policy"); (2) pension reform to improve a dire fiscal outlook; (3) "transitional justice" measures aimed at past KMT abuses; (4) deepening international cooperation; and (5) taking a less integrationist approach to cross-Strait relations. In the context of this ambitious agenda, President Tsai added a pledge to undertake judicial reform:

> At this juncture, this is the issue the people of Taiwan care the most about. The general sentiment is that the judicial system is not close to the people, and is not trusted by them. It is unable to fight crime effectively, and has lost its function as the last line of defense for justice. To demonstrate the new government's resolve, we will hold a national congress on judicial issues this coming October. By allowing public participation and letting in social forces, we will advance judicial reform together. The judicial system must respond to the needs of the people. It will no longer be a judicial system for legal professionals only, but for everyone. Judicial reform is not only the business of legal professionals; it must be inclusive. These are my expectations for judicial reform.[1]

1 Inaugural Address, Office of the President (May 20, 2016), https://english.president.gov.tw/Page/252.

The President's comments on judicial reform elicited the most applause of any part of her speech.

Yet there were reasons to suspect judicial reform would again be thwarted. In July 2016, President Tsai nominated two career judges to the presidency and vice presidency of the Judicial Yuan. Neither was famous for a commitment to judicial reform, and the presidential nominee was allegedly involved in the repressive Formosa Magazine Incident in 1979. Outsiders suspected that such establishment-type judges would be unsuited to the task of overhauling the court system, and a controversy ensued. The nominees were soon withdrawn.[2] Such nominations raised questions about President Tsai's level of engagement with judicial reform amidst her already-full agenda. Nonetheless, the Judicial Reform Foundation (JRF, 民間司法改革基金會) and other reformists remained optimistic. In the end, Hsu Tzong-Li (許宗力), a respected German-educated law professor and moderate reformist, was made President of the Judicial Yuan. President Hsu's role in the reform process has been significant. Generally, he has steered the judiciary toward a milder vision of reform that is still based on the civil law tradition but is more sensitive to public opinion.

Preparations for the promised conference indicated changes in the strategic vision for accomplishing reform. In July 2016, the Presidential Office announced the creation of a preparatory committee (籌備會議) for an October conference.[3] Then, the conference was delayed until mid-November 2016.[4] Finally, in late November, President Tsai presided over the first meeting of the preparatory committee. She announced that the committee would invite members of the public to send in reform suggestions that would be used to set the agenda, relying on the principle of "diverse voices and broad popular participation" (多元聲音, 全民參與).[5] Behind these delays, there seem to have been discussions between the Presidential Office and the JRF. In August 2016, a senior figure at the JRF told the author that they were trying "to sell our model to the government." This called for a three-step process: gathering opinions from the public, having experts analyze and convert them into discussion topics, and then turning them into concrete proposals.[6] The JRF actually undertook this task itself, complete with three meetings, two conferences, and videos of the events published

2 Sophia Yang, "President Withdraws Judicial Leadership Nominations," *Taiwan News* (August 15, 2016), www.taiwannews.com.tw/en/news/2966494.

3 "President Tsai Launches Judicial Reform in Taiwan," *Taiwan Today* (July 12, 2016), https://taiwantoday.tw/news.php?unit=2,6,10,15,18&post=3923.

4 Wen Yu-te and Jake Chung, "Foundation Anticipates Judicial Reform Conference," *Taipei Times* (November 4, 2016), www.taipeitimes.com/News/taiwan/archives/2016/11/04/2003658552.

5 "President Tsai Presides over First Meeting of Preparatory Committee for National Conference on Judicial Reform," Office of the President (November 25, 2016), https://english.president.gov.tw/NEWS/5032.

6 民間司法改革基金會 [Judicial Reform Foundation], 全民司法改革運動 [Nationwide Judicial Reform Movement] (Taipei: Judicial Reform Foundation, 2016).

online. Given the similarities with the eventual course of events, it appears that the JRF did successfully "sell" its processual model to the Tsai government.

Meanwhile, some judges and prosecutors, presumably voicing the anxiety of their institutions, denounced President Tsai's leadership of the preparatory committee. They claimed this infringed upon the separation of powers and judicial independence,[7] considerations that had prevented President Lee Teng-Hui from heading the 1999 National Conference on Judicial Reform (NJRC). But it was clear that strong executive support was needed for judicial reform to succeed. The lack of such executive leadership frustrated implementation of the NJRC's resolutions. And executive involvement was crucial to the success of judicial reform in Japan and South Korea.

From February 28 to July 10, 2017, there were six meetings of the preparatory committee, which began with 17 members. It solicited public suggestions for reform, screened them, and then reshaped them into workable proposals. Five "conference panels" (分組會議) were created to serve as subcommittees to discuss areas of reform. These met about six times each, were composed of 18–20 people per panel, and discussed reform ideas for about three hours at a time, with the proceedings broadcast live online. Decisions were reached by consensus or voting. On August 12, 2017, ten months of preparations culminated in a "summary meeting" (總結會議) of the National Conference on Judicial Reform (司法改革國是會議). Over half of the 101 participants had no legal background. This final meeting of the Conference adopted the panels' decisions and produced 87 resolutions on a variety of issues.

The three most important issues at the Conference were the restructuring of the judiciary, adoption of lay participation in courts, and judicial personnel policy. First, with regards to restructuring, the old "position" or *dìng wèi* (定位) debate, on the unification of jurisdictions under a "tribunalized" Judicial Yuan, was abandoned. Rather than such a frontal attack on entrenched institutions, the Conference decided a set of piecemeal changes: most importantly, the Constitutional Court's jurisdiction would be expanded, allowing it to hear more cases, and the number of judges at the Supreme Court and Supreme Administrative Court would be reduced to 14 and 7, respectively.[8] Their combined total was over 90 at the time of the Conference.

Second, it was decided that some form of civil participation in adjudication should be adopted, but that details would be decided later, based on the study of civil and common law systems, at the implementation stage.[9]

Third, the Conference proposed major changes to judicial selection and training. It called for judges and prosecutors to be selected by a unified examination

7 "Tsai Leading Judicial Reform will be Risky: Judges," *Taiwan News* (August 16, 2016), www.taiwannews.com.tw/en/news/2967194.

8 Resolution 20. See, 司法改革國是會議 [National Conference on Judicial Reform], 司法改革國是會議決議主/協辦機關分工表 [National Conference on Judicial Reform Resolution Table].

9 Ibid., Resolution 46.

(for lawyers, judges, and prosecutors) and trained for one year, but not in the Judges Academy (法官學院) or the Academy for the Judiciary (司法官學院).[10] Rather they would receive practical training within their organizations – apparently a kind of revival of the German *Referendar* internship.[11] After this year, still considered part of the examination, there would be a selection by oral test for the position of "candidate judge" (候補法官), whose period would last for five years. Candidate judges would not be permitted to deal with cases on their own. During their first two years, candidates would have to work in an institution outside the court, in order to gain experience. In the latter three years, candidate judges would need to serve as drafting assistants to full-time judges, in order to mitigate the loss of manpower caused by the adoption of this system.[12]

It is worth noting that the above also would apply to prosecutors. The fact that the same resolution dealt with judges and prosecutors together indicates that reformists were unable to push the separation of judges and prosecutors further. Additionally, the JRF had drafted a "Prosecutors Act" (檢察官法), analogous to the Judges Act, to increase prosecutorial accountability, but it appears that this high-priority reform was abandoned. It seems that prosecutorial resistance to reform was at least partly successful, although other resolutions recommended some less significant prosecutorial reforms.

Unfortunately, several other important reforms cannot be discussed here for considerations of space.

In her speech closing the Conference, President Tsai acknowledged that implementation would be critical to the success of judicial reform.[13] At the writing of this chapter, one-and-a-half-years later, implementation has been a mixed success. For the judicial reorganization reform, the Constitutional Court Litigation Act (憲法訴訟法) was passed in December 2018 and will come into effect after three years. This law upgrades Taiwan's Constitutional Court to the level of other German-style, Kelsenian courts. It creates a constitutional complaint process, amicus curiae system, simple majority rule for reaching decisions, reorganizes the body as a court rather than the "council" it has been heretofore, abolishes the collective writing process, and recasts the Court's decisions as judgments rather than "interpretations." This was a relatively easy reform to achieve, given that it maintains continuity with Taiwan's Continental tradition,

10 The Judges Academy, operated by the Judicial Yuan, mainly provides continuing education for judges. The Academy for the Judiciary is managed by the Ministry of Justice, and, as the successor to the JPTI (Judges and Prosecutors Training Institute), it has trained new judicial officers. Both institutions can trace their recent history to the entering into force of the Judges Act in 2013.

11 However, a key difference is that in Germany aspiring lawyers must also undertake the internship, which will not happen in Taiwan.

12 Resolution 41.

13 "President Tsai Delivers Closing Remarks at Summary Meeting of Presidential Office National Conference on Judicial Reform," Office of the President, August 12, 2017, https://english.president.gov.tw/News/5190.

benefits the Judicial Yuan, and essentially adversely affects no other institution. However, the radical downsizing of the Supreme Court and Supreme Administrative Court has not yet been passed by the Legislative Yuan. Those institutions can be expected to strenuously fight such a change.

The final form of civil participation has remained a public controversy. The Judicial Yuan proposed a "citizen judge" (國民法官) system that resembles Japan's lay judge model. Six citizens would deliberate and vote with professional judges in certain criminal cases. Judicial Yuan President Hsu's moderate reform inclinations are evident in this proposal. Opponents believe that this system does not go far enough in empowering the people and suggest that professional judges will be able to dominate in decision-making. Many reformists, such as Huang Kuo-Chang, advocate a more radical idea: a US-style jury system. A new group, the Taiwan Jury Association, has surfaced to publicly fight for adoption of the jury system. Tapping into populist pro-democratization sentiment, it has asked, "Taiwan's executive and legislative branches are already democratic – what is the judiciary waiting for?"[14] Civil participation reform has been unimplemented, although "citizen judge" experimental trials are underway.

The reform of judicial personnel policy is also unfinished. The Judicial Yuan insists it will push for the changes, but the list of steps in its "latest progress" report are meetings and discussions that have lasted over a year.[15] Meanwhile, the JRF and Huang Kuo-Chang have demanded that the majority of a proposed committee to supervise judges have no legal background. This runs counter to the Judicial Yuan's proposal that a majority be lawyers, judges, or prosecutors.[16] They rejected Huang's proposal because it was feared that non-specialist laymen might, through misunderstanding, punish judges that make decisions that do not satisfy the public. This debate captures the dichotomy between judicial organization according to expert knowledge versus community norms. The battle for judicial personnel policy goes on.

President Tsai's 2017 National Conference on Judicial Reform shrewdly adapted the bottom-up tendencies of modern Taiwanese politics for a process that must in some way be top-down. Allowing citizens to determine the reform agenda while employing legal elites to clarify their concerns has created a distinctively democratic judicial reform process. However, implementation has been slow, and the longer reform waits, the less likely it becomes. Resistance

14 台灣陪審團協會 [Taiwan Jury Association], 我們在做什麼? [What Are We Doing?], https://jurytw.wordpress.com/%e7%b0%a1%e4%bb%8b.

15 司法院 [Judicial Yuan], 司法改革 方案 & 進度 [Judicial Reform Program and Progress], 五、法官的多元進用、監督與淘汰 [5, Judges' Diverse Intake, Supervision, and Elimination], www.judicial.gov.tw/ten/ten.html#5.

16 民間司法改革基金會 [Judicial Reform Foundation], 法官、 檢察官淘汰機制, 人民不能再等了~ 呼籲加速審議《法官法》暨公布職務監督草案記者會 [Judge and Prosecutor Elimination Mechanism, the People Cannot Wait Again! Press Conference to Call for the Acceleration of Review of the Judges Act and to Publicize the Job Supervision Draft], March 19, 2019, www.jrf.org.tw/articles/1618.

has come mainly from institutional inertia. In terms of legal diffusion, aspects of the new reforms demonstrate a commitment to learning from the Continental tradition (e.g., Constitutional Court reform) or not straying far from it, as with "citizen judge" lay participation and judicial personnel policy reforms that introduce internships and probationary periods for new judges. Yet, if Taiwan adopts some form of the American jury system, rather than a lay judge-style system, it would represent the infusion of a populist, Jacksonian-style democratic ethos into the judiciary. At this point, *de minimis* judicial reform or failure to reform can only preserve a deeply unpopular status quo and would likely increase demands for more radical reform.

Index